D1587997

Fritz Lang's Metropolis

Studies in German Literature, Linguistics, and Culture

Edited by James Hardin
(*South Carolina*)

Fritz Lang's *Metropolis*

Cinematic Visions of Technology and Fear

Edited by
Michael Minden
and
Holger Bachmann

CAMDEN HOUSE

First published 2000
by Camden House

Camden House is an imprint of Boydell & Brewer Inc.
PO Box 41026, Rochester, NY 14604–4126 USA
and of Boydell & Brewer Limited
PO Box 9, Woodbridge, Suffolk IP12 3DF, UK

ISBN: 1–57113–122–1

Library of Congress Cataloging-in-Publication Data

Fritz Lang's Metropolis : cinematic visions of technology and fear / edited by Michael Minden and Holger Bachmann.
p. cm. – (Studies in German literature, linguistics, and culture)
Includes bibliographical references.
ISBN 1–57113–122–1 (alk. paper)
1. Lang, Fritz, 1890–1976—Criticism and interpretation. 2. Metropolis (Motion picture) I. Minden, Michael. II. Bachmann, Holger, 1969–
III. Studies in German literature, linguistics, and culture (Unnumbered)

PN1997.M436 F75 2000
791.43'72—dc21

00-031170

A catalogue record for this title is available from the British Library.

This publication is printed on acid-free paper.
Printed in the United States of America.

CONTENTS

Illustrations

Preface

THIS VOLUME IS DIVIDED into a two-part introduction and four main parts. The Introduction consists of Holger Bachmann's substantial historical account of the genesis, production, and first reception of *Metropolis*, and Michael Minden's overview of the film's subsequent critical reception. Part One, "Materials and Documentation," contains three different sorts of primary sources. The first sources are reprints of publicity material in which an extract from Thea von Harbou's novel was placed alongside the equivalent treatment in the screenplay. In fact, this excerpt from the screenplay is all that survives of the original, although an earlier draft was found among the papers of Gottfried Huppertz, who composed the film's first musical score for Lang. Two excerpts from Thea von Harbou's novel are also included in order to give a flavour of her prose and moral attitude, but also to cast light on one of the murkiest aspects of the film's plot: exactly what does Fredersen intend by sending the robot Maria among the workers? The second kind of documentation included consists of reports about the making of the film that give information concerning the production process, but perhaps more interestingly and reliably, convey an impression of the public relations and marketing effort made on behalf of its highest-budget venture by the film's production company, Ufa. The final section of primary sources provides examples of reviews, not only from Germany but from around the world, including the famous justification — from the *New York Times* — of the cuts made to the film for American distribution and the full texts of the oft-quoted reviews by H. G. Wells and Luis Buñuel.

Part Two, "Metamorphoses of *Metropolis*," recognizes that the lack of the original text of this film is inseparable from any discussion of it. Enno Patalas, the former Director of the Munich Film Museum and the man most responsible for the sustained detective and restoration work that has been devoted to Lang's film, provides an up-to-date report on the state of knowledge about and the current holdings and versions of the film, together with hopes and plans for its future. Thomas Elsaesser's essay, published here in this form for the first time in English, is an excellent analytical introduction to the film, but since it takes the Moroder makeover as its point of departure, also firmly establishes the film's "openness to its own afterlife," as Elsaesser puts it in his essay, as one of its defining characteristics. Giorgio Bertellini's article is a counterbalance to that of Patalas, for, while stressing the indispensable nature and undisputed value of the work of the film restorers, it also emphasizes how the meaning of those labours can ultimately never be to restore a lost original, but rather to highlight how the study of early film, in its dependence upon the palimpsestic nature of its texts, reveals with particular clarity the conditions of all historiography.

Part Three of the book, "Classic Texts and Context," reprints four major essays on Lang's film: Alan Williams' careful structuralist analysis of the film, and three essays from the period when the insights of structuralism and poststructuralism came to be reapplied to a specific historical context. The central theme of these three essays is the ambivalent character of technology. Thus Ludmilla Jordanova, who is interested in the relation between the representation of science and gender, sees the film as expressing how precarious the boundaries are in the popular imagination between good and bad science, the good and the bad woman, and good and bad power. The image of technology as an expression of power is opposed to, but finally complemented by, the mediating human function of the woman. Not, however, before the destructive side of woman and the destructive side of technology have been identified with one another, both posing a threat to political stability. Whereas Jordanova is working in the context of the history of science, Andreas Huyssen, in a seminal essay, is more specifically interested in Weimar culture. He argues that the film displaces the (expressionist) male fear of technology onto the male fear of women — both masculine "others" with a rich genealogy — in order to exorcize them both, and to align itself with the purified technology of *Neue Sachlichkeit*. What made Huyssen's essay so resonant was the way in which not only these matters, but also questions of psychoanalysis, religion and the cinematic apparatus itself are deftly woven together into a single argument. R. L. Rutsky takes issue with Huyssen by pointing out that dividing technology into dystopian or utopian forms, as Huyssen does, masks a more essential distinction: that between, on the one hand, technology as rational and functional and, on the other, as dynamic, irrational, and libidinal. Italian Futurism and *Neue Sachlichkeit* are both utopian in their understanding of technology, but the latter understands it as rational and functional, the former as dynamic and irrational. *Metropolis* displays both views of technology, the Taylorist mechanization of the workers and the wild sexual energy of the robot. Yet they are both dystopian, and the film can only conceive of utopia by mediating between them. It is through this *mediation* between modern industrial rationality and connotations of familiarity and the home traditionally associated with women, that *Metropolis* reveals the nature of the special appeal of National Socialism.

Part Four, *"Metropolis* Now," offers three entirely new essays. Andrew Webber's piece provides a psychoanalytical reading. There are certain scenes in the film that cry out for analysis from this point of view. Webber's essay reflects the symbiosis that has developed over the years between film theory and psychoanalysis. He explores that area of the film's effectiveness that, by definition, does not map perfectly onto political and social affiliations. His essay also has the virtue of considering the film in the context of other outstanding examples of early German cinema. Whilst *Metropolis* is unique in certain ways, it also has its place among the other stylized German studio films of its time. Julia Dover's polemic is important because, by linking *Metropolis's* enthusiastic pessimism about the relation between man and machine to that of Baudrillard and other contemporary theorists of culture and communications, she both highlights the film's relevance to contemporary debates about the place of human subjectivity threatened with replacement by prosthetic electronic consciousness, and underlines that the issue demands an ethical response rather than a merely academic one. Finally, Ben Morgan's surprising and highly original essay goes against an assumption that colours all the other contributions in this book, namely that the film is marred by its sentimentality. By referring to Jung, rather than Freud, and aligning himself in some ways with Patrice Petro's increased differentiation between types of spectator in the Weimar period, he urges a different view of the film's main characters who are, after all, Freder and Maria. Morgan wishes to dissociate himself, and the film, from the sort of regulation of emotional life that invalidates areas of experience by calling them sentimental. Instead, while allowing that the ending is a regrettable short-circuit, Morgan suggests that the film asks us to take the transformation of Freder and his relationship with Maria seriously as a critique of, and an alternative to, the stern, controlling view that characterises not only Fredersen, but also the many excellent analyses of the film to be found in the rest of this volume.

M. M.
H. B.
July 2000

Acknowledgements

The editors wish to thank all the contributors for their cooperation. All the contributors, whether their work was being reprinted, published in a new form, or published for the first time, were enthusiastic and supportive. Patrice Petro and Yves Laberge, and, from the beginning, Jim Hardin, were also extremely ready to help. We wish to record our thanks for a generous grant from the Tiarks Fund of the German Department, Faculty of Modern and Medieval Languages, University of Cambridge, which paid for the illustrations, and to the research fund of Jesus College, Cambridge, for help with expenses for permissions and other purposes. Meg Tait provided some indispensable editorial and linguistic assistance in the final stages, and without Adrian Asher, Rob Feakes, Ashley Meggitt and Rhona Watson in the Jesus College Library and Computer Centre, the conversion of such disparate material into a more or less homogeneous electronic form would have been so much more difficult than it actually was.

M. M.
H. B.
July 2000

Fritz Lang's Metropolis

Cinematic Visions of Technology and Fear

Introduction

I: The Production and Contemporary Reception of *Metropolis*

Holger Bachmann

"THE SILLIEST FILM"[1] — or "the most remarkable and unique spectacle ever shown on the screen"?[2] Fritz Lang's *Metropolis* has always provoked extreme responses. Widely acknowledged as a bravura display of film craftsmanship, *Metropolis* has been equally widely denounced as unbearably trivial, naive, sentimental and — in Kracauer's hindsight — even fascist. Unlike in the case of *Der müde Tod* (Destiny, 1921) and *Die Nibelungen* (1924), even Lang himself wasn't too fond of the film, stating in retrospect that he found *Metropolis* "silly and stupid" and even "detested it after it was finished."[3]

Nevertheless, it is clear that *Metropolis* represents a significant moment in film history. Recent studies have even suggested that *Metropolis* marks not only a culmination of Lang's early style, but a condensation of all that Ufa — and by extension German silent cinema — was about: "if there was an 'aesthetics of Ufa' . . . it found its most convincing incarnation in a film which could only have been created in Germany, only at the height of the Weimar republic, and only at Neubabelsberg: in Fritz Lang's *Metropolis*."[4] A film that epitomizes

---

[1] H. G. Wells, "Mr. Wells reviews a current film," *The New York Times Magazine*, 17 April 1927, 4 and 22 (4). The text is included in Part One of this volume.

[2] Review of Metropolis, *Bioscope*, 24 March 1927, 59.

[3] Lang speaking in 1965, cited in Peter Bogdanovich, *Fritz Lang in America* (London: Studio Vista, 1967), 124.

[4] Klaus Kreimeier, *Die Ufa-Story. Geschichte eines Filmkonzerns* (Munich: Heyne, 2nd ed 1995), 183. Unless otherwise noted, translations from original German passages are mine — H. B. Ufa (*Universum-Film Aktiengesellschaft*) was founded on 18 December 1917 and, not least by strategic mergers with important studios such as *Decla-Bioscop* in 1921, quickly rose to become the major film production company in Weimar Germany. Ufa built its fame on silent classics such as *Metropolis* and *Faust,* film musicals such as *Die Drei von der Tankstelle* (Three Good Friends, Wilhelm Thiele, 1930) and *Der Kongreß tanzt* (Congress Dances, Erik Charrell, 1931), as well as melodramas (*Der blaue Engel*/The Blue Angel, Josef von Sternberg, 1930) before gaining notoriety for Nazi propaganda films (*Kolberg*, Veit Harlan, 1945). The conglomerate was dismantled after 1945 and re-founded in the 1950s; in 1963, the assets were taken over by Bertelsmann.

Ufa's vices and virtues — and, fittingly enough, is often said to have contributed in no small part to the company's fall — in such a way could not have come about by coincidence. *Metropolis* was not only a creation of Lang's sheer genius; it was also the product of studio policies, production techniques, representational paradigms, and not least marketing strategies that characterized the biggest German film company that ever existed. Similarly, the combination of technical brilliance with thematic kitsch can hardly be explained as a temporary lapse of reason on Lang's part; it is rooted in the phenomenon that was Ufa. Before turning to the manifold critical and analytical views of *Metropolis* represented in this volume, an inquiry into why and how the film was produced will help to shed light on the very idiosyncrasies that make it such a fascinating piece of modern culture.

Metropolis, Ufa, and Weimar Cinema

The most straightforward explanation for Lang's vision of the future is contained in a well-known anecdote. In October 1924 Lang went to America to attend the premiere of *Die Nibelungen*, a film that represented a vital "prestige object and an export article" for the German studios.[5] Lang later described his first view of the Manhattan skyline by night as seen from the ship's deck as the inspiration for his next film: "I looked into the streets — the glaring lights and the tall buildings — and there I conceived *Metropolis*."[6]

Having returned from the U.S.A., Lang published "Was ich in Amerika sah" [What I saw in America], a travelogue he wrote for the leading German trade journal *Film-Kurier*. In the very first of these essays, he outlined his impressions in more detail, giving a description that already mirrors his inner vision of the city of the future and his clear intention to make a film about it:

> [Where is] the film about one of these Babylons of stone calling themselves American cities? The sight of Neuyork [*sic*] alone should be enough to turn this beacon of beauty into the center of a film . . . Streets that are shafts full of light, full of turning, swirling, spinning light that is like a testimony to happy life. And above them, sky-high over the cars and trams appear towers in blue and gold, in white and purple, torn by spotlights from the dark of night. Advertisements reach even higher, up to the stars, topping even their light and brightness, alive in ever different variations . . . Neuyork by day is the definition of sobriety, nevertheless fascinating by its movement. Neuyork by night is of such beauty that, if one experienced nothing

[5] Michael Töteberg, *Fritz Lang* 3rd ed. (Reinbek: Rowohlt, 1994), 50.

[6] Bogdanovich, *Fritz Lang in America*, 15.

> but the arrival in the harbor at night, one would still have an unforgettable impression for one's whole life.[7]

What Lang did not tell his German readership was that New York had a deeply ambivalent effect on him, a combination of attraction and repulsion, of fascination and fear; when he walked the streets the day after his arrival, Lang noted that "[the city] was the crossroads of multiple and confused human forces [irresistibly driven] to exploit each other and thus living in perpetual anxiety."[8] So the city of lights had a darker side for Lang, an undercurrent, a threatening second layer — the "undercity" he would depict in *Metropolis*. In fact, it was the notion of a covered-up, repressed, uglier face of the modern city that fuelled his imagination: "at night the city did not give the impression of being alive; it lived as illusions lived. I knew then that I had to make a film about all of these sensations."[9] According to his own version of events, then, Lang was inspired to create the film both by what he called the sensations and by a deeply divided attitude toward the modern city, elements that would characterize *Metropolis*.

To be sure, even the most superficial glance at *Metropolis* confirms the profound influence New York had on the film's visual design (the swirling lights, the sky-high buildings are all there in the breathtaking vistas towards the skyline of Metropolis). Nevertheless, as with many of his retrospective accounts, Lang's frequently told tale of his sudden flash of inspiration has to be seen as a part of his carefully cultivated myth in which he liked to depict himself as a creative genius. Lang's alleged revelation at the sight of New York may have been decisive for the film's ultimate look, but certainly does not represent the only reason for the creation of *Metropolis*; neither can Lang's autocratic version of the film's genesis account for *Metropolis* coming to exemplify Ufa and German silent film as such. In fact, in his recent biographical study, Patrick McGilligan points out that plans for *Metropolis* were already forming at the time Lang was about to finish the *Nibelungen*. The architect Erich Kettelhut even states that he read a first sketch for Lang's next monumental film in April 1924, immediately after the premiere of

[7] Fritz Lang, "Was ich in Amerika sah — Neuyork und Los Angeles," *Film-Kurier*, 11 December 1924 (unpaginated). A reprint can be found in Fred Gehler, Ullrich Kasten, eds., *Fritz Lang. Die Stimme von Metropolis* (Berlin: Henschell, 1990), 207–11.

[8] Lang as quoted in Frederick W. Ott, *The Films of Fritz Lang* (Secaucus: Citadel, 1979), 27; Ott gives no specifications as to his source.

[9] Lang as quoted in Ott, *The Films of Fritz Lang*, 27.

the *Nibelungen* in Berlin; as early as July 1924, Lang and Harbou had definitely started to work on a *Metropolis* script.[10]

At this point it is necessary to scrutinize the role of the man who accompanied Lang on his trip to America, producer and Ufa director Erich Pommer. As head of Decla, Pommer had assisted in creating the benchmark of what became known as German expressionist film when he produced *The Cabinet of Dr. Caligari* in 1919–20; after Ufa merged with Decla-Bioscop in 1921, Pommer was effectively in charge of Ufa before he officially became head of production from 1923 until 1925. Pommer's task was doubly challenging. His first task was to provide likely export hits, as German films after 1918 were not least an attempt to re-establish Germany's wartorn identity by generating products whose success would earn respect abroad — a strategy naturally also motivated by the lucrative business potential of an internationally renowned film industry. In addition, by the mid-1920s, American film studios had managed to break into the European film markets by exploiting their unparalleled monetary resources, production facilities, technical achievement, a populist star system, and not least aggressive, expansionist distribution policies.[11] European audiences were thrilled by Hollywood's entertainment-oriented, contemporary style that offered slick escapism shot through with suspense, comic relief and the inevitable happy ending. As a result, the domestic film industry in Germany came under severe pressure to produce better, bigger and more spectacular pictures.[12]

In order to counter this domestic competition and also to ensure success abroad, Pommer fostered a distinctly German filmic discourse that he had already mapped out in his Decla-productions of *Caligari* and *Genuine* (1920), Lang's *Destiny* (1921) and Murnau's *Schloß Vogelöd* (The Haunted Castle, 1921). As the Americans increasingly dominated realistic subject matter, Pommer headed in the opposite direction: the stylized art film. What is usually referred to as the expressionist discourse of German films in the mid-1920s thus never represented an *ars gratia artis*-type aestheticism; Pommer rather saw art and commercial appeal as directly related in his production strategy. He was convinced that

---

[10] See Patrick McGilligan, *Fritz Lang. The Nature of the Beast* (London: Faber and Faber, 1997), 108–09. On 4 July 1924, the *Illustrirtes Wiener Extrablatt* reported that Lang and Harbou were about to a finish a first version of the script; cited ibid.

[11] This American dominance culminated in Germany in the Parufamet contracts, in which Paramount and MGM exploited Ufa's financial difficulties to obtain major distribution advantages.

[12] Thomas J. Saunders, "History in the Making: Weimar Cinema and National Identity," in *Framing the Past. The Historiography of German Cinema and Television* (Carbondale/Edwardsville: Southern Illinois UP, 1992), 42–67 (50).

"an artistically accomplished film can do first-rate business;" therefore, the aim of his production policy was "to develop the highest artistic means and goals in order to do at least as much business as others do when they manufacture crude sensations for the masses."[13] Under his leadership, German film and Ufa thus became synonymous with neoromantic, mythical, or historical plots in exotic, artificial settings, illuminated by stark, evocative contrasts of light and shadow combined with sprawling, slow-moving, probing narratives focusing on the darker sides of the human psyche, often interspersed with elements of the supernatural.[14]

The development of this commercial art film idiom was rooted in Pommer's remarkable ability to discover and support those directors best suited to fulfil his vision. By offering massive budgets and seemingly limitless production time frames, Pommer encouraged directors such as Wiene, Murnau, Lang, Dupont, and von Gerlach to develop their visual style and to introduce aesthetic and technical innovations, a policy that is reflected in the vast scope and technical brilliance of his productions. The landmark design of *Caligari*, the pictorial arrangements of the *Nibelungen*, the stunning set pieces in *Zur Chronik von Grieshuus* (The Chronicles of the Grey House, von Gerlach, 1925), the unchained camera in *Der letzte Mann* (The Last Laugh, Murnau, 1924), and the groundbreaking perspectives and expressive angles in *Varieté* (Variety, Dupont, 1925) would not have been possible without Pommer's financial backing, aesthetic support, and patience, which allowed Lang and von Gerlach in particular to go to every directorial extreme imaginable.

Significantly, Pommer's directors themselves were quite aware that the art films they produced were a direct reaction to the threat posed by American entertainment cinema, as Lang pointed out as early as 1924:

> Germany has never had, and will never have, access to the giant human and financial resources the American film industry can employ. And that is her good fortune. For it is precisely this that forces us to respond to this purely material superiority by our spiritual superiority [*geistiges Übergewicht*].[15]

---

[13] Erich Pommer, "Geschäftsfilm und künstlerischer Film," *Der Film* 50 (10 December 1922).

[14] See Hans-Michael Bock and Michael Töteberg, *Das Ufa-Buch. Kunst und Krisen, Stars und Regisseure, Wirtschaft und Politik,* (Frankfurt: Zweitausendeins, 1992), 101.

[15] Fritz Lang, "Wege des großen Spielfilms," *Die literarische Welt* 40 (1 October 1926), 5–6 (5).

Nevertheless, Pommer was professional enough to realize that by the 1920s, the technical standards in the film industry were set by Hollywood. Therefore, Pommer's and Lang's visit to the U.S.A. in 1924 was intended as a study trip which would give Lang the opportunity to visit the leading American studios and gather impressions he could incorporate into his next film project. At Universal, Warner Brothers, and United Artists, Lang learnt about American production style and technical facilities at first hand. He witnessed the shooting of Universal's *Phantom of the Opera* and was impressed by the massive set in which, as he told his German readers in "What I saw in America," "the great French opera in Paris was reconstructed";[16] in *The Lost World,* he could study Willis O'Brien's groundbreaking use of stop motion effects. What he rejected, however, was the subject matter of most American films, which, in his view, was characterized by the "monotony of the plots [and] ignorance of historical processes."[17]

Within the German art film paradigm, precisely these themes — history and myth — had led Lang (and Pommer) to success twice before, and after the triumph of *Destiny* and the *Nibelungen,* a new, similarly "Germanic" vision was called for to top these achievements. However, the influential contemporary critic and theorist Kurt Pinthus had already voiced dissent on the occasion of Lubitsch's *Das Weib des Pharao* (The Loves of Pharao, 1922): "The romantic historical mass spectacle has passed its peak and cannot be developed any further."[18] *Destiny* and *Nibelungen* were in themselves variations on the historical film, but according to Pinthus only a truly new approach could now pave the way for future German film making: "We have to distance ourselves from themes that are not only historically but also emotionally of the past. We have to find themes for the present, and for the future . . . . "[19] In New York, and with one eye on the American market, Lang found that theme — the city of the future.

So, in 1925 and in accordance with Ufa's production policy, the time for *Metropolis* had come: Pommer wanted another stylized megaproduction and was ready to finance it; Lang discovered a futuristic imagery that expanded and added to his filmic vision; and the technical state of

---

[16] Fritz Lang, "Was ich in Amerika sah — Neuyork und Los Angeles," *Film-Kurier,* 11 December 1924; cit. in Gehler and Kasten, *Fritz Lang,* 210.

[17] Fritz Lang, "Was lieben und hassen wir am amerikanischen Film?" *Deutsche Filmwoche,* 2 October 1925, 35.

[18] Kurt Pinthus, "Lubitsch in Ägypten" (review of *Das Weib des Pharao*), *Das Tage-Buch,* 18 March 1922, 416–20 (419).

[19] Review of *Metropolis, Das Tage-Buch,* 3 May 1924, 605; see Töteberg, *Fritz Lang,* 51.

film making had reached a stage at which this vision could be realized. Naturally, the vision of the American city was to be presented in the manner typical of Pommer's art film — mythical, suggestive, symbolic, Germanic. In keeping with the Teutonic spirit of film making, there had to be the *idea* of a deeply significant message, leading to what English reviewers called "two hours of grim, remorseless preaching."[20] There was, however, a major obstacle to these attempts at probing psychology and ideology. Even contemporary voices suggested that "Germany lacked stable and generally held social and moral conventions, thus a meaningful present";[21] Weimar offered no fixed cultural makeup to underpin the Germanic pathos. As a result, rather than presenting a coherent message, "in the absence of a consistent, representative world view, [Weimar film] reflected [. . .] the ideological and social confusion of the nation."[22]

In Ufa's monumental films, this tendency was reinforced by the scriptwriter who provided the plots for all of Lang's silent films from *Destiny* to *Frau im Mond* (Woman in the Moon, 1928/9): Lang's wife Thea von Harbou. Harbou's mixture of sentimentality, reactionary tendencies, "inner" piety and trivial, populist sensationalism had earned her the title of "Lady Kitschener," the countess of kitsch of German cinema.[23] In her screenplays and stories, she reduced various myths and literary sources to their potential for commercially successful, melodramatic sensationalism full of pseudoreligious pathos, as is evident in her scripts not only for Lang, but also for other Ufa directors such as Murnau (*Phantom*) or von Gerlach (*Chronicles of the Grey House*).[24] In the case of *Metropolis*, Harbou used her pastiche technique to create a disparate, trivialized collection of motifs from various literary sources, such as Wells's *Time Machine* and *The Sleeper Wakes* (the underworld of the workers), Shelley's *Frankenstein*, Villiers d'Isle Adam's *L'Eve Future* and Karl Capek's *R.U.R.* (an inventor creating artificial life), and con-

[20] "Sinister City of the Future," *Daily Express*, 22 March 1927, 9.

[21] Saunders, *Framing the Past*, 58, referring to Otto Kaus, "Guter und schlechter Kitsch," *Film-Kurier*, 28 July 1924 (unpaginated).

[22] Saunders, *Framing the Past*, 38–39.

[23] See Jürgen Kasten, *Film schreiben. Eine Geschichte des Drehbuchs* (Vienna: Hora, 1990), 24.

[24] On von Harbou, see Reinhold Keiner, *Thea von Harbou und der deutsche Film bis 1933* (Hildesheim: Georg Olms, 1984), and Karin Bruns, *Kinomythen 1920–1945: Die Filmentwürfe der Thea von Harbou* (Stuttgart: Metzler, 1995). On von Harbou's travesty of a literary source, see my *"Über die Heide ins Herz der Nation." Theodor Storms Novelle "Zur Chronik von Grieshuus" und ihre Verfilmung durch die Ufa 1925* (Essen: Die blaue Eule, 1996).

temporary German drama such as Georg Kaiser's *Gas* and Ernst Toller's *Masse Mensch.* The result was a "theme" whose eclecticism could hardly be surpassed, including a random mixture of socialism (workers versus capitalists), expressionism (the fascination and horror of machines, the modern city as Moloch, a father/son conflict, a vision of the renewal of mankind by a savior in the future), myth (the alchemist, Gothic visions), and romantic love story.

Because of the unique situation outlined above, *Metropolis* could indeed have been created only by Ufa, only in 1925, and only in Germany. As a commercialized art film, *Metropolis* was the climax of Pommer's strategies; as a vision of the future, it complemented Lang's filmic imagination; with the passion-laden but ultimately noncommittal stance manifest in Harbou's script and Lang's realization of it, *Metropolis* transposed contemporary social dislocation into filmic imagery and thus formed "an exact seismic reflex of the structural flux in the psychological and ideological stature of society".[25] Precisely because it turned into what Herbert Jhering perceptively calls an "ideological film without ideology"[26] *Metropolis* can be seen as representative of Weimar cinema and culture as such.

Significantly, Lang seems to have realized this process to some extent, as is evident in his comment "maybe there has never been a time that has looked for new forms to express itself with such ruthless resolve."[27] Similarly, one contemporary reviewer clearly understands this wider significance and points out that even though the film was subtitled *Schicksal einer Menschheit im Jahre 2000* (Fate of a Human Race in the Year 2000), *Metropolis* was far from being a mere science fiction film; rather, it was "official Germany in its entirety, as we know it and as we experience it first-hand every day."[28]

From Novel to Film

Metropolis epitomizes German silent cinema under the sign of Ufa, not only by virtue of its place in Pommer's production policy and the structures of Weimar society, but also in the very manner of its creation. What today would be called Ufa's "premarketing strategies" began

---

[25] Kreimeier, *Die Ufa-Story* 184.

[26] "Ein Weltanschauungsfilm ohne Weltanschauung;" Review of *Metropolis,* originally in *Berliner Börsen-Courier,* 11 January 1927; reprinted in Herbert Ihering, *Von Reinhardt bis Brecht. Vier Jahrzehnte Theater und Film,* vol. 2, *1924–1929* (Berlin: Aufbau-Verlag, 1959), 523–24 (523).

[27] Lang, "Wege des großen Spielfilms," 5.

[28] Hans Siemsen, "Eine Filmkritik, wie sie sein soll," *Die Weltbühne* 24 (14 July 1927), 947–50 (949).

with the novel on which the film was to be based. In 1925 Thea von Harbou wrote a novel about the city of the future, and she made no attempt to conceal its sole purpose of serving as the source for a film: "I place this book in your hands, Fried," Harbou stated in the preface.[29] The publication of the novel represents a textbook example of Ufa's marketing department at work: the novel was first serialized in the journal *Illustriertes Blatt*, where it appeared "amply illustrated with pictures from the film."[30] Only then did the novel appear as a book from the publishing house August Scherl, a company owned by Alfred Hugenberg. This sequence is typical of Ufa's multimedia marketing strategy for the so-called *Uco* films: Decla and later Ufa had signed a contract with the publisher Ullstein according to which successful novels planned as prospective film subjects would be serialized in the *Illustriertes Blatt*. The serial appeared while the film was already being shot, and the final installments were generally illustrated with film stills. The book version would finally be published by Ullstein or August Scherl in time for the premiere; it too constituted a movie "tie-in" and was illustrated with stills. This marketing technique had proved successful not only for Harbou's own novels, but also for adaptations, such as Norbert Jacques's *Dr. Mabuse*, which Lang had filmed in 1922.[31]

Before the actual shooting could begin, Lang had to form his own ideas and Harbou's script into a working basis for his film project. During this process, several motifs and plot elements originally envisaged were removed. Lang's description of the plans and of the changes may be regarded as a reflection of the ideological and spiritual diffuseness and confusion that was typical of Weimar cinema:

> I dabbled in so many things in my life, and I also dabbled in magic. Mrs. von Harbou and I put in the script of *Metropolis* a battle between modern science and occultism, the science of the medieval ages. The magician was the evil behind all the things that happened: in one scene all the bridges were falling down, there were flames, and out of a Gothic church came all these ghosts and ghouls and beasties. I

[29] Thea von Harbou, *Metropolis* (Frankfurt a.M.: Ullstein, 1984), 4.

[30] Press Department of Ufa, *Metropolis, Sondernummer des Ufa-Magazins*, ed. Stefan Lorant (Berlin: Bukwa, Presse Abteilung der Ufa, 1927), unpaginated. Hereafter cited as *Ufa-Magazin*.

[31] On *Uco*, see Kreimeier, *Die Ufa-Story*, 88 and 105, and Töteberg, *Fritz Lang*, 35–37. There seems to be some confusion as to the name of the newspaper: Kreimeier writes of the *Berliner Illustrierte*, whereas Töteberg refers to the *Berliner Illustrierte Zeitung*. The contemporary Ufa program, however, states that the serial appeared "in the 'Illustriertes Blatt.'"

> said, "No, I cannot do this." Today I would do it, but in those days I didn't have the courage.[32]

What remained of this apocalyptic scenario was a disparate mixture of high-tech upper world and medieval underworld, some isolated scenes in a Gothic cathedral, and Freder's dream vision of the dance of death — a collection that did not add up to a coherent vision, as Lang himself regretted in retrospect: "slowly we cut out all the magic and maybe for that reason I had the feeling that *Metropolis* was patched together".[33] Elements survived in the novel, which features a widespread Gothic cult and in which some apocalyptic visions occur; however, *Metropolis* would hardly have been more thematically convincing with these supernatural elements, as they only heighten the trivial romanticism of Harbou's novel. A further discarded plan focussed on the science fiction elements of the plot and foreshadowed Lang's subsequent film: "in our original version of *Metropolis*, I wanted the son of the Master to leave at the end and fly to the stars. This didn't work out in the script, but it was the first idea for *Woman in the Moon*".[34]

Lang and His Actors

Finally, in April 1925, the German trade journals informed their readers: "Fritz Lang has made such progress with the preparations for his film 'Metropolis,' based on a novel of the same title by Thea von Harbou, that he will begin shooting at the beginning of May."[35] Amidst similar public relations activities by Ufa, shooting of *Metropolis* began on 22 May 1925, with a budget of 1.5 million reichsmarks. Lang had cast relatively little-known actors in leading roles, as he had done in *Dr. Mabuse* and *Die Nibelungen*. For the role of the guardian of the heart machine, Lang had hired Heinrich George, who had been a theatre actor at Erwin Piscator's *Volksbühne* and who had appeared in Richard Oswald's historical spectacle *Lucrezia Borgia* (1922); the youthful hero Freder was to be played by Gustav Fröhlich, a former journalist who had only been planned for a supporting role.[36] A true newcomer was Brigitte Schittenhelm in the role of Maria. Although Schittenhelm, who shortened her name to "Helm" for her film career, had already attended trial shots for *Die Nibelungen*, she had no film experience. Lang, who

---

[32] Lang in Bogdanovich, *Fritz Lang in America*, 124.

[33] Lang in Bogdanovich, *Fritz Lang in America*, 124.

[34] Lang in Bogdanovich, *Fritz Lang in America*, 125.

[35] "Vertrieb und Verleih: Die Ufa-Produktion," *Der Film*, 19 April 1925, 45.

[36] See Kreimeier, *Die Ufa-Story*, 346, and Ludwig Maibohm, *Fritz Lang und seine Filme* 2nd ed. 1985 (Munich: Heyne), 100.

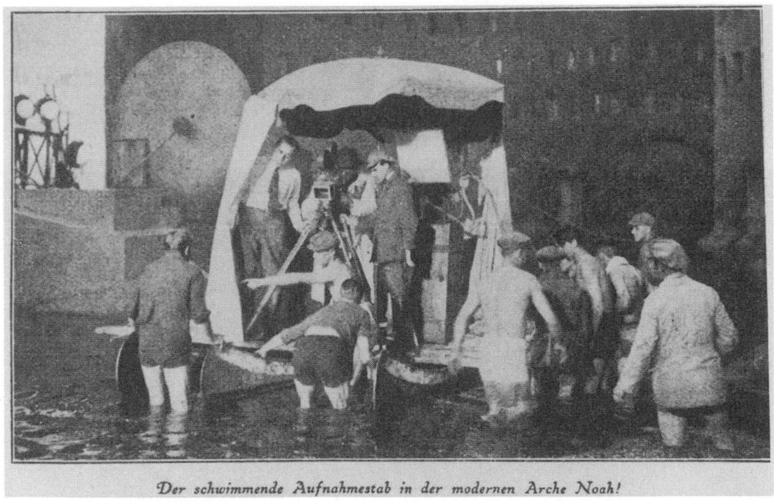

Der schwimmende Aufnahmestab in der modernen Arche Noah!

1. "The swimming filmcrew in a modern Noah's Ark." Lang directs the flooding sequence.

2. Lang prepares a shot with the moving camera. [Both photos courtesy of Deutsches Institut für Filmkunde, Frankfurt]

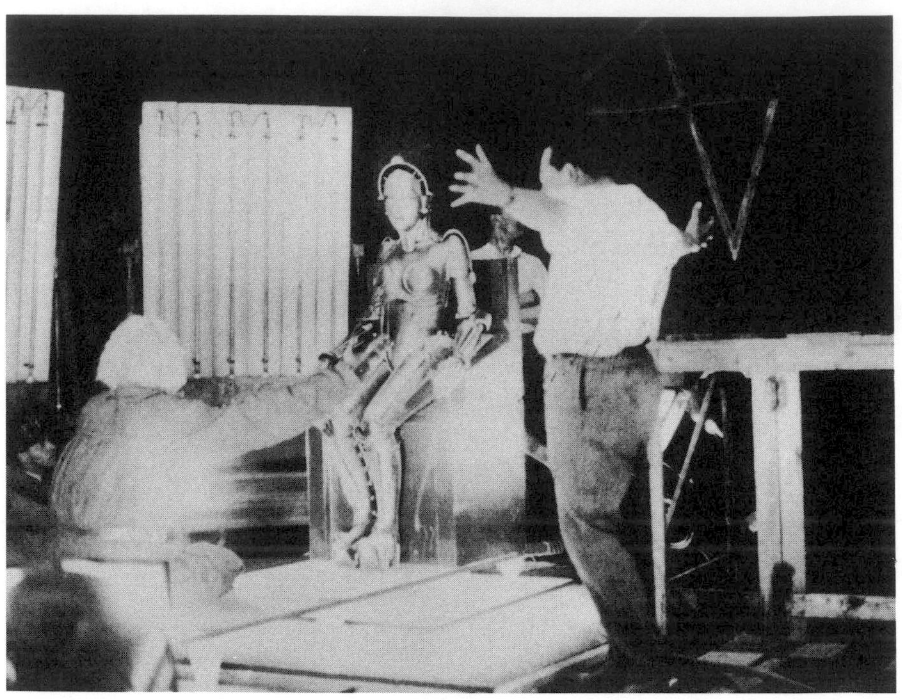

3. Lang gives instructions to Helm and Klein-Rogge.
[Deutsches Institut für Filmkunde, Frankfurt]

was always on the lookout for young actors, nevertheless hired her for the central role of the film, a carte-blanche decision reminiscent of Murnau, who around the same time opted for the relatively inexperienced Camilla Horn as Gretchen in his *Faust*.[37]

Both castings are symptomatic of Ufa's focus on the director as opposed to America's star cult: for Pommer's directors, actors were merely resources that became valuable as soon as they could be formed into their visions. Lang's (and Murnau's and von Gerlach's) directorial methods are directly related to this attitude, as Helm's account of her audition reveals: "I was given a letter to read, and while I was reading, the light was switched on, and the cameraman started cranking. In short: I was filmed. Then the actor Alberti came up to me, shouted at me, insulted me. This little incident was necessary so that Fritz Lang could test my ability to express emotions."[38]

What this so-called little incident also reveals is a hallmark of the whole production of *Metropolis*: an almost manic obsession with perfection that Lang himself extolled as one of the virtues of German film. According to Lang, film would develop into art only in Germany because cinema could only find its true form "with a German perseverance that is fed by an obsessive mental preoccupation with the 'work' [*das Werk*]."[39] The "work" did indeed obsess Lang, and the shooting of *Metropolis* probably represents the climax of this fixation, which is evident both in his directorial style and in the perfectionism with which his team realized the vision of the future.

In the edition of the *Ufa-Magazin* devoted to *Metropolis*, Gustav Fröhlich, Rudolf Klein-Rogge, Fritz Rasp, Alfred Abel and Theodor Loos recount their experience on the set of *Metropolis*.[40] Naturally, the accounts were meant to be light-hearted, anecdotal sketches, but Lang emerges from between the lines as a rigorous, ruthless dictator driving his actors to ever new extremes. Lang wanted every scene to be exactly the way he imagined it, which is why he always demonstrated the scene to the actors and even interfered in makeup and costumes on the set. Mostly, however, he strove for the utmost filmic effect. In a scene in which Theodor Loos (Josaphat) was meant to hit Fritz Rasp (Der Schmale), Loos was "egged on by Fritz Lang, who wanted to film the

---

[37] Lang describes his — often frustrating — search for new talent in Ludwig Spitzer, "Fritz Lang über den Film der Zukunft," *Die Filmtechnik*, 15 July 1925; see Part One of this volume.

[38] Brigitte Helm, "Wie ich entdeckt wurde," *Ufa-Magazin*, unpaginated.

[39] Lang, "Wege des großen Spielfilms," 5.

[40] See Part One of this volume for the accounts by Alfred Abel and Theodor Loos.

sudden reaction in my face, to hit me [Rasp] so hard that I passed out. As everyone told me, I had never acted so true to life." For the flooding scene, Brigitte Helm, Theodor Loos and five hundred children from the poor quarters of Berlin had to shoot for fourteen days in a pool of water that Lang "kept at quite a low temperature, to nip excessive demonstrations of our youthful gaiety in the bud." Lang, who directed the scene from a specially built raft, "encouraged us . . . to seek out the biggest jets of water" in order to gain the most terrifying effects. Lang's manic perfectionism is probably illustrated best by Gustav Fröhlich's account, which reveals that under Pommer's directive, Lang could afford to spend two days on a single scene:

> [The shooting] takes hour after hour, until we are so exhausted and tired that we enter a trance like state in which we begin to believe in our love ourselves . . . And again, because the embrace still wasn't affectionate enough . . . This time, the kiss was too short . . . On my knees, from morning to midnight! The camera shoots us from a different angle every time. And every time we repeat the scene even more fanatically, even more ardently. For two days . . . [41]

A film journalist who had visited the set put Lang's way of working in a more objective perspective: "Lang repeats the takes so frequently that only the professionalism of his actors prevents the shooting from becoming a suicidally hazardous enterprise."[42]

Mirrors and a "Kind of Sandwich Paper" — Special Effects

While Lang's radical way of directing his actors remained to a large extent behind the scenes, the same compulsive drive to perfection also produced the film's most memorable characteristic: its profound visual impact. What no critic could deny was that *Metropolis* showed cinema as it had never been seen before, with images only modern cinema could produce. The two surviving pages from the shooting script show that Lang immediately visualized a scene.[43] The resulting visual quality, which to this day distinguishes *Metropolis*, however, derived not only

---

[41] Gustav Fröhlich, "Eine Liebesszene wird gedreht," *Ufa-Magazin* (unpaginated).

[42] A. Kraszna-Krauß, "Wo man 'Metropolis' dreht . . . ," *Die Filmtechnik* 4 (5 August 1925), 75–76 (76).

[43] The *Metropolis* screenplay held in the *Stiftung Deutsche Kinemathek* in Berlin represents an earlier version of the script that was found in the papers of Gottfried Huppertz, the composer who supplied the score for *Metropolis*. The actual shooting script containing Lang's meticulous notes and sketches seems to be lost; however, the two pages referred to above were published in the *Ufa-Magazin* and have survived in this form. See Enno Patalas, "The City of the Future — A Film of Ruins," in Part Two of this volume.

from Lang's own vision but also from the creations by Lang's camera team Karl Freund and Günther Rittau and by his architects Otto Hunte, Erich Kettelhut, and Karl Vollbrecht.

As in the case of *Die Nibelungen*, *Metropolis* relied in part on massive full-size sets constructed at Neubabelsberg, including "extensive and complicated interiors" and a huge water tank for the flooding scene on the back lot.[44] However, *Metropolis* mostly represents an apotheosis of the use of special effects not only in German silent film, but in German film as a whole. Due to its predilection for the supernatural, Ufa had always specialized in special effects, but in *Metropolis* Lang's team broke new ground by combining state-of-the-art techniques: the Schüfftan process, the stop motion effects Lang had witnessed in America, and superimposition.

Named after its inventor Eugen Schüfftan, the *Spiegeltrickverfahren* (mirror trick process) created the possibility of combining models with live action. A mirror was placed in front of the camera to reflect objects behind or next to the camera, such as models of buildings or landscapes; this mirror was either half-transparent or placed at an angle that allowed the camera to film both actors and models at the same time.[45] The result was a convincing fusion of actors and special-effect objects that was used to tremendous effect in *Metropolis*. Günther Rittau, the cameraman who was responsible for the use of the mirror special effects, points out:

> With the help of parts of sets and smaller-scale Schüfftan models, we created parts of the gigantic street scenes and the atmospheric scenes in the cathedral . . . Most complicated were the visionary images of the Moloch machine, which were also made with the help of the mirror trick process.[46]

The Schüfftan process was also used for the city of the workers, the "Stadium of the Sons," the club Yoshiwara, the machine room, the tower of Babel, Rotwang's house and the sculpture of the head of Fredersen's wife Hel.[47] For scenes in which the Schüfftan process could not have been employed due to movement required throughout the frame, Rittau resorted to stop motion, the clearest example of this procedure being the famous long shot of the main street full of pedestrians,

---

[44] Kraszna-Krauß, "Wo man 'Metropolis' dreht . . . " 75.

[45] A detailed description is given by Rolf Giesen, *Special Effects* (Berlin: edition 8½, 1985), 34.

[46] Günther Rittau, "Trickaufnahmen in *Metropolis*," *Mein Film* 60 (1927), 6. An English translation of an extract from this piece can be found in Part One of this volume.

[47] Giesen, *Special Effects*, 36.

cars and airplanes. In these special-effect shots, which are probably indebted to Lang's witnessing of the use of stop motion in American studios, the "perseverance" Lang had demanded for an art film reached a climax,[48] as is evident in Rittau's description:

> One illustration of how difficult such shots are is the fact that we worked for almost 8 days in order to shoot 40 metres of film showing model scenery; every single frame had to be shot individually, and 40 metres of film contain 2,100 individual frames. In the film, this whole scene does not last longer than 10 seconds.[49]

A whole subdivision of technicians had to be employed to achieve the motion effect Lang imagined for the long shots, as Erich Kettelhut recalls in his unpublished memoirs:

> Based on the test shots we found out that after every single frame, planes had to be moved by one and a half centimetres, trams by one centimetre, cars by roughly three quarters of a centimetre and the pedestrians only by minimal steps in order to create a flowing movement at a realistic speed . . . Only reliable people could carry out this job.[50]

One of the most lasting and impressive images of the whole film, however, was created by the more traditional effect of superimposition: the light rings by which the robot is turned into the "false" Maria. For this famous scene, Lang merely shot the image of the sitting robot, while the special effects — often celebrated as Lang's superb vision — were the contributions of Rittau's team. Rittau placed a black velvet silhouette of the robot in front of the camera and shot two moving light rings that were pulled up and down alongside the silhouette; the same piece of film had to be exposed six times to create the twelve rings of light around the figure. His assistant, H. O. Schulze, recalled that the light rings themselves "were made of a kind of sandwich paper [*Stullenpapier*] distributing the light."[51] His words give some idea of the ingenuity with which Rittau's team produced entirely convincing, spectacular visual effects.

The reason for this fixation on overwhelming visual special effects was only partly a consequence of the fact that *Metropolis* was set in the future. Much more importantly, the groundbreaking technical achievement of the film is representative of the conviction that the "fantastic, mysterious events absolutely had to be made *visible* (my

---

[48] Lang, "Wege des großen Spielfilms," 5.

[49] Rittau, "Trickaufnahmen," 6.

[50] Cited in Giesen, *Special Effects*, 37.

[51] Giesen , *Special Effects*, 39.

italics)," as Rittau put it.[52] For both Lang and his camera crew the visual impact was not only paramount, but in itself the meaning and the message of the film as a pictorial realization of emotions and visions; in Lang's own words, the realization of "the storming rhythm" of machines and the city.[53] When Lang, together with Freund, employed a swinging camera to render the shock of an explosion or when he used a series of symbolic superimpositions to signify Freder's agony and hallucinations, he was driven by the same obsession as when he laboured over technical effects — an obsessive urge to visualize completely what was to be conveyed. The object, as Karl Freund put it, was "to express the horror in visual terms [and] to create that illusion, that visual impression in the spectator that, rhythmically and subjectively, corresponds exactly to the content of the scene."[54] In more universal terms, Lang summarized his intentions in making *Metropolis* as the desire to prove, "even more than in *Dr. Mabuse*, . . . to prove that . . . film has the potential to lay bare processes of the soul and so to give psychological grounding to the events."[55] It was this fanatical search for the perfect "psychological," emotional, and symbolic image that made Lang demand an army of 1,000 bald men for the visionary scene of the Tower of Babel and that made him shoot it six times; that made him order realistic (and dangerous!) explosions for the rise of the workers; and that drove him to act like a torturer towards his actors.

The result of this extreme approach was an outrageously lengthy shooting period during which Lang repeatedly exceeded his budget, until the final production cost of *Metropolis* had reached the notorious 5.1 million reichsmarks that turned *Metropolis* into the most expensive German silent film ever. This technical and artistic obsession and megalomania was not unique to Lang, although critics have frequently distinguished him for it. Rather, it haunted all of Pommer's best directors: Murnau, who, like Lang, attempted to express emotions by moving camera and treated his actors ruthlessly; Dupont, who presented the same radical angles that Lang demanded from Freund and Rittau; and von Gerlach, who needed seventeen months to finish *Chronicles of the Grey House*, for which a complete castle was constructed on the back lot. These similarities in production technique again suggest that *Me-*

---

[52] Rittau, "Trickaufnahmen," 6.

[53] Spitzer, "Fritz Lang über den Film der Zukunft," 230.

[54] Karl Freund, "Die fliegende Kamera," *Ufa-Magazin* (unpaginated).

[55] Spitzer, "Fritz Lang über den Film der Zukunft," 230. Significantly, at around the same time, G. W. Pabst similarly used filmic imagery and advanced special effects photography to uncover psychological processes in the so-called psychoanalytic film *Secrets of a Soul*.

tropolis may be seen as an epitome of Weimar cinema. The urge to force every detail and nuance into the overall aesthetic vision — even if the thematic groundwork was lacking, as in *Metropolis* — "characterizes Ufa as cultural syndrome and aesthetic workshop . . . this interplay between perfectionism and [thematic] inarticulateness is part of the 'aesthetics of Ufa' and its role between culture and politics in the years of the Weimar Republic."[56]

4. The special effects crew set up a stop motion shot.
[Deutsches Institut für Filmkunde, Frankfurt]

[56] Kreimeier, *Die Ufa-Story*, 188.

5. German poster for the film's run at the Ufa-Pavillon.
[Deutsches Institut für Filmkunde, Frankfurt]

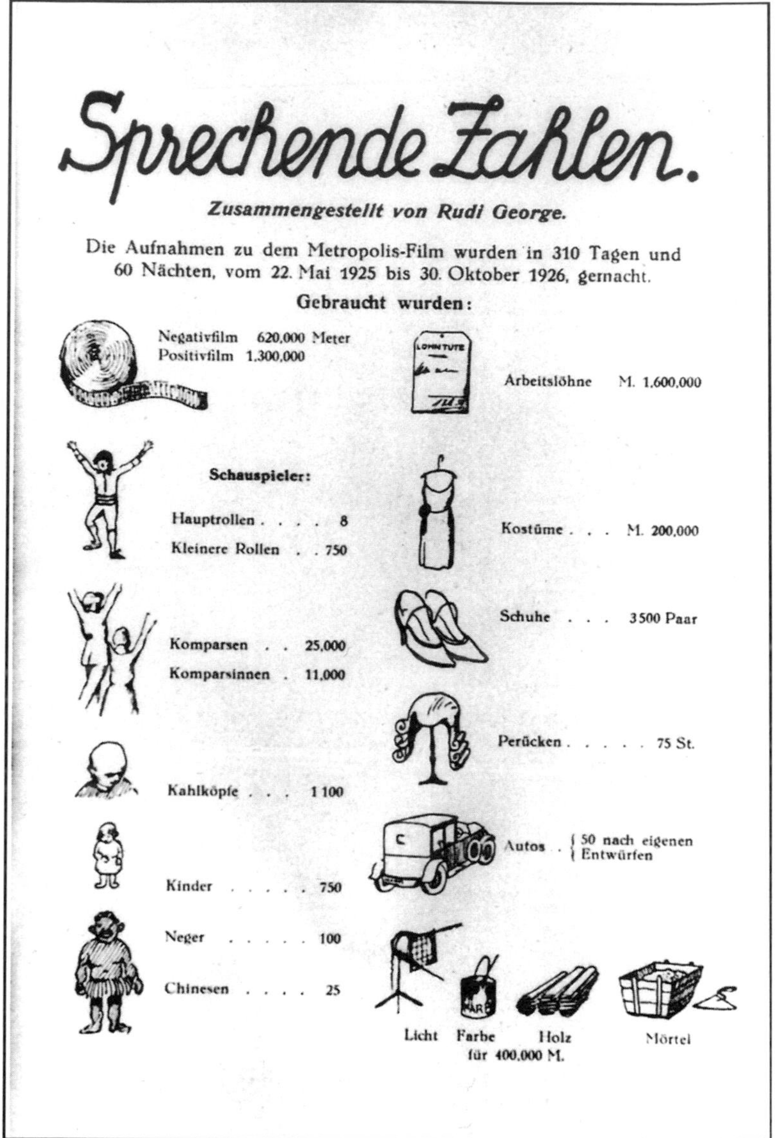

Sprechende Zahlen.

Zusammengestellt von Rudi George.

Die Aufnahmen zu dem Metropolis-Film wurden in 310 Tagen und 60 Nächten, vom 22. Mai 1925 bis 30. Oktober 1926, gemacht.

Gebraucht wurden:

Negativfilm 620.000 Meter
Positivfilm 1.300.000

Arbeitslöhne M. 1.600.000

Schauspieler:

Hauptrollen 8
Kleinere Rollen . . 750

Kostüme . . . M. 200.000

Schuhe . . . 3500 Paar

Komparsen . . 25.000
Komparsinnen . 11.000

Perücken . . . . . 75 St.

Kahlköpfe . . . 1100

Autos . . 50 nach eigenen Entwürfen

Kinder 750

Neger 100

Chinesen 25

Licht Farbe Holz Mörtel
für 400.000 M.

6. The film's notorious "vital statistics" from the *Ufa-Magazin*. [Deutsches Institut für Filmkunde, Frankfurt]

DIE FILMWOCHE

SCHRIFTLEITUNG: PAUL ICKES

BERLIN, 12. JAN. 1927 | Herausgeber: Filmschriften-Verlagsgesellschaft m. b. H. Berlin SW 11, Bernburger Straße 13 · Telephon: Nollendorf 7526/27 | HEFT 2

Aus
„METROPOLIS"
Fritz Lang-Film der
UFA
im Verleih der Parufamet

(Phot.: Ufa)

Oben:
BRIGITTE HELM als Maschinen-mensch

Darunter:
ALFRED ABEL und RUDOLF KLEIN-ROGGE

7. *Metropolis* in the trade press. The front cover of *Die Filmwoche*, 12 January 1927. [Deutsches Institut für Filmkunde, Frankfurt]

Reception in Germany

Metropolis was first shown in Berlin on 10 January 1927, but as we have seen, Ufa's propaganda machinery had kicked into gear long before that date. During the actual shooting at Neubabelsberg, the company invited representatives of the leading trade journals to witness the most spectacular moments of the film's production. These public relations events were an integral part of Ufa's marketing strategy, which used the attraction of the studios to encourage enthusiastic "work shop" reports in the trade press that in turn created widespread interest even before the film was released by offering a fascinating glimpse behind the scenes. This technique had proved successful in attracting attention to *Die Nibelungen* (journalists had been present during the shooting of the dragon fight and the burning of the castle of the Huns) and to *The Chronicles of the Grey House*; a stunned Willy Haas wrote an account of the unchained camera in action on the set of *The Last Laugh*.[57] For *Metropolis*, the journalists were invited to witness scenes such as the flooding, the explosion of the main machine room and the burning of the robot at the stake; the critics were also able to study every other aspect of the production, such as Freund's and Rittau's extreme angles, the swinging camera, and even the size of the sets and the special effect models used. Production reports appeared from 1925 onwards throughout the leading trade publications, and they were illustrated by preliminary stills supplied by Ufa as early as 1926.[58] These articles clearly fulfilled Ufa's publicity purposes by printing plot summaries and vivid accounts of the shooting that were used to underline the superiority of German studios:

> A glaring flash of light, a terrifying detonation, one of the gigantic escalators breaks down with a terrifying crash. Licking flames, smoke, splinters, destruction. — The explosion is a splendid success. A daring deed that simply could not be permitted to fail . . . a tremendous step ahead in the gargantuan work on "Metropolis." One can already rest assured today that Fritz Lang and Ufa are creating a piece of work

---

[57] See Willy Haas, "Was wird gearbeitet? Ein Besuch im Ufa-Gelände Neubabelsberg," *Film-Kurier*, 19 July 1924, and Alex Kossowsky, "Die Berliner Ateliers," *Film-Kurier*, 25 September 1924 (both unpaginated).

[58] See for instance "Das Film-Modell," *Mein Film* 28 (1926), 11, which published shots of the Tower of Babel model, and "Wo 'Metropolis' gedreht wird . . . ," which described the outdoor sets, the plot, Lang's direction, and Freund's and Rittau's camerawork. Working for Ufa, Lang had to accept these promotional activities, even though he felt that stills explaining trick photography destroyed the cinematic illusion; see Spitzer in Part One.

> here that once again will prove that German film is among the world's best productions.[59]

The prerelease articles also show that the German film world clearly realized the film's raison d'être as a perfect specimen of Pommer's production policy — an "art" counterweight to American dominance at home and abroad. The Austrian journal *Mein Film* even took *Metropolis* as an opportunity to muse on American and German film production in general:

> The two film industries of global significance have been in competition with each other for years now: the German industry and the American one . . . [Germany] strove hard to equal American technical standards. This has not been achieved so far. But German directors have surpassed the Americans in the artistic aspects of film making. And these are perhaps the decisive aspects . . . The film "Metropolis," on which Fritz Lang, director of "Die Nibelungen," has been working for over a year now, seems to surpass everything previously produced in terms of sheer monumentalism: the monumentalism of its artistic, technical and architectural achievement. What was been created here (Lang is just about to finish shooting) exceeds even the wildest dreams of the Americans when they try to conceive of the potential of German film.[60]

Ufa's propaganda machinery thus made sure that expectations were high when the film did actually have its premiere in Ufa's flagship cinema, the *Ufa-Palast am Zoo.* With over 2,100 seats and an orchestra of seventy-five, with its spectacular lighting and pompous design, the *Ufa-Palast* was the perfect venue for Pommer's grandiose spectacles such as *Faust, Chronicles of the Grey House* or *Variety*. It created the mythical, stylized atmosphere that also permeated the films presented there. Moreover, for the biggest productions, both the interior and the exterior of the cinema were decorated with key visual elements corresponding to the style of the particular film; for *Chronicles of the Grey House,* for instance, a model of the stylized castle Grieshuus and a huge oak tree adorned the façade of the cinema.[61] These elaborate decorations were not simply a means of advertising, but also, by setting a pervasive atmosphere, subliminally manipulated the audience and thus "made it

[59] "Hinter Filmkulissen," *Kinematograph,* 25 October 1925, 16.

[60] "Der zukunftsphantastische Film *Metropolis,*" *Mein Film* 25 (1926), 9–10 (9). See Part One of this volume for the full text in translation.

[61] See Holger Bachmann, *"Über die Heide ins Herz der Nation." Theodor Storms Novelle Zur Chronik von Grieshuus und ihre Verfilmung durch die Ufa 1925* (Essen: Die blaue Eule, 1996), 156.

receptive to the film's message."[62] The screening of *Metropolis* saw the massive *Ufa-Palast* "transformed to this end into a silver building that gleams like a beacon into the night,"[63] so that the cinema itself became part of Lang's vision of a futuristic city — a fitting link considering the intricate connection linking not only *Metropolis*, but also Weimar cinema as such, with the city made manifest in Berlin (compare the films by Walter Ruttmann, Joe May, and Robert Siodmak). In the inner foyer, a copper-coated reproduction of the giant alarm bell rung by Helm during the flooding set the atmosphere for one of the most spectacular scenes of the film.

As usual for Ufa premieres, *Metropolis* attracted a distinguished audience. The company had efficiently turned the film's release into a major cultural event by inviting representative members of Weimar society, such as "the leading public officials, the *Reichskanzler*, ministers, aldermen and various prominent names from the worlds of art and literature;"[64] one reviewer simply stated "'Ganz Berlin' war da."[65] The presentation of the film was accompanied by a score by Gottfried Huppertz, Ufa's prolific composer, who made use of the trivial leitmotif technique that also characterized his work for *Die Nibelungen* and *Chronicles of the Grey House*.

What this audience — and probably only this audience — saw was the original, uncut version of *Metropolis*. This version, which had been classified by the censors on 13 November 1926 as "Nicht für Jugendliche zugelassen" (Not permitted for young persons), consisted of nine acts and was 4,189 metres long; the film ran for roughly 150 minutes, excluding one intermission. The influence of Ufa had gained the film the distinctions "Volksbildend" (A film of educational value) and "Künstlerisch wertvoll" (Artistically valuable), thereby further boosting its claim to cultural significance — and, on a more practical note, making the film exempt from large parts of the entertainment tax, which was an additional incentive for cinema owners to show it.[66] Nevertheless, the

[62] Kreimeier, *Die Ufa-Story* 141.

[63] Review of *Metropolis*, *Kinematograph*, 16 January 1927, 21.

[64] Review of *Metropolis*, *Kinematograph*, 16 January 1927, 21.

[65] *Deutsche Tageszeitung*, cited in "Pressestimmen über Metropolis," *Kinematograph*, 16 January 1927, 17–18 (17).

[66] On the length and rating of the censored version, see "Filmschau: *Metropolis*," *Der Bildwart* April/May 1927, 326–29 (326). The running time, which indicates that the film was shown at a projection speed of twenty-four frames per second, is stated in two contemporary reviews and can also be deduced from the score by Gottfried Huppertz. For the basic calculation of running time according to length and projection speed, see the film measurement tables in Paolo Cherchi Usai (ed.), *Burning*

response of the audience was mixed: according to the contemporary reviews, the visual elements of the film generally impressed, while "the reaction to the film's plot was (to put it mildly) divided."[67] While some reviewers, including the critic writing for the *Berliner Morgenpost*, reported "seemingly endless applause which, in the intermission and at the end, again and again called for the director, his team, and the actors,"[68] the truth seems to be that there was only "faint applause in which some boos and hisses could be heard."[69]

These conflicting accounts are representative of the entire coverage *Metropolis* received in the German press. A whole range of German newspapers from across the political spectrum praised the film as a remarkable achievement: the liberal-democratic *Berliner Morgenpost* admired an "awesome work," *Der Tag* even stated "One can sense it: this is the film of all films — the *Über*-film!" and the right-wing papers *Berliner Lokal-Anzeiger* (owned by Alfred Hugenberg), *Deutsche Zeitung,* and the nationalistic *Neue Preußische Kreuz-Zeitung* elevated the film into the "major event of the season" and "the greatest German film so far."[70] In the midst of this chorus of praise, however, there were dissonant voices led by the most influential film critics of the Weimar republic: Willy Haas, Herbert Jhering, Paul Ickes and Rudolf Arnheim. These analytically probing reviews mostly attack a mindless megalomania that had resulted in "a massive effort shamelessly wasted" on a sentimental, trivial plot.[71] None of them denies the sheer spectacle and cinematic craftsmanship. "Fritz Lang has created many images that are indeed impressive," as Rudolf Arnheim points out;[72] Willy Haas even begins his review by playing Ufa's game and sets the film off against American competitors: "What has been achieved in this German film leaves American camerawork far behind and is entirely unique in the

---

Passions. An Introduction to the Study of Silent Cinema (London: British Film Institute, 1994), 93–96.

67 Review of *Metropolis, Die Filmwoche,* 19 January 1927, 56.

68 *Berliner Morgenpost,* cited in "Pressestimmen über Metropolis," *Kinematograph,* 16 January 1927, 17–18 (18).

69 "Filmschau: *Metropolis,*" *Der Bildwart,* 326.

70 "Pressestimmen über *Metropolis,*" 17–18.

71 "Filmschau: *Metropolis,*" *Der Bildwart,* 326.

72 Rudolf Arnheim, review of *Metropolis, Das Stachelschwein,* 1 February 1927, 52–53 (52). Arnheim's review has been reprinted in Helmut H. Diederichs, ed., *Rudolf Arnheim. Kritiken und Aufsätze zum Film* (Munich: Fischer, 1977), 184–86.

history of cinema."[73] As we have seen, Lang was obsessed with visualizing the idea of "the city," and in so doing he had, in Luis Buñuel's words, successfully created a beautiful, gargantuan ballet;[74] more complex thematic implications were secondary for Lang. Nevertheless, it was with some justification that contemporary critics relentlessly uncovered the banality and even reactionary tendencies of von Harbou's script. Their reviews inaugurated the widespread evaluation of *Metropolis* as a visually accomplished but thematically dismal hybrid to which Lang himself also subscribed later on, stating that "the main thesis was Mrs. von Harbou's, but I am at least fifty per cent responsible because I did it . . . I was interested in machines . . . "[75]

Herbert Jhering, for instance, states that *Metropolis* was an utter failure from the outset, since "a modern *Großfilm* [high budget film production] and the regressive, novel-oriented imagination of Thea von Harbou have nothing to do with each other."[76] Similarly, Willy Haas feels that the strange eclecticism of medieval and futuristic, of mythical and pseudoreligious is nothing but an evasion of the questions tackled, a "noncommittal stance of belles lettres desperately drawing on tomorrow and yesterday in order to avoid today"[77] — a tendency we have already identified as representative of Ufa's policy in general. Rudolf Arnheim particularly castigates the anachronistic, reactionary tendencies of Harbou's script and warns of the danger inherent in her seemingly naive approach to the so-called social question:

> Fashionable genre scenes and medieval depictions of ghosts and ghouls, painted in machine oil. No trace of *Neue Sachlichkeit*. . . . [von Harbou] went forth in search of our times — her territory was a novel that was also meant to be the source for a film. On the program, her impish face shines out below the bobbed hair, but she is dangerous, nonetheless. For she plants sentimentalities in a bed in which they already grow like rank weeds and from which they must be rooted out

---

[73] "Zwei große Filmpremieren," *Die literarische Welt*, 21 January 1927, 7. For the full text of Haas's review in translation, see Part One of this volume.

[74] Review of *Metropolis*, *Cahiers du cinéma* 223 (August/September 1970), 20–21 (21). See Part One of this volume for the full text.

[75] Bogdanovich, *Fritz Lang in America*, 124.

[76] "Der Metropolis-Film," *Berliner-Börsen Courier*, 11 January 1927; reprinted in Ihering, *Von Reinhardt bis Brecht*, 523–24 (524). For the text in translation, see Part One of this volume.

[77] Haas, "Was wird gearbeitet?" 7.

> ruthlessly if progress is to be made in this world . . . Beware: manicured hands should not meddle with socialism![78]

Probably most surprisingly, even *Die Filmwoche*, a trade journal owned by Alfred Hugenberg, had the courage to speak up against *Metropolis*. As had been the case when *Die Nibelungen*, *Grey House* and *Variety* opened, the front page of the magazine was dedicated to Ufa's recent megaproduction, with a detailed account of the plot, but the review by Paul Ickes, editor in chief, is nothing less than a direct and sustained attack on von Harbou and Lang. Ickes criticizes the disjunction between technical perfection and thematic emptiness:

> Dear *gnädige Frau* von Harbou: I am profoundly concerned by this film; I haven't watched a film that so dispelled my enjoyment and compelled me to demur to such an extent in a long time. And dear Herr Fritz Lang: Despite the inhuman amount of work put into it, the film is as hopeless — as far as [thematic] perspective is concerned — as it could possibly be . . . Dear Herr Lang, do pay more attention to sober common sense — for it is what really matters, *do not always think only of the individual images*! It is your undoing that it is the image for you, and not the idea, that counts: you are held prisoner by the images. And, to be sure, many of your images are wonderful, the technique is excellent — but the whole must have meaning and content, must make sense to us![79]

Following these severe attacks, Ufa must have realized early on that the film would not become the success it had hoped for. In a bid to convince cinema owners that the film would do big business, whatever the critics wrote, the company not only produced a film program, it also compiled a special press booklet with stills, a synopsis, and a representative collection of positive reviews; thc company also published this in

---

[78] Rudolf Arnheim, *Kritiken und Aufsätze*, 52. Rudolf Arnheim's views on the lack of *Neue Sachlichkeit* in *Metropolis* are challenged by Haas, who criticizes von Harbou precisely for fusing "a little socialism with the new, spic-and-span cult of the machine [*der neue tipptoppe Maschinenkult*];" see Haas's review in Part One of this volume. In considering the relevance of the city and the machine in *Metropolis*, Haas seems to come closer to a key element of the film than does Arnheim. More importantly, however, these diametrically opposed statements by two perceptive critics illustrate how *Metropolis* amalgamated disparate stylistic and thematic elements. The significance of *Neue Sachlichkeit* elements in *Metropolis* is still a major point of debate for modern analytical readings. Different interpretations of this aspect of the film are given by Andreas Huyssen, "The Vamp and the Machine: Fritz Lang's *Metropolis*," and R. L. Rutsky, "The Mediation of Technology and Gender: *Metropolis*, Nazism, Modernism"; see Part Two of this volume.

[79] Paul Ickes, "Kritik der Leinwand: *Metropolis*," (*Die Filmwoche*, 19 January 1927, 60–61 (60).

the *Kinematograph*[80] — doubtless with the aim of manipulating public opinion of the film. In fact, recent essays on Weimar film criticism have suggested that by printing possible headlines and entire text blocks, Ufa directly influenced a great number of the reviews of its films. It seems probable that just such a carefully directed critical response may have been behind the positive reviews of *Metropolis* — a hypothesis that would explain the curiously polarized coverage we have observed above.[81]

Moreover, Ufa's marketing department resorted to techniques usually associated with prewar Italian historical spectacles and attempted to sell the film by its sheer size. In the special edition of the *Ufa-Magazin* dedicated to *Metropolis,* the company published the now notorious so-called telling figures concerning the film's production: 1,300,000 metres of positive film; 758 actors; 36,000 extras; 1,100 bald men; 750 children; 100 black people; twenty-five Chinese people; 1,600,000 reichsmarks for salaries; 200,000 reichsmarks for costumes; 3,500 pairs of shoes; seventy-five wigs; fifty specially designed cars; and lighting, paint, wood, and mortar worth 400,000 reichsmarks. Similarly, the program pictured the most spectacular sets and claimed "all this had to be built!"

Publications close to Ufa, such as the *Kinematograph,* took up this cue and argued that *Metropolis* ushered in "a new age of film production. This alone must be motivation enough for German theatre owners, who must give prominence to this great film."[82] In the more objective reviews, however, this rather blunt attempt on Ufa's side to impress audiences and critics by size backfired and was denounced as a "manipulative snobbery of numbers" that was rejected as a plain "attempt at bribery."[83] As a consequence, and despite all attempts on Ufa's side to salvage the film, *Metropolis* became not only the most expensive, but also the most disastrous of the company's productions. This failure was exacerbated by the Americanized version of the film which also came into German cinemas soon after the premiere of the original cut.

---

[80] "Pressestimmen über Metropolis," 17–18.

[81] Paul Ries argues that such clearly calculated public relations measures were used to promote Pabst's *Geheimnisse einer Seele* (Secrets of a Soul, 1925/26); "*Geheimnisse einer Seele*: Wessen Film und wessen Psychoanalyse?" *Jahrbuch der Psychoanalyse* 39 (1998), 46–80 (68–69).

[82] Review of *Metropolis, Kinematograph,* 16 January 1927, 21.

[83] Reviews by Theodor Heuss, cited in Kreimeier, *Die Ufa-Story* 184, and by Rudolf Arnheim, *Kritiken und Aufsätze,* 52.

THE MORNING POST, TUESDAY, MARCH 15, 1927.

ARE BRITISH FILMS MENACED BY A GERMAN "HOLLYWOOD"?

"THE GARDEN OF THE SONS OF RICH MEN."—This picture shows the immensity of the setting. The runners on the track are dwarfed by surroundings as vast as those of the Wembley Stadium.

METROPOLIS.—The workers live in an underground City of their own, and are here preparing to ascend to their labours in huge lifts. The motif of the story is the reconciliation of Capital with Labour.

The German "wonder film" "Metropolis" is shortly to be given a "special presentation" at the Marble Arch Pavilion; and behind that bare announcement lies much which may be of serious importance to the British film Industry. The film has not yet been viewed in England, and its merits, therefore, must be left to the critics when it is staged. The issue, however, is a larger one than the merits of this particular German film. The real point is the determined effort on the part of Germany to wrest from America her hold on the British Market, and the ambition of the young producer, Fritz Lang, to turn the Ufa studios into the Hollywood of Europe for exploiting German films. With "Metropolis" he has spared no effort. The story is by his wife, Thea von Harbou, a "best seller" of the Jules Verne type, and concerns life in the year 2027. The settings, therefore, demand treatment which is "futuristic" in the actual sense of the word, and the resources brought to bear are amply demonstrated in the immense model—half the size of the studio—shown immediately above. There traffic moves on bridges hundreds of feet above the roadway, while aeroplanes circle over the fantastic super-skyscrapers. It is claimed that the production cost a quarter of a million sterling, and that from first to last 37,000 paid actors and actresses were employed. The film may or may not appeal to British tastes, but there can be no doubt as to the gigantic nature of the effort. In any case, these are the days of "big things," and the spectacle of German production on such colossal lines is not a comforting one. While we in England dream of building a "Hollywood" the Germans are building one in actual fact.

LANG'S CONCEPTION of a Female Robot.

CREATING A "STAR."—Herr Lang does not believe in employing world-celebrated "Stars." He found Brigitte Helm when she was 16 and made her famous.

A SECTION OF THE UFA STUDIO.—When shall we build in England gigantic frameworks for settings such as these?

8. *Morning Post*, 15 March 1927.
[University Library, Cambridge]

9. Back cover of *Kinematograph Weekly*, 17 March 1927.
[University Library, Cambridge]

"Its Weirdness Will Stand Up" — *Metropolis* in America and England

The subsequent heavy American interference with the distributed version of *Metropolis* is symptomatic of the fact that despite Ufa's accusations against Lang, the company was not ruined by this film alone; *Metropolis* was merely the straw the broke the camel's back. Klaus Kreimeier has shown that Ufa had run into financial difficulties as early as 1925 — due in part to Pommer's production policies, but also to Ufa's endless acquisitions and a relatively stable currency, which made export increasingly difficult. As a result, losses amounted to almost 36 million reichsmarks in 1925.[84]

In December 1925 American film producers became interested in Ufa, as the financial problems of the company offered a welcome opportunity to weaken this powerful competitor. Representatives of MGM and Paramount visited Berlin and negotiated a deal in which Ufa obtained a loan of $4 million. In turn, Ufa had to reserve seventy-five per cent of its cinema capacity for American productions and was obliged to distribute twenty films of each partner per year, for which the mutual distribution company Parufamet was founded. In addition, Universal granted Ufa a loan of $275,000, for which the company had to accept fifty Universal films a year. Even though Ufa was promised access to the American markets in return, there could be no doubt that the Parufamet and Universal contracts represented nothing less than Ufa's unconditional surrender to its American competitors.[85]

When *Metropolis* was distributed in 1927, the Parufamet contract ensured that Paramount and MGM had considerable influence on the version that was to be shown in America. Because Pommer had left Ufa early in 1927 in the midst of allegations of financial carelessness, there was no creative head to prevent tampering with the production. The American distributors were therefore free to "adapt" the film to what they thought was their audience's taste, and they did not hesitate to do so: Parufamet commissioned the American writer Channing Pollock (and his team Julian Johnson and Edward Adams) to abridge the film, and the distributor made no secret about the revisions.[86] On 13 March 1927, the *New York Times* even published an article describing the ma-

[84] Kreimeier, *Die Ufa-Story* 152. Kreimeier refers to the figures given by Hans Traub, *Die Ufa. Ein Beitrag zur Entwicklungsgeschichte des deutschen Filmschaffens* (Berlin: Ufa-Buchverlag, 1943), 60.

[85] Kreimeier, *Die Ufa-Story* 153.

[86] Kreimeier, *Die Ufa-Story* 153. Detailed analyses of the various cut and re-arranged versions of *Metropolis* are provided by Enno Patalas and Giorgio Bertellini in their contributions to this volume.

jor cuts that were meant to make the film more appealing; these "revisions" were "upheld as needed," and the German producers said to have exhibited either a "lack of interest in dramatic verity or an astonishing ineptitude."[87]

To rectify these "flaws" and in order to make the film more palatable to Americans, Pollock removed all the scenes in the nightclub Yoshiwara (where the robot Maria appears as a seductive vamp), probably because he thought the alcohol and drug orgies celebrated there were unfit for an American audience in the time of Prohibition; similarly, Pollock deleted the scenes in the "Stadium of Sons."[88] As both Enno Patalas and Giorgio Bertellini point out the most decisive changes concerned a major aspect of the novel and the original film: the relationship between Rotwang, the inventor, and Fredersen, the master of Metropolis. In what is probably the best-known version of the film we have today,[89] Rotwang is a typical mad scientist with an inexplicable hatred of Fredersen and a fundamentally malicious, vicious nature, a characterization that jars with Klein-Rogge's performance, which frequently suggests torment, self-doubt, and grief. In this version, Rotwang has created a robot in female form for no special reason, and Fredersen asks him to give the robot the face of Maria in order to incite the workers to revolt. This rather confusing element of the plot, along with the fact that Klein-Rogge's performance doesn't fit Rotwang's character in the Parufamet version, is the direct result of heavy editing, as is illustrated by the contemporary account of the cuts:

---

[87] Randolph Bartlett, "German Film Revision Upheld as Needed Here," *New York Times*, 13 March 1927, section 7,3. See Part One of this volume.

[88] The cuts for the American version were first outlined by Paul Jensen, "Metropolis," *Film Heritage* 2, no. 3 (winter 1967/68), 22–28 (24). They are also summarized in Ott, *The Films of Fritz Lang*, 129. The sound version by Giorgio Moroder contains some restored Yoshiwara footage showing two men fighting for the favours of the robot Maria. In Part Two of this volume, Patalas provides a description of further Yoshiwara scenes on the basis of a contemporary review and the censorship card of the film's trailer in "The City of the Future".

[89] Both Patalas and Bertellini suggest that *Metropolis* was so heavily changed that the film should not be read as a definitive version, but rather as a palimpsest marked by ongoing modifications, re-arrangements and reductions. Patalas carefully describes the genealogy of the different versions in which the film survives and argues that at least four manifestations of the film should be distinguished when attempting a reconstruction: the "original," full-length premiere version, the cut Parufamet variation, a tinted British version, and the second German version based on the Parufamet cuts. Bertellini suggests the Moroder rock video clip produced in 1984 can be seen as another valid interpretation. For another critical reading of the Moroder version, see the contribution of Thomas Elsaesser in Part Two of this volume.

> [One shot showed] a very beautiful statue of a woman's head, and on the base was her name — and that name was "Hel." Now, the German word for "hell" is "hoelle" so they were quiet [*sic*] innocent of the fact that this name would create a guffaw in an English speaking country. So it was necessary to cut this beautiful bit out of the picture, and a certain motive which it represented had to be represented by another.[90]

As Enno Patalas has shown with his careful reconstruction of the original scene, these cuts seriously disturbed the narrative flow. In the novel and the original film, the mysterious Hel played a prominent role: she was Fredersen's deceased wife and Freder's mother. Most importantly, she had been in love with Rotwang; Fredersen had made Hel leave Rotwang, and she died in giving birth to their son Freder. Rotwang felt betrayed and developed what von Harbou describes in the novel as "a hatred [for Fredersen] that bordered on insanity;"[91] he also became obsessed with recreating Hel for himself, if only as a massive stone sculpture kept in his laboratory or as an artificial human being — the robot he has manufactured.[92] In the rebellion incited by the robot, his revenge seems to be complete: he has recreated Hel, who destroys Fredersen's city; but he has also complete control over the woman he thinks has betrayed him. Finally, by lending the robot the looks of Maria, the lover of Fredersen's son, he "takes his revenge not only on his rival, but also on the son who denied himself to Rotwang when his mother conceived him by another."[93]

In Channing Pollock's version, this whole complex was removed, thus leading to the one-dimensional characterization of Rotwang as the mad scientist who is a mere puppet for Fredersen. The American version was reedited so heavily that it also required new intertitles; Pol-

---

[90] See Bartlett, "German Film Revision Upheld as Needed Here," reprinted in Part One of this volume.

[91] *Metropolis*, 45.

[92] According to von Harbou's novel, the inscription underneath Rotwang's stone sculpture of Hel's head reads "HEL/Born to make me happy and a blessing for all mankind/Lost/To Joh Fredersen/Died/When she gave birth to his son Freder." Surviving stills show that these scenes were carried out as described in the novel; see Enno Patalas, "*Metropolis*, Scene 103," trans. Miriam Hansen, *Camera Obscura* 15 (autumn 1986), 165–73. In his reconstructed version of the film, Enno Patalas included stills of the lost Hel scenes as inserts, which Giorgio Moroder also used for his rock video version in 1984.

[93] Patalas, "*Metropolis*, Scene 103," 171. An incisive interpretation of the Hel scenes is also given by Georges Sturm, "Für Hel, ein Denkmal, kein Platz," *Bulletin CICIM* 9 (1984), 54–78. For comprehensive reading of the Hel motif, see Rutsky, "The Mediation of Technology and Gender," in Part Two of this volume.

lock promptly supplied them, frequently toning down the social issues addressed in the film. In this process, the names of Joh and Freder were changed to the blunt "John" and "Eric" "Masterman," as Pollock obviously thought these names more straightforward; the American reviews, confusing the father's name with the son's, even stated that "Eric [is] a much better German name than John for a young chaser."[94] What Pollock destroyed, however, was the religious symbolism of the names permeating and structuring the film — Joh/Jehova, Freder/father and brother, Mary/mother and saint — and in so doing he removed one of the more interesting aspects from von Harbou's trivialized archetypal character constellations.[95] What reviewers clearly realized as a "subtitular dialectic compounded for American comprehension"[96] met with a mixed response; in its edition of 16 March 1927 *Variety* praised Pollock's new titles as having a "dignity in language and phrasing that lends greatly to the impressiveness," whereas other commentators saw Pollock's editing and reformulation of the titles as a major drawback, since the titles were deemed "only fair, and towards the end rather stupid in their reiterated sentiment."[97]

Some confusion about the dramatic construction ensued during the same process. In the original novel and film versions, for instance, the master of *Metropolis* ultimately wants the robot to incite the workers to revolt (even though his motivation for this aim remains unclear);[98] in the revised American version, "this manufactured Mary [. . .] is employed to quell the dissatisfied workers," but by "some queer freak" suddenly turns on her creators and preaches destruction, thereby rendering her actions entirely arbitrary.[99]

---

[94] Review of *Metropolis*, *Variety*, 16 March 1927.

[95] Similarly, the name of Hel, the original mother in the film, carries symbolic connotations, as it refers back to the mythical goddess of death (see Sturm, 58–59). Finally, the name of the city itself can also be seen as signifying the *metro-polis*, the ultimate mother-city. See Roger Dadoun, "*Metropolis*: Mother-City — 'Mittler' — Hitler," trans. Arthur Goldhammer, *Camera Obscura* 15 (autumn 1986), 136–63. See also Rutsky's essay in this volume.

[96] Evelyn Gerstein, Review of *Metropolis*, *The Nation*, 23 March 1927; cited in Ott, *The Films of Fritz Lang* 134.

[97] Lionel Collier, review of *Metropolis*, *Kinematograph Weekly*, 24 March 1927, 57; see also Gilbert Seldes, review of *Metropolis*, *The New Republic*, 30 March 1927; cited in Ott, *The Films of Fritz Lang*, 140.

[98] In the film, Fredersen simply commands Rotwang: "Let it create dissent."

[99] Mordaunt Hall, "A Technical Marvel: Metropolis," *New York Times*, 7 March 1927. The English reviews likewise stated: "Masterman bids his scientist complete the new robot in the image of the human girl, that it may preach submission to the underground race. But the robot runs counter to the wishes of its maker and

All in all, Pollock's version cut the film's seventeen reels to a mere ten, reducing its length from the original 4,189 metres to 2,841 metres, which equals a running time of just 107 minutes.[100] British trade journals wrote that the film was 10,000 feet long (approximately 3,048 metres or 111 minutes), which indicates that still another version was prepared for the British market. In fact, Enno Patalas draws attention to a surviving, tinted English print of the film that differs from the American cut by several scenes.[101] It must be stressed that these substantial changes for the various international versions are far from unique; rather, they make *Metropolis* representative of ruthless distribution practices tolerated or even enforced by Ufa and other European film companies. In order to enhance a film's chances on the international market, changes of film titles, names, intertitles and even profound revisions of the narrative without any considerations for the film's artistic coherence were the rule rather than the exception in the 1920s.[102]

The American premiere of this truncated version at the Rialto cinema in New York on 5 March 1927 was eagerly awaited by a crowd of 10,000 people.[103] In England, *Metropolis* was first shown at the Marble Arch Pavilion on 21 March 1927.[104] Here, the premiere was celebrated as the "precedent" for a "first night [of a new motion picture] as a social

---

preaches revolution to the submerged race." Review of *Metropolis, Daily Mail,* 22 March 1927, 17.

[100] On the length of the American version, see Patalas, "*Metropolis,* Scene 103," 170. The running time in minutes is stated in *Variety,* 16 March 1927. As in Germany, this suggests that the film was shown at a projection speed of 24 frames per second.

[101] See the review of *Metropolis* in *Bioscope,* 24 March 1927, 59, and Patalas, "The City of the Future," in Part Two of this volume.

[102] On changes of European films for international versions, see Bachmann (1996), 184 (on the American version of *Chronicles of the Grey House*); see also my "Arthur Schnitzler's *Der junge Medardus* as Drama, Screenplay and Film" (Doctoral dissertation, University of Cambridge, 1997), 225–35, which describes the substantial revisions for the English and French release of Michael Curtiz's Austrian production *Young Medardus* (*Der junge Medardus,* 1923). Significantly, in his article "German Film Revision Upheld as Needed Here" (see Part One of this volume), Randolph Bartlett not only defends the changes for the American version of *Metropolis,* but claims that any German film exported to America has to be edited before its release due to serious flaws marring virtually all German films.

[103] Jenkins, *Fritz Lang. The Image and the Look,* 22.

[104] See the advertisement on the back cover of *Kinematograph Weekly,* 17 March 1927. A selection of American and British reviews can be found below in Part One of this volume.

function": "the seats had been sold long in advance, and any available space was filled with people standing [and] there was a crowd [waiting] outside."[105] Once more, this immense interest had been efficiently created by Ufa's promotion strategies, as Ufa's marketing department had used the same public relations measures in England and America as in the domestic market. The trade journals had been supplied with stills and the "telling figures" well before the premiere;[106] as a substitute for the German workshop articles about the film's production, reports about the production techniques and special effects had been sent to the most important trade journals.[107] In the 16 March 1927 edition of *Variety*, for example, a reviewer wrote that

> A letter recently received by Variety (this paper) and written by the Aktiegesellschaft fur Spiegeltechnik [*sic*] of Berlin advised that in the UFA picture "Metropolis," shortly to be shown in New York, appeared 13 scenes of the firm's system called the Schufftan process.

Interestingly enough, Ufa was not aware that the mirror trick was largely unknown in America — *Variety* pointed out that nobody could tell exactly what the system was; the reviewer rightly guessed however that "[it must be] some sort of a process introduced to make the immensity of the effect or to aid it." In England, Ufa's public-relation measures worked better, as Lionel Collier, the critic writing for *Kinematograph Weekly*, stated that "the Schüfftan process has been used to its fullest advantage."[108] In fact, on the British market, Ufa's propaganda machinery, which presented the company as a powerhouse of innovation, artistic craftsmanship and incomparable size, was so successful that the newspapers that received — and published — stills of the production saw Ufa exactly as the company wanted to appear: as a substantial competitor for American productions, as is evident in headlines such as "Are British Films menaced by a German 'Hollywood'?"[109] Shortly before the premiere, Ufa relied most heavily on aggressive, "loud advertisement,"[110] calling *Metropolis* "The Screen Sensation of the

---

[105] "The Talk of the Town," *Daily Express*, 23 March 1927, 4.

[106] The *Bioscope* tried to visualize the size of the film by pointing out: "No fewer than 37,808 paid performers appear in [*Metropolis*], a number equivalent to the entire population of a good-sized town, such as Bedford or Maidstone." "Cast of 37,000 — 'Metropolis' an Amazing German Film," *Bioscope*, 17 March 1927, 53.

[107] See "The Creator of 'Metropolis' — Thea Von Harbou's Imaginative Work," *Bioscope*, 3 March 1927, 49.

[108] Lionel Collier, review of *Metropolis*, *Kinematograph Weekly*, 24 March 1927, 57.

[109] Production report on *Metropolis*, *Morning Post*, 15 March 1927, 7. See Figure 8.

[110] H. G. Wells, "Mr. Wells reviews a current film," 4.

Age!"; in England, this advertising campaign was combined with collections of enthusiastic reviews of the American premiere in advertising pages.[111]

However, despite all enthusiasm and forceful premarketing, a review of the German premiere carried by *Variety* on 23 February 1927 had already warned: "Nothing of the sort has ever been filmed before; the effect is positively overwhelming. [So it is] too bad that so much really artistic work was wasted on this manufactured story." In fact, for the same reasons as in Germany, *Metropolis* turned out to be a flop on the international market.

Like their German counterparts, the American reviewers admired the spectacle as a remarkable achievement that stood out because of its impressive visual design, overwhelming architecture, convincing special effects and masterly mass choreography. The critic writing for *The New York Times* on 7 March 1927 however perceived the film as "a technical marvel with feet of clay, a picture as soulless as the manufactured woman of its story." Interestingly enough, precisely the same comparison was drawn by English trade journals: on 24 March 1927, *Bioscope* carried a review arguing that "Herr Lang has produced a film like his own automaton, bold in imagination, marvelous in accomplishment, awe inspiring in its effect, only lacking in human sympathy and heart appeal."[112] One decisive difference between the American and British reviews concerns the appraisal of Pollock's version. Whereas *Variety* endorsed his cuts on 16 March 1927 as having created "quite good continuity," the British *Kinematograph Weekly* clearly realized the damage done by the revision: "The picture has had to be considerably shortened, and to this is also perhaps attributable the jerkiness of the continuity, which also militates against a dramatic intensity of plot."[113]

What the reviewers universally commended was the film's "pictorial composition," which was regarded as "frequently superb"; Lang was praised for "think[ing] in terms of sheer visual beauty . . . and

---

[111] See the reviews of *Metropolis* in *Bioscope*, 17 March 1927, front page, and on the back page of *Kinematograph Weekly*, 17 March 1927. As the title ("Chorus of Praise") and the comments chosen are identical in both journals, it is highly probable that these advertisements were compiled and supplied by Ufa. In an interesting exception to this active public relations work by Ufa, the American trade journals were not sent a press sheet by the American distributors, as *Variety* complained (16 March 1927). This indicates that despite the promises made to Ufa in the Parufamet contracts, the company's American partners were not particularly interested in promoting Ufa productions in their domestic market.

[112] Review of *Metropolis*, *Bioscope*, 24 March 1927, 59.

[113] Lionel Collier, review of *Metropolis*, *Kinematograph Weekly*, 24 March 1927, 57.

group rhythms rather than of dynamics,"[114] which in Lionel Collier's view turned *Metropolis* into "the apotheosis of that producer's methods of pictorial presentation."[115]

The reviews thus reveal that Pommer's strategy of developing a specifically German filmic discourse succeeded at least in artistic terms; the critics found the film interesting for its "Germanic" qualities, precisely the stylized approach that was seen as synonymous with Ufa productions such as *Die Nibelungen, The Last Laugh* and *Variety*. American journals pointed out "Houses that played 'Variety' won't miss with 'Metropolis.' It's the same UFA and its weirdness will at least stand up";[116] the English trade press likewise recommended "The magnitude of the production; the producer's reputation; the unusual type" — i.e. exactly the hallmarks of Pommer's policy — as the "selling angles" of the film.[117]

Perceptive reviewers even anticipated the modern appraisals of the film as a splendid visual achievement representing a landmark of stylized silent cinematography:

> [the film] is spoiled by lack of balance; the story is absurd in spots . . . I forgive all that. For *Metropolis*, with its beautiful shots of fantastic buildings, and its terrific use of electrical phenomena as elements in a dynamic composition which actually becomes the climax of the picture, in its correct and complete exploitation of the camera, will again do for us what Germany has done twice before [namely teaching us] the virtues of *Caligari* and *The Last Laugh*.[118]

These balanced assessments demonstrate that what is probably the most famous review of *Metropolis* is not entirely representative of the film's reception outside Germany: H. G. Wells's slating of *Metropolis* in *The New York Times* as the "silliest film" he had ever seen.[119] Well's hammering of *Metropolis* is by turns brilliant, polemical, and misguided. Wells objects to von Harbou's technique of "borrowing" themes from world literature and draws attention to Shelley's *Frankenstein*, Capek's

---

[114] Iris Barry, "The Cinema: *Metropolis*," *The Spectator*, 26 March 1927, 540; Evelyn Gerstein, review of *Metropolis, The Nation*, 23 March 1927, cited in Ott, *The Films of Fritz Lang*, 134.

[115] Lionel Collier, review of *Metropolis, Kinematograph Weekly*, 24 March 1927, 57.

[116] *Variety*, 16 March 1927.

[117] Review of *Metropolis, Bioscope*, 24 March 1927, 59.

[118] Gilbert Seldes, review of *Metropolis, The New Republic*, 30 March 1927, cited in Ott, *The Films of Fritz Lang*, 140.

[119] "Mr. Wells reviews a current film," 4 (see note 1 above). The following quotations are from this source, which is reproduced in its entirety in Part One of this volume.

R.U.R. or his own *The Sleeper Wakes* as sources. As we have observed, von Harbou's "soupy whirlpool" of a story moreover took the basic division of the city into an upper world and an underworld from Wells's *Time Machine* (interestingly enough, Wells does not mention this novel in the review). Wells rejects this transfer of his own "juvenile" literary ideas to a contemporary film as anachronistic and naive, so that to him, "Metropolis, in its forms and shapes, is already as a possibility a third of a century out of date."

Wells also criticizes the plot's simplistic exploration of the social question, arguing that the contemporary social and economic development of American cities pointed in entirely different directions from those suggested by Lang's film. Instead of being mindless slaves, workers of the future would need refined technical skills and have "spending power" to fuel the capitalistic system. According to Wells, Lang's "idiotic spectacle . . . contradicts these facts . . . with a sort of malignant stupidity" and thus represents a reactionary polemic against technology and progress. Nevertheless, Wells regrets that the film "wastes some very fine possibilities," which probably formed the nucleus for his own filmic vision of the future — *Things to Come* (GB 1936), possibly a direct answer to what he regarded as Lang's "old-fashioned balderdash."

German reviewers opposed to *Metropolis* were delighted with Wells's attacks and reprinted excerpts from the review, which had appeared in translation in the *Frankfurter Zeitung* on 3 May 1927.[120] While Wells is perceptive in his attacks on von Harbou's reactionary, naive script, it is in the economic aspects that Wells's criticism misses the point. What Lang created was not a well-reasoned vision of the economic future of modern states; as we have seen, it was rather a condensation of both a fear and an attraction to technology and machines, rendered in an expressive, abstract, and stylized manner with the archetypal, utopian perspective of a new human race.

Moreover, whereas Wells expected a sound treatment of the future, Lang offered a symbolic and visual exploration of basic issues and hierarchies — mythical versus technical, male versus female, eroticism versus love — that, in Buñuel's words, mostly illustrated a "sensation" by a "symphony of movement."[121] When Lang did want technical accuracy, he was entirely capable of it, as is evident in *Woman in the Moon*, in which the sequence of the rocket's construction and launch was so prophetic that the Nazis banned the film when they started their rocket

[120] See Hans Siemsen, "Eine Filmkritik, wie sie sein soll," *Die Weltbühne* 24 (14 July 1927), 947–50, and "Filmschau: *Metropolis*," *Der Bildwart* April/May 1927, 326–29.

[121] Töteberg, *Fritz Lang*, 55.

development program.[122] By contrast, in *Metropolis*, Lang's aim was pure filmic expression. Whilst Wells's forceful debunking of the theme of *Metropolis* is incisive, his fervor blinds him to the decisive aspect of the film — its profound, lasting visual impact.

The Failure of *Metropolis*

What Wells's review also reveals is that due to Ufa's propaganda machinery, *Metropolis* seemed on the verge of becoming a tremendous success at the beginning of its run in America and England. Wells observes that "the theatre when I visited it was crowded. All but the highest-priced seats were full, and gaps in places filled up reluctantly but completely before the great film was begun." Similarly, one week after the film's premiere in London, English trade journals stated that "at every performance many people have had to be reluctantly refused admission owing to the theatre being filled to capacity"; as a result of "enormous bookings" and "lengthy waiting queues," the film's run at the Marble Arch Pavilion was extended indefinitely.[123] Ultimately, however, Ufa's gamble with Lang's multimillion production failed. It seems that *Metropolis* suffered the fate of many modern blockbusters: an enormous advertising effort created widespread interest and huge box office takings in the first few weeks, but as soon as news of the film's flaws were spread by word of mouth, the audience's interest waned. The advent of sound film in 1927 with *The Jazz Singer* dealt another blow to *Metropolis* in the eyes of a public thrilled by the marvels of the new "talkies."

As early as April 1927, Ufa realized that *Metropolis*, which was supposed to generate revenues of one million reichsmarks, would turn out to be a financial failure. In a last attempt to rescue the project, the directing board of Ufa decided on 7 April 1927 to persuade Parufamet that

> *Metropolis* should keep up its run in the American version in ten to twelve large cities in the provinces, after deleting as many intertitles as possible with communist overtones. In the autumn or, in the case of bad weather, as early as late summer, the film should be re-released in Berlin [in this version].[124]

---

[122] Töteberg, *Fritz Lang*, 65.

[123] "*Metropolis* Draws the Crowds," *Bioscope*, 31 March 1927, 11.

[124] Transcripts of meetings of Ufa Board of Directors; Transcript 3, Meeting 7, April 1927; see Kreimeier, *Die Ufa-Story*, 189, and Patalas in Part Two, who describes the various distributed versions in some detail.

This statement illustrates that by April 1927, the cut American version had been supplied not only internationally, but also to cinemas in Germany, so that most audiences had seen only the truncated version of the film. Although Ufa planned to re-release the film, Parufamet now had other plans and suggested that the film's run should be terminated throughout Germany; the American version of *Metropolis* was to be released nationwide in August. Ufa hoped to recoup some of the losses and agreed to this proposition on 8 April, but it stipulated that "the pietistic revisions" added to the American version be removed.[125] On 5 August, the film was thus effectively censored again for German distribution. It was cut from the original 4,189 metres to a mere 3,241 metres; that is, its showing time was reduced from an original running time of 150 minutes to 117 minutes. The abridged version adopted American cuts such as the deletion of most of the Yoshiwara material and, most seriously, the Hel sequences; according to Patalas, in this process "about half of approximately 200 original intertitles survived, more or less exactly, the other half were dropped; fifty new intertitles were added."[126]

But revision was to no avail; or rather, by completely destroying the narrative cohesion of the film, revision actually exacerbated the thematic weaknesses of *Metropolis*, as is evident in the confusion concerning the dramatic construction that still mars the versions we have today.[127] Not least due to its total failure in America, which represented a considerably bigger potential market than Germany, *Metropolis* never recouped the money invested in it, even though the film repeatedly cropped up in cinemas. For instance, in 1932, *Metropolis* was re-released in Berlin due to a universal shortage of high-quality films in Germany; significantly, the trade journals stated that the film merely scored a "curiosity success," which typifies its commercial fate in general.[128] After several years only a seventh of the production costs of *Metropolis* had been recovered.[129]

As Ufa's biggest gamble, risked in order to rescue the company from the clutches of the competition, *Metropolis* had failed completely. Ufa

---

[125] Transcript 4, Meeting 8, April 1927; see Kreimeier, *Die Ufa-Story*, 189, and Patalas in Part Two below.

[126] Patalas, "*Metropolis*, Scene 103," 170; see also Patalas, "The City of the Future," in Part Two below.

[127] This situation might be remedied in part by the "synthetic version" Enno Patalas proposes, which would be a collection of all available material assembled as an attempt to come closer to the film's original form (see Part Two below).

[128] "'Metropolis' im Palace," *Kinematograph*, 3 August 1932, 3.

[129] Töteberg, *Fritz Lang*, 61.

now needed scapegoats for this disaster and found them in Lang and Pommer, who were publicly blamed for the financial problems of Ufa. Lang protested and demanded that a court of arbitration should point out that "the production costs of the film did not even come close to such a sum [five million reichsmarks]."[130] Even if Ufa was right about the sum stated, we have seen that it was not *Metropolis*, but Pommer's strategy of giant "art" productions, coupled with the company's megalomaniac policies, that ruined Ufa. *Metropolis* was a symptom, not the sole cause of Ufa's downfall.

Ufa nevertheless drew the consequences and resolved that any new productions with Lang should be under strict budgetary supervision. Lang was appalled by the accusations and founded his own production company, *Fritz Lang Films*, which produced *Spione* (The Spy, 1928) and *Frau im Mond*; Ufa merely distributed Lang's last silent films. After a further confrontation concerning the use of sound in *Woman in the Moon*, the falling out was complete. Clearly thinking back to the failure of *Metropolis*, Ufa's board of directors decided in a meeting held in 1929 that

> considering previous differences in opinion and the corresponding huge losses for Ufa, there is to be no further business contact with Fritz Lang concerning the production of Ufa films for or in cooperation with Ufa.[131]

Töteberg points out that unofficially, Ufa distanced itself even more decisively from Lang; he cites a handwritten addition to this resolution commanding that "all the leading members of Ufa should treat L.[ang] with 'cool reserve'!"[132] In 1929, one of the great co-operations in film history thus had come to an end due not least to a film which remains celebrated to this day.

Despite all controversy, *Metropolis* has managed what few silent films have achieved: it has embedded icons into the popular imagination that recur with irresistible power. Lang's vision of the megacity has returned to cinema again and again, Ridley Scott's *Blade Runner* (1982) being the most notable example, with more than just a homage to the new Tower of Babel dominating the skyline of Metropolis; the robot returns in farcical mode as C-3PO in George Lucas's *Star Wars* (1977)

---

[130] "Fritz Lang wehrt sich," *Die Filmbühne*, 15 May 1927, 20.

[131] Töteberg, *Fritz Lang*, 66.

[132] Töteberg, *Fritz Lang*, 66.

and, indeed, has become almost synonymous with the science fiction film as such.[133]

Probably one of the best contemporary appraisals of *Metropolis* was, fittingly enough, given by Lang himself in "Was ich noch zu sagen habe" [What I still have to say], an essay he wrote for the *Ufa-Magazin* on *Metropolis*. When he was asked for a comment on his film after he had finished it, he explicitly stated that the film summed up his filmic vision. It should not, he continued, be approached verbally or thematically, but rather in terms of its sheer visual impact:

> I once knew a young violin player [. . .] who was not capable of humming or singing the simplest of melodies. In order to express himself, he needed the instrument with which he was familiar. Well, everything I have to say and will never be able to express in words is written down in the black and white film writing of "Metropolis," and if I did not succeed in expressing myself there, I will certainly not find the expression here [in words].[134]

---

[133] See J. P. Telotte, *Replications. A Robotic History of the Science Fiction Film* (Chicago: U of Illinois P, 1995), esp. 55–71.

[134] Fritz Lang, "Was ich noch zu sagen habe," *Ufa-Magazin* (unpaginated).

Introduction

II: The Critical Reception of *Metropolis*

Michael Minden

THE IMMEDIATE CONTEXT OF *METROPOLIS* is Weimar Germany. When it comes to the question of context, however, the film has a peculiar property. Because of its specific thematic linking of technology, politics and sexuality, it leads commentators to try and define exactly what *kind* of context is required to read and criticize it adequately. This property is what makes Lang's film such a suitable subject for a collection of materials and essays.

The Weimar social theorist Siegfried Kracauer set the post-war agenda for the critical scrutiny of early German cinema in general and Fritz Lang in particular in his 1947 book *From Caligari to Hitler*.[1] The question to which he sought an answer was how to understand the relation between the phenomenon of popular film and the life of society at large. Of course, this question was so crucial because the survivors of the Second World War needed to understand the human and social origins of the catastrophe. This need perhaps led Kracauer to insist too keenly on the possibility of reading the psychology of a society through its mass media. In the new fact of popular culture and particularly film, Kracauer felt he had found a point at which the social and the human could be read in relation to each other in such a way as to inform political and historical analysis. But in pursuing his thesis that film revealed how Weimar society was beset by a crisis of retrogression blighting men's sense of their masculine identity, and thus by a crisis of authority and lack of rational political responsibility, Kracauer oversimplified and somewhat regimented the dozens of films he analyzed. He emphasized content over formal and medial considerations.

Metropolis is a film with an obvious difficulty: from its first reception there has been the judgement that the film had strong images but a weak plot. Kracauer's view of the film certainly reflects this. While he is sensitive to the power of the film's images — the city, the machine room, the crowd scenes, the robot transformation scene — even pointing out how they at times contradict the sentimental conservative ten-

[1] Princeton: Princeton UP. Several of the essays included in this volume take issue with and develop Kracauer's arguments, see especially the contributions by Elsaesser, Huyssen, and Rutsky.

dency of the film, he is not prepared to allow that they need to be taken into account when analyzing the film's "social imaginary," to borrow the term from Andreas Huyssen, which is after all Kracauer's main concern.[2]

On the other hand, there is no doubt that Kracauer does have a point about *Metropolis*. His argument is that one can read the Weimar Republic as an anticipation of the Third Reich by means of the collective psychology expressed in its film culture. The film is important for his argument because he can point to the interest shown in Lang's work by prominent Nazis. This connection is more than just anecdotal,[3] it is also perfectly logical. Kracauer persuasively points out how the film conveys the very principle that informed Goebbels' ideal of propaganda, namely the importance of seduction alongside coercion as a means of control exercised by the state.[4] The form of authority so powerfully established in the film is finally not weakened but strengthened by the challenge it sustains in the story. By the end, the Master of Metropolis, Joh Fredersen, has gained access to control not just of the workers' bodies, but of their minds as well, by means of the mediation of his — only temporarily — rebellious son Freder.[5] Indeed, the point is not simply thematic, since what clearly happens is that visual pleasure, to use Thomas Elsaesser's phrase, is deployed in the cause of political acquiescence.

Kracauer's example of a sociological-psychological study of a certain body of films led to a series of case studies on what came to be known misleadingly as German Expressionist Cinema (misleading because what appears to be a description is in fact the naming of a problem: how exactly do expressionism and cinema relate to each other?).[6] The particu-

---

[2] See Andreas Huyssen, "The Vamp and the Machine: Fritz Lang's *Metropolis*," reprinted in Part Three of this volume.

[3] For an historically authenticated account of the relation between Lang and the Nazi propaganda establishment, see Werner Gösta, "Fritz Lang and Goebbels — Myths and Facts," *Film Quarterly* 43, 3 (summer 1990), 1989/90, 24–27.

[4] For the film in relation to Nazi propaganda, see also Huyssen, and Rutsky in Part Three of this volume.

[5] Kracauer, *From Caligari to Hitler*, 163–164. But cf. Ben Morgan's quite different reading of Freder in the last contribution in this volume!

[6] This identification of a certain corpus of films as a recognizable entity also owed something to the other classic study of early German cinema besides that of Kracauer, Lotte Eisner's *The Haunted Screen*, trans. Roger Greaves (Berkeley: U of California P, 1973, first published in French in 1952), which dealt with the early German cinema as visual art, taking as its theme "Expressionism in the German Cinema," to quote from the book's subtitle; Eisner's book also refers to the influence (in

lar phenomenon of early German cinema (or at least certain particularly celebrated examples of it) came to support one answer to how the theoretical and multi-perspectival demands of the study of film could be met. This answer was sociology. The requirement was to identify a movement, because then it was possible to go on to demonstrate a social causality. There was a clutch of studies in the sixties and seventies that built on Kracauer's lead, often adding to or differentiating what he had claimed. These studies nevertheless also contributed both to the homogenization of this corpus of films and to the institutionalization of a sociological approach that was bound, given the historical context, to subordinate the films to a role as the precursor of fascism.[7] On the other hand, in addition to establishing that these films had to be seen in a political way, they also established a great deal about the commercial environment in which they came about as well as about the defining effect of the American film industry upon the German one. Huaco's 1962 interview with Erich Pommer is an important example.[8]

The sociological model was taken a step further by John Tulloch who chose precisely *Metropolis* in an editorial of a new film studies journal in 1976 to sketch out a methodology for the study of film.[9] It is characteristic that here too it is the method that is the real topic, the need for reflection about context, that drives the discussion, rather than the film text in isolation. Nevertheless, in Tulloch's adaptation of structuralism which he grafts on to sociology somewhat in the manner of Lucien Goldmann, the complex patterns of imagery — he has, for instance, a brilliant short discussion on the play of hands, me-

---

lighting and staging) of the leading theatre director of the period, Max Reinhardt, and of German literary Romanticism.

[7] George Huaco, *The Sociology of Film Art* (New York: Basic Books, 1965); Paul Monaco, *Cinema and Society: France and Germany During the Twenties* (Amsterdam: Elsevier,1976); Eric Rhode, *A History of the Cinema From its Origins to 1970* (Harmondsworth: Penguin, 1976); Andrew Tudor, *Image and Influence* (London: George Allen & Unwin, 1974)

[8] The industrial context has recently been significantly extended and differentiated by Klaus Kreimeier, *Die Ufa-Story: Geschichte eines Filmkonzerns* (Munich: Heyne, 2nd ed. 1995), and Bruce A. Murray and Christopher J. Wickham, eds., *Framing the Past: The Historiography of German Cinema and Television* (Carbondale: Southern Illinois Press, 1992).

[9] "Genetic Structuralism and the Cinema. A Look at Fritz Lang's Metropolis," *Australian Journal of Screen Theory* 1 (1976), 3–50.

chanical, human and symbolic, in the film[10] — does not get short shrift, but is persuasively worked out as a system of antinomies involving the film's plot structure as well. Tulloch thus restores the film's integrity as a complex entity, but proposes the dialectical synthesis of his antinomies (spiritual/materialist, organic/mechanistic, empathetic/exploitative etc.[11]) not by reference to aesthetic considerations, since the aesthetic weakness of the synthesis offered by the film is not in doubt, but by reference to quite sophisticated sociological ones. He identifies Lang and the others in the art world of the so-called German expressionist film as belonging to a class of German mandarins who rightly felt their traditional role as mediators between spiritual and practical matters to be gravely threatened by the new technological culture with which they found themselves confronted. It is this cultural and social circumstance that makes its impression upon the complex structure of images informing the film and driving its plot.

For all the real merits of Tulloch's piece, one weakness of the case concerning the sociological dream of a film movement which is also a scientifically coherent whole, needs to be pointed out. The technological elements without which his system of antinomies, and indeed his whole sociological-semiotic argument, does not really work are of course central to *Metropolis*, but they are much harder to substantiate in early German cinema as a whole.[12] Those critics, on the other hand, who in the seventies were released from the categorical imperative of sociology were free to pursue the complex sexual-technological semiology of this particular film. Moreover, in the transition from structuralism to post-structuralism, the increased interest in the subject position within the structures investigated had important effects for this film too. It at once encouraged the auteur theory, and thus released Lang (albeit somewhat indirectly, via the French rediscovery of the *American* Lang[13]) from the simplifying political judgement cast upon him by Kracauer, and provided the language with which to talk about the stake of the subject — whether the subject as understood by psychoanalysis or by feminism — within the structuring determinants of desire and technology.

---

[10] Tulloch, "Genetic Structuralism," 13.

[11] Tulloch, "Genetic Structuralism," 15–16.

[12] Indeed, it is noticeable how Murnau's version of *Dracula, Nosferatu,* edits out all the references to technology — typewriters, Winchester rifles and above all blood transfusions — that play a crucial part in Bram Stoker's novel.

[13] See E. Ann Kaplan, *Fritz Lang. A Guide to References and Resources* (Boston, MA: G. K. Hall & Co, 1981), 3–6.

The psychoanalyst Roger Dadoun published an essay in French in 1974,[14] in which he explored the differing ways in which the unconscious is touched by the film. His reading is weakened by the circumstance that the lack of a mother in the economy of the film — a lack obviously of huge importance in psychoanalytic terms and to which Dadoun therefore attaches great significance — is in fact largely the effect of American intervention and can thus not coherently be used to examine the minds of Lang or Hitler. Nevertheless, Dadoun is certainly justified in pointing to the psychoanalytical aspects of *Metropolis*. Hitherto sexuality had been seen as a thematic issue in the film: it is what erupts when order breaks down. Now, sexuality is rightly seen as a structural matter as well. By stressing the significance of versions of "the primal scene," Dadoun consciously draws attention to the act of seeing. No reading of the film can really ignore the pivotal moment at which Freder comes upon what he thinks is the object of his own deepest desires (the good Maria) in the arms of his father (who is in fact inspecting the robot), and suffers a collapse. Freder is called upon to endure and correct this disorder in the relation between sexuality and technology. The viewer shares his disorientation, and the need to deal with it, when the film's virginal heroine becomes both a technological object (a robot), and an aggressively sexual figure. Dadoun also deepens the connection between Nazi ideology and visual seduction alluded to by Kracauer by pointing out how the rich libidinal fascination of the film informs the dull ideology at its surface.

Feminist analysis has a particularly sharp eye for the manipulation of subject position in culture, especially in that of popular film. Patricia Mellencamp's article of 1981 programmatically puts the sex back into the film's structure and effects, a sexuality the film disavows but also depends upon in the form of the cinema as a technology of desire.[15] The containment of the sexual as problem (a problem represented by the son's discomfort at the primal scene) entails ensuring the continuing safety of the male subject position and the projecting at the same time of the divisive and discontinuous effects of sexuality onto the female body, which is split and fractured, indeed doubled and quadrupled in the film.[16] A secure and coherent masculine position entails the denial of a place in either subjectivity or history to women.

---

[14] "Metropolis Mother-City — 'Mittler' — Hitler," trans. Arthur Goldhammer, *Camera Obscura* 15 (autumn 1986), 137–63.

[15] "Oedipus and the Robot in Metropolis," *Enclitic* 5, no.1 (spring 1981), 20–42.

[16] Mellencamp, "Oedipus and the Robot," 32.

In the 1980s this highly theoretical type of film studies, organized around the question of subject position within the specific material determinants of the medium of film, was re-integrated into historical context. This gave a rich yield as far as the cinema of the Weimar Republic is concerned. In a couple of important articles Thomas Elsaesser returned to Kracauer in order to insist, against him, upon a more differentiated relation between the socio-historical context of these films and their narrative import.[17] Once again, what is at stake is the whole question of what "context" means, that is to say, of how the phenomenon of film/cinema can be thought about in such a way as to embrace both its artistic and industrial specificity, as well as all the other determinants, for instance of a social, historical, economic or political nature, that demand to be considered.

Reflection about subject positions dependent on modes of narrative, montage, and *mise-en-scène*, and characteristic of all narrative cinema, which had been developed to such a high degree of sophistication by the critics of the seventies we have just discussed, now becomes reflection about the *specific* subject positions of an actual historical time and place; those of the directors, and of the implied and the real audiences.[18] Kracauer was wrong to reduce these films to narrative paradigms in order to indicate a relation between them and a certain historical narrative, because in doing so he was imposing upon them (and upon history) anachronistic norms of classical realist narrative which became institutionalized for film in Hollywood. The effect of this was to mask the very respect in which these films were genuinely avant-garde, namely the consciousness implied by their non-Hollywood, disjunctive and fantastic, register of that *reification of immediacy* that the Hollywood film paradigm so magisterially practices but hides at the same time.

Elsaesser's argument also has the virtue of taking up and placing in a new context the central contention of the other classic study of Weimar film, Lotte Eisner's *The Haunted Screen*, namely that alongside expressionism there is a significant link between *Romanticism* and the

---

[17] "Film History and Visual Pleasure: Weimar Cinema," in *Cinema Histories/Cinema Practices*, ed. Patricia Mellencamp and Philip Rosen (Frederick: University Publications of America, 1984), 47–84; "Social Mobility and the Fantastic: German Silent Cinema," *Wide Angle* 5, no.2, (1982) 14–15. In addition to revisiting Kracauer's argument, Elsaesser returns to Lotte Eisner's founding contention that the recourse to Romantic motifs characterizes the early German cinema.

[18] Patrice Petro takes this progression a step further along by specifying the female constituencies within this specific historical spectatorship. *Joyless Streets. Weimar and Melodramatic Representation in Weimar Germany* (Princeton: Princeton UP, 1989).

early German cinema. What can crudely be called the subjectivism of historical Romanticism confronts us in an alienated form in the figures of the fantastic that characterize this cinema. The manner in which the cinematic imaginary, like Romanticism before it, blocks out (and thus, properly analyzed, obliquely expresses) historical determinants such as the real social disabilities effecting spectators and producers, is *visible* in the Weimar cinema.

The motif of the sorcerer's apprentice, "one of the most typical figures of the fantastic in the German Cinema"[19] is not simply an allegory of technology that has got out of hand. It is an image of the dismay of artist-intellectuals at the splitting off of a part of themselves, the products of their own creativity and insight, to become fetishes and commodities and therefore reified in the new industrial mass culture. Thus in Elsaesser's analysis, Tulloch's sociological analysis is wedded to a yet more differentiated and medium-sensitive reading of the construction of subject positions in Weimar cinema.

In the particular case of *Metropolis,* this has significance for our understanding of the theme of technology. In the film's explicit treatment of technology many of the submerged patterns of early German cinema come to the surface, particularly the contradiction that can emerge when a culture traditionally distrustful of, and resistant to, technology seeks ways of appropriating a medium intrinsically technological and market-related. It is clear that the series of episodes involving the robot Maria closely resembles the topos of the sorcerer's apprentice, since her activities outstrip any obvious intention of her creators. This affinity is disavowed by the (more or less distinct) plot strands which seek to explain the creation and deployment of the robot version of the virginal heroine either politically (Fredersen) or psychologically (Rotwang). The defective coherence, and indeed redundancy of the plot strands, however, the very absence of a seamless narrative continuity, serves to uncover this topos of self-alienation.[20]

This particular form of self-alienation, the reification of immediacy of which Elsaesser speaks, resonates far beyond Weimar. This larger context was brought out with particular emphasis by Peter Wollen in 1989 in an essay called "Cinema/Americanism/The Robot."[21] In the era of modernism intellectuals, artists and politicians face the problem of reconciling the positive potential of technological rationalization with

[19] Elsaesser, "Social Mobility," 19.

[20] This applies as much to what one knows about the lost original as to the American attempt at producing a simpler and more popular narrative.

[21] "Cinema/Americanism/The Robot." *New Formations* 8 (summer 1989), 7–34.

political emancipation and with pleasure. Their grappling with this problem is embodied and explicit in *Metropolis*, although not of course theoretically resolved. A view of a rationalized world, the kind of view exemplified by Taylorism and Fordism, needs to find ways of dealing with pleasure, if for no other reason than for the sake of efficiency. Yet any linkage between technology and sexuality,[22] threatens to turn technology into a rampaging uncontrollable monster, an overthrowing of the rational ordered world by the brute materiality that slumbers within human beings as well as machines. The sexualized machine Maria — to bring out the analogy bluntly — is the sexualized machine film, that "bewitches the mind and the passions,"[23] threatening to subvert the interests of the industrial rationalization which gives rise to it.

As a result of its series of interconnecting contexts *Metropolis* both resists this bewitching passion and exploits it. Amid the contemporary aesthetic-social arguments to which Wollen refers, those that speak in favour of the technological imaginary as a tool of emancipation and those that urge the need for control and the amputation of passion from technology, this film occupies a threshold position. On the one hand it prominently disapproves of the technological imaginary as a vampish bachelor machine that unseats strong men, alienating their eyes from their brains and sending them spinning into erotic hallucination and nervous breakdown (to say nothing of its terrifying effect upon the otherwise servile working masses). On the other it is, more than any previous film of the early German cinema, aimed at a mass audience (and certainly not just at a German one), and committed to the spectacular and to special effects, all of which involves taking an industrially significant financial risk. The robot vamp is the metonym for the whole film as a *European* image machine: in its images and narrative it is intended as a critique of, but also an aesthetic transcending of, the United States star system and the United States pleasure industry. At the same time it is undoubtedly meant to be industrially and aesthetically powerful enough to make Neubabelsberg a real and effective rival to Hollywood.[24]

There are more links that extend the context of this film to include the United States. The film as we know it, or as we knew it until the reconstruction work of the Munich Film Museum, details of which are

[22] Such a link is already given in the history of the creation of "gynoids" such as in Villiers de l'Isle-Adam's *L'Eve future* (Future Eve, 1886).

[23] Wollen, "Cinema/Americanism/The Robot," 19.

[24] This is certainly how it was seen in contemporary reviews and previews. For the industrial circumstances surrounding the coming about of *Metropolis*, see Holger Bachmann's account in this volume.

provided by its erstwhile director Enno Patalas in this volume, is to a significant extent the result of American editorial input, details of which are likewise documented in various places in this volume.[25] It is here particularly that "context" irreversibly invades "text." From this point on we are dealing with a cultural event, and its lengthening history, without clear authorship. It is not a deconstructive platitude but a simple fact to say that with the American cuts and reediting we lose contact with the origin of the matter that we are discussing.

This dissolving of text into context took another, more creative, turn when Giorgio Moroder made the film over into an extended rock video in 1984. This remarkable revisiting of the old silent film reinstates some missing sequences and stills, and adds tinting, and a sound track of contemporary music.[26] With this turn, Lang's film, with its particular take on technology, enters the postmodern culture of the proliferating appropriation, recombining and recirculating of images, sounds, effects and so forth, that was in its early stages in 1984, and has reached seismic culture redefining proportions with the ensuing computer revolution.[27] Moroder's intervention in a way redeems the invasion by the first American revisers, because alongside a second ruthlessly capitalistic appropriation of Lang's images and narrative (or parts of it), there is the respect for Lang's lost original achievement evidenced both in the moments of restoration, and in the power and authority that the effects of subsequent technologies are able to confer.

As Paul Coates remarks in his 1991 study of the legacy of German cinematic expressionism, Moroder's "campladen, postmodern pastiche" is trading on a significant distance from the material it is reframing.[28] Coates has a real point when he goes on to say that this distance between material and treatment was already effective in Lang's original application of Thea von Harbou's story and themes. With the benefit of hindsight it does seem tenable to claim that the film in its first version, and before the first American adaptation, already had the effect of pastiche about it, a sense that the characters, narrative and themes of the film (and they include not only expressionism but many other varied

[25] See Bachmann, Bartlett, Patalas, Bertellini in this volume.

[26] There are also some intriguing omissions, see Yves Laberge, "Une mémoire filmique défaillante: oublis et plans manquants dans la version sonorisée (1984) du film *Métropolis* (1927) de Fritz Lang," *Champs visuels. Revue interdisciplinaire de recherches sur l'image* 4 (1997), 135–46.

[27] Wollen, "Cinema/Americanism/The Robot," 28–31.

[28] *The Gorgon's Gaze. German Cinema, Expressionism, and the Image of Horror* (Cambridge: Cambridge UP, 1991), 44.

motifs and references[29]), are not as important as the force of the effects used to convey them. These characters, themes and narrative are there, of course, and there is no ironic or subversive intention. There is just an indifference to the world of concerns they represent, the old European world, and an assent to the sheer effectiveness of the sexualized machinery, the technological imaginary, of the new mass industrial age.

---

[29] Indeed, one might even argue that this lack of underpinning commitment to any one style or theme was already present in von Harbou's original hotch-potch, which is not as homogeneously expressionist as Coates implies. In his account of the film's genesis in this volume, Bachmann aptly describes von Harbou's contribution as "passion-laden but ultimately non-committal."

Part One

Materials and Documentation

The following section provides a collection of contemporary material relevant to the production and reception of Metropolis. *It falls into three main categories: excerpts from novel and screenplay; production reports; and reviews. The purpose of this selection is to place* Metropolis *into its historical framework and to show how the film was seen in the 1920s by means of first-hand accounts — a perspective often overlooked when analyzing* Metropolis. *The passages from the novel and the screenplay give an idea of Harbou's style and demonstrate how she adapted the source novel into a film script. The production reports, mainly taken from German film journals and the official advertising booklet, show Ufa's public relations machinery at work; at the same time, these articles provide further material on the rationale behind the film's production as a weapon against Hollywood. Finally, the review section presents German, American and British reactions in order to demonstrate the film's various metamorphoses and its reception in different target countries. In that sense, the section provides the background against which the modern critical readings can be judged.*[1]

---

[1] A basic note on spelling conventions: in journals and newspapers from the 1920s, film titles are frequently cited not in italics, but in quotation marks, sometimes followed by the descriptive addition "film." This convention has been kept in order to convey better the tonality of the original passages.

The Novel and the Screenplay

THE FOLLOWING MATERIALS are intended to convey the texture of Thea von Harbou's novel, whose relationship to the film Holger Bachmann explains in his account of the genesis of the film in the introduction above. The novel *Metropolis* was first published in 1925 in installments in the "Illustriertes Blatt" (Frankfurt am Main); these were richly illustrated with stills from the film. The book edition was published by August Scherl Publishing House (Berlin).

The first two passages in this section are from the novel and the only surviving part of the actual screenplay. They were published by Ufa in the special *Metropolis*-edition of the *Ufa-Magazin* to illustrate the transition from novel to script and to advertise the book. In the *Ufa-Magazin* — where the passages from both novel and script appear under the collective title "Death to the Machines" — the excerpts are typeset in parallel in two columns in order to allow direct comparison of source and film adaptation. The texts show that von Harbou had considerable skill as a screenwriter, despite her deficiencies as a novelist. The third passage comes again from the novel itself and is an important source of information, since it represents the only explanation we have of why Fredersen actually *wills* the destruction of Metropolis. The fourth passage furnishes a detail that illustrates the sentimental morality of von Harbou's original text.

Death to the Machines!

*Thea von Harbou describes the rise of the workers in her novel and in her film manuscript:**

PASSAGE ONE:
THE NOVEL

Metropolis had a brain.
Metropolis had a heart.

---

* From Press Department of Ufa, *Metropolis, Sondernummer des Ufa-Magazins,* ed. Stefan Lorant (Berlin: Bukwa, Presse Abteilung der Ufa, 1927), unpaginated. The text reproduces the entire passage as published in the *Ufa-Magazin.* Translation by Holger Bachmann and Meg Tait. Excerpts from *Metropolis* by Thea von Harbou by permission of Ullstein Buchverlage. Translation based on the 1984 edition by Herbert W. Francke (Frankfurt: Ullstein, 1984).

The heart of the machine city Metropolis lived in a white, cathedral-like hall. The heart of the machine city Metropolis was guarded by one single man.

The man was called Grot, and he loved his machine.

This machine was a universe to itself. Above the mysteries of its delicate joints stood, like the sun — like the radiance of a deity — the silver whizzing wheel, and, as it swirled and whirled, its spokes seemed like one sparkling disc. This disc filled the back wall of the room in its entire breadth and height.

There was not a single machine in the whole of Metropolis which did not receive its power from this heart.

One single lever commanded this wonder of steel. Grot would not have exchanged his machine for all the treasures of the world, heaped up before him.

When Grot heard the great roar of Metropolis around the red hour of sunrise, he looked towards the clock on the front wall and thought: This is against all that is natural and right . . . [1]

When Grot saw the streaming mob surge towards him around the red hour of sunrise — in ranks of twelve, led by a girl who danced to the beat of the howling crowd, he switched the lever of the machine to "Safety," carefully closed the door of the hall, and waited.

The mob thundered against his door.

Go on, hammer away! Grot thought. The door can take it . . .

He looked at the machine. The wheel was spinning slowly. The beautiful spokes glinted distinctly. Grot nodded towards his beautiful machine.

They won't annoy us for long, he thought. He waited for a sign from the new Tower of Babel. For a word from Joh Fredersen. The word did not come.

He knows, Grot thought, that he can rely on me . . .

The door quivered like a giant drum, the masses threw themselves against it like a living battering ram.

There seem to be rather a lot of them, thought Grot. He looked at the door. It shook, but held up. And it seemed like it would hold up for a very long time.

Deeply satisfied, Grot nodded to himself. He would have loved to light a pipe, if smoking had not been forbidden here. He listened to the

---

[1] The frequent ellipses are part of Harbou's idiosyncratic style and appear in the original text.

howling of the crowd and impact after impact against the humming door with a kind of comfortable anger. He loved the door. It was his ally. He turned and looked at the machine. He nodded towards it tenderly: The two of us — eh?! . . . What do you say to the drunken fools, machine!

The storm in front of the door worked itself up to a typhoon. There was a panting rage in it at such prolonged resistance.

"Open up — !!"

"Open up, you scoundrel — !!"

That would suit you fine! Grot thought. How well the door held up. His stout door!

What were the drunken apes singing outside?

"We have passed judgement on the machines! We have sentenced the machines to death!"

Oh-ho — ! He, Grot, could sing, too! He could sing drunken songs wonderfully well! With his heels he kicked the base of the machine he was sitting on. He pushed his black hat further towards the back of his head. With his red fists in his lap, he sang at the top of his voice, his mouth gaping, his little, wild eyes turned towards the door:

"Come here, you drunken rabble, if you dare! Come here, if you want the living daylights beaten out of you, you lousy apes! Your mothers forgot to give you a spanking when you were small, you snot-noses! You're not fit for pig's fodder! You fell off the back of the refuse lorry! And now, you chicken lice, you are standing outside the door, my stout door screaming: 'Open up — ! Open up — !'"

The base of the machine resounded to the drumbeat of the heels of his boots . . .

But suddenly both ceased: the drumming and the singing. A very strong, very white light flashed three times beneath the cupola of the hall. A sound, tender and piercing like the stroke of the gong of a temple bell, became audible and overpowered every other noise.

"Yes!" said Grot, the guardian of the heart machine. He jumped to his feet. He lifted his broad face, which gleamed in joyful eagerness to obey. "Yes — here I am!"

A voice said slowly and clearly: "Open the door and surrender the machine!"

Grot stood and did not move. His two fists hung from his arms like plump hammers. He blinked frantically. He swallowed. But he remained silent.

"I repeat the command," the calm voice said.

The guardian of the heart machine shook his head fiercely from side to side as though it were a heavy burden.

"I . . . I don't understand," he gasped.

The calm voice spoke in a heightened tone: "Open the door and surrender the machine!"

But the man still remained silent and stared upwards stupidly.

"I repeat the command," the calm voice said.

The guardian of the heart machine sucked in a deep breath.

"Who is this?" he asked. "What dirty swine is this — ?"

"Open the door, Grot . . . "

"The devil I will — !"

" . . . and surrender the machine!"

"The machine — ?" Grot said, "the —— my machine ——?!?!"

"Yes," the calm voice said.

The guardian of the heart machine began to shake in every limb. His face turned blue and the eyes stood out like white balls. The masses, throwing themselves against the door like a battering ram, howled, hoarse from howling:

"The machines must die, — to hell with them!"

"Death! — Death! — Death to the machines!"

"Who is this?" the man asked, in a voice so loud that it became a shriek.

"This is Joh Fredersen."

The guardian of the heart machine stood like a block. Then the block turned around awkwardly, staggered towards the door and pulled at the bolts.

The mob heard it. They howled in triumph. The door flew open, and the mob swept aside the man who met them at the threshold. The mob flooded forward towards the machine. The mob wanted to violate the machine. A dancing girl led the mob.

"Behold — !" she screamed, "behold — ! The beating heart of Metropolis! What should we do to the beating heart of Metropolis — ?

We have passed judgement on the machines! We have sentenced the machines to death!"

PASSAGE TWO:
THE FILM SCRIPT

Shot 263.
Heart Machine

Long Shot:

> Almost filling the image, the giant steel frame of the heart machine. The whole colossus standing against the spokes of an enormous steel wheel — these are like a disc.

A tangle of switchboards, lever systems, scales, safety valves. The machine working, all its enormous limbs moving steadily. The wheel behind it is like a radiant sun. Grot occupied with his machine, secure, calm, attentive. One cheek swollen with chewing tobacco.

Single shot:

Grot working on the machine, suddenly looks up.

Long Shot:

Flush-mounted into the wall, box with glass screen. On the screen, flashing in constant rhythm, the word DANGER.

Detail:

Grot. Jumps with a single leap towards a giant lever, turns it with enormous exertion of all his muscles.

Shot 263 / 1.

Different Camera Position:

Heart machine in the background.

Two doors, one rising, one falling, mightily enclosing the full breadth of the room.

Single Detail:

Grot runs to a kind of telephone. Speaks into the receiver.

Shot 264.
Joh Fredersen's Room.

The room is empty . . . on the desk, there is a column of light which, flashing constantly, calls and calls. Strips of paper roll from an appliance similar to the one Grot works at. Endlessly, endlessly . . .

Shot 265.
Heart Machine

Single Detail:

Grot at the appliance from shot 263/1.

He speaks, shouts, screams, roars into the appliance . . . no reply. Finally, dripping with sweat, furious, panting like an irritated bull, he throws down the receiver. He runs his hands through his hair, shakes his head.

Shot 266.
Machine Room I.

Workers at the machines.

The machine woman Maria and a throng of men and women from the mob floods from the appliance towards the machine room. Howling:

Title:

"Away from the machines — !
Let them race themselves to death — !"

The workers are brought down from the machines, swept away. The mob swallow them. All roaring:

Title:

"To the Heart Machine — !
To the Heart Machine — !"

[They pour] outside like a wave of mud sucked away by a maelstrom.

The machines alone, alive . . .

Shot 267.
Joh Fredersen's Room.

Long Shot:

Joh Fredersen enters, looks around. The recording appliance, next to it the confused heap of paper strips. Joh Fredersen moves into the frame, picks up one of the paper strips, reads it, reaches towards the speaking appliance.

Shot 268.
Heart Machine.

Part of Detail: towards the speaking appliance.

Grot looking up.

On the appliance, a sign is flashing in characteristic succession. Grot rushes towards the appliance, picks up the receiver, listens.

Shot 269.
Joh Fredersen's Room.

Detail:

Joh Fredersen at the recording appliance. He speaks into it with the rigid expression of command:

"Open the Doors!"

Shot 270.
Heart Machine.

Part of Detail:

Grot at the speaking appliance. He thinks he has not understood correctly, screams something into the appliance, at the same time pointing towards the doors with his other hand . . .

Different Camera Position:

The doors closed, in front of them, howling, thundering against the doors, the mob.

Shot 271.
Joh Fredersen's Room.

Detail:

Joh Fredersen at the speaking appliance. With heightened expression of unmistakable command he repeats:

"Open the Doors — !!"

Shot 272.
Heart Machine.

Close Up:

Grot at the speaking appliance. His eyes seem to be popping out of his head, red as a bull he screams into the appliance:

"If the heart machine perishes, the machine quarter will be destroyed — !!"

Shot 273.
Joh Fredersen's Room.

Close Shot:

Joh Fredersen at the speaking appliance.

He stamps his foot:

"Do as I tell you — !!"

Shot 274.
Heart Machine.

With a blasphemous curse, Grot throws down the appliance. The man is like a bomb about to explode. Pulls open the door lever.

Different Camera Position:

The mob outside the door, in front the machine woman Maria. Suddenly pointing upwards: Look — look !!

Single Shot:

The one door begins to sink down slowly.

Single Detail:

Grot, half insane with rage, like a bull in a cage up and down, to and fro: Swine! Swine! Swine — !

Different Camera Position:

The doors are already moving apart, leaving a small aperture.

Individuals from the crowd try to jump upwards, to swing themselves up in howling impatience.

Single Shot:

Grot turns around as if stung by an adder. —

Shot 275 / 1.

Shot from inside: towards the doors.

The one door vanishes upwards, the other is half sunk to the ground, hands are reaching over it, faces appearing above the hands. Workers swing themselves over the sinking door.

Camera towards Grot:

Grot, who cannot restrain his helpless rage any longer, seizes a crowbar. Stands there, his breath rattling in his throat, body bent forward, the epitome of deadly menace.

Camera at a distance:

People climbing over the door, beyond which [stands] Grot, roaring with rage.

Single Shot:

Grot climbs over a few stairs, upwards to the base of the machine. Led by the machine woman Maria, the mob storms from the appliance towards the heart machine, roaring:

"Death to the machines — !"

PASSAGE THREE: WHY FREDERSEN WILLS THE DESTRUCTION OF METROPOLIS*

"Father," Freder called aloud, "your city is being destroyed."

Joh Fredersen did not answer. Billowing branches of flames seemed to erupt from his temples.

"Father, don't you understand? Your city is being destroyed! Your machines have come to life, they're rampaging through the city! They're tearing Metropolis to pieces! Do you hear me? Explosion after explosion! I saw one street where the buildings were dancing on the broken ground like little children dancing on the belly of a laughing giant. A lava stream of molten copper poured out of the shattered tower of your smithy down the city streets and a man ran before it, naked, his hair singed, and he screamed: 'It's the end of the world!' But then he stumbled and the stream of copper caught up with him . . . There's a hole in the earth where the Jethro works used to be and it's filling up with water. Shreds of steel bridges hang between disemboweled towers. Cranes swing from their crossbeams like hanged men. And the people, unable to flee or to try to resist, wander among the buildings and the streets, which all seem doomed to destruction . . . "

He encircled the trunk of the cross with his hands and threw back his head to look into his father's face.

"Father, I can't imagine that there's anyone more powerful than you! I used to curse your inordinate power with all my heart, for it filled me with fear. Now I go down on my knees to ask you: Why do you allow Death to lay his hand upon the city which is your own?"

"Because it is my will that Death should come over the city."

"It is your will?"

"Yes."

"The city is to die?"

"Freder, do you not know why?"

There was no answer.

---

* Translation by Meg Tait. Excerpts from Thea von Harbou's *Metropolis* by permission of Ullstein Buchverlage. © 1926 by August Scherl GmbH, Berlin. Translation based on the 1984 edition by Herbert W. Francke (Frankfurt: Ullstein, 1984), 152–53.

"The city must fall, Freder, so that you may build it up once more . . . "

"I?"

"You."

"So you would place the murder of the city at my feet?"

"The murder of the city lies solely at the feet of those who trampled Grot, the Keeper of the Heart Machine, to death."

"Was that also your will, Father?"

"Yes."

"Then it was you who forced guilt upon the people?"

"For your sake, Freder, for you shall redeem them."

"And what about those, Father, who must die along with your dying city before I can redeem them?"

"Concern yourself with the living, Freder, not with the dead."

"And if the living come to murder you?"

"That will not happen, Freder. That will not happen. For there was only one who was able to find the way among the rampaging God Machines, as you called them. And he has already found it. He was my son."

PASSAGE FOUR: A PAINTED WOMAN IS REDEEMED*

[Maria] stood in the room in which she had stood before when she saw Freder for the first time, when she led the procession of small grey waifs to the children who were happy in their play, when she spoke to Freder's heart with her soft cry: "See these are your brothers!"

But not one of those sons, most beloved of their immeasurably wealthy fathers, to whom this building belonged, was to be seen.

A few candles burned, and they lent an air of intimate familiarity and cozy warmth to the mighty room. The room was filled with the gentle chatter of sleepy children's voices, chirruping like swallows before they return to the nest.

They were answered by the less muted voices of the women, beautiful in brocade and face paint, who had once been the playthings of the sons. Equally horrified by the prospect of fleeing as of remaining here, their indecision had finally caused them to remain in the "House of the Sons," and Maria had brought the children to them because she could have found no better refuge; for a beautiful yet terrible coincidence of events had transformed a flock of delicate little whores into a flock of

---

* Translation by Meg Tait. Excerpts from Thea von Harbou's *Metropolis* by permission of Ullstein Buchverlage. © 1926 by August Scherl GmbH, Berlin. Translation based on the 1984 edition by Herbert W. Francke (Frankfurt: Ullstein, 1984), 169.

delicate little mothers burning with a new flame of fulfillment in their new duties.

Not far from Maria the woman charged with preparing the drinks knelt next to a bowl of warm water and was about to wash the thin, small-boned body of Grot's daughter, who stood before her. But the child had taken the sponge from her hand and, silently and earnestly, deliberately and tirelessly, begun to wash the woman's beautiful face of its paint.

10. "The Stadium of the Sons" — the full scale set . . . [Deutsches Institut für Filmkunde, Frankfurt]

11. . . . and the film image, completed by means of Schüfftan's mirror trick. [Deutsches Institut für Filmkunde, Frankfurt]

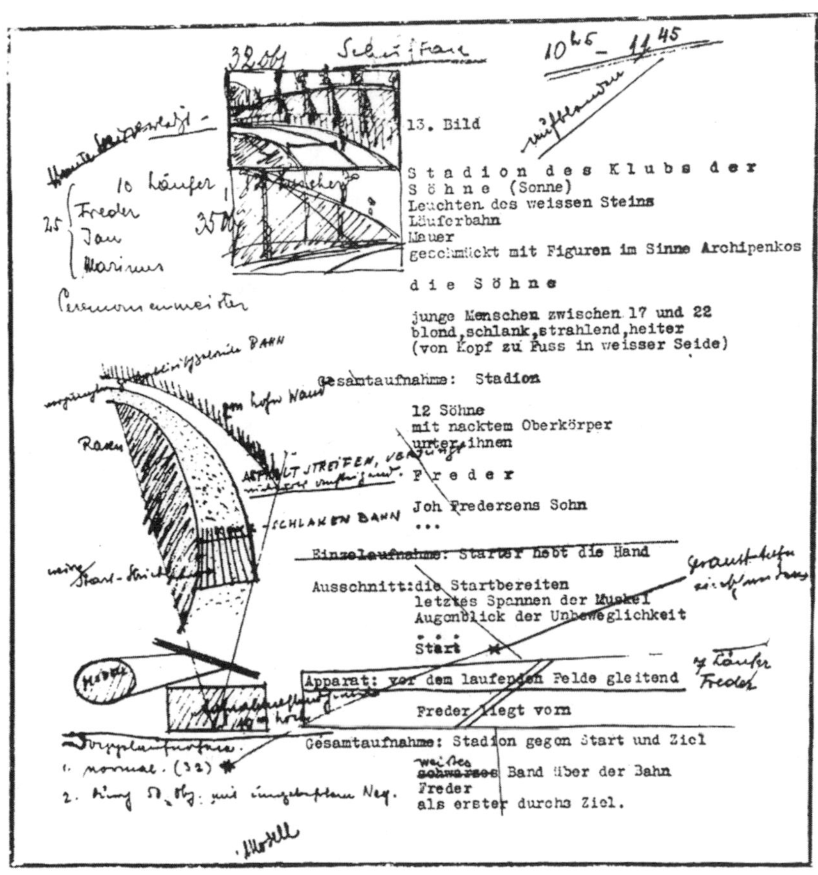

13. Bild

Stadion des Klubs der Söhne (Sonne)
Leuchten des weissen Steins
Läuferbahn
Mauer
geschmückt mit Figuren im Sinne Archipenkos

die Söhne

junge Menschen zwischen 17 und 22
blond, schlank, strahlend, heiter
(von Kopf zu Fuss in weisser Seide)

Gesamtaufnahme: Stadion

12 Söhne
mit nacktem Oberkörper
unter ihnen

Freder

Joh Fredersens Sohn
...

~~Einzelaufnahme: Starter hebt die Hand~~

Ausschnitt: die Startbereiten
letztes Spannen der Muskel
Augenblick der Unbeweglichkeit
...
Start

Apparat: vor dem laufenden Felde gleitend

Freder liegt vorn

Gesamtaufnahme: Stadion gegen Start und Ziel

~~schwarzes~~ weisses Band über der Bahn
Freder
als erster durchs Ziel.

12. Stadium of the Club of the Sons. The only surviving page from the shooting script as reprinted in the Ufa program. Lang's detailed notes and sketches define the design, the time of shooting (10.25–11.45), the required actors and the precise set-up of the Schüfftan trick. [Deutsches Institut für Filmkunde, Frankfurt]

Production Reports

THE FOLLOWING REPORTS from the production process of *Metropolis* give an idea of the way in which Ufa promoted its blockbuster, as well as providing insight into Lang's dictatorial direction and the obsession with visual perfection that characterized Ufa under Erich Pommer. We also learn from them about the creation of the special effects for which the film was, and has remained, famous. They were created by the most distinguished craftsmen the German film industry of the 1920s had to offer — Otto Hunte, Erich Kettelhut, Karl Vollbrecht, Günther Rittau, and Karl Freund.

PASSAGE ONE:
LUDWIG SPITZER, FRITZ LANG ON THE FILM OF THE FUTURE*

Let's be clear from the outset: Fritz Lang was in a very peaceable mood when I visited him at his home at a rather early hour, and he answered all my questions with the engaging modesty that has always distinguished the now world-famous director of "Die Nibelungen." He passed over the aspects he did not want to divulge with the smiling ease he has acquired in the course of the numerous interrogations he has had to endure. He was, for instance, understandably reticent when I wanted to know some details about his new work "Metropolis":

"I don't want to say anything about this at the moment. You will certainly know that the film is based on the novel of the same title by Thea v. Harbou, who has also written the script. The theme: the enormous progress of technology in future times. A sequel to "Dr. Mabuse," so to speak. Whereas that film attempted to portray our time with all its adventures, in my new work I try to capture the storming rhythm of a highly intensified rate of the progress of civilization. Maybe in "Metropolis" I will manage, even more than in "Dr. Mabuse" (just think of the house number that rushed in front of the public prosecutor when he drove to Mabuse's talk about his experiments) to prove that film too has the potential to lay bare the workings of the soul and so to give psychological basis to events — a fact that is often denied.[1]

This is new filmic territory we have to conquer.

---

* "Fritz Lang über den Film der Zukunft," from: *Die Filmtechnik*, 15 July 1925. Translation by Holger Bachmann and Meg Tait.

[1] In *Dr. Mabuse*, Lang used superimpositions to convey psychological processes. Here, he is referring to a superimposed number that seems to rush in front of the face of the prosecutor hunting Mabuse, signifying his obsession with his enemy — H. B.

To be sure — we have to be aware of this — the problems that arise here touch on questions leading us into the field of psychoanalysis and require a certain psychological training of those who would interpret them correctly. Because it is not enough to master the technology. If you want to give a psychological basis to the events; if you are trying to show the 'inner' processes of the man who, say, falls down a roof, you also have to — know these inner processes. And this, of course, requires a degree of psychological training."

"You mean," I interjected, "to stay with the example you have chosen, in that case you have to know that the falling man sees his whole life pass before him as if in a kaleidoscope — whereas, without such knowledge, you would arrive at wrong 'explanations' of the inner process?"

"Exactly," the director replied.

What Fritz Lang said here does indeed open interesting perspectives on the film of the future, which, regarded in this way, may also be able to bridge the borders that exist to this day — and by necessity — between works of literature (that are shaped by language) and works of the screen (that are created by the camera lens). And maybe we will reach a stage at which translating a great creation of world literature into film language will no longer mean stripping it of its psychological content (by transferring to the screen solely the naked events, that is the "external" action), but will rather mean a genuine rendering, albeit one with a new form. Then, in the finished film, we will finally and truly feel the spirit of the writer who has created the adapted work, whereas up to now, this spirit has at best only been perceptible through the contributions of the actors. And then, too, it will be possible for works that are created directly for the screen (something I have always advocated, as film has its own laws and possibilities), to have an entirely different format. Someone like Carl Mayer, for instance, will then be able to tell us things quite different from those he has already told us. And "the" screen artist, who at present perhaps has not stepped forward because he thinks film has not yet reached the level of maturity at which he would be able to give everything he's capable of, will come into his own. Maybe then we will be able to speak of a true art of film (whereas at the moment, at best there are art films).

"And the means by which psychology can be introduced into film?"

"Special effects in the widest sense of the word," Lang replied. "This comprises both increased and decreased taking speed, major modification of the construction of the camera itself (as, for instance, when the dwarves in "Die Nibelungen" are turned to stone; photography: Carl Hoffmann and Günther Rittau), and this also comprises the use of the Schüfftan mirror process — but on the other hand, one should not talk too much about how special effects are achieved, as this robs the audience of the illusion. For this reason, it also seems misguided to me when illustrated journals sometimes publish stills of special effects. Why should everyone be allowed to look behind the scenes? Why take away the naive joy with which we face the world of film — why show that the 'colourful fantastic atmosphere' of the events that, for the vast majority, are frequently inexplicable, often have a rather profane origin? However, to come back to special effects: in order to put the technological possibilities of film completely into the service of his production, I am convinced that the director has also to master — the camera. Maybe I'm not giving away a secret if I reveal that director Erich Pommer — to whose perceptive expertise all his artistic colleagues owe a great deal (as it grants them numerous opportunities to develop their vision) — told me when I came to him, as a young painter from Paris with the intention of becoming a film director: 'If you want to become a good film director, first of all you have to learn how to master the camera.' And — as my preceding words show — he was only too right."

"And where do you see young artistic talent?"

"We have architects — everything else is hopeless. This is my personal experience: about 500 young people have visited me so far. They all wanted to work in the film industry. I listened to them all, very willing to help in any way where there is but the shadow of a hope, of a possibility. I did not find one who knew what he wanted. They came to me with unclear, confused, fantastic stories that did not demonstrate a trace of suitability. For instance: 'I am an opera singer, without an engagement; anything he (here he named a well-known film actor) can do, I can do better.' Or the girl aged sixteen or seventeen, who 'sooo wants to be in the movies.' Or the author of several articles (nineteen years old), in which he bitterly complains that the film industry systematically shuts itself off from young people. I ask him to come to me, I put him to the test, and receive only an unclear stammering for an answer. Finally the confession: he has written a magnificent script. The title: 'Snow White'!!! Why should I bore you with any more examples?" Lang concluded the description of his experiences. "Give me young talent, let young people come forward who know what they want, and who can show what they are made of. They won't be turned away from my door. But — I fear, I fear, I will have to wait a long time for them."

[. . .]

PASSAGE TWO: THE FUTURE-FANTASTIC FILM *METROPOLIS**

The two film industries of global significance have been in competition with each other for years now: the German industry and the American one. In the period just before the war and during the great conflict of the peoples, the American film industry underwent outstanding technical development and created the genre of the monumental film. But Germany too brought forth films of respectable production values in the years in which the two states did not have much to do with each other, and she strove very hard to equal American technical standards. This has not been achieved so far. But German directors have surpassed the Americans in the artistic aspects of film making. And these are, perhaps, the decisive aspects. This — and not the technological advances — has caused the Americans to take German film seriously, to study it and finally also to use its artistic methods and its artists. The American film industry would never have taken its directors and actors from a foreign country in such huge numbers as it has taken them from Germany had it not come to believe that German film was about to surpass American film in every respect. And so, it has jumped at the solution of "mixing" before Germany could steal a march on America.

It is well known that the heads and owners of the biggest American film studios paid a visit to Germany a short time ago in order to sign reciprocal contracts with the great German companies and to take the opportunity to entice away the best film actors and directors.

German film production of the past four years had inspired great awe in Americans. This is particularly true of Ufa's top productions, films of outstanding artistic and technical merit, such as the "Nibelungenfilm" and "Variety," and monumental films, such as "Faust" and "Metropolis," which were begun under Erich Pommer's direction (who has himself been hired overseas).

The film "Metropolis," on which Fritz Lang, director of "Die Nibelungen," has been working for over a year now, seems to surpass everything previously produced in terms of sheer monumentalism: the monumentalism of its artistic, technical and architectural achievement. What has been created here (Lang is just about to finish shooting) exceeds even the wildest dreams of the Americans when they try to conceive of the potential of German film studios. And they do not hide their admiration, calling the "Metropolis" film — the shooting of which

* "Der zukunftsphantastische Film *Metropolis*," from: *Mein Film* 25 (1926), 9–10; author not stated. Translation by Holger Bachmann and Meg Tait.

the American film directors have also attended several times — a superfilm, an authoritative work of film art and film technology.

Apart from the witty and imaginative writer of the novel and the screenplay, Thea von Harbou, the men who created this film are director Fritz Lang, cameraman Karl Freund and architect Otto Hunte. The leading parts in the film are played by the newly discovered stars Brigitte Helm and Gustav Fröhlich, and other parts are played by Alfred Abel, Rudolf Klein-Rogge, and Walter Rilla.

Today, we are delighted to be able to show our readers a series of stills from the most recent shots of the "Metropolis" film, a work that we hope will also be released here [in Austria] as well in the coming season.[2]

Concerning the "burning of a witch in the year 2000," a scene for the film "Metropolis," which took place in the film city of Metropolis, we have been told:[3]

Not long ago, the paroxysm of the mob had reached its climax one night in the doomed city of Metropolis. Rotwang, the modern magician, had caused tremendous mischief with his devilish idea of giving a machine woman the looks of Maria. Madness forges ahead, unstoppable, unleashed. Goaded on, the workers were about to lynch the true Maria, just as she was carrying the last of the children saved from the catastrophe into the House of the Sons. In mortal fear, the hunted girl hid between the stone saints at the entrance to the cathedral. It would have been useless, if the mechanical Maria had not by a lucky coincidence appeared at this very moment. All the rage and desperation of the maddened crowd was now vented on her. Chaos at the foot of the column of the tower. The rampaging mob has heaped up wrecked cars, torn silk furniture, valuable books and paintings. A hecatomb of hell. And high up above, Lucifer himself sits upon the throne. A devil in human form, a worker who is still young. His rolling, popping eyes, his face contorted with rage and surrounded by wild strands of hair, seem to excite the hordes even more than the inarticulate sounds with which he stirs up their unleashed passions ever more. An orgy of hatred and passion. A Witches' Sabbath that even the most hideous imagination could not conceive of in a more horrifying way.

And the witch is there, too. She is dragged near, her hair loose, her clothes torn, her eyes bloodshot and crazed. In front of them all the giant Grot, who drags her mercilessly up the hideous pile, where willing hands seize her and tie the poor creature to the column with ropes. Just

---

[2] The article contains seven illustrations, including a still that shows Lang shooting a scene with Maria and Rotwang.

[3] In the following passage, the text mixes different tenses, probably to create immediacy and excitement.

a machine, but her hysterical laughter drowns out the roaring noise from a thousand rough, hoarse throats. A thousand torches are instantly at hand to set fire to the one, the living torch. And then suddenly, a deep, piercing voice which has no human quality, which comes from a giant funnel.

"Stop, back!" thunders — Fritz Lang through the megaphone. "Less tense, more movement. A long skull is throwing back a shadow from over there — I don't want it . . . " The magic spell is broken. We return to reality. It is rough and cold, because the nights at Neubabelsberg are anything but summery. And then — the sounds of a jazz band ring out. Film country, the country of contrasts. The crowd, which just a moment ago was thronging wildly, now turns peacefully in a round dance and laughs. And Thea von Harbou smiles too. It was her idea to fill the short breaks in between the individual takes with music in order to refresh the tired extras, who have been at work for nine nights already. For this, she acquired the title of a "Cosima of Babelsberg" — free of charge.

PASSAGE THREE: ALFRED ABEL, AAA . . . WHAT HAPPENED TO ME IN YOSHIWARAAA . . .*

Yoshiwara! Elegant men in dinner jackets, truly charming ladies in magnificent outfits.

Shooting at night! Shots! Made-up bodies tremble slightly, feathers are drawn closer to the unclad bosom, one coat grants two beauties some shelter from the bitter cold at the same time. Attention! Action! More merriment, more rapture, "ladies and gentlemen!" Fritz Lang's voice sounds through the night, "this is Yoshiwara in Metropolis and not your grandmother's fancy-dress ball." And now, four stunning young Yoshiwara ladies step forth from the group. They step in front of the Almighty's throne: "We are so bitterly cold, please, please, give us something to warm us up." The monocle flashes: "Puttchen, quick, a bottle of brandy, it's on me!" — One bottle of brandy for one hundred trembling, freezing girls? "Stop," sounds the voice of the mighty one. "Ten bottles of brandy." Jubilant cries race through Metropolis. — No trace of grandmother any more; everything works fine. *He* is satisfied. Hooray! Here's to you, Fritz Lang! Here's to you, guys and girls!

Silence on the large set! Only the production manager paces out the area once more. A tall, strong man. Ha — what is this? The strong man shivers! There's an animal lurking in the gloomy dawn. What should

* "Aaa . . . was ich erlebte in Yoshiwaraaa . . . ," from: Press Department of Ufa, *Metropolis, Sondernummer des Ufa-Magazins*, ed. Stefan Lorant (Berlin: Bukwa, Presse Abteilung der Ufa, 1927), unpaginated. Translation by Holger Bachmann and Meg Tait.

we do? Slowly, the beast sneaks closer. No revolver to hand. Sound the alarm? Closer and closer comes the beast. What on earth is it? All wild beasts in the world rush through his mind. Stop! Aren't these feathers? Oh, how it hisses! A terrible roar sounds through the night! A panther! — Now it's grunting; so it must be a wild boar! Have at it, and pray God is with you. Seize it with strong arms. "Ouch!" . . . A human sound? "Please, please, fetch dressing room, can't stand, blasted brandy, drank whole bottle on my own!" A Yoshiwara lady crawled on all fours through the alleys of Metropolis, a phantom beast in a see-through feather dress.

The cockerel belonging to the Ufa zoo crowed a joyous "Good Morning" as a strong man carefully led a freezing, beautiful woman adorned with diamonds to her dressing room.

PASSAGE FOUR: THEODOR LOOS, MY FEET GOT WET!*

I spent the nicest seaside holidays of my life last year at the al fresco pool of "Metropolis" in Neubabelsberg. For fourteen days the water was kept at a pretty low temperature especially for us actors, to nip excessive demonstrations of gaiety in the bud.

So we bustled about from morning to evening with 500 little boys and girls. In between, there was mulled wine, chocolate, and gingerbread, and the occasional little shower. Fritz Lang cruised to and fro between us with his staff on a big pontoon. Through his big megaphone he encouraged us time after time to seek out the biggest jets of water.

But however hard it may have been, I can assure you that I'd hate to have missed these days in my life. Because, even though my feet got wet, at least I know that it was worth it.

PASSAGE FIVE: GÜNTHER RITTAU, SPECIAL EFFECTS IN *METROPOLIS**

The cameraman is the modern magician. There is no such thing as "impossible" for him. And yet, for all his magic, one must not notice that it is "magic." The less noticeable this is, the better his work. And because I hope you do not detect the manifold work of the "magician" in the "Metropolis" film, I would like to give away some secrets of the "magician" here.

A special story among the special effect shots were the shots using Schüfftan's trick process [*Spiegeltrickverfahren*]. To construct all the gi-

* "Ich habe nasse Füße bekommen!" from: Press Department of Ufa, *Metropolis, Sondernummer des Ufa-Magazins*, ed. Stefan Lorant (Berlin: Bukwa, Presse Abteilung der Ufa, 1927), unpaginated. Translation by Holger Bachmann and Meg Tait.

* "Trickaufnahmen in *Metropolis*," from: *Mein Film* 60 (1927), 6. Translation by Holger Bachmann and Meg Tait.

ant sets demanded by "Metropolis" in full size would have swallowed up enormous sums of money and, above all, a lot of valuable time. Here, the Schüfftan process offered the only possibility of a practical solution, and we made ample use of it. With the help of parts of sets and smaller-scale Schüfftan models, we created parts of the gigantic street scenes and the atmospheric scenes in the cathedral. During Schüfftan shots, special attention has to be given to the way the camera is set up and to the lighting of the model sets. The visionary images of the Moloch machine, which were also made with the help of the mirror trick process, were particularly complicated to create. Other shots, for which the Schüfftan method could not be used due to movements occurring within the scene, were made with the help of model sets. Among these were the shots of the main street, as well as those of the explosion of the main machine hall and the reservoirs. Model shots require special precision both in constructing the model and in lighting the shot, as well as in adjusting the camera. An illustration of how difficult such shots are is the fact that in order to shoot forty metres of film showing model scenery, we worked for almost eight days; every single frame had to be shot individually, and forty metres of film contain 2,100 individual frames. In the film, this whole scene does not take longer than ten seconds. For another model shot (the explosion of the machine hall), the construction and preparation of the model took four weeks; the shot itself (which could only be carried out once) only one and a half minutes. The slightest mistake during the shooting would have ruined the work of four weeks. For the shots of the main road, in which roughly 300 small model automobiles were used, every single car had to be moved a few millimetres forward after every single frame in order the create the impression of movement in the film. Other overview shots of the city of Metropolis were made with the help of painted pictures that were given a three-dimensional look by suitable lighting. A panoramic shot of the Eternal Gardens was created with the help of a small model in the shape of a painted vista. As the model was shot from very close range due to its small size, the camera could not be moved. In order to achieve the panorama effect, the model was therefore moved past the camera. In order to accomplish a completely steady taking speed, in this shot, as in many others, the camera was operated by a small electrical motor. A further interesting problem was the shot of the television set; this was solved by a projection machine that, from behind, projected the image of the machine master Grot onto the television screen, which in turn was filmed by a camera in front. In order to obtain a flawless image, projection machine and camera were linked by axles in this shot, so that both operated at the same speed.

The most interesting tasks for the cameraman, however, arose out of the creation of the various lighting effects, most importantly during the scene in which the machine woman takes on human form in the laboratory of the inventor Rotwang. The anthropogenesis is accomplished by transferring the human form of Maria by means of electric currents. Now, electric currents have the habit of being invisible. But on the other hand, the fantastic-mysterious event taking place here absolutely had to be made visible. The only way of achieving this was to make the effect of the electric currents visible. Liquids in strange receptacles took on a shine and started to simmer, the electric apparatus enclosing Maria began to scintillate and was eventually completely covered by giant, shining chains of sparks moving to and fro; simultaneously, shining rings of electric current start to form on different levels around the machine woman and begin to glide up and down. The incipient anthropogenesis is illustrated by making visible a shining system of circulating blood streams. The realization of these shots required many weeks of preparatory tests in the laboratory and equally lengthy periods of practice shots. The chemistry of photography played no small role in obtaining these shots, and the strangest kind of auxiliary material was used.

A more detailed explanation would go too far here and would also not be to the point. Suffice it to say that special frames, striae [*Schlieren*], soft soap, vignettes, and extremely complicated machines especially constructed [for these shots] played a decisive role. For days, the workers had to be trained in operating the appliances, which required split-second precision. Individual pieces of film were exposed up to thirty times. Everyone who knows anything about photography will understand immediately what this means. In these shots, everything depended on the most exact calculations, on the utmost precision of the work and the appliances, and most of all on the nerves and the patience of the cameraman. I can confidently claim that shots like the ones in the "Metropolis" film have never been shown in any film so far. May this film be proof, if proof is needed, that the technology of the artistic German *Großfilm* [high budget film production] can stand comparison with that of any other country.

PASSAGE SIX: OTTO HUNTE, MY WORK ON *METROPOLIS**

The preparations for "Metropolis" took up as much time as the work on both parts of "Die Nibelungen." And the amount of work grew with the technical details. Luckily enough, the architect is enabled by the

* "Meine Arbeit bei 'Metropolis,'" from: *Berliner Zeitung am Sonntag*, 7 January 1927. Translation by Holger Bachmann and Meg Tait.

current state of film technology to use a technique that makes the work substantially easier and that until lately could hardly have been imagined: the Schüfftan process, of which I made ample use in "Metropolis."

Most of the time and effort was taken up by the construction of the main road of Metropolis, at the end of which the new "Tower of Babel" rises; the tower was meant to be 500 meters high and therefore could in no way be constructed in full size. I had to use a miniature model and represent the traffic passing through this street by means of a trick shot. It would go too far to explain all these things in detail, but the kind of toilsome, minutely precise work needed to put airplanes, high-speed railways, automobiles and people into this shot can easily be imagined. This work took almost six weeks, and the result flits past the eyes of the spectator in twice six seconds.

One scene in which a trick shot was completely out of the question was the flooding, where the cement and iron concrete pavement of the streets is broken open and destroyed by the masses of water. The large quantities of water needed for this had to be dammed up and kept on a higher level in order to achieve the necessary pressure. For this purpose, four reservoirs with a capacity of 1,600 cubic metres were built, and in addition to that several smaller tanks for special shots. To be on the safe side, I also had a large motor spray installed, just in case the water did not have enough power to burst through the concrete pavement. When we were actually taking the shot and a massive jet of water was catapulted eight metres into the air, we all believed it was the motor spray; but in fact there was no need for it even to begin to function.

The explosion that destroys the giant escalators of the workers' city looked much more dangerous than it actually was, because the escalators were set in motion by a safety-catch and crashed down in such a way that only at the moment when they hit the ground did we create the impression of an explosion using pyrotechnic means.

These are a few details of the work on "Metropolis," a work that is pioneering both in technical and artistic respects, and in which the one cannot be imagined without the other. That these difficulties, of which I have given some examples, could be surmounted, proves the unlimited possibilities and potential of the future development of film.

Reviews

Germany

THE FIRST, UNCUT VERSION OF *METROPOLIS* opened in Berlin on 10 January 1927 in the Ufa-Palast am Zoo. The critical reaction was divided and ranged from the reverent praise that Ufa had carefully prepared by its public relations to thoroughly negative, sarcastic slatings that uncovered the gap between the film's technical achievement and the triviality of its plot. The following reviews illustrate this broad spectrum.

Review of *Metropolis**

Metropolis

Production: Universum-Film
Distribution: Parufamet
Leading Roles: Helm, Fröhlich, Abel, George, Klein-Rogge
Length: 4,189 Metres (nine Acts)
Premiere: Ufa-Palast am Zoo

In the Ufa-Palast, Fritz Lang's long-awaited film from the wonderland Metropolis is being shown in a great gala performance.

It is the film version of the science-fiction novel written by Thea von Harbou that was published by Scherl Publishing House. In the year 2000, a city of light rises up over the darkness of a workers' city. Day and night, uncanny, gigantic, complicated machines whirr beneath the earth and work for the inhabitants of Metropolis, who live in massive, infinitely high buildings, send their sons to eternal gardens and while away their own time in Yoshiwara, the temple of lust.

Master over life and death in this legendary city is Herr Fredersen, whose heart is set on one thing: on his son, who one day wants to help the people his father oppresses, and who innocently causes a kind of revolution — the workers' city sinks, but the people are saved, and they are possibly even led to a happier future. The young hero and the heroine, who bears the romantic name "Maria," find each other for life.

---

* From: *Der Kinematograph*, 16 January 1927, 21; author not stated. Translation by Holger Bachmann and Meg Tait.

It may be that several aspects of the plot remain somewhat problematic in the film. This, however, is not important in this film, because even the great accomplishments of Alfred Abel, George, Klein-Rogge, Fröhlich's capable performance and the excellent Brigitte Helm are secondary in comparison with the purely decorative and technical aspects of the film. What we see in purely visual terms is admirable. And it remains a brilliant and astounding achievement even if one knows that it was all filmed by means of the Schüfftan process.

The boldness of the script and its technical realization mean that in "Metropolis" we have a work that defies comparison with almost every other German production.

Despite several reservations concerning individual aspects, this is the greatest film ever made in this country. It may well be that a composition of this kind will not be considered extraordinary in a few years from now. But here and now we are standing at the beginning — and an awe-inspiring beginning it is — of a new age of film production. This alone must be motivation enough for German theatre owners, who must give prominence to this great film. The technical aspects alone make it worth seeing, not to mention its many other merits. In addition to the director and the actors, particular mention must be made in this instance of the cameramen. Karl Freund and Günther Rittau were facing entirely new challenges in every respect. They mastered the photographic and technical problems in a virtuoso manner. They created a convincing appearance of realism, which is maintained whether they were working with a full-scale construction after the old method or a model. Finally mention should be made of the score by Gottfried Huppertz, perhaps not overwhelming as a composition in its own right, but remarkably skillful and commendable as a musical illustration of the grand theme.

The leading public officials, the Reichskanzler, ministers, aldermen and various prominent names from the worlds of art and literature were to be seen at the premiere. Currently the film is being shown at the Ufa pavilion, which has been transformed to this end, into a silver building that gleams like a beacon into the night.

Willy Haas, Two Major Film Premieres*

Metropolis

Even one and a half years before its release, there were rumors that a miracle of film technology was in the making here. And the facts surpass even the greatest expectations. What has been accomplished in this German film leaves everything achieved in American camerawork far behind and is unique in the history of film technology. Not only in terms of pure craftsmanship; in many scenes this technical expertise is perfectly transferred into elements of musical imagery, of symphonic imagery; it obeys the subtlest wishes and suggestions of the most sensitive nerves — even of such an extraordinary master of the art of movement composition as Fritz Lang. Take Maria fleeing through the catacombs, for example, constantly pursued by the spotlight of a tiny electric torch — a mouse caught in the trap of a minuscule patch of light; or the will-o'-the-wisps and semi-visions that glide up the screen and provide a visionary illustration of Freder's fading consciousness as he passes out and sinks to the ground; all this is well worth setting hundreds of complicated machines to work for weeks. I could easily continue this list for quite some time. Wonderful, for instance, is the light, playful tempo of the fantastic overviews of Metropolis, the airplanes swimming lightly in the air, the cars that almost float as they glide over gigantic, suspended steel bridges — the pianissimo, musical expression of a luxury industry so refined that it operates in discrete silence. And so on.

But this must not be the last, or even the decisive, word about a film of such dimension and such pretensions.

What might we, should we, expect of a film for which 36,000 extras, 1,100 bald men, 750 children, 100 Negroes, 3,500 pairs of shoes, 75 wigs, 50 futuristic cars, 500 to 600 skyscrapers of 70 floors apiece, a few thousand utopian motors, 620,000 metres of negative and 1,300,000 metres of positive film, — and above all else a director's brain in a state of superhuman concentration had to be mobilized for one and a half years?

Not a lot — dear reader, don't laugh.

Simply a motif that requires and demands such an effort. In his drama "The Undivine Comedy" the poet Krasinski needed roughly the same effort in order to demonstrate, while pushing against the limits of language and form, that the revolution of the lower classes is akin to an odorous, repulsive plague. Mr. Lenin, not a bad director himself,

* "Zwei große Filmpremieren," from: *Die literarische Welt* 3 (21 January 1927), 7. Translation by Holger Bachmann and Meg Tait.

needed ten times the effort to prove the opposite. There are indeed motifs that can hardly be developed with less than 60,000 leading actors, simply because their passions and themes derive from world history. When Christ himself must remain silent, it may well be that 100,000 people are necessary if he is to be portrayed adequately. The same goes for Napoleon to express the idea of the leader. The same is true for socialism. And basically there is nothing, absolutely nothing, that militates against the notion that Frau Thea von Harbou too, author of this film, cannot realize her creative ego with anything under 36,000 extras, 750 children, 100 Negroes and 3,500 pairs of shoes.

But not by taking tiny, carefully measured-out portions from every aspect of world history and mixing it together in an allusive, allegorical way. A little Christianity, with the idea of the "mediator," of religious services in the catacombs, of the holy mother of humankind Maria ("Suffer the little children" — as a substitute for the absent son); a little socialism, with the thoroughly modern cult of the machine, the proletariat enslaved and robbed of their souls, and the perfect "accumulation of capital," to put it in entirely Marxist terms, which makes a single person the invisible master of the world; a little Nietzscheanism, with the worship of the superman. Everything is mixed together so carefully in such a way that the script manages neatly to evade any suggestion of an uncompromising idea, and no "tendency" — Heaven forbid — is able to develop. And yet only an idea that is cruelly, heavenly defiant, uncompromising in its very nature, could justify such gigantic production demands. And this is the curse of the *Großfilm* [high budget film production], this is the reason why nine-tenths of every *Großfilm* seems empty and superfluous: because the *Großfilme* in themselves represent nothing but a state of attention to the tastes of every part of the audience, a desire to be wholly inoffensive and utterly uncommitted, to give a little of everything and nothing of anything. A thinker, a creator, needs everything; but a gourmet requires only a tiny dish of hors d'oeuvre.

Everything else is a consequence of this basic fact.

The deep inner lack of style. A hyper-American, science-fiction city set in the year, say, 3000 A.D. — and in its midst, a collection of Biedermeier souls, all roaring drunk, and a constructed "femme machine" (Edison's "Woman of the Future" as imagined by Villiers d'Isle Adam), but not a single living human being in this mechanized world who is conceived in a creative way, projected into the future in a manner that shows psychological understanding. Instead, an emotional strangeness and distance, with an inner life incomprehensible to us, and maybe an even more bizarre anatomy, just as Wells has attempted so often, although he too has failed to achieve any kind of convincing creativity. In addition to all this we are once again presented with medieval church romanticism — in the midst of futuristic dynamos, turbines, airplanes, cars. The problem is not simply that all this puts an intolerable strain on the nerves of every cultivated person with a sense of style — it is symptomatic of something far more disquieting. This is the noncommittal stance of belles lettres, desperately drawing on tomorrow and yesterday in order to avoid today. What kind of barely definable humour is at work when the slightest glimpse of tangible today appears by chance in this wild swing of the pendulum between a romantic day before yesterday and a romantic day after tomorrow? When the youthful hero, for instance, reads a copy of the "Apocalypse" in an edition that was published only a few years ago by the *Avalunverlag* in Hellerau, and I just briefly imagine that one of these dead chess figures could actually read a book that is part of my own library. The entire clockwork mechanics of this carefully calculated world stops at once, because it can bear nothing that reminds one of real life, nothing that is perceptible, tangible, empirical — precisely because it is not life. Neither the life of the day before yesterday nor of the day after tomorrow, because real life could never be ruined so terribly by the appearance of life. Because it is — and now I beg your pardon — the romanticism of a high society lady. It is another example of the genre that will not have anything to do with life's bitterness and sweetness, with real worries, real longing, the truly burning questions of our existence; no matter if it gushes of the sweet countess Wally or the handsome junior lawyer, or if, Kurfürstendamm style, it has the forget-me-not suddenly blossom amidst raging giant motors.

There is a single, more significant symbol here — although it is not to the author's liking and certainly not intended by her: a certain depth to the motif of the female doppelganger, which embodies both the unleashed hell of lust and the most tender virtue of the . . . but now we are straying down devious paths indeed!

Herbert Jhering, The *Metropolis*-Film*

I went to see this film with great expectations. Individual elements were fascinating, but as a whole it was disappointing. Film — even this one, in fact particularly this one — is no longer merely a matter of technical expertise. A great deal can be accomplished these days. Fritz

---

* "Der Metropolis-Film," from: *Berliner Börsen-Courier*, 11 January 1927; reprinted in Herbert Ihering, *Von Reinhardt bis Brecht. Vier Jahrzehnte Theater und Film*, vol. 2, *1924–1929* (Berlin: Aufbau-Verlag, 1959), 523–24. Translation by Holger Bachmann and Meg Tait.

Lang is capable of a great deal, too. But producing an ideological film without an ideology, that is something that no expertise in the world can carry off.

A technical city of the future and the romanticism of the shady bower; a world of machines and ridiculous individual fates; social worlds in contrast, and as mediator between "brain and hand the heart," Georg Kaiser and Birch-Pfeiffer; "Mountains, Oceans and Giants"[1] and a legendary Maria, Alfred Döblin and Thea von Harbou — it doesn't work. Workers and entrepreneurs, this battle presents itself in filmic terms on its own merits, even when it is transposed into a futuristic city such as "Metropolis." But here we have invention and stylization. Thea von Harbou invents an absurd plot bursting at the seams with themes and motifs. Fritz Lang stylizes this foundation and lets the images fight each other. Medieval Dance of Death here, modern Dance of Death there. Allusions to our time here, allusions to our cultural heritage there, but the orientation never arises out of the subject matter.

The workers, even the machines that carry their supra-realistic reality in themselves, are sometimes stylized (Moloch!). The film works with emotional clichés throughout. Horrible. A factual theme turned to atrocious kitsch. Effects not because ideologies urge towards explosions, but because the film wants its effects. The ending, the tear-jerking reconciliation of employer and employee — dreadful.

It is hard to use harsh words in the face of something that has been the subject of intensive efforts over several years. But because the failure of "Metropolis" will be attributed to high-quality films as such, it is important that we should indicate the reasons why this film *had* to fail. A modern *Großfilm* [high budget film production] and the regressive, novelistic imagination of Thea von Harbou have nothing in common. If in "Metropolis" it had not been Alfred Abel who played the industrialist, if it had not been Heinrich George who played the machine master, if a new talent, Brigitte Helm, had not played the impossible female lead, if it had not been Fritz Rasp who, as a new Kühne, played a detective, who in turn had not fitted in with the others stylistically — the film would have been totally appalling. As it was, Herr Klein-Rogge as the inventor over-acted, while Gustav Fröhlich as son of the millionaire seemed talented, but still too restless.

---

[1] [Editors' note: *Berge, Meere, Giganten* is the title of a futuristic novel by Alfred Döblin, published in 1924.]

America

As a major production clearly designed to rival Hollywood's efforts, *Metropolis* had already attracted the attention of American reviewers with its premiere in Berlin. When the revised Parufamet version was first shown in New York on 5 March 1927, the film met with remarkable public interest and was widely discussed in the trade press and daily newspapers. Universally denouncing the theme of *Metropolis* as naive and sentimental, the reviewers nevertheless acknowledged the film's visual accomplishment and its "Germanic" stylization, which was seen as representative of Lang and Ufa. Randolph Bartlett's piece in *The New York Times* gives an indispensable insight into the American re-editing of the German original.[2] In what is arguably the most famous review of *Metropolis*, H. G. Wells, as part of a series on "The Way the World Is Going" also for *The New York Times*, denied the film any merit, dismissing it outright as an antiquated and downright silly plagiarism.

"Metropolis"*

Berlin, Feb. 5.
The long-awaited film for which Ufa has been beating the gong for the last year. It is said to have cost 7,000,000 marks (about $1,680,000), and the picture looks it.

Nothing of the sort has ever been filmed before: its effect is positively overwhelming. From a photographic and directorial standpoint it is something entirely original. Brigitte Helm, in the leading feminine role, is a find. If she has never really acted before, Fritz Lang, directing, certainly did an extraordinary piece of work with her.

Also Heinrich George, Fritz Rasp and Gustav Froehlich deliver exceptional performances. The weakness is the scenario by Thea von Harbou. It gives effective chances for scenes, but it actually gets nowhere. The scene is laid in the future, one hundred years from now, in the mighty city of Metropolis, a magnified New York. It is ruled by a mil-

[2] For its American release, *Metropolis* was substantially revised according to what Parufamet thought fit for the American public. In charge of the film's reworking was a team led by Channing Pollock, an American writer who had provided the screenplay for *The Fool*. In Pollock's version, *Metropolis* was cut from 4,189 metres to a mere 2,841 metres, and most intertitles were rewritten. See Bachmann, Patalas and Bertellini in this volume for more details.

* From: *Variety*, 23 February 1927; author not stated.

lionaire, who lives in the upper city and whose son falls in love with a girl of the workers, who lives below in the city of the toilers. This girl is preaching good will to the workers in the catacombs below the city. An inventor has discovered a way to make artificial human beings, and at the request of the millionaire gives this creation of his the form of the girl. She preaches destruction to the workers, and they destroy the machinery which regulates everything in the city. Only through the aid of the boy and the real girl can the children of the workers be saved from inundation in the lower city. The workers turn against the evil marionette and burn her on a scaffold. The boy and the girl are united, and peace is closed between the millionaire and the workers.

Too bad that so much really artistic work was wasted on this manufactured story. However, if put across with strong publicity, it may be possible to get out the money invested in it.

Randolph Bartlett, "German Film Revision Upheld as Needed Here"*

I am getting just a little bit tired of the attitude taken by certain writers and other commentators, that anything done to a German moving picture to prepare it for American audiences is automatically and inevitably wrong. I am prepared to support in some detail the opposite position — that with possibly two exceptions, the successes of the German productions in America have been largely due to expert editing in this country.

In certain elements of picture making the Germans have achieved outstanding supremacy. First of all, in the element of force. In productions like "Metropolis" there is breath-taking power. In others, such as "Danton" ("All for a Woman") and "Quo Vadis," this force was almost crude and boisterous, but there was in these films a sincerity and relentlessness that held the audiences in its grip. In these pictures, as in "The Loves of Pharaoh," that force was expressed in the sweep of large bodies of men and women, giving a momentum best described in the physical formula, mass multiplied by velocity and by distance.

In the handling of light the Germans have been well abreast with the times, and their cleverness in working out unique effects, such as the traveling concentric rings of light moving through one another in the metamorphosis scene in "Metropolis," has often baffled the American experts.

It has been amazing to those who have handled German productions and recognized these and other touches of genius, that when it came to

* From: *The New York Times*, 13 March 1927, section 7, 3.

the telling of the story there seemed to be either a lack of interest in dramatic verity or an astonishing ineptitude. Motives were lacking for the most important developments in the narrative, or were extremely naive. Yet all that was required was a little ingenuity to work into the scenes the missing elements. It is no answer to this criticism to say that in many of the pictures made in this country the same faults are to be found.

Concerning "Metropolis," it is not in my province to speak in detail of what was done, but I saw the whole seventeen reels before they were touched, and watched the film take form under the hands of Channing Pollock, Julian Johnson and Edward Adams, and I have never seen a greater achievement of the editing art. And all they were trying to do was to bring out the real thought that was manifestly back of the production, and which the Germans had simply "muffed." I am willing to wager that "Metropolis," as it is seen at the Rialto now, is nearer Fritz Lang's idea than the version he himself released in Germany.

Then there are incidents that are almost hilariously amusing. In "Metropolis" there was originally a very beautiful statue of a woman's head, and on the base was her name — and that name was "Hel." Now the German word for "hell" is "hoelle" so they were quite innocent of the fact that this name would create a guffaw in an English speaking audience. So it was necessary to cut this beautiful bit out of the picture, and a certain motive which it represented had to be replaced by another.

A laugh-inspiring bit in a tragic moment was removed from "The Loves of Pharaoh." The hero and heroine were being stormed by a mob, and whenever a "stone" hit any person or any hard substance, it bounced. It was perfect Keystone.

These are mild samples. In the last seven or eight years I have been closely in touch with most of the important productions brought to America from Germany, and I have yet to see one which, in its original state, did not contain some sore spot that protruded like a wart on the end of a nose. I will add that I did not see "The Last Laugh" and "Variety" until they were in the theatre.

So much for the actual, intrinsic values. When we add to this the fact that American audiences require fare far different from that of the European, we multiply the necessity for adaptation.

Most of this worship of German films is of a piece with milady's pride in her Paris hat, which, with the exception of the label, can be duplicated in a dozen shops on Grand Street.

If you don't believe that German films need to be edited, ask the man who owns one.

"Metropolis"*

UFA production, German-made, released through Famous Players Lasky. No player starred or featured in American presentation. Without press sheet as yet available, technical information not at hand. Opened at Rialto (Publix), New York, March 5, indefinitely. Running time, 107 minutes.

John Masterman	Alfred Abel
Eric, his son	Gustav Froelich [*sic*]
Rotwang, the inventor	Rudolf Klein-Rogge
Joseph	Theodor Loos
No. 7	Heinrich George
Mary	Brigitte Helm

"Metropolis" has mass appeal over here, but without class appeal of any character. It's a weird story, visionary all of the time, without any degree of unusual imagination and ofttimes monotonous. Withal, a puzzling film that might deceive the most expert picture showman, either way. Yet it holds something that holds the picture audience and will draw to a picture house.

That may be its weirdness or its production or photography or subject matter of 100 years hence or so, or its attempted massiveness of scenes — or that it reels off like a Henry Ford dream — mechanical — human labor of the future.

With press sheet exactly what is striven for must be doped out. It appears to be that the mechanical can never wholly substitute for the human labor, nor must Capital entirely exhaust its working people or that the human physical elements may never be mechanically transposed.

These things will fling an ordinary picture audience at their limitations into a turmoil of thought, meanwhile held to some suspense by the supposed vastness of it all; big machinery halls, the huge crowds of labor people; mythical ultra-modern city of one hundred years hence with its underground living abode for the laborers, or the perpetual lock step with its dirge that runs throughout the film.

After all of this for the serious side and before the picture has been running very long one is inclined to laugh at its plain absurdities, its open face scheme of story and the merciless persecution of poor Mary. Mary is probably the most chased girl of the screen. They chased her everywhere every minute, up alleys, into rooms, over roofs and what not. If Mary saw a chance to escape the open door closed just before she

* From: *Variety*, 16 March 1927; author not stated.

reached it. The only thing muffed was a blackface comedian to get the laughs in this stupendous scene of a "Haunted House."

And Eric, the son of his father, who went down into the subterranean town for the first time in his twenty years to see the village and Mary. Caught by the skirt as he was wrangling with some vamps in burlesque wheel costumes, Eric fell for the dame. That was Mary, also about twenty and the first time she ever had been inside of a two-story home. Mary had large blue eyes. Someone had told her to stare and plenty. Mary did.

Down in the village to which the workmen went in elevators holding 1,000 people or more, from appearances, Mary was a sort of Aimee McPherson evangelist without the scandal. Mary preached peace, before and after she landed Eric (a much better German name than John for a young chaser).

But Eric wasn't Mary's only chaser. The other was Rotwang, an inventor. After he had perfected Metropolis as a one-man town belonging to John Masterman, Rotwang, who looks like David Belasco did fifteen years ago, started to pull the final surprise upon his Masterman. He had fashioned a human figure of metal. All required was to get his lights working properly, to send or pour any human he pleased into the figure — and he selected Mary, but before capturing Mary, Rot [*sic*] had to chase her about eighteen miles of hallways.

He put everything of Mary's into the figure, excepting Mary's peace loving soul, but a caption said a soul couldn't be placed into steel, probably having in mind a few theatrical managers. So when the No. 2 Mary came forth, she was a hellraiser, preached socialism to the workmen and started the machinery going the wrong way.

It led to a flood, to the workmen going upstairs, to the real Mary saving the children, to Eric getting his Mary and to the Masterman taking a tumble to himself.

In all of this is trick photography and trick production. Probably there never has been a picture made with so much seemingly trick production stuff. Nothing appears to be on the level in this film. In the trick photography is one bit of swirling electric lights that can't be figured out by any method.

In the production end seems [*sic*] to be several massive sets that either were magnified from miniatures or drawn as sketches and vitalized. The impossible unison of the movements of human beings suggests this. In any event the effect is big for the seventeen percenters. But the photography of "Metropolis" does not compare with that of "Variety," which it slightly suggests, although the production end here lies over the other like a tent, whether it's faked or no.

A letter recently received by Variety (this paper) and written by the Aktiegesellschaft fur Spiegeltechnik [*sic*] of Berlin advised that in the UFA picture "Metropolis," shortly to be shown in New York, appeared 13 scenes of the firm's system called the Schufftan [*sic*] process.

No one in New York who could be reached had heard of the Schufftan System. It may be like the "Valley of the Lepers" in "Ben-Hur." But "Metropolis" appears to have some sort of a process introduced to make the immensity of the effect or to aid it, in much the same way pictures have found how to multiply crowds, as must have been done here also. At times the crowds look enormous.

But "Metropolis" will make the commoners talk if no more than to say, "You must see that crazy picture."

From understanding the German version was a pretty clumsy affair. Over here and especially recut by Channing Pollock, there is quite good continuity, as far as that could be gotten, while Mr. Pollock's captions have a dignity in language and phrasing that lends greatly to the impressiveness. Without impressiveness this picture would have to fall down because of its blooeyness.

Brigitte Helm as Mary did nicely in acting when assuming the No. 2 dual role. That forced her to the other extreme of expression. Alfred Abel as the boss of the works did well as the cold stern driver of men and money. Gustav Froelich [*sic*], the son, had a heavy part he played lightly for value and must have been selected for his juvenile appearance. Theodor Loos was Joseph or No. 7, probably Joseph, and with plenty of beard. He made it resemble Russian more than German, also beating off a mob of several thousand, as did Eric at one time. How those Germans, single handed, can handle mad mobs in pictures is pretty close to a mirthful miracle.

For UFA to say this picture cost almost $2,000,000, if not meaning marks, sounds like the bologna, unless the actors got it or the processes were unusually expensive. It is more easily believable that the picture was comparatively cheap for the eyeful results obtained.

Some sex stuff here and there and a cooch dancer! Yes, sir, a coocher. In the revigorated mechanical figure, and a pretty good coocher, too, but not so thick around the hips as German coochers generally are. But then you must remember that this young lady was made to order.

Houses that played "Variety" won't miss with "Metropolis." It's the same UFA and its weirdness will at least stand up. But don't invite the readers of "The American Mercury" to see it.

H. G. Wells, "Mr. Wells Reviews a Current Film"*

I have recently seen the silliest film. I do not believe it would be possible to make one sillier, and as this film sets out to display the way the world is going, I think "The Way the World Is Going" may well concern itself with this film. It is called "Metropolis," it comes from the great Ufa studios in Germany, and the public is given to understand that it has been produced at enormous cost. It gives in one eddying concentration almost every possible foolishness, cliché, platitude and muddlement about mechanical progress and progress in general, served up with a sauce of sentimentality that is all its own.

It is a German film, and there have been some amazingly good German films before they began to cultivate bad work under cover of a protective quota. And this film has been adapted to Anglo-Saxon taste, and quite possibly it has suffered in the process, but even when every allowance has been made for that, there remains enough to convince an intelligent observer that most of its silliness must be fundamental. Possibly I dislike this soupy whirlpool none the less because I find decaying fragments of my own juvenile work of thirty years ago, "The Sleeper Awakes," floating about in it.

Originality is Lacking

Capek's Robots have been lifted without apology, and that soulless mechanical monster of Mary Shelley's, who has fathered so many German inventions, breeds once more in this confusion. Originality there is none, independent thought none; where nobody has imagined for them the authors have simply fallen back on contemporary things. The airplanes that wander about above a great city show no advance on contemporary types, though all that stuff could have been livened up immensely with a few helicopters and vertical and unexpected movements. The motor cars are 1926 models or earlier. I do not think there is a single new idea, a single instant of artistic creation, or even of intelligent anticipation, from first to last in the whole pretentious stew. I may have missed some point of novelty, but I doubt it, and this, though it must bore the intelligent man in the audience, makes the film all the more convenient as a gauge of the circles of ideas and mentality from which it has proceeded.

The word "Metropolis," says the advertisement in English, "in itself is symbolical of greatness" — which only shows us how wise it is to consult a dictionary before making assumptions about the meaning of words. Probably it was the adapter that made that shot. The German

* From: *The New York Times Magazine*, 17 April 1927, pages 4 and 22.

"Neubabelsburg" [*sic*] was better, and could have been rendered "New Babel." It is a city, we are told, of about 100 years hence. It is represented as being enormously rich, and all the air and happiness are above, and the workers live, as the servile toilers in blue uniforms in "The Sleeper Awakes" lived, down, down, down below.

Now, far away in dear old 1897, it may have been excusable to symbolize social relations in this way, but that was thirty years ago, and a lot of thinking and some experience intervene. That vertical city of the future we know now is, to put it mildly, highly improbable. Even in New York and Chicago, where pressure upon central sites is exceptionally great, it is only the central office and entertainment region that soars and excavates. And the same centripetal pressure that leads to the utmost exploitation of site values at the center leads also to the driving out of industrialism and labor from the population center to cheaper areas and of residential life to more open and airy surroundings. That was all discussed and written about before 1900. Somewhere about 1930 the geniuses of the Ufa studios will come up to a book of anticipations which was written as recently as a quarter of a century ago. The British census returns of 1901 proved that city populations were becoming centrifugal, and that every increase in horizontal traffic facilities produced a further distribution. This vertical social stratification is stale old stuff. So far from being a hundred years hence, "Metropolis," in its forms and shapes, is already as a possibility a third of a century out of date.

But in its form is the least part of its staleness. This great city is supposed to be evoked by a single dominating personality. The English version calls him John Masterman, so that there may be no mistake about his quality. Very unwisely he has called his son Eric instead of sticking to good, hard John and so relaxed the strain. He works with an inventor, one Rotwang, and they make machines. There are a certain number of other rich people, and the sons of the rich are seen disporting themselves with underclass ladies in a sort of joy conservatory rather like the Winter garden of an enterprising 1890 hotel during an orgy. The rest of the population is in a state of subject slavery, working in "shifts" of ten hours in some mysteriously divided twenty-four hours and with no money to spend or property or freedom. The machines make wealth. How is not stated. We are shown rows of motor cars all exactly alike, but the workers cannot own these, and no "sons of the rich" would. Even the middle classes nowadays want a car with personality. Probably Masterman makes these cars in endless series to amuse him. One is asked to believe that these machines are engaged quite furiously in the mass production of nothing that is ever used and that Masterman grows richer and richer in the process.

This is the essential nonsense of it all. Unless the mass of the population has spending power there is no possibility of wealth in a mechanical civilization. A vast, penniless, slave population may be necessary for wealth where there are no mass production machines, but it is preposterous with mass production machines. You find such a real proletariat in China still — it existed in the great cities of the ancient world — but you do not find it in America, which has gone furthest in the direction of mechanical industry, and there is no grain of reason for supposing it will exist in the future. Masterman's watchword is efficiency, and you are given to understand it is a very dreadful word, and the contrivers of this idiotic spectacle are so hopelessly ignorant of all the work that has been done upon industrial efficiency that they represent him as working his machine minders to the point of exhaustion so that they faint and machines explode and people are scalded to death. You get machine minders in torment turning levers in response to signals. Work that could be done far more efficiently by automata. Much stress is laid on the fact that the workers are spiritless, hopeless drudges, working reluctantly and mechanically. But mechanical civilization has no use for mere drudges. The more efficient the machinery the less need there is for the quasi-mechanical minder. It is the inefficient factory that needs slaves, the ill-organized mine that kills men. The hopeless drudge stage of human labor lies behind us. With a sort of malignant stupidity this film contradicts these facts.

Man and His Machines

The current tendency of economic life is to oust the mere drudge altogether, to replace much highly skilled manual work by exquisite machinery in skilled hands, and to increase the relative proportion of semi-skilled, moderately versatile and fairly comfortable workers. It may, indeed, create temporary masses of unemployed, and in "The Sleeper Awakes" there was a mass of unemployed people under hatches. That was written in 1897, when the possibility of restraining the growth of large masses of population had scarcely dawned on the world. It was reasonable then to anticipate an embarrassing underworld of underproductive people. We did not know what to do with the abyss. But there is no excuse for that today. And what this film anticipates is not unemployment, but drudge employment, which is precisely what is passing away. Its fabricators have not even realized that the machine ousts the drudge.

"Efficiency" means large-scale production, machinery as fully developed as possible and high wages. The British Government delegation sent to study the success in America has reported unanimously to that effect. Increasingly the efficient industrialism of America has so little need of drudges that is has set up the severest barriers against the flooding of the United States by drudge immigration. Ufa knows nothing of such facts.

A young woman appears from nowhere in particular to help these drudges. She impinges upon Masterman's son, Eric, and they go to the "catacombs," which, in spite of the Masterman's steam machines, have somehow contrived to get over from Rome, skeletons and all, and burrow under this city of "Metropolis." She conducts a sort of Christian worship in these unaccountable caverns and the drudges love and trust her. With a nice sense of fitness she lights herself about the catacombs with a torch instead of electric lamps that are now so common. That reversion to torches is quite typical of the spirit of this show. Torches are Christian, we are asked to suppose; torches are human. Torches have hearts, but electric hand lamps are wicked, mechanical, heartless things. The bad, bad inventor uses quite a big one.

Builder of the Tower of Babel

Mary's services are unsectarian, rather like an afternoon Sunday school, and in her special catacomb she has not so much an altar as a kind of umbrella full of crosses. The leading idea of her religion seems to be a disapproval of machines and efficiency. She enforces the great moral lesson that the bolder and stouter human effort becomes the more spiteful Heaven grows by reciting the story of Babel. The story of Babel, as we know, is a lesson against "pride." It teaches the human soul to grieve. It inculcates the duty of incompetence. The Tower of Babel was built, it seems, by bald-headed men. I said there was no original touch in the film, but this last seems to be a real question — you see bald-headed men building Babel. Myriads of them! Why they are bald-headed is inexplicable. It is not even meant to be funny and it isn't funny: it is just another touch of silliness. The workers of "Metropolis" are not to rebel or do anything for themselves, she teaches, because they may rely on the vindictiveness of Heaven.

But Rotwang, the inventor, is making a Robot, apparently without any license from Capek, the original patentee. It is to look and work like a human being, but it is to have no "soul." It is to be a substitute for drudge labor. Masterman very properly suggests that it should never have a soul, and for the life of me I cannot see why it should. The whole aim of mechanical civilization is to eliminate the drudge and the drudge soul. But this is evidently regarded as very dreadful and impressive by the producers, who are all on the side of soul and love and such like. I am surprised they were not pinched for souls in the alarm clocks and runabouts. Masterman, still unwilling to leave bad alone, persuades Rotwang to make this Robot in the likeness of Mary, so that it may raise an insurrection among the workers to destroy the machines by which they live and so learn that it is necessary to work. Rather intricate that, but Masterman, you understand, is a rare devil of a man. Full of pride and efficiency and modernity and all those horrid things.

Then comes the crowning imbecility of the film — the conversion of the Robot into the likeness of Mary. Rotwang, you must understand, occupies a small old house embedded in a modern city richly adorned with pentagrams and other reminders of antiquated German romances, out of which its owner has been taken. A faint smell of Mephistopheles is perceptible for a time. So even at Ufa, Germany can still be dear, old, magic-loving Germany. Perhaps the Germans will never get right away from the brocken. Walpurgis Night is the name day of the German poetic imagination, and the national fantasy capers securely forever with a broomstick between its legs. By some no doubt abominable means Rotwang has squeezed a vast and well-equipped modern laboratory into this little house. It is ever so much bigger than the house, but no doubt he has fallen back on Einstein and other modern bewilderment. Mary has to be trapped, put into a machine like a translucent cocktail shaker and undergo all sorts of pyrotechnic treatment in order that her likeness may be transferred to the Robot. The possibility of Rotwang just simply making a Robot like her evidently never entered the gifted producer's head.

The Robot is developed in wavering halos. The premises seem to be struck by lightning repeatedly, the contents of a number of flasks and carboys are violently agitated, there are minor explosions and discharges. Rotwang conducts the operations with a manifest lack of assurance, and finally to his evident relief the likeness is taken and things calm down. The false Mary then winks darkly at the audience and sails off to raise the workers. And so forth and so on. There is some rather good swishing about in the water after the best film traditions, some violent and unconvincing machine breaking and rioting and wreckage, and then rather confusedly one gathers that Masterman has learned his lesson and that the workers and employers are now to be reconciled, and by "love."

Never for a moment does one believe any of this foolish story; never for a moment is there anything amusing or convincing in its dreary series of strained events. It is immensely and strangely dull. It is not even to be laughed at. There is not one good-looking nor sympathetic nor funny personality in the cast; there is, indeed, no scope at all for looking well or acting like a rational creature amid these mindless, imitative absurdities. The film's air of having something grave and wonderful to communicate is transparent pretence. It has nothing to do with any social or moral issue before the world, or with any that can even conceivably arise. It is bunkum and poor and thin even as bunkum. I am astonished at the toleration shown it by "a number of film critics on both sides of the Atlantic," and it cost, says The London Times, 6,000,000 marks. How they spent all that upon it I cannot imagine. Most of the effects could have been got with models at no great expense.

The pity of it is that this unimaginative, incoherent, sentimentalizing and make-believe film wastes some very fine possibilities. My belief in German enterprise has had a shock. I am dismayed by the intelligent laziness it betrays. I thought Germany, even at its worst, could toil. I thought they had resolved to be industriously modern. It is profoundly interesting to speculate on the present trend of mechanical invention and of the real reactions of invention upon labor conditions. Instead of plagiarizing from a book thirty years old and resuscitating the banal moralizing of the early Victorian period, it would have been almost as easy, no more costly and far more interesting to have taken some pains to gather opinions of a few bright young research students and ambitious modernizing architects and engineers about the trend of modern invention and develop these artistically Any technical school would have been delighted to supply sketches and suggestions for the aviation and transport of 2027 A.D. There are now masses of literature upon the organization of labor for efficiency that could have been boiled down at very small cost. The question of development of industrial control, the relation of industrial to political direction, the way all that is going, is of the liveliest current interest. Apparently the Ufa people did not know of these things and did not want to know about them; they were too dense to see how these things could be brought into touch with the life of today and made interesting to the man in the street. After the worst traditions of the cinema world, monstrously self-satisfied and self-sufficient, convinced of the power of loud advertisement to put things over with the public, and with no fear of searching criticism in their minds, no consciousness of the thought and knowledge beyond their ken, they set to work in their huge studio to produce furlong after furlong of this ignorant old-fashioned balderdash and ruin the market for any better film along these lines.

Six million marks! The waste of it! The theatre when I visited it was crowded. All but the highest-priced seats were full, and gaps in places filled up reluctantly but completely before the great film was begun. I suppose every one had come to see what the city of a hundred years hence would be like. I suppose there are multitudes of people to be "drawn" by promising to show them what the city of a hundred years hence will be like. It was, I thought, an unresponsive audience and I heard no comments. I could not tell from their bearing whether they believed that "Metropolis" was really a possible forecast or not. I do not know whether they thought the film was hopelessly silly or the future of mankind hopelessly silly, but it must have been one thing or the other.

Great Britain

Metropolis was distributed in Britain by Wardour Films Ltd.; it premiered in the Marble Arch Pavilion on 21 March 1927 in a version that differed from the Parufamet cut in several scenes. Surrounded by Ufa propaganda, the film attracted widespread interest in the British press, especially in the trade journals such as *Kinematograph Weekly* and *The Bioscope*, which singled out the film's "points of appeal" and "selling angles" from a cinema owner's perspective. The assessment of the film as such mirrors the American appraisal of a technically impressive, but thematically weak spectacle.

"Metropolis"*

Offered by: *Wardour.* **Directed by:** *Fritz Lang.* **Length:** *10,000 feet.* **Release Date:** *Not fixed.* **Type:** *Spectacular Drama, from a story by Thea von Harbou.* **Cast:** *Brigitte Helm, Alfred Abel, Gustav Frolich [sic], Rudolf Klein-Rogge, Fritz Rasp, Theodor Loos, Heinrich George.*

IN BRIEF: Highly imaginative story of the conflict between Brain and Muscle in the future. A production of extraordinary imagination and power on a colossal scale, lacking only human interest. A triumph of technical efficiency.

Suitability: A unique production which will chiefly appeal in the best-class houses.

Selling Angles: The magnitude of the production; the producer's reputation; the unusual type.

Plot: A city of the future is controlled by the dominating brain of one John Masterman, who confines the working classes in an underground city of machinery for the purpose of enabling the upper classes to live in idleness and luxury in a city of palaces and gardens. Learning that Mary, a beautiful girl of the people, is preaching the doctrine of love and charity to the workers, Masterman employs Rotwang, a scientist, to create an automaton in Mary's likeness to counteract her influence. Perfect in every physical attribute, the automaton is without a soul and, seeking only to disseminate the principles of evil, stirs up the

---

* From: *The Bioscope*, 24 March 1927, 59; author not stated.

workers to revolt, when they destroy city, scientist, automaton and themselves. The principal characters are inexplicably saved to deliver a moral tag on the necessity of sympathetic feeling between the classes.

Comment: Fritz Lang has surpassed all his previous achievements as a producer of extraordinary imagination and power. Nothing has ever been done on the screen to convey the suggestion of such vastness of resource, such magnitude of design, such efficiency of technical skill. It is an awe-inspiring picture of what might possibly happen in a hundred years' time if mechanical science were developed to its extreme limit. It also conveys a warning as to what may be the outcome of film entertainment if technical efficiency is to be the main objective. Herr Lang has produced a film like his own automaton, bold in imagination, marvelous in accomplishment, awe inspiring in its effect, only lacking in human sympathy and heart appeal. The story is of too speculative a nature to be carried to its logical conclusion, and in order to preserve his principal characters for a conventional happy ending the producer has had to resort to melodramatic methods which at time perilously approach banality. In spite, however, of the weakness of the story, the production is unique in conception and accomplishment and is one that no exhibitor should fail to present to his patrons.

Acting: The artists are handicapped to a great extent by the unconvincing nature of the story and overwhelmed by the magnitude of the production. Brigitte Helm is sweet and beautiful as the girl of the people and as a *tour de force* her performance of the automaton is theatrically effective. Gustav Frolich [*sic*] plays with sincerity as the hero and has a pleasing personality. Heinrich George makes the part of the foreman of the workers stand out with effect. Alfred Abel as John Masterman lacks the strong personality of the ruler of thc city, and Rudolf Klein-Rogge as the crazy scientist plays on somewhat conventional lines. It is the masses of workers, men, women and children, who supply the dramatic touch, and the way in which the crowds are handled is the producer's greatest triumph.

Production: The wonder city of the future; the underground intricacies of mechanical device; the process by which the automaton is created; the upheaval and destruction of the whole fabric; all show a fertility of invention and efficiency of presentment which stamps the film as the most remarkable and unique spectacle ever shown on the screen.

Lionel Collier, "Reviews of the Week — *Metropolis*"*

[Editorial Comment:]

Advance reports have in no way magnified the remarkable spectacular effects achieved by Fritz Lang in "Metropolis;" it is the apotheosis of that producer's methods of pictorial presentation. I doubt if the screen has ever seen such crowd handling as in the scenes depicting the rise of the workmen and the smashing of the machines, followed by a flood in the underground tenements in which they are forced to live in the year of grace two thousand and twenty-seven.

While Fritz Lang has succeeded in drawing an awe-inspiring picture of a visionary city and by his detail has showed the domination and monotonous regularity of the machines to which the men are slaves he has not made his symbolical meaning entirely gripping; it just somehow misses its force, perhaps by being over-sentimentalized.

The picture has had to be considerably shortened, and to this is also perhaps attributable the jerkiness of the continuity, which also militates against a dramatic intensity of plot. Channing Pollock's subtitles are only fair, and towards the end become rather stupid in their reiterated sentiment.

Again, the producer has not been nearly so well served by his artists as he was in "Destiny" [*Der müde Tod*, editor's note], "The She-Devil" [*Kriemhilds Rache*, editor's note], and "The Nibelungs," although the new young actress, Brigitte Helm, gives an entirely interesting performance, especially as the "Robot" woman who heads the revolt. Incidentally, the birth of this soulless human is one of the high lights [*sic*] of the production.

Few people will be able to resist, however, the sweep of kaleidoscopic events, and the picture should prove an enormously novel attraction anywhere. [. . .]

[Review:]

Metropolis.

Wardour. German (A). Featuring Gustav Frolich [sic] and Brigitte Helm. 10,000 feet. Release date not fixed.

A conception of a big city a hundred years hence, which is irresistible in its sweeping representation of mechanical control and its overthrow. The theme which Fritz Lang has developed from his wife's, Thea von Harbou's, story, is the need of a heart to mediate between hands

* From: *Kinematograph Weekly*, 24 March 1927, 57. Collier's comments begin with a general overview over the week's films, in which he also mentions *Metropolis* (Editorial Comment), followed by a review dedicated exclusively to *Metropolis*.

and brain. Fritz Lang's most famous productions are "The Nibelungs," "The She-Devil," and "Destiny." Brigitte Helm was a young girl of sixteen and new to the screen when the picture was commenced, and it took two years to complete. There has been nothing so stupendous in architecture, crowd control, and camera work as in this production.

Story. — [*plot synopsis*] [. . .]

Acting. — Brigitte Helm is extremely interesting as Mary and as her "robot" counterpart; she distinguishes admirably between the two. There is a tendency for her to be over-emotional, which is also noticeable in the acting of Gustav Frolich [*sic*] as Eric. Alfred Abel is sound as John Masterman, while Rotwang is excellently played by Rudolf Klein-Rogge.

Production. — Fritz Lang has made a picture that takes one's breath away by its technical excellence, but does not rise to great heights from a story point of view. Its theme is good and well pointed, but there is a certain jumpiness in the continuity — probably due to cutting — which militates against it.

From the spectacular point of view nothing greater has been achieved on the screen. This octopus of a mechanical city is admirably expressed, and one can almost feel that one has visited it after seeing the picture, while the whole atmosphere of dependent subjection to the machine is most brilliantly depicted.

The disaster following the smashing of the machines when the underground homes are flooded is on a huge scale, and all through the crowd handling is a masterpiece of directorial skill.

The making of the "robot" is also fascinating to a degree, and scene after scene of kaleidoscopic impressions are almost bewildering in their ingenuity.

Setting and Photography. — The city with its overhead and underground ways, its aeroplanes and lighting and mechanism, is a thing to wonder at, while the photography is brilliant. Wonderfully effective angles are used, and lighting is remarkable. The Schüfftan process has been used to its fullest advantage.

Points of Appeal. — A spectacular booking which will astonish wherever shown. There are unlimited points to stress in the wonderful settings and extraordinary crowd handling. Fritz Lang's name should be used, and also the pith of the theme.

Iris Barry, "The Cinema: *Metropolis*"*

If "Metropolis" fails to be quite a great film, the fault lies, not with brilliant German producers, nor with its subject matter, nor with the actual treatment of this picture-parable of life next century. It fails because the cinema as yet fails to be quite adequate as a means of expression.

Here on the screen is a concrete picture of a great city of the future, with its soaring skyscrapers, its aerial traffic-bridges, its clouds of little aeroplanes buzzing about like gnats, its smokeless air, its labour-saving dwellings, its intricate electrical devices and its dependence on machinery. The imagination of Fritz Lang, the director, and of the studio-architects and designers who have brought this vision to "life" proved adequate enough here. The film shows us the making of an artificial human being: shows us television. We can accept these miracles. It shows us, grimly, the standardized mankind which a future civilization keeps buried deep in the bowels of the earth, and uses only as machine-fodder, mere slaves to the machinery on which — we can quite believe — everything depends. These too we can believe in, for we know and recognize and accept these manual workers with their weary backs, heavy hands and dull, hopeless eyes. We can feel with them and for them, when they rebel and destroy the machinery that enslaves them.

But I fear that the intelligent part of the audience that see "Metropolis" will find very difficult to admire the peacock-strewn pleasure gardens of the future, in which the free and gilded inhabitants of the skyscrapers of the future disport themselves, heedless of the tragic workmen down below. It is sad, too, to find that men of the future dress just as hideously as do those of to-day [*sic*]. But the costume is not very convincing, anyhow, in "Metropolis": and though part of the film is conceived in an expressionist mood, and part of it quite naturalistically, some of it is mere picture-postcard. The expressionist parts are far and away the best, and the workmen turn out better than their masters.

The weaknesses of the cinema are most apparent in the story. It is pure melodrama on the D. W. Griffiths [*sic*] plan, and frankly treated as such. So grandiose a theme as that which "Metropolis" attempts to develop demanded, of course, something on the epic scale. The cinema, even here at its best, and full as it is of invention and thrill, is still only at the mental age of seventeen. It is still — quite rightly — far more

---

* From: *The Spectator*, 26 March 1927, 540. The author of this review, Iris Barry, became the first head of the Film Library of the Museum of Modern Art and in this function played a major part in preserving the Parufamet version of *Metropolis* as released in Germany in 1927.

concerned with its medium than with what its medium may most magnificently express. We cannot delude ourselves about this: for it is a fact.

Yet "Metropolis" is by far the most nearly adult picture we have seen. There are moments when it touches real greatness: in its handling of crowds, not for the sake only of the spectacle, but for what emotion the movement of the crowd can express. Its architecture is beautiful, its pictorial composition frequently superb. The clothing of a robot in human flesh provides as great a thrill as anyone could wish: and there are two other great moments. One comes when the robot, presenting the appearance of the heroine exactly but for a subtle spiritual difference, winks at John Masterman. This gesture, which might so easily have been merely comic, has the effect of some highly dramatic, rhetorical phrase in an Elizabethan play. It tells us everything about the robot. The other moment, which passes half-unperceived, comes when No. 7, the sturdy foreman of the workers, seeing them reveling amid the ruins of the machinery, recalls them to their slave-mood by a shrill whistle. This tells us everything about the workers.

The photography of "Metropolis" is absolutely brilliant: some of the acting is fine, particularly when it is stylized. Most of the sub-titles are quite atrocious and many of them highly unnecessary. The one which was essential — explaining though the robot was created to preach submission to the workers, it in fact preached revolution — was omitted. The moral is, of course, that though man might create mechanical man, even the degree of humanity the machine possessed would endow it with that capacity for disobedience and revolt which has distinguished man since Adam.

I wonder how the audiences in cinemas in the South Wales mining districts and in Glasgow will regard this film? And whether the members of the Coal Owners' Association have been invited to see it?

Spain

Luis Buñuel, *Metropolis**

Metropolis is not a single film. *Metropolis* is two films joined at the hip, but with divergent spiritual necessities that are diametrically opposed to each other. Those who understand cinema as an unassuming storytelling mechanism will be deeply disappointed in *Metropolis*. That which it recounts is trivial, overblown, pedantic and outdatedly romantic. But, if to the tale we prefer the "plastico-photogenic" background of the film, then *Metropolis* will fulfil our wildest dreams, will astonish us as the most astonishing book of images it is possible to compose. It is made, thus, of two contradictory elements, keepers of the same sign in the zones of our sensibility. The first of these, which we could term "pure lyric" is excellent, the other, anecdotal or human, is occasionally irritating. The two together, in their simultaneity or their succession, constitute the final creation of Fritz Lang. It is not the first time that we can observe such a disconcerting dualism in Lang's work. Example: the ineffable poem *Destiny* contained disastrous scenes sublimely lacking in taste. If the rôle of accomplice in this is taken by Fritz Lang, it is his wife, the scenographer Thea von Harbou who must stand condemned for being the author of these eclectic efforts, of a dangerous syncretism.

The "film," like the cathedral, should have been anonymous. People of every class and artists of every order were involved in the elevation of this monstrous cathedral of modern cinema. Every industry, every technician was represented, along with extras, actors, scriptwriters; Karl Freund, the greatest of the German cameramen, and his stellar group of collaborators; among the sculptors, Ruttmann, the creator of the absolute "film." Chief among the architects figures Otto Hunte: it is to him and to Ruttmann that we in fact owe the most successful "visualizations" of *Metropolis*. The set designer, last of the relics abandoned by the theatre to the cinema, is hardly in evidence at all. His involvement in the film has only really been identified in the worst moments of *Metropolis*, in that which has been emphatically and appropriately named the "eternal gardens," extravagantly baroque and in unprecedentedly bad taste. From now on, and forever, the set designer will be replaced by the architect. Cinema will become a faithful interpreter of architecture's most audacious visions.

---

* From: *Cahiers du cinéma* 223 (August/September 1970), 20–21. The review originally appeared in *Gazeta Literaria de Madrid* in 1927. Translation from the French by Carol O'Sullivan.

The clock in *Metropolis* only counts ten hours; those of work. The life of the whole city proceeds in time with this double rhythm. The free men of *Metropolis* tyrannize the slaves, who are like niebelungen [*sic*] of the city and who work in a perpetual electric daylight, in the depths of the earth. The only thing missing in the simple mechanism of the Republic is heart, the sentiment with the power to unite such hostile extremes. And in the dénouement, we will see the son of the director of *Metropolis* (the heart) unite his father (the brain) and the chief foreman (the arms) in a fraternal embrace. Mix these symbolic ingredients with a lavish dose of terror, add an overwhelming and theatrical acting style, mix well and you will have obtained the theme of *Metropolis*.

But on the other hand, what a fascinating symphony of movement! How the machines sing in the midst of splendid transparencies, "Arc de Triomphed" by the bursts of electricity! All the chandeliers in the world, romantically shivered into myriad reflections, have come to take their place in the canons of the modern screen. The brightest gleam of steel, the rhythmical succession of wheels, of pistons, of never yet created mechanical forms create a magnificent ode, a brand new poem for the eyes. Physics and Chemistry are miraculously transformed into Rhythmics. Not a single static moment! Even the intertitles, rising, descending, turning, swiftly braking into shards of light or fading into shadows, become part of the general movement: they too succeed in being images.

In our opinion, the chief fault of the film lies in the fact that its author did not follow the idea illustrated by Eisenstein in his *Battleship Potemkin*, that he forgot one actor, an actor full of novelty and possibilities: the crowd. However the theme of *Metropolis* demanded it; instead, we have to endure a series of characters full of arbitrary and vulgar passions, asked to convey a symbolism for which they are not adequate — indeed, far from it. This does not mean that the multitudes are absent from *Metropolis*; but they seem to fill a decorative role, that of a huge ballet; they aim to impress us by their beautifully choreographed and balanced movement rather than allow us to see their soul, their subordination to more human, more objective agencies. In spite of this there are moments — Babel, the workers' revolution, the final persecution of the android — in which both extremes reach their full potential.

Otto Hunte annihilates us with his colossal vision of the city in the year 2000. His vision could be false, and even out of date, if we consider the latest theories on the city of the future; but, from the point of view of the photogenic, its emotive force and its astonishing and innovative beauty remain unequalled. His technique is so perfect that even in the course of an in-depth examination the existence of a model is never suspected.

Metropolis cost forty million gold marks to make: between actors and extras, some 40,000 people participated. The finished film is 5000 metres long, but in all nearly two million metres of film were used in its making. On the day of the premiere in Berlin, the seats cost eighty gold marks. Does it not seem depressing that with all this at its disposal, Lang's work was not a model of perfection? If we compare *Metropolis* and *Napoléon,* the two biggest films of modern cinema, with other, more modest, but also more perfect and purer films, we may learn the profitable lesson that money is not the sine qua non of modern cinematographic production. Compare *Rien que des heures,* made at a cost of only 35,000 francs, with *Metropolis*. First must come sensibility, and intelligence: everything else, including money, is secondary.

Part Two

METAMORPHOSES OF *METROPOLIS*

The City of the Future — A Film of Ruins

On the Work of the Munich Film Museum*

Enno Patalas

IF THERE WAS A REPRESENTATIVE SURVEY asking for the best known title of a German silent film, *Metropolis* would undoubtedly make the running. But which film would people mean? The one shot by Fritz Lang in Berlin in 1926 and only ever shown there at the beginning of 1927? The one shortened, rearranged, newly titled for Hollywood by one Channing Pollock? The second German version, fashioned after the American model, which could be seen in Germany from the end of 1927? The same, shortened once more, with different English intertitles again, which the Museum of Modern Art in New York has made accessible to the cinephiles of many countries since before the war? The German sound version from the sixties, which goes back to the one mentioned before? The attempt at a reconstruction made around the same time by the film archive in the then GDR? Giorgio Moroder's postmodern interpretation with colour and music from 1984? The "Munich version" now always running at one or other of the Paris cinemas and available on VHS? Madonna's video clip "Express Yourself"?

None of these to the exclusion of the others: rather a vague idea encompassing them all, memories, rumours, overlapping, correcting, contradicting. No object: projections.

Around 1975 the Münchener Filmmuseum (Munich Film Museum) started to collect German films of the twenties and early thirties, not in order to create an archive and still less in order to restore or to reconstruct them, but simply to ensure that the organizers of retrospec-

---

* The following is the text of a lecture, extended and updated by the author, drawing on his earlier publications: "*Metropolis,* Scene 103," trans. Miriam Hansen, *Camera Obscura, A Journal of Feminism and Film Theory* 15 (autumn 1986), 165–75; "*Metropolis* in/aus Trümmern," in *Fritz Lang. Eine Publikation des Münchener Filmmuseums und des Münchener Filmzentrums E.V.,* ed Fritz Göttler (Munich: Münchener Filmmuseum, 1988), 15–17; "*Metropolis* nasce delle schegge," in *Via col tempo,* ed Vittorio Giacci (Rome, 1994), 153–60. Translated from the original German by Holger Bachmann and Meg Tait. Enno Patalas was head of the Munich Film Museum from the early 1970s until 1993. In this function, he was especially active in the reconstruction of silent films; one of his major ongoing projects is the restoration of *Metropolis*. Patalas has written widely on film history, including a history of film in three volumes, *Geschichte des Films,* which he co-wrote with Ulrich Gregor (Reinbek: Rowohlt, 1962).

tives would no longer be dependent upon what the distributors had to offer — 16mm copies of films shot on 35mm; sound versions of silent films with images cut left, top, bottom, which had to be shown twenty, thirty per cent faster than they were meant to be shown; duplicates of duplicates of duplicates, more grey on grey than black and white, cut by a fifth, a third, by half, with intertitles translated back from English, Czech, Dutch.

At that time, a number of versions of *Metropolis* were available. The first was the sound version submitted to the *Freiwillige Selbstkontrolle* (the West German film censorship agency) by the Nordwestdeutscher Filmverleih (a West German film distribution company) in 1962 and released in 1964: 2,535 metres based on material from the National Film Archive in London, with titles translated back from English and musical accompaniment after the piano version of the original score by Gottfried Huppertz. A second version was the result of the first attempt at a reconstruction by the East German Staatliches Filmarchiv (State Film Archive) at the end of the sixties, again based primarily on the London material, with additional footage taken mostly from a short version of the American distribution version obtained by the East German archive from the Reichsfilmarchiv (Imperial Film Archive) as well as from copies from the Czechoslovakian and Soviet film archives. In the seventies, the Deutsches Institut für Filmkunde (The German Institute for Film Studies) distributed a copy of this version that had accidentally been made using sound film stock.

After an exchange of new West German films for Soviet film classics (three metres of Eisenstein in black and white for one metre of Herzog in colour) had established a relationship of trust between ourselves (the Munich Film Museum) and Gosfilmofond in Moscow, the Russians presented us with our first films dating from the twenties — some of them copies of material looted after the National Socialist defeat in 1945, some of them copies imported earlier, still others old Russian distribution versions, sometimes only fragments of them. Moscow had held the Paramount version of *Metropolis*, cut from an original length of roughly 3,100 metres to 2,816. How it came to Moscow cannot be clarified — a recent written enquiry on my part elicited the response that "the material had been preserved by Gosfilmofond for a long time."

On 30 August 1979, Kenneth Anger, who had successfully shown his films (*Fireworks, Scorpio Rising,* and so forth) in Munich and had seen some material from our collection, wrote to me about a visit to the collector Harry Davidson in Melbourne. "Mr. Davidson ran his print of *Metropolis* for me in his home . . . It is a magnificent print. It has scenes and sequences missing from all the 'augmented' prints, including the recent compilation by the East Germans. It also has the original colour toning, with night scenes toned blue and interiors and the machine rooms, etc. toned in warm amber . . . Since I am a scholar particularly of Lang's *Metropolis,* I can speak with some authority when I say *here are the scenes missing* in all other prints. Here is a fist-fight among the men in a night-club over the favours of Maria-the-Robot-Girl, here is one of the men committing suicide over the False Maria. Here, at last is the real Maria swinging on the bell-rope in the cathedral in the last sequence of the film."

And: "of all the archives in the world, I have thought of you first of all in the consideration of the preservation of this unique original print of *Metropolis* and the incorporation of the unique scenes in it, that are missing from all other prints, into a definitive long version of the film, similar to the work done on the magnificent print of *Siegfried* you kindly had shown for me in Munich."

Also in 1979, the Deutsche Kinemathek in West Berlin obtained a copy of the screenplay (in addition to his scores for *Die Nibelungen, Metropolis,* and *The Chronicles of the Grey House*) from the papers of the composer Gottfried Huppertz, a document that until then was considered lost; not the definitive shooting script (of this, only one page has survived by its publication in the Ufa advertising booklet, the *Ufa-Magazin*),[1] but an earlier version. The Deutsche Kinemathek let the Munich Film Museum have a copy.

At the same time we also received the Huppertz score from the Deutsches Institut für Filmkunde (the German Institute for Film Studies) in Wiesbaden, complete with 1,027 cues for the conductor, from which the succession of scenes and shots in the original version can be deduced, in many instances in great detail.

And in the following year, the East German State Film Archive copied a censorship card of the film for us — one of those booklets of grey cardboard containing, in addition to information about the film's length, complete lists of intertitles for each reel. This card too was based on the original version.

This version, written by Thea von Harbou and directed by Fritz Lang, was passed by the Filmprüfstelle (film censorship office) on 13 November 1926 with a length of 4,189 metres, and was first shown on

[1] The surviving script page describes the race in the Stadium of the Sons. The advertising booklet reprints two versions of the page, one of them including extensive handwritten notes by Lang. Press Department of Ufa, *Metropolis, Sondernummer des Ufa-Magazins,* ed. Stefan Lorant (Berlin: Bukwa, Presse Abteilung der Ufa, 1927), unpaginated. Passages from this booklet are reprinted in translation in Part One of this volume.

10 January 1927 — at 24 frames per second, and thus in 153 minutes — in the *Ufa-Palast am Zoo* on the *Kurfürstendamm*. It was only seen by the Berliners present for that short initial run. At the same time, diligent hands commissioned by Paramount-Famous Players-Lasky, which in accordance with the Parufamet contract of 1926 had the US rights to the film, were already busily cutting the negative destined for American release.[2] On 13 March, under the headline "German Film Revision Upheld as Needed Here," one read that these cuts and rearrangements were necessary if the film was to be shown to an American audience. Motifs of the plot were removed, titles added, names changed. Freder became Eric, Joh Fredersen became John Masterman.[3]

On 7 April, after a not particularly successful start in Berlin, the Ufa Board of Directors agreed to encourage the distributors to show *Metropolis* "in the American version [. . .] after deleting as many intertitles as possible with communist overtones" — at first in the provinces and then, in the fall, in Berlin as well. The next day the gentlemen received a communication from the distributors asking them to cancel the film's run altogether and release it again as late as August. "As it can be assumed that in this way, additional earnings of several 100,000 marks can be achieved," say the minutes, "this suggestion is accepted. The pietistic revisions added to the American version should perhaps be removed, similarly, changes suggested by theatre men shall be carried out."[4]

On 5 August, the Filmprüfstelle passed a second version of the film for release, cut by over a fifth, to 3,241 metres, rearranged, most of the titles reformulated and rewritten; this was the only version in which the film could be seen from that time onward. Balthasar (Roland Schacht) wrote in September 1927 in the *Blaues Heft* where he had already reviewed the premiere version: "This *Metropolis* is not at all, in fact not in the least, the film we saw three quarters of a year ago in the

---

[2] The production company Famous Players, later Famous Players-Lasky Corporation, had been founded by Adolph Zukor in 1912 and was absorbed by Paramount in the mid-1920s. Paramount kept the well-known brand name and acted as a distribution arm of the company. When Erich Pommer left Ufa in 1926, his first assignment in the USA was the production of *Hotel Imperial* for Famous Players-Lasky Corporation. See Klaus Kreimeier, *Die Ufa-Story. Geschichte eines Filmkonzerns* (Munich: Heyne, 2nd ed. 1995), 146.

[3] See Randolph Bartlett, "German Film Revision Upheld as Needed Here," *New York Times*, 13 March 1927, section 7, 3. The article is reprinted in Part One of this volume.

[4] Transcripts of meetings of Ufa Board of Directors; Transcript 3, Meeting 7 April 1927, and Transcript 4, Meeting 8 April 1927; see Kreimeier, 189.

Ufa-Palast am Zoo. [. . .] A few motifs remain from the music by Gottfried Huppertz, and he is still credited as the composer, but with these exceptions, the accompaniment has switched to the tried and tested medley of Chopin, *Freischütz* and *Traviata* along with popular songs from the Kinothek [. . .] The difference between the two versions is comparable to the difference between the Tannenberg monument and the war memorial stone in Alt-Ruppin." The new tower of Babel as an architecture of ruins.

When, ten years later, Iris Barry, the first head of the Film Library of the Museum of Modern Art — which, together with the Cinémathèque Française, the National Film Library in London and the Reichsfilmarchiv became a founding member of the Fédération Internationale des Archives du Film (FIAF), the international association of film archives — asked Ufa for a copy of the second German version of the film, this version had a length of 2,250 metres, to which one must add three hundred metres of intertitles (the negative only had flash titles); so seven hundred additional metres were missing, bringing the total to 1,650 metres.

Few films have been cut, rearranged, reinterpreted so persistently, systematically, and rigorously as *Metropolis,* yet this case is so richly documented that one can read the film, in its multi-layered form, like a palimpsest.

Harry Davidson, the collector in Melbourne, never responded to my attempts to coax the copy described so enticingly by Kenneth Anger from him. In 1981, Tom Luddy, who at that time was the head of the Pacific Film Archive in Berkeley, wrote to me that Davidson had died, and I obtained the address of the administrator of the estate from Kenneth Anger. Then the National Film and Sound archive in Canberra bought the collection and agreed to let us have a duplicate negative of the *Metropolis* copy, gratis, since they were not satisfied with its quality. It arrived in Munich in 1983, 2,654 metres long, and in our view there was nothing wrong with it.

In the same year we received yet another version from the National Film Archive (NFA) in London. This version was incomplete in a different way; it was 2,602 metres long and made from another copy of the version that the Associated British Picture Corporation (ABPC) had distributed and left to the NFA in 1961. Obviously there had been a British version of the film that differed from the American version, with different intertitles and shots and sequences that were missing from the American one — and the same held true the other way round.

I came across the London version when I tried to duplicate the previous efforts made by the East German archive. In so doing, I found that the material that the London archive had made available to the East Berlin archive mainly consisted of negative that went back to a lavender (a print made from a copy of the film originally exposed in the camera) that it had obtained in 1938 from the Museum of Modern Art in a FIAF exchange. This copy had been made of a negative produced there that was based on the copy that Ufa had sent to the Museum of Modern Art in 1936. This suggested that we should make efforts to obtain not only the original material that had survived in Canberra and in London, but the New York material as well.

At first the only access we had to this material was from within the version prepared by the East German archive, which let us have a copy in 1981. This copy is 2,917 metres long, including an introductory text in the credits. This version kept the intertitles of the MoMA version, in alternation with titles it added from the American and English distribution versions, so that the hero was sometimes called Freder Fredersen, sometimes Eric Masterman. "The final version," our East German colleagues wrote in 1970 in their final report for FIAF, "can only be produced when screenplay and censorship cards are found," which, as mentioned above, was the case ten years later. The screenplay from Huppertz's papers, the censorship card that had survived in the East German archive itself, and the piano score with its 1,027 cues became the most important written documents for our operation.

Yet another valuable document was discovered in the Cinémathèque Française in 1983 by Georges Sturm, then head of the Centre d'Information Cinématographique de l'Institut Français de Munich (CICIM), the film department of the Institut Français in Munich: two albums of stills by Horst von Harbou, Thea's brother, which Fritz Lang had given as a present to Henri Langlois in the fifties. When I told Lang's widow Lilly Latté about this during a visit to Los Angeles (*Metropolis* was being screened in the L.A. County Museum), she knew of a third album which was indeed discovered and which we were also able to use. From this album, we took two pictures of the Hel monument that had fallen victim to the revisions and incorporated them into our version as inserts.

After we had made a copy of the Paramount version from Moscow and gathered together the negatives from Canberra and London along with a copy of the East German reconstruction, we began to reconstruct the original German intertitles as far as they could be placed in the extant sequences — based on faithfulness to the text and following the censorship card. At that time, we did not know anything about the graphic design of the intertitles. In addition, we inserted synopses of missing passages on the basis of the list of intertitles, screenplay, and score; these were kept as short as possible, just providing enough detail to enable viewers to comprehend the remaining segments.

Precisely the quality of those sequences which, as the East German archivists had already realized, went back to the German version still left much to be desired. Of these sequences, we had only the East Berlin copy of the London duplicate negative of the MoMA nitrate lavender of the duplicate negative of the Ufa copy, but we were still unsure of the genealogy. The process of solving this problem dragged on — practically up to this day.

In 1980, the Hollywood composer Giorgio Moroder (*Midnight Express*) came to visit me and told me that he wanted to add an electronic score to a silent film — he asked whether I had an idea — a German one? Surely there could only be one: *Metropolis.*

Then, when Moroder was working on his rock music clip version, I drew his attention to the fact that the best original material was probably to be found at MoMA; the copy lent to Moroder by the copyright owner, the Murnau foundation, could only be a duplicate of this material, of the next or even of the following generation. When I heard the Ufa history of the nitrate negative from Eileen Bowser, Iris Barry's successor in the MoMA Film Department, and when I heard further that it had still not been copied to safety film, I persuaded her to do business with Moroder, to let him pay for an interim positive and then to let him draw his negative from that. This is the way they did it. During the next FIAF meeting she thanked me for my advice. What would happen now to the nitrate negative, I asked her, now that she had her fine grain? She replied with another question: "You wanna have it?"

We only had to pay for the transport to Germany back in 1986 to have the MoMA negative of 2,632 metres, including the inserted MoMA intertitles, shipped to the Bundesarchiv in Koblenz, which made the copy for us that became the basis of our further work. In 1987, Gerhard Ullmann and Klaus Volkmer mounted a 3,153-metre working and screening copy (the "Munich version"). All material and information we had collected was incorporated into this copy on the basis of a montage plan that was in turn based on the piano score, the screenplay, and the censorship card.

In 1985, Joachim Bärenz accompanied the working copy of *Metropolis* for the first time in the Munich Film Museum on the piano — according to the surviving cut of the film, which had also served us as a basis for producing the montage of the extant bits and pieces, but arranged according to the sequence of our newly assembled version. Up to that time, it was not customary to provide musical accompaniment for films screened in the Film Museum. In 1977, when designing the new black cinema — one with no reflective surface but the sharply delineated white rectangle of the screen, so that nothing could be seen but the film — I insisted on acoustics in which the silence would complement a silent film instead of seeming awkward as it had been in the case in the old, provisional hall. Only when the frequent discoveries of scores and the activities of people such as Joachim Bärenz made clear that music often was an important part of the original shape of a film did we make an effort to screen silent films with music, if possible with the original music; we let Rudolf Augstein and Gunther Sachs donate a new Bösendorfer for us and nurtured Aljoscha Zimmermann as house pianist, arranger, and composer. Since 1989, he has also accompanied *Metropolis* in the Film Museum with his arrangement of the Huppertz score.

In 1988 we calculated that up to that time we had had twenty-four screenings of a *Metropolis* copy prepared by the museum, with ongoing changes to the copies; 3,512 paying spectators had been registered (in the following six years the number of screenings rose to thirty-five, that of the spectators to 5,257). In the same year, on 24 and 25 October, there were two screenings of the "Munich version" in the Philharmonie in the Gasteig in Munich, accompanied by sixty members of the Graunke orchestra conducted by Bernd Heller, who had adapted the Huppertz scores for this purpose. "The music," as Michael Althen wrote in the *Süddeutsche Zeitung* on 28 October, "reinforces the action. [. . .] The multiplied movement helps to bring out the plot, combines the disparate elements of the story in an instrumental way. Paradoxically, the accompaniment does not bring out more strongly the pathos that is often hardly bearable; on the contrary, it draws attention away from it."[5] And: "In imaginative power *Metropolis* remains unsurpassed to this day. Other works in the same architectural tradition, such as *Blade Runner* or *Brazil*, would not only be inconceivable without *Metropolis*, they have not surpassed Lang's classic by a single step."[6]

In 1989, there were screenings of the "Munich version" in, among other places, Edinburgh, Rome, Bologna and Barcelona, in 1990 in Le Havre, Los Angeles (accompanied there for the first time by the Defa symphony orchestra, and later also in Berlin);[7] in 1991 in Vienna, Paris, Budapest, Brussels, Nancy, Montreal, Amsterdam; in 1992 in Kyoto, Ottawa, Milan, Schwerin; in 1993 in Turin, Tokyo, Toulouse, Branden-

---

[5] Michael Althen, Review of *Metropolis*, *Süddeutsche Zeitung*, 28 October 1988.

[6] Althen, Review of *Metropolis*.

[7] The abbreviation Defa stands for Deutsche Filmaktiengesellschaft, the major East German film company founded in 1946.

burg; in 1994 in Mexico, Madrid, Lisbon, Potsdam. In 1995, after a kind of dress rehearsal in Helsinki, the version was screened in the Paris Théâtre du Châtelet, accompanied by a new score that the Argentine Martin Matalon had been commissioned to write by IRCAM; it was a partly electronic, partly instrumental composition for sixteen musicians. The film has been distributed in France since 1996 — with French subtitles for the Munich intertitles — and not a week passes when the film is not on the repertoire of a French cinema.

Following achievements such as the *Metropolis* project, the Munich Film Museum has gained a reputation for pioneer work in the field of film restoration or reconstruction (or "editorial restoration," as our colleagues in London call it). It seems quite odd that a rather secondary institute should have been granted this reputation, a regional cinematheque with staff and financial resources that are modest in national terms, let alone international ones. This is furthermore an institute that is subordinate to the administration of a city museum, which by the way is the reason why FIAF did not even want to acknowledge it as a "correspondent" for quite some time — it was only promoted from "observer" to a mere "provisional member" in 1997. Precisely these limitations, the shadowy existence, the amateur status of its staff, the barely developed and evolving division of labour (projectionists mutated into restorers, programme directors into archivists), along with the fact that the audience has always been involved as an accomplice: all this made unconventional methods possible. Consequently, when in April 1998 during its annual congress in Prague FIAF organized a symposium that dealt with the restoration of film and other art forms and its ethics and asked me to give a paper, I called it: "On 'Wild' Film Restoration, or Running a Minor Cinematheque."

Gian Luca Farinelli of the cinematheque in Bologna introduced a colloquium on the same topic in Paris in November 1997. In his opening address he expressed the hope that "necessarily hasty decisions and improvised restoration activities" — our "wild" restorations! — would finally "give way to a practice based on both well-considered and carefully documented criteria and philological selection principles."

How fortunate then that during the Berlin Film Festival in February 1998 the restoration committee of the Kinemathekverbund, the association of cinematheques, resolved to give special attention to *Metropolis* once more. Since then, the work of the *Metropolis* research group of the Kinemathekverbund has led to new insights. Most importantly, the holdings of the former Reichsfilmarchiv — left to the Bundesarchiv in Berlin by the East German Staatliches Filmarchiv — included the camera negative of the Paramount version. This version was obviously cut further in the USA, and one reel was replaced by a duplicate negative.

Nevertheless, probably in the 1930s after the distribution rights had expired, it was returned to Berlin (to Ufa, and from there to the Reichsfilmarchiv), complete with all the *trims*. The optical quality of this material is better than that of any other existing version.

That the "Munich version" was never meant to be the last word on the reconstruction of the film is obvious. In general, any restoration of films, just like any other piece of art, simply has to be conducted as a reversible and open process.

First of all, the incorporation of material hitherto unused by or inaccessible to the Munich Film Museum will necessarily lead to better results as far as picture quality is concerned.

Secondly, research is necessary to find out whether film material currently held in the archives in Lausanne, Milan, Montevideo, and a dozen others, can add something to the reconstruction of the premiere version.

Thirdly, information previously not exploited would have to form the basis of some decisions, such as how to use the flash titles featured in the torso held by the Murnau Foundation, among them twenty-eight titles of the original version, and the tinting of the Australian copy. The fact that this copy in the meantime has wound up in the George Eastman House in Rochester has finally given me the opportunity to inspect it. Interior shots and artificially lit scenes are tinted in orange (Kenneth Anger's "warm amber"), and night scenes are in blue-green — especially in the next to the last and last act, following the explosion of the "heart machine." Yellow stands for "exteriors/day": the stadium, the skyline montage, the final sequence in front of the cathedral portal. The "Eternal Gardens" are tinted in pink, the catacombs in violet, the duel and the fist fight in Josaphat's account in red (for rage).

Most of all, however, discussion must centre on which criteria a new version of *Metropolis* should meet. The major questions here are whether a synthesis of elements from different versions should be allowed, and how the *lacunae*, the 1,000 metres that are sill missing, should be handled; whether those thirty-five intertitles which are extant in the original form (but only as stills, as non-animated titles) should be incorporated into the reconstruction — and whether only these titles should be used or whether others, of which only the text is known, should be graphically designed to match the extant titles. Another question to be answered is how missing sequences, shots, and parts of them should be represented: whether by text descriptions, stills, black film, or not at all; whether the colours of the "Australian" copy (on Agfa material, and thus probably drawn in Germany) can be used as the basis for the reconstruction of the German version.

My suggestion is to aim at several versions:

The first version should be a reconstruction of the American Paramount version based at least on the nitrate negative from the East German archive, maybe also on the Gosfilmofond duplicate.

Secondly, a reconstruction of the British version based on the "Australian" copy, which in the meantime has wound up in the George Eastman House in Rochester, augmented by the version held in London, and with colour at least for those parts that are extant in the original tinting.

The third should be a reconstruction of the second German version of 1927, as far as it is extant in the MoMA and Murnau variation — with the intertitles contained as flash titles in the latter; in addition, those titles that are not extant in the original graphic form should be reconstructed faithfully according to the original text based on the censorship card.

Fourthly a synthetic film version that comes as close as possible to the 1927 premiere release, what could be called an "improved and augmented new edition" of the Munich version, adequately secured and accessible (lavender, duplicate negative, screening copies), a version which takes into account all the extant material without hampering the impact of the work by non-filmic notes — in the sense of a "visible restoration," just as progressive restorers practice it in other fields.

(Fifthly: who, precisely, is to take care that the Moroder version is properly secured?)

Finally, one could imagine a book with an equal distribution of text and image that also conveys the insights afforded by a critical, comparative reading of screenplay, score, censorship card, and stills — in more detail than is suitable for the screen.

There is a very thin line between a restoration that leaves or gives back an old film its own, specific quality and power, and a renovation that tries to remove its wrinkles with makeup, just as antique dealers do with old furniture. As important as the conservation of the old may be, it is also wrong to cover up the losses, the distance, the difference. An active handling of the past includes grief over that which is lost.

Grief over the one thousand metres, more than half an hour, of *Metropolis*. Grief over the following sequence, described again according to Balthasar in the *Blaues Heft*, February 1927: "The worker [No. 11711, after Freder has switched clothes with him] gets into the car. A coquette in a car nearby — a Dix figure, tremendously suggestive and ravishingly shot — the announcement of Yoshiwara, a pleasure bazaar en gros, makes his blood boil."[8] Two shots are described on the censorship card of the film's trailer: "A young man is covered by falling paper," —

[8] Balthasar (Roland Schacht), review of *Metropolis, Das blaue Heft*, February 1927.

advertising slips for Yoshiwara — "in the foreground a number of balloons appear rising into the air and turning into human heads; piano keys, dancing couples, a roulette, embraces, a dancer." Balthasar: "In the 'absolute' films of Léger and Picabia, we have already seen something resembling the special-effect shots of this pleasure haunt, but never so brilliant, so synthetic, so characteristic in their phoney, blinding wax makeup . . . ."[9]

[9] Balthasar (Roland Schacht), review of *Metropolis, Das blaue Heft*, February 1927.

Innocence Restored?

Reading and Rereading a "Classic"

*Thomas Elsaesser**

Introduction

"GERMAN CINEMA" STILL RECALLS the 1920s, expressionism, Weimar culture and a time when Berlin was the avant-garde capital of Europe. Yet oddly enough, neither the films nor their directors are as vividly present to the popular memory as the often eponymous larger-than-life protagonists: *Dr. Caligari, Dr. Mabuse, The Golem, Nosferatu — the Vampire,* and the two Marias from *Metropolis* are the icons and the anti-heroes of the epoch. They have entered not just movie mythology but live on — parodied, pastiched and recycled — in very different guises, serving as either models for modern villains (*Dr. No, Goldfinger*), become the undead of count(less) Dracula and vampire films (From Universal's thirties horror films to Coppola's *Bram Stoker's Dracula*), or they provide the imagery for music videos by stars as diverse as Madonna, Michael Jackson and David Bowie, and among which Mick Jagger's take on Conrad Veidt's Cesare from *The Cabinet of Dr. Caligari* is by no means the least remarkable. In these remixes of decor and motifs, of figure, pose and attitude, this German cinema of the 1920s speaks of vitality and electricity, fusing human and machine energy, showing sinuous bodies animated at once by electric currents and dark urges.

Nowhere does the neon-Gothic heart beneath these streamlined surfaces of Berlin modernism revamping German romanticism beat more vibrantly than in *Metropolis*, Fritz Lang's flawed masterpiece from 1926, and no other classic has trailed quite the clouds of glory from its own time into the present. In a turn of events as paradoxical as it was unpredictable, *Metropolis* has now become the veritable archetype for a new movie genre: post-Fordist kitsch techno-noir. From *Blade Runner* to *Batman Returns*, from *Brazil* to *Seven*, Lang's fatal Ufa suicide mission — notorious in the history of the cinema for the extravagance of

---

* This essay incorporates material from a review and an essay ("Innocence Restored") that originally appeared in *Monthly Film Bulletin* 51 (December 1984), 363–366. The material is used by permission of the publishers. A German version has appeared in "Endlosschleife Metropolis" in Irmbert Schenk, ed., *Dschungel Grossstadt* (Marburg: Schueren, 1999), 29–56.

its production values, the number of extras in the crowd scenes later excised, the millions of meters of celluloid shot and the millions of reichsmarks spent — has taken on the status of an *Urtext* of cinematic postmodernity, a position confirmed when one remembers that it, too, has inspired outstanding music videos by Freddy Mercury ("Radio Gaga") and Madonna ("Express Yourself"). And true enough, there is plenty for contemporary anxieties to thrill to: the cyborg figure of the robot Maria now takes on features of empowerment where its original audience might only have sensed malevolence. The boldly outlandish sets of *Metropolis'* futuristic cityscape pulsate and pullulate with postmodern life, compared to the stark modernist high-rises gone soulless and drab that once were its real-life contemporaries. In the contrast between the master of the city's high-tech office — the penthouse dream of every yuppie trader — and the alchemist's lab that is home to the scientist Rotwang, multinational corporate culture meets new-age ecology, while in the catacombs of *Metropolis* the sweatshops of Asia or Latin America are only a shout and a prayer away from the religious fundamentalisms, the media evangelisms, and voodoo revivalisms now fevering towards the millennium.

Giorgio Moroder's *Metropolis*

The return of *Metropolis* as cult film had its first apogee in 1984, when at the Cannes Festival a curious hybrid of archival restoration work, sacrilegious tampering with a venerated classic, and iconoclast popmodernism had its outing: Giorgio Moroder's newly minted, ruthlessly tinted rock opera, in which the robot Maria lasciviously strips to a disco beat. As the *Nouvel Observateur* reported, mock-outraged, but also half in awed disbelief: "Un rocker nommé Fritz Lang."[1] Moroder's reissue at a cost of almost as much as Ufa lost,[2] with a New Wave soundtrack written by Moroder himself and performed by such chart-toppers as Freddy Mercury, Bonnie Tyler, Adam Ant and Pat Benatar was bound to offend the purists if only because it smacked of such crass commercialism and seemed so evidently calculated to jump the culture barrier. Yet whatever pained expressions might cross one's face when confronted with lyrics like "Here She Comes" (when the saintly Maria first makes her entrance) or "Cage of Freedom" (when Freder mingles among the machine room slaves), Moroder's sound serves Lang curi-

---

[1] *Le Nouvel Observateur*, 6 July 1984. The article also features an interview with Gustav Fröhlich, who shows himself "delighted" by the new version.

[2] Moroder, apparently, pipped David Bowie to the post with his new version. "In his effort to prevail over Bowie, Moroder admitted that, 'I raised my bid and in all probability paid too much for the rights'." Lenny Borger, "Moroder's *Metropolis*," *Variety*, July 1984.

ously and worryingly well.[3] Especially in the set pieces (the city-scape, the machine room, the transformation of Maria, the flooding of the workers' homes) *Metropolis* retains a breathtaking and awesome sense of spectacle that puts to shame much of the special-effect work one has come to associate with contemporary Hollywood. The thrills, of course, have less to do with the suitability of the score as theme music for this particular narrative. Refusing to "inhabit" the fiction, the music's impact is a function of the sound's power to enhance the image and open it up to another dimension altogether. In this respect, Moroder's instinct was right: the film looks terrific and feels as though all it had ever needed was stereophonic sound, in order to help it to a new audience. The tinting in different shades of pink and blue gives the black-and-white the high artifice of colour while preserving the richness of tonal values one associates with mint-condition silent prints: but part of the luminous brilliance that is now so seductive to the eye is probably a synthetic illusion due to the metallic crispness of the Dolby-enhanced synthesizer score. All this in the service of surface, of tactile as well as specular values.

It has become commonplace to point out that the silent cinema was very rarely silent. *Metropolis,* too, originally had a score, composed by Gottfried Huppertz, which in the 1970s was used to showcase the restored archive version on German television. But Huppertz's music — a medley of Liszt, Wagner, and Tchaikovsky performed mainly on the piano — is salon music, curiously irrelevant to the film because it is devoid of associations other than to the pomposity of first-night audiences at mid-1920s movie palace premieres.[4] In this context, it is worth recalling that *Metropolis* made under the so-called Parufamet agreement (intended to secure American distribution for German prestige films) was invested with such extravagant production values because this was Neubabelsberg wanting to out-Hollywood Hollywood. But by a peculiar historical irony, *Metropolis* finally opened in New York barely three months before *The Jazz Singer* had its premiere, so that like many other remarkable silent films from the end of the decade, it went under in the new craze for sound. Moroder, an Italian who made his reputation in the U.S.A. both in the record business (he launched Donna Summer) and in movies (he won Academy Awards for the scores of *Midnight Express* and *Flashdance*), might justifiably claim that Lang did get a kind

---

[3] One such pained expression and horrified gasp comes from Claude Beylie. See "Dédales de *Metropolis,*" *Cinématographie,* July 1984, 24.

[4] On sound in early cinema, see for instance, the essays in Rick Altman, ed., *Sound Theory/Sound Practice* (New York: Routledge, 1992) and especially Altman's extensively documented article "The Silence of the Silents," *The Musical Quarterly* 80, no. 4 (1997), 648–718.

of revenge on Hollywood and the coming of sound: with his version, *Metropolis* finally had its long-frustrated American premiere.

Moroder probably took the courage for his conviction from the phenomenal success of Kevin Brownlow's restored print of Abel Gance's *Napoleon*, in the version shown by Francis Ford Coppola in New York with a score by Coppola's father. Brownlow and Coppola refurbished a silent film to fit into the concert hall, for a highbrow gala audience that wanted to relive — through the transport of nostalgia or the archivist's phantom of integral history — what might have been the original experience of spectators at a metropolitan (London, New York, Paris, Berlin) first-run house.[5] Moroder, more naively or more cunningly, did not go in search of a lost aura of authenticity to indulge his enthusiasm for silent movies. He took it where he probably found it — on television, with a tinkly sounding, archly cute pianola score — and made it big again — big screen, big sound. If one is unsympathetic to the enterprise, one could say that Moroder's work started at the opposite end from Brownlow's: instead of seeing history as a return to origins, Moroder abolished distance (the "aura" of the original work) and opted for appropriation, treating the film (deliberately and provocatively) as a "found object," while expending much archival time and technical effort on preserving or restoring what could be called the film's "innocence." In the light of what we (think we) know about *Metropolis*, this is more than a gamble and would seem to be nothing short of heresy piled upon blasphemy. But it was also a bold move, for it recognized that the norm for an audio-visual experience today is not only television, but distracted viewing of television. Moroder made the more peremptory but also diffuse kinds of synchronization between sound-source and image track familiar to the distracted spectator the basis of his extremely meticulous and competent workmanship. The model here is indeed the contemporary rock video where, at the expense of a more complex narrative, much of the undoubted sophistication goes into devising both sound-image echoes and image-sound echoes, so that the sound sometimes cues the image and vice versa. Classical sound continuity respects a strict allocation of roles and tasks: the musical accompaniment cues the narrative image discreetly, and almost always in order to efface itself. Dolby sound and the disco beat are anything but self-effacing; with them, time-honoured hierarchies of sound cinema were beginning to crumble, as can be observed in the editing techniques of films like *Apocalypse Now*, *Mad Max* or *Blade Runner* (not to mention the films that Moroder himself has worked on) that often fol-

[5] An annotated bibliography of the reception of *Metropolis* can be found in E. Ann Kaplan, *Fritz Lang. A Guide to References and Resources* (Boston: G. K. Hall, 1981), in particular 145–55.

low the sound-track, even if it means violating the norms of visual continuity or creating what appear to be bad matches.[6] In the case of *Metropolis,* Lang's idiosyncratic visual style with its sudden changes of angle, the startling montage-effects, the shifts in size, and the futurist play on shape and line — which in the "silent version" often feels like irritating ornament and a distraction from the narrative — is now not only visible to the trained eye, but palpable as an immediate, bodily experience. If, as *Variety* wrote, a fully instrumental score without the songs would have been better, the reason is (among other things) that the sound space Moroder creates through electronic sound effects and the synthesizer penetrate, model and modulate very intriguingly the visual space of Lang's film, giving it a kind of movement in three dimensions. Moroder was evidently aware of this, for he prefaces the film with a quotation from Lang: "I perceive the world through the eye and only very rarely through the ear, much to my regret."

While the live orchestra behind and around *Napoleon* was grandiose in its way, it remained a distinct musical experience matched to a distinct visual experience. Moroder's score, perhaps by its deliberate anachronism in relation to the film, made one see Lang's images as taking place not on a two-dimensional screen but in the stereophonic space created by the sounds, without the film thereby becoming more "illusionist" or "hyper-real" (as in film productions relying on digital special effects). On the contrary, the element of abstraction, the tension between the functional and the ornamental in Lang's mise-en-scène of spaces, objects, and people (for which he was duly taken to task by Siegfried Kracauer) once more communicate some of the vitality that international modernism's forms possessed for artists like Léger or Picabia, and when Taylorization and biomechanics appealed to both V. I. Lenin and Henry Ford. It is not easy to explain what punk fashion, disco-music, and strobe-light stage acts have in common with the constructivist ethos of the 1920s (except perhaps a pessimism that is both energetic and sentimental), but the shaven heads of the Babylonian slaves, the workers' clothes with trousers bunched at the ankles, leather-clad figures guarding the mouth of Moloch, or Klein-Rogge's inspired mad scientist Rotwang are instantly recognizable icons of the 1980s, whatever they may have meant in and for the 1920s. After seeing Moroder's *Metropolis,* it is more than apparent that Fritz Lang was a stylist, eclectic and decorative, but one who could design a consistent

---

[6] An extensive discussion of modern sound design can be found in J. Belton and E. Weiss, eds. *Film Sound* (New York: Columbia UP, 1986). See also, on the sound designs of Francis Ford Coppola, T. Elsaesser and M. Wedel, "The Hollow Heart of Hollywood: *Apocalypse Now* and the new sound space," in Gene Moore, ed., *Conrad on Film* (Cambridge: Cambridge UP, 1997) 151–75.

look, from dressing a huge set to arranging the tiniest accessories on a bedside table, and give it enough variation to convey a quite particular visual rhythm. Even in static compositions he counterpoints a dominant visual motif by repeating it several times in echoing shapes but playing on difference of size and surface texture. Moroder's version is able to pick up much of this — the correlation of visual composition with syncopated sound and the translation of editing effects into rock harmonies, as in the opening scene when the music works with uncanny precision towards the climax of the steam-whistle blowing to announce the end of the shift.

Moroder's formula, however, may not be repeatable, and there are probably not many silent classics where the addition of Dolby sound could so convincingly bring out the aestheticizing tendencies of a culture transforming itself into a technology of spatial sound and tactile vision, especially a culture that exercises power simultaneously through spectacle and surveillance. The rediscovery and persistent fascination with *Metropolis* raises interesting questions about what happens when a new technology takes in hand the products and forms of an earlier one.[7] We know that television has quite radically transformed the cinematic heritage, down to computer-generated tint-coding of old black-and-white movies for colour transmission. With Moroder's *Metropolis*, video techniques and digitized image-making seem poised to take television out of its domestic closet and back onto the big screen. Perhaps one of the reasons Lang's film survives the treatment so well is that it has the stature and robustness of a grand narrative. As in the myths that Claude Levi-Strauss's analyses, such stories survive the rough handling they necessarily receive by an oral tradition thanks to their redundancies and archetypal configurations.[8] What *Metropolis* set out to be was not only an American film in terms of its production values and special effects: it also wanted to be a "birth of the nation" film, a foundation film a modern, "synthetic" fairy tale, a *Märchen* for the machine age.

---

[7] Luc Besson's *The Fifth Element* constructs its New York of the future along the visual axes of Lang's cityscape, with a tower very much like that in *Metropolis* to focus the gaze in the distance — a necessary device when one considers the three-dimensionality Besson needed. See Nigel Floyd's interview with the art director of *The Fifth Element* in *Sight and Sound* 7 (June 1997), 6–9.

[8] Film scholars such as Alan Williams and John Tulloch have provided typically structuralist analyses of the film in the 1970s: Alan Williams, "Structures of Narrativity in Fritz Lang's *Metropolis*," *Film Quarterly* 27, no. 4 (1974), 17–24 (reprinted in Part Three of this volume) and John Tulloch, "Genetic Structuralism and the Cinema: A Look at Lang's *Metropolis*," *Australian Journal of Screen Theory* 1 (1976), 3–50.

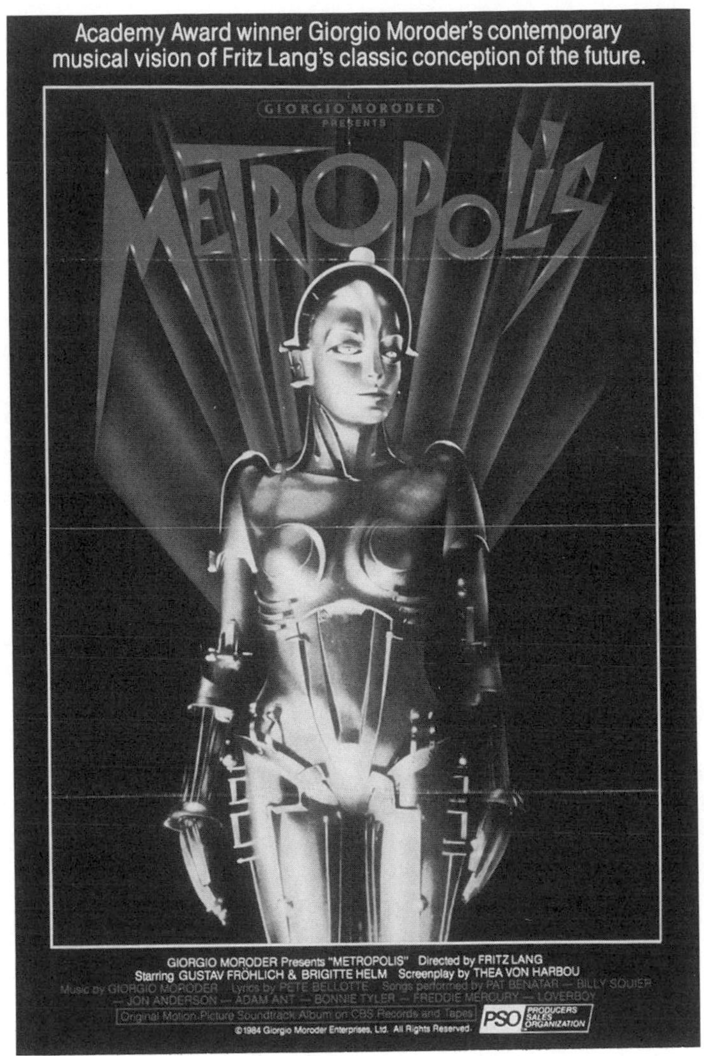

13. Poster for the 1984 Giorgio Moroder version of *Metropolis.* [Museum of Modern Art/Film Stills Archive]

Telling and Retelling *Metropolis*

A brief reminder of what Thea von Harbou's story was supposedly about: in the year 2020 A.D. the city of Metropolis is dominated by a giant administration and leisure complex, serving and controlling the technocratic empire that surrounds the central tower. Above, close to the clouds, there is an open-air stadium; somewhere below, an electric power station. Social classes are sealed off from each other. While the sons of the rulers play decadent games in the timeless pleasure gardens, the shift change in the power station releases rows of uniform worker-slaves into the lifts that take them even further underground to their tenement blocks.

One day Freder, son of Fredersen, the absolute master of Metropolis, falls in love at the sight of a girl from the lower classes surrounded by wide-eyed children who suddenly appear at the entrance to the eternal gardens. Freder drops everything, but instead of catching up with the girl he finds himself in the machine room of the power station, just as an explosion erupts, killing scores of workmen. When he tries to tell his father about the incident, he realizes that administrators are more worried about security than safety. Fredersen dismisses Josaphat, his assistant, partly for having allowed an outsider to stray into the lower levels, partly because it is the foreman who informs the master of the city about mysterious drawings found on the dead workers. With Josaphat, whom he dissuades from killing himself, as his accomplice, Freder returns to the machine room and takes over from a worker who has collapsed at the controls. Intoxicated by his freedom, and wearing Freder's clothes, the worker heads straight for the Yoshiwara, the city's exclusive nightclub.

Now a worker among workers, Freder follows them to a clandestine meeting in the catacombs. There he discovers that the girl he has fallen in love with is none other than Maria, the workers' spiritual leader. Their eyes meet as she promises the workers the advent of a mediator and saviour.

Meanwhile, disturbed by the maps found circulating among the workers, Fredersen goes to see his former rival in love and power, Rotwang. The scientific brain behind Metropolis, he is now a recluse inventor working on a robot replica of Hel, the woman he lost to Fredersen. Flattered by Fredersen's admission of helplessness, Rotwang takes him to the workers' meeting and agrees to kidnap Maria in order to give the robot her likeness and make the robot lead the workers in a self-destructive uprising. While searching for Maria, Freder is himself trapped by Rotwang, and cannot prevent what turns out to be the creation of her double. Soon, the false Maria is everywhere: she whips the men at the Yoshiwara into sexual frenzy or murderous duels and in the catacombs incites the workers to smash the machines. Freder himself surprises her in his father's arms and comes down with brain fever, during which he has nightmares of a lascivious Maria dancing naked before a sea of devouring eyes. Despite the remonstrations of the foreman, the workers wreck the generator (the "heart machine") and thus flood their own homes.

Nursed back to health, Freder sets out to find the real Maria, whom he discovers in the middle of the workers' city, once more surrounded by children, half immersed in the rising flood. With the aid of Josaphat the lovers manage to send the children back up to the safety of the eternal gardens. Below, in the machine rooms, the workers realize too late the danger to their children: grief-stricken, they turn into a lynch mob, turning on the false Maria, dragging her in front of the cathedral, to be burnt at the stake.

Freder watches in horror, unaware that inside the cathedral, Rotwang is pursuing the real Maria whom he believes to be Hel. As the robot goes up in flames, Freder catches sight of Rotwang carrying the limp and faint Maria on his back along the Cathedral parapet. He rushes after him, and in the ensuing fight Rotwang falls to his death while Freder manages to pull Maria to safety. On being told that his son saved their children, the workers spare Fredersen. Taking his father's hand, Freder moves towards the foreman, who is once more prepared to shake hands with his boss. Industrial peace and the status quo have returned, while a newly united couple exchange the final kiss.[9]

Weimar Cinema's Bad Object: Fritz Lang and *Metropolis*

No other filmmaker has sparked off and at the same time focused the ambivalences surrounding classic German cinema as powerfully as Fritz Lang. Not only have his films from the 1920s received a fair share of symptomatic, psycho-social readings and retellings by Lotte Eisner, Siegfried Kracauer and subsequent critics.[10] Kracauer's remarks on Lang in *From Caligari to Hitler* tie virtually every significant trend and tendency of his book's thesis to one of Lang's Films, making him, beyond the key figure, into something like the evil genius of Weimar cinema. Kracauer set the tone for what remained the same critical configuration in the psycho-historical literature devoted to Lang: that his films proj-

---

[9] For a psychoanalytic reading of the plot and its resolution, see Roger Dadoun, "*Metropolis*: Mother City — 'Mittler — Hitler,'" trans. Arthur Goldhammer, *Camera Obscura* 15 (autumn 1986), 137–64.

[10] An especially brilliant post-Kracauer analysis is Andreas Huyssen, "The Vamp and the Machine: Technology and Sexuality in Fritz Lang's *Metropolis*," *New German Critique* 7, no. 24–25 (winter 1981–82), 221–237. This essay is reprinted in Part Three of this volume.

ect authoritarian attitudes, support irrationalist and mythical readings of society and history, and construct fables offering social-fascist solutions to political and economic crises.[11] The name Lang became synonymous with films where tyrants tried to enslave the world and where the individual was a puppet of alien inhuman powers. At best (that is to say, at their least politically compromising) Lang's films were said to exemplify the doomed struggle against these forces, but neither the protagonists nor the director were judged capable of unravelling the chaos or of demystifying the social and political interests hiding behind them. Kracauer complained:

> Dr. Mabuse's family likeness to Dr. Caligari cannot be overlooked. He, too, is an unscrupulous master-mind animated by the lust for unlimited power . . . The film succeeds in making of Mabuse an omnipresent threat that cannot be localized, and thus reflects society under a tyrannical regime — that kind of society in which one fears everybody because anybody may be the tyrant's ear or arm . . . Here as well as in Caligari not the slightest allusion to true freedom interferes with the persistent alternative of tyranny and chaos.[12]

The accusation of political naivety has often been repeated: the social romanticism of *Metropolis* has been dismissed as stupid and silly, where it was not bluntly accused of being dangerously proto-fascist and class-collaborationist propaganda.[13] H. G. Wells, from premises rather different than those of Kracauer, wrote a famously dismissive review, which already at the time was quoted with unconcealed Schadenfreude by a number of German journalists.[14]

Equally damaging was Kracauer's analysis of what he termed the "mass ornament" in Lang's film, and which he saw as having inspired Leni Riefenstahl's *Triumph of the Will*. According to Kracauer, the impact of the cinema has been to blur the opposition between myth and reason in modern, industrialized societies. They have become two sides of the same coin: the drive for abstraction at all levels of social as well as economic existence. This abstraction finds its most pleasurable but

---

[11] As Ann Kaplan remarked: "*From Caligari to Hitler* attempting to combine political and sociological approaches with psychological ones, effectively damaged Lang's critical reputation for at least a decade." *Fritz Lang: A Guide to References and Resources*, 2.

[12] Siegfried Kracauer, *From Caligari to Hitler* (Princeton: Princeton UP, 1947), 82–3.

[13] Fritz Lang himself later tended to dismiss the "message" as naive. See Peter Bogdanovich, *Fritz Lang in America* (London: Studio Vista, 1967), 124.

[14] H. G. Wells, 'Mr. Wells Reviews a Current Film', *New York Times*, 17 April 1927, 4 and 22. Hans Siemsen quotes Wells in "Eine Filmkritik wie sie sein soll," *Die Weltbühne* 24 (14 June 1927) 947–50. The full text of Wells' review is reprinted in Part One of this volume.

also most politically ambiguous form in spectacles and public occasions in which crowds participate, as subjects and objects of the event. Kracauer had in mind military parades, spectator sports, or political rallies, but he meant something more than merely the regular or geometrical patterns such crowds offer to the (photographic) eye. Rather, what in our televisual age we might call the fascination of "being there," where one takes pleasure in the knowledge of having been filmed, Kracauer sees more ominously as the constitutive moment where the modern audience as part of a crowd see themselves subject to an alien gaze, a gaze they welcome, because on it is founded the sense of community and belonging in a mass society. By representing the relation of individual to community in terms of self to body, and both in terms of vision and display, the mass ornament creates a powerfully social space contaminated by a new kind of (media-made) subjectivity, cut loose from history and social relations. For Kracauer, Lang's films paradigmatically enact the fascination of seeing oneself seen in the mass-ornament, so that

> In *Metropolis,* the decorative not only appears as an end in itself, but even belies certain points made by the plot. It makes sense that, on their way to and from the machines, the workers form ornamental groups; but it is nonsensical to force them into such groups while they are listening to a comforting speech from the girl Maria during their leisure time. In his exclusive concern with ornamentation Lang goes so far as to compose decorative patterns from the masses who are desperately trying to escape the inundation of the lower city. Cinematically an incomparable achievement, this inundation sequence is humanly a shocking failure. [15]

That *Metropolis* is a "shocking failure" has thus been echoing down the ages in many different versions. Not only did Kracauer's moral judgement provide a parallel to the film's "flopping" at the box office and sealing the fate of Ufa, its production company, which would have landed in the hands of the receiver had it not been "rescued" by the right-wing newspaper magnate Alfred Hugenberg. The supposedly inadequate humanist dimension of the film also served as a shady emblem of the tragic inadequacies of the Weimar Republic in the face of imminent fascism. [16]

---

[15] Kracauer, *From Caligari to Hitler,* 149

[16] More recent research both on Ufa and on the finances of *Metropolis* have considerably modified if not altogether disproven the bases for such analogies. See Klaus Kreimeier, *Die Ufa-Story. Geschichte eines Filmkonzerns* (Munich: Heyne, 2nd ed. 1995), and H.-M. Bock and M. Töteberg (eds) *Das Ufa Buch* (Frankfurt· Zweitausendeins), 1992.

Hollywood vs Weimar Narrative

One "benefit" of Moroder's *Metropolis* is that it complicates ideological readings such as Kracauer's. While Moroder's disco score underlines the autonomy and separateness of the episodes, his editing gives the film's lack of overall coherence a different ideological meaning. For if the cinema's urge to construct self-contained narratives has exhausted itself on television in favour of serial models that permutate a limited number of elements, the deep structure of *Metropolis* may not quite be the proto-fascist social fable or the oedipal story of the missing mother. The narrative becomes rather more comparable to a Dallas-type struggle for power over several generations, centered on the connection of business and sexuality, rivalry and ancient feuds, private empires and the exchange of women, itself a celebration of capitalism's power to divide and join, separate and recombine: a process of which the fragmented and recycled, reedited and rock-video'd torso of *Metropolis* seems an appropriately apocalyptic instance.

Most of the 16mm copies of *Metropolis* still in circulation are taken from the American release print of 1927, which was cut by more than a quarter from 4,181 to 3,100 metres and supplied with intertitles specially written to make sense of the mutilations. In recent years both the East German Film Archive and the Munich Film Museum have assembled versions that, while still incomplete, run to two-and-a-half hours.[17] They give the impression the film probably always had rather a murky story line that in the words of Richard Combs "largely leaves the audience to make its own connections."[18] Moroder's solution was to go back to the original intertitles and use the explanatory ones as narration over freeze-frames inserted from scenes presumed missing, with the others turned into dialogue and printed as subtitles. Stills that are familiar from old publicity material and as production shots — a plunging view of the skyscrapers, the shell-shaped entrance to the Yoshiwara nightclub, Rotwang's memorial to the woman he lost to Fredersen — are incorporated as establishing shots and to link sequences.[19] The effect is to smooth transitions and to suggest a more precise (but also more limited) sense of location and of action spaces for the narrative to move in back and forth.

---

[17] On the Munich version, see Enno Patalas, "*Metropolis*, Scene 103," trans Miriam Hansen, *Camera Obscura* 15 (autumn 1986) 165–73, and the more recent account in Part Two of this volume.

[18] Richard Combs, "*Metropolis*," *Monthly Film Bulletin* 43, (April 1976).

[19] On the central role played by Hel, see Georges Sturm, "Für Hel ein Denkmal," *Bulletin CICIM* (München) no. 9 (1984), as well as his earlier "Auf der Suche nach der verlorenen Szene," *Bulletin CICIM* no. 5–6 (1983), 88–95.

Moroder's *Metropolis,* down again to 89 minutes, is therefore not a cut version from an archive print but itself the result of reediting. Anyone interested in the original and in the differences between German film-making and Hollywood will find it a fascinating document because it illustrates two possibly quite distinct experiences of cinema or ways of thinking about narrative. What I mean by this is already hinted at in the plot synopsis. More than is usually the case, it is already a retelling, or rather an interpretation of an interpretation. It underlines what in Moroder's re-release is perhaps no more than the consequence of streamlining the narrative, in order to provide the characters with credible motives, where previously they either had none or too many conflicting reasons. *Metropolis* is now a love story between Freder and Maria, with all the classic complications and delays. "He" can only win "her" by defeating the Father, which he does by first taking the side of the workers in their struggle and then by engaging in a proxy fight with the "bad" father, Rotwang, over the possession of the Mother. The references to Hel, now that they have been put back, make the real Maria the symbolic double of Freder's mother, Rotwang's lost love and Fredersen's wife. The false Maria is simply the "other woman" — femme fatale, whore, and rabble-rouser. Centered on the absent mother and thereby multiplying the father-son relationships, the intrigue transforms the woman into an object of desire without having to acknowledge her sexuality, a strategy typical of narratives constructed around male narcissism. For Rotwang, Maria is a substitute of the dead Hel, fetishized in the robot, itself a phallic representation of his missing hand; for Freder, she is the mother he never knew; and for his father, the woman who can be controlled and manipulated wholly as image.

In a sense, of course, such a symbolic reading was already contained in Lang's original, but Moroder's editing has somewhat altered the balance of the narrative logic. The 1926 version had as its hero a Freder who was weak, ineffectual, never quite at the right time at the right place, and despite charging impulsively with his head thrust forward, always backing off in horror at what he sees. It contributed much to the sense of impasse, the impossibility of his fulfilling the role of mediator in anything other than a derisory or deliberately ironic fashion. The Freder of this version — the object of whose quest is now the girl and no longer the knowledge about how and where the other half lives — pushes ahead because of his passion and only recoils at the enormity of the detours that the law of the father puts in the way of gratification. To achieve this shift of emphasis, and make Freder a more active protagonist, Moroder gives the narrative a unilinear direction, via establishing shot, scene-dissection, close up, by the simple expedient of relying on reverse field editing and point of view shots to generate continuity, cutting out most of the inserts that in Lang's version had separated — in time and space — the character's gaze from its object.

To admirers of Lang, this is an unpardonable interference in the text, for the hallmark of his style is precisely the interpolation of disorienting or disrupting visuals into the classic match-cut, making what is represented seem ambiguously motivated and always happening at one remove.[20] For one additional aspect of the image's non-identity with the represented is that in Lang a shot seems to have no weight of the real, no extension and no depth, and above all, no illusion of presence. What defines an image is its frame, and by reframing an object or a scene, as Lang often does at moments of imperceptible but vital drama, he creates a new object, or a new scene, and not merely a different view of the same. It is a feature noted by Bellour:

> in *Siegfried*, for instance: three warriors occupy almost the entire surface of the screen; they are so close that they cannot be seen in their entirety; between them are blank spaces, in the background a bare wall; the image is perfectly flat and the soldiers look like cardboard cut-outs; when Kriemhild's women pass behind them, following her, perspective suddenly returns so vividly that one feels it as being too deep, and it seems like another illusion. (Bellour, 35–36)

Thus, narrative in Lang is generated not so much by the logic of the actions, but out of the mise-en-scène of part objects, or rather, narrative is nothing other than an effect of the camera's ability to frame and reframe an object or scene and displace itself in relation to that object or scene.[21]

This may sound like the nit-picking of a cinephile, but it can also confirm that the German silent cinema of the 1920s — what I have earlier defined as "Weimar (art) cinema" — was based on a different visual grammar than what we have all come to accept as the norm, namely Hollywood-type continuity editing. Ultimately, however it affects the way one reacts to the ideological message offered by the narrative. Historically, Lang's film may seem symptomatic of the fears of a technocratic élite sensing itself incapable of managing both modern technology and the class that arose in response to it. At the same time, private needs remain irreconcilable with public objectives: in the original, the domestic melodrama of Freder is overtaken by the spectacle of the crowd and the machines, so that the parable of the hand and the head joined together by the heart becomes a purely formal solution.

---

[20] See Raymond Bellour, "On Fritz Lang," in S. Jenkins (ed.), *Fritz Lang, The Image and the Look* (London: B. F. I. Publishing, 1981) 26–37.

[21] The effect of French interest in Lang has been to demonstrate the consistent way in which Lang's films are not a mise-en-scène of spectacle, but in the words of Bellour "the mise-en-scène of vision itself," "On Fritz Lang", 28.

Moroder's version, built around the simple structure of boy-meets-girl, boy-loses-girl, boy-gets-girl, makes both the politics and the spectacle of technology an extended metaphor, a grandiose and not-quite-serious back-projection of the agonies and ecstasies of young love. This gets rid of much of the disagreeable naivety and clumsiness of the final reconciliation scene because it suggests a different kind of apotheosis. The film is now flamboyantly erotic, unashamedly camp, delightfully fetishistic, and gloriously perverse in the scenes between Rotwang and Maria in the catacombs, or whenever it plays with religious imagery. What Lang might have made of this Jeff Koons quality that Moroder brings into the film is difficult to guess; but that it is a "strong misreading" (in the sense of Harold Bloom) and not just a trivializing, postmodern pastiche is undeniable.

A Critique of Cynical Reason?

If the pseudo-class struggle with its pseudo-revolution/resolution is seen as merely an orchestration of the love theme, the film becomes in a sense ideologically even more cynical than Lang and Harbou's facile optimism. The question is, however, whether the force of the images in *Metropolis* had not always exceeded the requirements of the narrative and thus subverted any directly ideological reading of the story line? Moroder's paring down actually makes it easier for the visuals to work on their own, because the love story, as so often, for instance, in the Hollywood musicals of the 1950s, becomes virtually invisible except as a convenient device for motivating the choreographed numbers and spectacular set-pieces. The erotic frisson that this releases into the film is finally an eroticism of the image, a fascination not with the now obsolete futurism of steam-driven mega-machines (whose representation in the film is more decorative than dramatic), but with the technology of the processes of representation, i.e. the technology of the cinematic spectacle itself. Not least Lang's own, quite distinct way of handling (classical) narration gives the film — from our present perspective — its collage quality, making it the blueprint of so many postmodern city-symphonies for the MTV generation and opening up the story-line for camp appropriations such as Moroder's.

Must we call this openness of *Metropolis* to its own afterlife "a shocking failure," or is it the sort of prescient insight, translated into aesthetic form, that makes us think of Weimar Germany as one of the most extraordinary decades in modern history? I would like to think that it is a sign of how we can see the (naive) readings of "history" in Kracauer to be themselves deconstructed by a new technology reviving the film (in this case, Moroder's techno-version), thereby making it available to another cultural moment (postmodernism, neon-noir). This moment, too, however, does not stand "outside" history, because it must in turn be historicized, allowing us to grasp both the "postmodern" element in Weimar (and National Socialism), as well as the "fascist" element in our own "late capitalist" (Jameson) cyborg technoculture . . .

It is as if Weimar culture, here embodied in Lang, was not so much "anticipating" postmodernism, as already taking a critical, self-critical and in Peter Sloterdijk's sense, "kynical/cynical" view also of postmodernism itself, affecting in turn our "ideological" critiques of Lang's film and of Weimar culture, which, according to Sloterdijk, "have remained more naive than the ideology they set out to unmask."[22] Thus Moroder's version of *Metropolis* is in the end nothing but an "extension" into (reception) history of Lang's own, and Moroder himself might be regarded as Lang's pre-programmed "ready-made," to take up a phrase which Marcel Duchamp, another modernist of "cynical reason," once applied, only half in jest, to the efforts of his more assiduous archivists, gallerists and exegetes. The "rocker" Fritz Lang, after first "rolling in his grave"[23] at the sight of Moroder, Jagger, Bowie, Madonna or Freddy Mercury strutting their stuff and striking a pose on top of it, might be content to join in the fun. As the first and last man of Weimar cinema, he surely has the last laugh on modernist critics and postmodern parodists alike: he is always already back from where they are heading to.

---

[22] Peter Sloterdijk, *Kritik der zynischen Vernunft* (Frankfurt: Suhrkamp, 1983), vol. 2, 708. For Sloterdijk's sense of the word "cynical" in relation to the Weimar republic, see Sloterdijk, vol. 2, 709: "the different areas of Weimar culture reached a summit of cynical structures that only now, from the vantage point of the disillusioned, kynical/cynical [kynisch-zynisch], crisis-conscious zeitgeist of the late seventies and early eighties, can be brought into view." For Sloterdijk the difference is between "top down," institutional and political cynicism and "bottom up" cynicism, as in the sarcastic laughter of the people, Bakhtinian carnival irreverence and resistance.

[23] "If Fritz Lang is not rolling in his grave, then the late Henri Langlois, who outlawed any musical scores for silent films at the Cinemathèque Française, certainly is," Borger, "Moroder's *Metropolis*," 5

14. Rotwang and Fredersen confront one another before Hel's inscription in Scene 103.

15. Rotwang raises his arms to Hel in Scene 103.

16. The shooting of Scene 103. [This and the above two photos from Giorgio Bertellini's Private Collection]

Restoration, Genealogy and Palimpsests

On Some Historiographical Questions

*Giorgio Bertellini**

> If we are indeed doomed to the comically convergent task of dismantling the universe, and fabricating from its stuff an artefact called The Universe, it is reasonable to suppose that such an artefact will resemble the vaults of an endless film archive built to house, in eternal cold storage, the infinite film.
>
> Hollis Frampton[1]

> I didn't touch the original because there is no original.
>
> Giorgio Moroder[2]

History and Archaeological Eloquence

IN 1847, HISTORIAN AND DEPUTY PUBLIC RECORD KEEPER Francis Palgrave commenting on the planned restoration of the Bordeaux cathedral, wrote to his antiquarian friend Dawson Turner: "You cannot grind old bones new. You may repeat the outward form (though rarely with minute accuracy) but you cannot the material, the bedding and laying, and above all the tooling . . . There is an anachronism in every stone."[3] From the middle of the nineteenth century — a period known for being one of the most concerned with historical explorations and reconstruction — such a lucid condemnation of any attempted "literal" restoration is quite revealing. Telling, in fact, of an epistemological impasse with which we are still engaged — namely, the fact that writing history is a *present* critical endeavour about *past* events — Palgrave's verdict appears to hold a provocative truth for contemporary historiography.

---

* Reprinted from *Film History* 7 (1995), 277–290, by permission of the author and publisher.

[1] Hollis Frampton, *Circles of Confusion: Film, Photography, Video: Texts 1968–1980* (Rochester, N.Y.: Visual Studies Workshop Press, 1983), 115.

[2] Quoted in Annet Insdorf, "A Silent Classic Gets Some 80s Music," *New York Times*, 6 August 1984.

[3] Francis Polgrave to Dawson Turner, 19 July 1847, in "Biographical memoir," *Collected Historical Works*, ed. R. H. Inglis Palgrave (Cambridge MA: Cambridge U P, 1919–1922), vol. 1, xlv; quoted in David Lowenthal, *The Past is a Foreign Country* (Cambridge: Cambridge UP, 1985), 278.

In the last decade film restoration practices have become objects of scientific and institutional attention, events with dedicated festivals (Los Angeles, Paris, Bologna), and critical issues worthy of historiographical interest. The practice of restoring films, in fact, may effectively challenge the usual and mystifying concept of the history of cinema as a mere succession of movie productions. Whereas, as Raymond Borde described in his seminal account of the history of cinémathèques in the early 1980s, the technological and economic developments of the film industry have constantly caused a parallel and extensive history of legal footage destructions.[4]

In this paper I would like to attempt a critical reading of the heuristics of *film restoration* against the background of current debates in early film historiography. My interest revolves mainly on early cinema for two reasons: rhetorical and (inter)disciplinary. First, although most historical studies attempt to (re)describe and (re)visit the past, at times with the intention of a critique, silent cinema is one of those scholarly domains where the issue of material loss and destruction holds an overt archaeological eloquence.[5] Secondly, early cinema represents a site of competing discourses where film history, encountering a heterogeneous set of historical and critical researches (for example social history, gender and race discourse, urban mass psychology, and so forth) questions its own disciplinary borders, problematizing its method and goals.

---

[4] Raymond Borde, *Les Cinémathèques* (Lausanne: L'Age d'Homme, 1983), 15–27. Borde, curator of the Cinémathèques of Toulouse, showed that film producers, being the only legal possessors of film rights, have cyclically initiated waves of destruction of their ever-growing and dangerous stocks. Constant necessities of storage space, combined with security requirements and difficulties of running primitive formats (such as 17.5 mm or 28 mm) contributed to extensive footage annihilation.

[5] In this sense, I am aware that early cinema could be paired with other archaeological studies of "repressed knowledge," such as matutinal feminist cinema and literature, censored queer artistic production, or unexplored "Third cinema." Yet, the agency of waste or repression of these unrecovered sites are often associated with complex ideological constraints and not directly with adverse decomposing processes, with institutional incurance and fear of anonymous nitrate footage, or even with uncertainties about edited or tinted versions. By no means do I intend to distinguish early cinema studies from other film researches merely on statistics or rhetorics of archival urgency. The rhetorics deployed for lost or "original" versions of some of Orson Welles' films seems a good counterexample. Rather, it seems important to me to observe that early cinema historiography is *naturally* and *necessarily* confronted with institutional languages and practices where terms like "restoration" and "preservation" indicate normal and systematic activities of curators and scholars and not simply incidental operations. One of the historical reasons for such discursive emphasis is connected with the "late" birth of Cinémathèques and Film Libraries in Europe and North America, occurring from the mid-30s.

The recent emphasis on early film spectatorship (G. Bruno, M. Hansen, J. Mayne, but also E. Ewen and R. Rosenzweig) for instance, has encouraged the rise of a methodological arena where different procedures and standards of evidence (such as production charts or film reviews versus ethnic, or gendered public spheres) test standard disciplinary proceedings.[6] I believe that it is in such an arena of different cultural and ideological investments (visual apparatuses, national filmographies, film consumption, modernity) that the supposedly peculiar modalities of historical writing may find their poetic difference from other written discourses (statistical reports, novels, diaries).

If a history of early cinema does not confine itself to a mere computing of (new) titles, credits, and period reviews, but rather attempts wider and more ambitious *cultural restorations*, then fundamental questionings need to be formulated. What is the text-object of a restoration? It is a *past* object? Which kind of language should we use to utter that past? In an epoch that until recently has seemed to widely support a kind of social historical amnesia, what does it mean to write a text that converses with the past, and what sort of conversation could that be?

From Michel Foucault's reading of Nietzsche's genealogy, a particular image emerges as an apt *figuration* of the historian's writing the past: the palimpsest. This multilayered structure implies the loss of aural "original" textualities, but also the horizontal and pluridisciplinary expansion of sources of cultural evidence. Thus, the genealogical modulation of a work of art, that is, its artistic and cultural relevance, results not only from its specific critical accumulation but also from the heterogeneous assembly of its confining textualities.

In this regard, a brief account of the intricate genealogy of Fritz Lang's *Metropolis*, which has been known and studied by critics and scholars in at least half a dozen different versions, illustrates the constitutive multiplicity of the film text. In particular, the exclusion of scene 103 from the American edition in 1927 and Giorgio Moroder's recent restored, reedited, and rescored 1984 version *literally* embody the structure of *Metropolis's* palimpsest, raising the questions of genealogies of cultural appropriations and of contemporary consumption of past "works of art." Both "adaptations," in fact, work as superimposed textualities that have been added in the spirit of a wider popular acceptance.

In the end, within the historiographical questioning of the practice of film restoration, Moroder's *Metropolis* does not represent a carica-

---

[6] Robert Sklar amplifies this question in his "Oh! Althusser! Historiography and the Rise of Cinema Studies," *Radical History Review* 41 (spring 1988): 10–35, now in Sklar and Musser, eds., *Resisting Images, Essays on Cinema and History* (Philadelphia: Temple UP, 1990), 12–35.

tured event in the life of a work of art. The composer in fact did what historians (and Benjaminian book collectors)[7] normally do; he discovered an object from the past and reshelved it into his own cultural library, according to personal visionary capabilities, yet toward a different understanding and appreciation of Lang's text(s).

Restoration, Antiquarians and Don Quixote

The restoration endeavour is essentially aimed at restaging a past context, a premiere version, an authorial uncut rendering, a critics' or an audience's most acclaimed edition.[8] Although restorers and archivists are generally aware of the historical illusions of their philological efforts, the attention displayed to technical *details* (sound score, colour contrasts, speed) and authenticity of *circumstances*, make them somehow resemble typical figures of Western investigation of the past: the antiquarians.

Brilliantly described in the early 1960s by historian Arnaldo Momigliano, antiquarians represent a particular breed of historians.[9] Their

---

[7] "To a book collector, you see, the true freedom of all books is somewhere on his shelves . . . for a collector — and I mean a real collector, a collector as he ought to be — ownership is the most intimate relationship that one can have with objects. Not that they come alive in him; it is he who lives in them." Walter Benjamin, "Unpacking My Library," in *Illuminations*, ed. Hannah Arendt, trans. Harry Zohn (New York: Schocken Books, 1968), 61–69 (66 and 69).

[8] In the problematics of the original version(s), a simple but efficacious taxonomy is offered by Eileen Bowser in her "Some Principles of Film Restoration," *Griffithiana* 38–39 (October 1990), 172–173. For instance, the claim for the "original" may refer to the film as it was conceived by its creator (at times through different decisions), or as it was seen by its audiences (which audiences and when exactly?). An earlier discussion was provided by Raymond Borde in "La Restauration des Films: Problèmes Ethiques," *Archives* 1 (September/October 1986), 1–10. In particular regarding the *Metropolis* case, Borde quite firmly opposed Patalas' virtuous and rigorous effort to unearth an "original version" to Moroder's amoral and irresponsible "electronic massacre."

[9] Momigliano's study on the birth and evolution of the antiquarians explains the rise of erudite research with Thucydides' restriction of historical practice to diplomatics and political thought in the fifth century B.C. From that point on, such different studies as local histories and geographies, family genealogies, urban chronologies, race mythographies, etc. developed outside the 'respectful' historiographical tradition. Their systematic descriptions, combined with a lack of rhetorical proficiency, made the antiquarian erudite research look useless, or worse, dangerously reverent of religious or nationalistic agendas. Arnaldo Momigliano, "The Rise of Antiquarian Research," in *The Classical Foundations of Modern Historiography* (Berkeley: U of California P, 1990), 54–79. Originally this essay was part of the Sather Classical Lectures Momigliano delivered at the University of California at Berkeley in 1961–62. It was also the prosecution of an earlier essay, "Ancient History and the Antiquarian," published in the *Journal of the Warburg and Courtauld Institutes*, 12 (1950) 285–315,

erudite research style has traditionally been ostracized by the dominant paradigms of history writing for its obscure and discordant topics and for its antichronological methods. Essentially, they were accused of being extremely (and mysteriously) interested in secondary facts and *minutiae* without being really interested in history. Nietzsche, in his 1873 *Use and Abuse of History*, also offered a lucid criticism of the pitfalls of what he called the "antiquarian kind of history," as opposed to a more appropriate critical attitude.[10] The typical reverence of the antiquarian, he wrote, is a way to obtain simple emotions of pleasure from the past, but this posture ends up hiding the "drab, rough, even painful circumstances of a nation's or individual's life."[11]

Conversely, within our discussion of the historiographical significations of restoration practices, it seems important to suspect that the mere technical act of restoring a past work of art may be as precise and detailed in method as it is obscure in its ultimate aims. What exactly are restorers and archivists eager to accomplish in their endeavours to return a film to its original form? If the act of writing about the past is in fact an operation which includes an interpretative mise en scène where past documents and events are framed by a present discursivity, restoring the original version of a film cannot be an objective and neutral procedure. Rather, it already constitutes an eclectic historiographical practice which may not acknowledge its present methodological obsessions.

With Michel de Certeau's discourse on the writing of the *other*, one might argue that antiquarians and restorers do not recognize the fundamental distance, break and limit that the past represents for a present understanding.[12] In other words, they may not apprehend the "real" in its twofold dimension:

---

later reprinted in A. Momigliano *Studies in Historiography* (London: The Trinity Press, 1966), 1–39.

[10] Friedrich Nietzsche, *Use and Abuse of History*, trans. Adrian Collins (New York: Macmillan, 1957). This work was conceived shortly after Bismarck's victory over France in a cultural climate that, according to the German philosopher, overemphasized the value of history, paralyzing the spirit of action and interrupting any true development in civilization.

[11] Moreover, he added: "The antiquarian sense of a man, a city, or a nation has always been a very limited field. Many things are not noticed at all; the others are seen in isolation . . . There is no measure: equal importance is given to everything, and therefore too much to anything." Nietzsche, *Use and Abuse of History*, 18–19.

[12] "A structure belonging to modern Western culture can doubtless be seen in this historiography: *intelligibility is established through a relation with the other*; it moves

> the real insofar as it is the known (what the historian studies, understands, or "brings to life" from a past society) and the real insofar as it is entangled within the scientific operations (the present society, to which the historians' problematics, their procedures, modes of comprehension, and finally a practice of meaning are referable).[13]

Like J. L. Borges's fictional character Ireneo Funes,[14] who embodies the ability (and the curse) of a perfect memory of obstinate and useless past details, antiquarians, and film philologists' need to justify the aims of their resurrection of dead voices from the past. In other words, they need to confute the risk of (falsely) pure "rescuings" of remote documents and memories, which feed an ideology of consensual historical heritages preserved in timeless establishments such as museums or archives.

On a different level of restaging the past is the sound allegory of another Borges novella, "Pierre Menard, author of the 'Quixote,'" which I find a fascinating and paroxysmal exploration of what we might call a "circular heterology," the exact rewriting of another text.[15] Borges fashions an hermeneutic mise en scène that embodies the impossibility of the antiquarian gestures — an exact and mummified "quotation" from remote times — while producing expanded discourses and effects in its "uttering the past."

Behind the precise and faithful restoring of Cervantes's novel, Menard's eccentric operation gives birth to an ambiguous and richer textuality. The new complexity of those exact words and paragraphs is the result of four centuries of literary and philosophical debates that have added readings and interpretations to the text, according to the

---

(or 'progresses') by changing what it makes of its 'other' . . . historiography separates its present from a past. But everywhere it repeats the initial act of division. Thus its chronology is composed of 'periods' (for examples, the Middle Ages, modern history, contemporary history) between which, in every instance, is traced the *decision* to become different or no longer to be such as one had been up to that time (the Renaissance, the French Revolution)," Michel de Certeau, *The Writing of History* (New York: Columbia UP, 1988), 3–4.

[13] de Certeau, *The Writing of History*, 35.

[14] Jorge Luis Borges, "Funes the Memorious," trans. E. Irby et al, in Donald A. Yates and James E. Irby, eds. *Labyrinths: Selected Stories & Other Writings*, (New York: New Directions, 1962), 59–66.

[15] Borges, "Pierre Menard, author of the 'Quixote,'" in Yates and Irby, eds., 36–44.

modalities, one might say, of the "history of effects" analyzed by the philosopher and exponent of modern hermaneutics, H. G. Gadamer.[16]

Menard's heroic attempt to *restore* identical lines of words and phrases seemed glorious, contradictory and provocative. It implied both Herculean labour and the instantaneous results of a Duchampian "ready-made." The overcoming of what we called with de Certeau the epistemological impasse of unreenactable past memories, or impossible heterology, is obtained through the paradoxical and literal restaging of the past on to an eloquent facsimile. While reproducing known textualities, Menard's operation plays the cultural circumstances of the present. Menard shows that no innocence is ever restored: the "new" Quixote imperfectly overlaps with the previous ones. The result metaphorically reproduces a *palimpsest.*

Assemblage of Visions: The Historical Palimpsest

Until now we have described the material centrality of film restoration within the "economy" of early cinema studies. Also we have discussed the paradoxical nature of its anachronistic and ideological efforts to "bring back" the past, supposedly *as it was* and *as it will always be.* Borges' paradoxical explorations of the textual relationships between past and present — in particular through Menard's gesture — have also provided provocative insights regarding the genealogical nature of textual memories. Reformulating a question we posed above, we can now ask what does it mean to *find* a text that "belongs" to the past, and what sort of *rescuing* that is.

Recent technological advances have enormously improved the capacity for film preservation and salvation. However, a great deal of the historical evidence that is being unearthed may not necessarily expand scholarly *visionary* capabilities. What counts, in fact, are the contexts where such historiographical rescuings occur. Using Giambattista Vico's attraction for etymologies and Foucault's reading of Nietzsche's geneal-

---

[16] The notion of "history of effects" portrays the historical sedimentation of different layers of interpretations of a given work. Any cultural tradition provides the literary prejudices and categories which govern the work's reading and understanding. For a further discussion, see Hans Georg Gadamer, *Wahrheit und Methode* (Tübingen; J. C. B. Mahr, 1960); English version: *Truth and Method,* trans. Joel Weinsheimer and Donald G. Marshall (New York: Crossroad, 1989), Part II, Chapter II.1B.iv., especially 300–306. Here is the most Gadamerian reference in Borges' "Menard": "To compose the Quixote at the beginning of the seventeenth century was a reasonable undertaking, necessary and perhaps even unavoidable, at the beginning of the twentieth, it is almost impossible. It is not in vain that three hundred years have gone by, filled with exceedingly complex events. Amongst them, to mention only one, is the Quixote itself," Borges, "Pierre Menard . . ." in Yates and Irby, eds., 41–42.

ogy, it seems possible to describe such hermeneutic contexts with the notion of the *palimpsest.*

Palimpsest (from Latin *palimpseston,* and Greek παλιμψηστος) literally means "scraped again," it indicates a parchment or a manuscript where the original writing has been erased or wiped out. The former text, also known as *scriptio anterior,* is often still visible at the margins or among the lines of the new textuality, since the interline is often opportunely redrawn. The most recent interpretation of the phenomenon is economic. Starting in the eighth century, due to lack of paper, 'palimpsests' were created to reproduce important manuscripts at the expense of — as the *Oxford English Dictionary* puts it — "less precious" ones. Beyond the mere material scarcity, issues of cultural selection and memory were obviously at stake.

In this sense, one may argue that the writing of history means a detailed and industrious rewriting on imperfectly erased textualities whose blank (or grey) spaces constitute the other, the void, and the loss that the historian, as modern scribe, constructs and fills with current cultural urgencies. Familiar with this etymology was Michel Foucault who, at the beginning of "Nietzsche, Genealogy, History," wrote its definition:

> 1. Genealogy is gray, meticulous, and patiently documentary. It operates on a field of entangled and confused parchments, on documents that have been scratched over and recopied many times.[17]

Through that multiple assemblage of textualities that is the palimpsest, the concept of restoration (both in its strict semiotic sense, that is referred to a single text, and in its wider cultural expansions) could maintain its heuristics in cinema studies only through a *genealogical perspective.* The conversation with the historical heritage that I previously questioned has to admit that its interlocutor is not a solidified and waxy possession, rather an unstable array of fragments, deviations, and false appraisals printed or scratched on the bodies of the past.[18] Genealogy does not only mean the abandonment of the metaphysical and political myth of origin, but also the discarding of the historicist notion of progress or development in civilization. The historical remembrance is as dynamic and occasional as its objects of attention, movement and change affect its natural functioning. Otherwise, with de Certeau, we

---

[17] Michel Foucault, "Nietzsche, Genealogy, History," in Donald F. Bouchard, ed., *Michel Foucault: Language, Counter-Memory, Practice* (Ithaca, N.Y.: Cornell UP, 1992), 139–164 (139).

[18] "What is found at the historical beginning of things is not the inviolable identity of their origin; it is the dissension of other things. It is disparity," Foucault, "Nietzsche, Genealogy, History," 142.

can say that memory falls into decay when no longer capable of alteration.[19] "Funes the Memorious" offered the definitive exemplum.

As a result, the historiographical acceptance of the genealogical perspective essentially transforms the restoration endeavour from a mere semiotic recovery into a more ambitious cultural rendering. It is in such a methodological expansion that early cinema studies questions its own borders and fundamentally enters into the more general venture of conceptualizing history.

Since a silent film — like any film — can be considered a palimpsest of plurivocal textualities (that include the sum of its dissimilar existing prints and the critical discourses it raised, as well as the "silent" cultural exchanges the film entertained with the social context of its exhibitions) then a mere searching or invention of "perfect" prototypes may end up assessing a philological essentialism. I would argue that such semiotic autocracy is mystifying and antispeculative. It assumes, in fact, that the present has the capacity to read through the opacities of the past, and that such reading out has to be consensual.

The assumption that a text speaks to us in the same way it spoke to earlier spectators relies on an equivalence among what Metz has termed "scopic regimes."[20] Such equivalence has to be demonstrated or refuted, not postulated. Besides, the operation of sorting out continuities and ruptures between the present and the past is hardly a unanimous enterprise; rather it is an interpretative practice which exposes the "visionary" skills of the historian.

To better focus the issue of textual multiplicity within a restoration project and of philological ineptitude in questioning film historical relevance, let us now turn our attention to an emblematic historiographical object, the famous German expressionist work *Metropolis*.

Fritz Lang's *Metropolis* (1926), Fifty Years of Multiple Texts

There are different kinds of restoration, or at least different degrees of historical relevance implied in every restoration project. It seems obvious to argue that restoring Febo Mari's *Il fauno* (1917), or even Hitch-

---

[19] Michel de Certeau, *The Practice of Everyday Life* (Berkeley: U of California P, 1984), 87.

[20] Christian Metz, *The Imaginary Signifier: Psychoanalysis and the Cinema* trans. Celia Britton et al. (Bloomington, Indiana UP, 1981), 61. More recently, art historian Jonathan Crary has quite clearly singled out this methodological tendency in his historical enquiry about traditional constructions of modern vision: "We have been trained to assume that an observer will always leave visible tracks, *that is, will be identifiable in relation to images,*" (emphasis added), Jonathan Crary, *Techniques of the Observer. On Vision and Modernity in the Nineteenth Century* (Cambridge, MA: MIT Press, 1990), 150.

cock's *Downhill* (1927) does not mean to encourage the same critical attention reserved for Gance's *Napoléon* (1927) or for the forthcoming new edition of Murnau's *Faust* (1926). Here I am not trying to argue that some films deserve more attention than other ones; I am only pointing to a typical phenomenon of artistic criticism, to the emergence of "classics" that we also find at work in that critical reinscription constituted by film restoration.[21] The example I would like to examine, in fact, is one of the most famous and influential classics in film history.[22]

The account of *Metropolis's* life is a history of reedited, retitled and shortened versions travelling throughout the world among production inconsistencies, fascist regimes, world wars, and distributors' discontents. This is why, until a decade ago, the number of different versions of *Metropolis* was probably inferior only to the multiple descendants of D. W. Griffith's *Intolerance* (1916), whose long-awaited restored version certainly did not end further discussions and polemics.[23]

Metropolis was first released in Berlin on 10 January 1927, under the Parufamet agreement between Ufa, Paramount-Famous Players-Lasky and MGM. That "first" version was already shorter than the one approved by the Censorship Commission on 13 November 1926, which was 4,189 metres long. In addition, as was a conventional habit for silent films, different "national" versions were prepared for distribution. In particular, the 3,170-metre American edition, shorter by one fourth and with remarkable new re-editings and intertitles, soon influenced German domestic versions, which were then rearranged according to the American revision. This second German edition (third at this point if we also consider the censorship edition) came out in the summer of

---

[21] On the institutional relevance of "film classics" see the *Records of the International Film Symposium, Tokyo,* 1989 whose main topic was "Film in the Context of Twentieth Century Culture — Are There Classics in Film?" (Tokyo: The National Museum of Modern Art, The Film Center, 1991), 51–96.

[22] As in the case of Walther Ruttmann's *Berlin. Die Sinfonie der Grosstadt* (Berlin, Symphony of a Great City, 1927) the influence of *Metropolis* is not confined to Western film translations. For instance, in 1929 Brazilians Adalberto Kemeny and Rodolfo Lustig directed *São Paulo: Sinfonia de uma Metrópole* (São Paulo: Symphony of a Metropolis, 1929) whose film style and production material (posters, slogans, paraphernalia) paid explicit homage to Lang's city film.

[23] For opposite opinions about this reconstruction, one might first see the account by Gillian B. Anderson of the Music Division of the Library of Congress, who played a major role in the reconstruction of Griffith's film "'No Music Until Cue'. The Reconstruction of D. W. Griffith's *Intolerance,*" *Griffithiana* 13, no. 38–39 (October 1990), 158–169. Among the negative criticism, two quite heterogeneous, yet to some extent convergent, contributions, by Russell Merritt and William K. Everson may be singled out. Merritt's "D. W. Griffith's *Intolerance.* Reconstructing an Unobtainable Text," *Film History* 4, no. 4 (1990), 337–375; and William K. Everson, "Intolerance," *Films in Review* 41, nos. 1–2 (1990), 16–20.

1927 with equivalent differences in form and content; it was 3,241 meters long, slightly longer than the American version.[24]

In the following years, neither the first nor the second German editions were satisfactorily preserved. In fact, when in 1936 the Museum of Modern Art bought a copy from Ufa, there were approximately 700 meters missing. The copy at MoMA, with English intertitles, was only 2,530 metres, 640 metres less than the first American release and 1,660 metres less than the German premiere version. It is from copies of this MoMA version, however, that *Metropolis* returned to Europe after the Second World War; initially to the National Film Archive in London and in the 1950s redistributed in Germany with retranslated intertitles. Meanwhile, the quality of the prints suffered heavily due to the numerous duplicate negatives that were made in different archives without any coordinated intention of preservation or reconstruction.

When in the 1960s the Staatliche Filmarchiv of the former German Democratic Republic began a reconstruction of the film, the reference versions used were two: a copy from the Museum of Modern Art and a copy of the American release version that the Staatliche Filmarchiv had acquired in 1945 from the Nazi Film Archive, the Reichsfilmarchiv. This copy was 2,826 metres long, that is 350 metres less than the US distribution edition. Furthermore, it differed from the American versions held by the London National Film Theatre and the Canberra National Film and Sound Archive, which ironically, differed remarkably from one another.

A similar reconstructive endeavour was initiated by the Munich Film Museum a decade later in the spirit of a scientific approximation of the German premiere version. Under the supervision of Museum Director Enno Patalas, the project took advantage of superior documentary resources, and thus won unanimous critical approval. Patalas's attempt was considered successful because he was able to rely on several slightly convergent sources that had just been discovered. They were: (a) the original score by Gottfried Huppertz, which contained an orchestral score, director's cues for the pianist, and instructions for particular arrangements for the synchronization of images and intertitles; (b) detailed censorship cards of the Berlin Film Censorship Office that passed the film for release 13 November 1926; (c) production stills of *Metropolis* that Fritz Lang donated to the Cinémathèque Française in 1959; (d) Thea von Harbou's script recently discovered in Huppertz's estate. As a result, Patalas's version (3,170 metres) lasts a few minutes more than two hours and represents the best philological approxima-

---

[24] For these and the following data, I am indebted to the contributions by Jure Mikuz, Michel Cieutat, Brigitte Cieutat, and Lorenzo Codelli, in *Positif*, no.285 (November 1984), 2–20.

tion in length to the version Ufa was able to show to the Berlin audience on a cold night in early January 1927.

I would now like to discuss two "accidents" to the body of *Metropolis;* one happened in 1927 and another in 1984. The first was the elimination of an entire scene due to the display of a jarring label; the second was the reedited, rescored and retinted version by composer Giorgio Moroder. Both appear to be part of the film's cultural expansion; their study expands the notion of text and problematizes the issue of film recovery.

Cutting Hel(l) and "Morodernizing" *Metropolis.* Truthful Accidents of a Multiple Body-Film[25]

In the existing prints of *Metropolis,* an important gender question was barely raised: if Rotwang, the inventor, creates a robot to replace the workers, why does he make that robot female? The narrative evolution of the story, in fact, appears to easily justify the female features of the robot with its diegetic mission:"To sow discord among the workers and destroy their confidence in Maria," as one of the American intertitles pronounces. Now that new and detailed documentation has become available, the gender identity of the robot requires more satisfactory answers: again and more specifically, what is the reason that propels Rotwang to construct the robot as a female, a choice made *before* Joh's decision to have the robot resemble Maria?

Patalas's fresh forms of evidence, in fact, have shed light on a revealing but missing sub-plot sequence numbered Scene 103, also called "Hel's room."[26] In that scene Rotwang is showing Joh Fredersen an enormous stone monument of his beloved and never-forgotten Hel, Joh's wife who tragically died giving birth to Freder. Unlike Joh, Rotwang was never able to forget her. The "new Hel," as perverse as she is obedient, literally and physically incarnates male fantasies of love, mastery, desire and revenge.[27]

[25] Here I am borrowing and playing with an ironic title used by Brigitte Cieutat in her reactive article "Fritz Lang 'Morodernisé,' ou, L'art du détournement," *Positif,* no 285 (November 1984), 12–14.

[26] For a poetic discussion of this discovery and of its significance see Enno Patalas, "*Metropolis,* Scene 103," trans. Miriam Hansen, *Camera Obscura* 15 (autumn 1986), 165–172.

[27] See Figures 14, 15, 16. Patalas only sets forth a brief discussion of the visual femininity in Metropolis: "The women in *Metropolis* are the projections of male fantasies, authorized by Rotwang, Fredersen, and Lang — the spectator in front of the screen recognizes himself among the spectators on the screen . . . Hel prefigures the new, artificial woman as her double. She would not merely be 'born for him,' she would be born 'of him' — daughter and lover in one," Patalas, Scene 103, 170–171. He then refers to other contributions, such as Roger Dadoun ("*Metropolis:* Mother City —

What matters here is not how Enno Patalas was able to reconstruct the scene from the new materials he could rely on, but why that scene, among others, was cut for the American release in 1927. Randolph Bartlett in an article published in the *New York Times* on 13 March 1927[28] explained the footage reduction of the German version by saying that the American audience needed more dramatic cogency and verisimilitude. In particular, Scene 103, literally translated "Hel's Room," was cut because the name Hel, inscribed on the base of her huge stone monument, had in English an unnecessary and misleading infernal connotation; its dominant visual centrality made it impossible to erase it or translate it, so the scene was to be cut.

Patalas comments on this exclusion by arguing that it was not simply the avoidance of a funny joke in the midst of a dramatic *momentum*, but that a gesture of moral and cultural censorship was also at work, aimed at avoiding any overt exposition of sadistic anxiety. This restrictive operation, together with numerous narrative condensations, effectively changed the poetic textural balance of the film. It was still *Metropolis*, but is was no more a "certain" *Metropolis*. Like Menard's rewriting of *Don Quixote*, the American version became another text, this time both philologically and culturally, fuelled by an interpretative apparatus which *literally* changed the body of the film.

At this point, if we ask what is the sense of a project of restoring *Metropolis*, we might respond that the technical recovery of its *original* edition has to make clear that such "originality" or "authenticity'" is not *Metropolis's* supertemporal essence. Rather, it is simply the semiotic verisimilitude of one of its German prints. I am sure that Patalas has specified his goal and the limits of his enterprise several times; I am not sure historians clearly acknowledge the lucid historiographical partiality of his initiative. Thus, I would argue that "restoring *Metropolis*" means to establish complex and plurivocal transactions between the film text(s) and the cultural sites of their historical production and consumption. Once more, I would like to stress that it is in such restagings of cultural and historical assemblages that film studies questions its specificity and encounters wider disciplinary references of historical study and intelligibility.

'Mittler' — Hitler," trans. Arthur Goldhammer, *Camera Obscura* 15 (autumn 1986), 137–163), and Andreas Huyssen, "The Vamp and the Machine: Technology and Sexuality in Fritz Lang's *Metropolis*," reprinted in Part Three of this volume.

[28] See the reprint of this article in Part One of this volume.

The second "accident" is constituted by the provocative operation of cultural reinvention performed by Giorgio Moroder in 1984. First of all, Moroder's version is an edition conceived for a commercial market and is thus indifferent to concerns of scientific coherence or philological adherence. Moroder partly owed his *Metropolis* reedition to Patalas' archival work[29] and partly took personal artistic initiative in the treatment of the film form. Not only did he replace the original score by Gottfried Huppertz with a contemporary pop soundtrack, he also edited several sequences on the basis of a "new" rhythmical (thus narrative) path, adding colors on the basis of typical silent movies principles (blue for night, red for dreams or fire sequences, etc.)[30] Finally, he replaced the stylized intertitles with subtitles better accepted by a modern audience. The result: eighty-two minutes of expressionistic and aural footage with an easy-listening soundtrack. Despite the initial prohibition of distribution in Germany, the film was widely appreciated internationally and became a success.

What I think is important for our discourse is not simply that we declare once more the loss of aura of the work of art in a postindustrial society, thus to accept Moroder's appropriation as a progressive (and fortunately unique) gesture. Although several discussions seem to repropose old categories,[31] other questions should be posed if early cinema wants to confront its process of revisiting the past and the actuality of its own motivations. Like the colourization of classics[32] or the irreverent recycling of found footage,[33] at stake is the discursive space of the *historical distance* that make us contradictorily protest the panning and scanning of *Lawrence of Arabia* on TV without raising any opposition to the current judgement of Phidias' decolourized sculptures of the Parthenon as fascinating "white" masterpieces.

---

[29] Patalas appears in the credits as "creative consultant," a homage by Moroder more than a real collaboration as Patalas explained to Lorenzo Codelli, "Entretien avec Enno Patalas," *Positif*, no. 285 (November 1984), 16–17.

[30] As a model for their reconstructions, both Patalas and Moroder employed the Canberra print, the only one that retained remnants of colours.

[31] For instance, Brigitte Cieutat vividly protests, claiming a "moral inalienable right" of the author. "N'est-ce pas faire bien peu de cas du droit moral, pourtant inaliénable, de l'auteur à la pérennité à l'intégrité de son oeuvre?" Cieutat, "Fritz Lang 'Morodernisé,'" 12.

[32] On the cultural problems of colourization, see the interesting article by Charles R. Acland, "Tampering with the Inventory: Colourization and Popular Histories," *Wide Angle* 12, no.2 (April 1990), 12–20.

[33] On this subject see William C. Wees, *Recycled Images. The Art and Politics of Found Footage Films* (New York: Anthology Film Archives, 1993).

If Scene 103 has taught us the historiographical relevance of geographical and cultural differences in the study of the critical expansions of a work of art, the "re-edited and rock-video'd torso" of *Metropolis*, as Thomas Elsaesser perspicaciously calls it,[34] irreverently questions the tension between authorship or past cultural heritage and contemporary popular culture.

I would like to read Moroder's commercial reinvention as an historiographical operation, not only aimed at showing, but also significantly affecting Lang's film. The composer, in fact, seems to treat *Metropolis* (1926) as found footage, and, by rearranging it into a re-scored series of recycled images, creates a new textuality, *Metropolis* (1984). It might not be the case to argue for an avant-gardish Brechtian estrangement, but surely the contrast between the old footage and the soundtrack draws attention to the bod(ies) of the film itself and the film's own constitution as image in the best tradition of the "recycled images" film style.

Despite the "philological murders," the Italian composer resurrects Lang's body-film into a live *quotation* of the past, and by embodying and juxtaposing different contexts of image-producing industries, displays an historical discontinuity that no *Napoléon* (1927) or *Intolerance* (1916), with their classic orchestral score, could ever achieve. Moroder quotes Lang by literally *interrupting* the narrative context of the German colossus, and creates a shorter but richer palimpsest where heterogeneous textualities (silent and electronic), being shaped together into a video-clip montage, display the historical construction of vision.[35]

Historiography and *Metropolis* Palimpsest

Lang's superproduction has been extremely influential in the history of international cinema for its expressionist film style, and its Golem-scientist Rotwang was soon developed by Universal horror productions and later by innumerable science-fiction master narratives. In Germany, once granted its utopian stylistic innovations, the psychological and ideological mirrorings of the film were denounced as rather contingent and opportunistic. Socially engaged in its idealistic reconciliation of labour and capital, Lang's film was at times described as a stylized par-

---

[34] Thomas Elaesser, "Innocence Restored," *Monthly Film Bulletin* (London) 51, no 611 (December 1984), 366. See the revised version, included in Part Two of this volume.

[35] It is important to recall here Walter Benjamin's observation referring to Brecht's epic theater: "Interruption is one of the fundamental methods of all form-giving. It reaches far beyond the domain of art. It is, to mention just one of its aspects, the origin of the quotation. Quoting a text implies interrupting its context." "What is Epic Theatre?" [Second Version], in *Understanding Brecht*, trans. Anna Bostock (London: Verso, 1983), 19. For this quotation I am indebted to Wees, *Recycled Images*, 53.

able on human solidarity in an epoch of modern and technological alienation.

However, from the very beginning, critical divergences were also connected to the heterogeneous diffusion of different prints. Regretfully and with sarcasm Paul Rotha wrote:

> Of *Metropolis*, more wilful abuse has been written than praise, partly because the version shown in Britain was unhappily edited, many sequences being deliberately removed. The British copy was "arranged" by Channing Pollock, author of *The Fool*. The film, when it made its London appearance, was not enthusiastically received. H. G. Wells, amongst others, damned it as "quite the silliest film . . . . " As a matter of fact, *Metropolis* was very remarkable, based on a brilliant filmic conception. Had it been shown in its entirety, it might have afforded a wonderful exposition of cinematography.[36]

Here I am not concerned with the "silent" restored copy that is now available for scholarly study. My interest in the issue of "film restoration," in fact, needs neither a scientifically restored film, nor a restored film at all. What has happened to *Metropolis* in its internationally commercial or archival distribution is not a series of isolated accidents for a silent movie. Early cinema studies, perhaps more consistently than other areas of film studies, often encounters the material ephemerality and vicissitudes of exhibition of its objects of study. It is a common situation, for instance, that fundamental titles of national filmographies or international "classics" have been seen, when available, in very different versions, including "suggestive" fragmented editions.

Metropolis has been no exception. The film's commercial and critical history is somehow the story of its different prints. Lang's work is a *palimpsest* of multiple textualities whose editing, tinting or toning, and sound differences are not to be considered betrayals of a (non)existent original. Patalas's "Scene 103" does not distinguish between a good and bad version. As I wrote above, if early cinema studies not only measures the lengths of opening night versions, but attempts to account for the effectual impact of its textualities, then divergences and shortcomings in montage, colour, or score constitute the positive ways through which to study how and to what extent a work has been differently consumed and appropriated.

Conversely, the result of Moroder's re-vision is not simply an "easier" experience for an untrained and exploitable audience, but an *inevitable new textuality*. Michel de Certeau would probably argue that *Metropolis* (1984), as an artistic reenactment or as an historiographical

---

[36] Paul Rotha, *The Film Till Now. A Survey of World Cinema* (New York: Funk & Wagnalls Company, 1930), 274–275.

operation, constitutes a *narrativization* of *Metropolis* (1926). In this respect, quite significantly some critics have written that the new videoclip editing style of Moroder's version, while emphasizing the autonomy and separateness of the episodes, deconstructs and reconstructs the visual pace of the film and catalyses its graphic matches and its figurative cut-ins.[37]

A Few Observations

Within an analysis of the historiographical heuristics of film restoration, Fritz Lang's *Metropolis* has resulted in an emblematic text. The dissemination of its different prints and the chronicle of its different critical receptions has shown that the only text to be restored by film studies is not simply a virginal nitrate edition, but rather a "history of effects." In this sense, *Metropolis'* "genealogy" is the history of a palimpsest, where different spectators have scratched their discursive effusions or their violent rejections. At issue is the contention that there is no stable heritage to preserve. Instead, a real critique might be performed through the maintenance of the dispersion of accidents, errors, deviations or faulty calculations that have determined the film's historical reception.

Thanks to Moroder's "quotation" and with Foucault's insights, we may say that as a critical object of discourse and, perhaps, even chemically, the body-film of *Metropolis* "manifests the stigmata of past experience and also gives rise to desires, failings, and errors . . . . [For *Metropolis,*] genealogy, as an analysis of descent, is thus situated within the articulation of the body and history. Its task is to expose a body totally imprinted by history and the process of history's destruction of the body."[38]

What can we restore, then, when we restore a film? Although I have not tried here to provide definitive answers, but simply to engage an institutional activity within wider historiographical concerns, I believe that through the problem of film restoration early cinema studies is, once more, called to follow interdisciplinary trajectories of historical

---

[37] In this sense, Elsaesser's comments are particularly eloquent: "the element of abstraction, of ornament, in Lang's mise en scène (for which he was duly taken to task by Kracauer) now communicates some of the vitality that Modernist forms once possessed . . . this is what Moroder's music is able to pick up; the correlation of visual composition and syncopated sound, and the translation of editing effects into rock harmonies, as in the opening scene when the music works with uncanny precision towards the climax of the steam whistle blowing to announce the end of the shift," Elsaesser, "Innocence Restored," 366. See also the revised version of Elsaesser's essay in Part Two of this volume.

[38] Foucault, "Nietzsche, Genealogy, History," 148 (insert added).

investigations. When we ask which is the most original and authentic version of *Metropolis,* we ask a philological question and a cultural question. The former deals with issues of authorship, production circumstances, and textual evidence. The latter with transactions between film poetics and the cultural density of contingent historical receptions.

For these reasons, we shall not dismiss Moroder's commercial experiment as an irreverent, disrespectful exploitation, but rather as a model for an *archeological* approach which maintains a distance from the past, and treats its documents as "discovered objects." Like a found-footage filmmaker who by recycling old images calls attention to them as images, as products of an intricate mosaic of information, entertainment, and visuality, the historian-collector I am imagining sees the freedom of past fragments in the shelves of his mind and in the archival vaults of his infinite *palimpsest*. An historian like this can only be a language, that is a *space* of writing and *place* of seeing.

Acknowledgement: I would like to thank Robert Sklar, Paul Sellors, and Valerie Walsh for their precious comments. This is for Ingalisa Schrobsdorff, with wonder.

Part Three

Classic Texts and Context

Structures of Narrativity in Fritz Lang's *Metropolis*

*Alan Williams**

THIS STUDY WILL ATTEMPT a narrative analysis of Fritz Lang's *Metropolis* using concepts developed by A. G. Greimas, particularly those of his "Eléments d'une grammaire narrative."[1] Greimas's system of analysis posits three fundamentally distinct levels in any text: a "deep" structure of meaning (similar to Levi-Strauss's notion in myth analysis but based on a dynamic model of generation rather than a static set of paradigms), an anthropomorphic level (shifts generated by the model become "actions" performed by "characters"), and finally the level of inscription in which the narrative is presented in whatever matter of expression chosen (in this case the filmic text as "read"). Rather than explain in detail Greimas's theory and then proceed to Lang, we will begin the analysis of *Metropolis*, introducing theoretical points as they become relevant. To this end we will begin with a preliminary "reading" of the film in Greimasian terms (primarily at the "anthropomorphic" level), then proceed to an attempt at formalization of the narrative structure (the "deep" level), and finally place the text in other systems of discourse, the "texts" of culture and ideology (using mainly the level of the inscription).

Metropolis begins with a segment (a self-contained bit of expression read as a separate unit) that appears totally expository although it has a definite function in the narrative. Greimas points out, after Propp, that all narratives must begin with a *manque*, a lack of some sort. In many of Perrault's fairy tales this is a lack of food; in the Russian folk-tales analyzed by Propp it is the kidnapping of the king's daughter. Lang's film begins with a depiction of the totally alienated condition of the workers, their lack of control or even contact with their own conditions of existence. This lack marks the workers as the film's first "subject" or hero (as a collective unit), although their function as actant, as performer of a set of operations, changes in the course of the film, as we will see. (The lack posited by Greimas is, of course, similar to the "problem" considered as the root of narrative in texts on the short story or on scriptwriting. Greimas's notion has the advantage, however, of being more concrete from the point of view of analysis and comparison, if not of story writing. It is easier to compare the lack of two specific

---

* Reprinted from *Film Quarterly* 27, no.4 (summer 1974), 17–24 by permission of the author and publisher.

[1] In *Du Sens* (Paris: Le Seuil, 1970).

objects than to compare two problems defined in different terms, giving a greater power of critical generalization.)

One of the other major devices of all narrative is also introduced in this first segment, but in a non-operative manner: the film is divided into various "spaces," making possible various transfers or disjunctions. The workers are seen descending from the machine rooms to their homes, using the giant elevators which form part of one of the film's ruling oppositions, movement by machine/self-movement, one aspect of the central opposition Machine/Human in the film's structure of meaning.

This notion of space is central to the most daring aspect of Greimas's theories of narrative, his definition of all narrative events as some sort of real or attempted *transfer* of an *object,* accompanied by or implying a spatial discontinuity. By this criterion the first narrative function in *Metropolis* occurs in the film's second autonomous segment. Maria, as "subject," takes the group of children (the object of value) from the worker city to the "pleasure garden" on the upper level. She is forced to leave, and the unit of narrative (and the segment) is ended by the failure of this attempted transfer. This narrative unit, isolated though it seems, does not remain unconnected with the narrative as a whole, by its creation of another hero, Freder, and its anticipation of the penultimate transfer of an object in the film which is the return of the children to the upper level (again to the "pleasure garden") by Maria, assisted by Freder and Josaphat.

This second segment of the film also introduces a second lack, this time individual rather than collective. This *manque* produces Freder as a "hero" of the narrative, for he discovers his lack of *knowledge* of the workers, which institutes the next portion of the narrative in which he descends to the machine rooms to observe the workers and witnesses the accident at the central power room. This constitutes, however, only the first stage of his acquisition of the knowledge which will enable him to act as a hero or subject in the film. The end of this portion of the narrative (and the third autonomous segment of the film) is indicated by his leaving the space of conflict, the machine rooms, to return to the upper levels with his (still incomplete) knowledge.

When Freder returns to the upper city, the residence of the ruling class, he attempts to give his father, Joh Fredersen, his understanding of the workers' condition. Fredersen at this point is simultaneously the intended destination of the object of value, knowledge, and anti-subject (traitor) who prevents its transmission. With the introduction of Fredersen at this point the narrative must be interpreted simultaneously on two levels, for as an actant Fredersen is the "subject" of another "story," in which the object of desire is the control (later the elimination) of the workers. For the discovery of the maps in the dead workers' clothing reveals another lack, similar to Freder's: the ruler of Metropolis lacks knowledge of the meaning of the maps, of the workers' intentions. From this point until the segment of the film in the catacombs the objects of desire sought by both father and son will be types of knowledge, which will enable them to function as hero and traitor in the decisive later stages of the narrative. In each case the knowledge will be acquired in stages. Thus, following the interview in Fredersen's office, Freder re-descends to the machines and Fredersen goes to the inventor Rotwang's house, each in search of more adequate knowledge. At the level of expression the film emphasizes this similarity by the use of parallel editing.

Their acquisition of knowledge, this stage of which is delineated by the spaces in which both hero and traitors remain, brings them both closer to the full knowledge necessary to the power to act. Freder discovers the gruelling effects of time and repeated effort by taking charge of a machine deserted by a failing worker. Fredersen is shown the Robot by Rotwang, who also partially deciphers the mystery of the maps, which are revealed to be guides to the catacombs below the worker city. Again parallels are established expressively between these acquisitions of knowledge by intercutting.

In the first segment in the catacombs (which we would number as seventh segment of the film) the acquisition of knowledge for both sides is complete. Freder, his father, and Rotwang observe Maria speaking to the workers. The initial lacks of knowledge are eliminated, but reveal in each case another lack: Fredersen discovers that he lacks control over the workers and Freder discovers his responsibility as "mediator." The new object of desire for both Freder and his father (through Rotwang) will be Maria, although she is desired by both as a means of obtaining another object, the workers, for their elimination (father) or liberation (son). Although Maria is still a subject or hero in the film, at this point she also becomes an object of desire.

The next narrative function in the film is the abduction of Maria by Rotwang from the catacombs to his house — a typical narrative transfer complete with spatial discontinuity. In the implied confrontation in the inventor's house between Freder and Rotwang (in the segment which follows) the latter triumphs by using machinery, which serves as helping agent to the traitors throughout the film. Freder is thus denied access to Maria whose features are transferred, quite literally, to the Robot. This is done in order to deceive Freder and the workers, that is, to transmit to them a *false knowledge*. The deception of Freder, in his father's office, removes his power to act. The function of the acquisition of knowledge in narrative is the creation of an ability to act, a *power.* Transmission of false knowledge is the classic means of neutralizing this power.

The individual deception of Freder is followed by the collective deception of the workers in the catacombs; this deception does not merely neutralize their power but converts them temporarily into traitors, allies of Fredersen and Rotwang. The Robot, contrary to the real Maria, convinces the workers to act by violence for themselves, not peacefully through others, a frequent distinction made in Western narratives between traitor and hero. The children left behind in the lower city will assume the workers' actantial function as hero, as metonymic representatives of the proletariat. In these deceptions, the Robot, though a machine, is an actant and fills the role of anti-subject or traitor.

The deception of the workers, however, is followed by the restoration of Freder's power to act, by his acquisition of the knowledge that the Robot is not Maria. The workers, as traitor, subdue him. Their object, the destruction of the machines, entails the destruction of their own children, who are the final object of value in the narration. The restoration of power to the heroes continues as Maria achieves her release from Rotwang's house and prevents the destruction of the children by moving them to the upper city with the help of Freder and Josaphat. The restoration of power to Freder and Maria is followed by the undeceiving of the workers and their return to the status of hero. The knowledge given them by the foreman of the powerhouse frees them from the traitors' domination. With this new status they seize and destroy the Robot, who becomes simultaneously anti-subject and object, as Maria was previously subject and object.

The second abduction of Maria by Rotwang creates one final lack to be dealt with by the hero Freder who by killing Rotwang eliminates the last of the traitors — Joh Fredersen being transformed from traitor to hero by his son's actions. It is Freder's having saved the children which saves his father from being killed by the workers. At the end of the film, therefore, the lacks (of the subjects, not the anti-subjects) are removed, the traitors destroyed, and the imbalance which set the narrative in motion eliminated.

We should add parenthetically that some of the problems raised by the narrative structure of *Metropolis* stem from the fact that much of the original version of the film is missing from the copies currently available.[2] Nonetheless the film as it exists has coherence and has been "read" easily enough by its audiences; thus our analysis has taken as its point of departure the text as we have it and not as it "should have been." In any case there is ample evidence that the original version has most of the inconsistencies which trouble the film in its current state.

Despite the apparent complexity of our preliminary reading, *Metropolis* does not have an inordinately complicated narrative design. The major difficulties of analysis come from the division of the functions of hero and traitor among six principal actants, with two of these switching function in the course of the film. The heroes appear in what we have considered the film's first two autonomous segments: the workers, Freder, and Maria. The traitors appear in segments five and six (in the office and Rotwang's house): Joh Fredersen, Rotwang, and the Robot. The distribution of actants and also their order of first appearance in the text is thus symmetrical — Fredersen and the workers will at times be both subject (anti-subject) and object, and Freder and Rotwang will function unambiguously as hero and traitor. This tripling of hero and traitor is maintained through a tripartite division of objects of value: the knowledge of the proletariat, the use of Maria, and finally the children of the workers, who metonymically represent the proletariat as social entity. These three objects function in the classic order of Western narratives: knowledge, power, action.

The final simplicity of the narrative structure of *Metropolis* comes principally from the central position (functionally and diegetically) of the abduction and release of Maria. It is as if the other major portions of the film's narrative structure had been grafted onto this double transfer, without which the story cannot function. The position of Maria as object follows the classic double transfer of Propp's tales (see his *Morphology of the Folktale,* The Hague: Mouton, 1968). The traitor abducts a woman, takes her to his own space, from which she is delivered by the hero and restored to the space of society (the hero who delivers Maria in *Metropolis* being Maria herself).

Propp, however, by retaining this series of events as fixed, produced a model only applicable to the specific body of texts which he studied. Greimas adopts a mathematical-logical model with a greater power of generalization, accounting for the Russian tales *and* other possible narratives. Based on a model originally developed for a theory of semantics,[3] it posits an "elementary structure of meaning" which may be schematized as follows:

---

[2] [Editors' note: this refers to the situation in 1974. See Bachmann, Bartlett, Patalas, Bertellini in this volume for the contemporary textual situation.]

[3] In *Sémantique structurale* (Paris: Larousse, 1966).

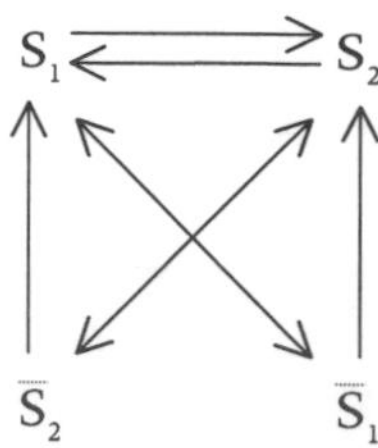

In this diagram ⇆ indicates a relationship of contrareity, ↔ a relation of contradiction, and → a relation of presupposition. In the structure of meaning constructed to account for the distinction Good/Evil, for example, S_1 = good, $\bar{S}_1$ = non-good, S_2 = evil, $\bar{S}_2$ = non-evil. The semantic aspects of this model will serve us here only as a point of departure. For Propp and for *Metropolis* what counts is the application of this model to narrativity.

If we take S_1 as the hero (subject) of a narrative and S_2 as the traitor (anti-subject) and consider that the object of value circulates in a structure of meaning defined by these terms, the object transfer of Maria, like the transfer of the king's daughter in the Russian tale, may be reduced to the following equation of: $F(S_1 \rightarrow O \rightarrow S_1) \rightarrow F(S_1 \rightarrow S_2)$, then $F(S_2 \rightarrow O \rightarrow S_2) \rightarrow F(S_2 \rightarrow O \rightarrow S_1)$. That is, Maria, originally in the space of society (S_1), is kidnapped by Rotwang ($\bar{S}_1$) and taken to the space of the traitors (S_2), the inventor's house. From this space ($\bar{S}_2$) the subject Maria takes the object Maria ($\bar{S}_1$) and returns to the space of society and the heroes (S_1).

One might reasonably demand at this point what purpose is served by this elaborate procedure; in a very real sense it "explains" nothing whatever. The object (of value, we might add) of the semiotic endeavor is not explanation, of course, but *description*, precise description with as high as possible a power of generalization. (Even highly refined sciences such as physics or biochemistry "explain" little, but rather provide more and more adequate models to describe particular objects). This description makes possible comparison and hierarchization of objects and processes studied. Greimas's model is thus superior to Propp's and to other descriptions of narrativity in that it is applicable to a greater body of texts and permits, for example, a comparison between narrative sequences within a particular text and between texts of different origins. Mathematically it may also be considered superior by the principle of elegance, for fewer and simpler terms are used to describe the same object.

These considerations lead us back to *Metropolis*. For using Greimas's model we may describe a curious feature of Lang's film. The circulation of Maria as object is accompanied and paralleled by that of the Robot, which moves as follows: $F (S_2 \rightarrow O \rightarrow \overline{S}_2) \rightarrow F (\overline{S}_2 \rightarrow 0 \rightarrow S_1)$, then $F (S_1 \rightarrow O \rightarrow \overline{S}_1) \rightarrow F (\overline{S}_1 \rightarrow O \rightarrow S_2)$. That is, the robot (a machine, S_2) is made to appear human ($\overline{S}_2$) and transferred to the space of society (S_1). The workers, discovering their deception, seize the robot and burn it ($\overline{S}_1$) whereupon it turns back into a machine (S_2).

One may easily see that the transfer of the robot is negatively symmetrical to that of Maria, that is, its starting point is shifted 180°. The transfer depends totally on the important opposition between being and seeming, *être* and *paraître*; a frequent distinction between hero and traitor in Western narrative is the latter's use of *deceit*. Because of this deceit, this non-conformity between being and seeming, the transfer of the Robot to the space of the workers is as "violent" an action as the abduction of the real Maria.

The transfer of the children to the upper city at the end of the film would appear at first consideration not to have the circular nature of the first transfer of the children as object in a structure of meaning in which the terms are lack and alienation and plenitude and control. In the transfer which opens the film they are taken by Maria from the worker city, characterized by non-plenitude, to the "pleasure garden" but are forced to return, giving the inverse of the double structure characteristic of the circular and stable narrative common to the Russian folktales. The alienated status of the proletariat, whom the children represent by metonymy, is affirmed. At the film's end, the children remain on the upper level, in the "pleasure garden." Yet their status is ambiguous, and their position at the close of the film gives *Metropolis* its subtle yet profoundly reactionary orientation. For although the children seem to remain in the state of plenitude they will, as a result of the accord reached between ruling class and workers, return yet again to their original space. The result of the narrative is only a relativization of its value system, its basic oppositions, which remain unchanged. Thus the film affirms the social structure presented at its beginning. The troubling experience created by Lang's film is thus in part explicable: what appears to be socially radical in the film's overt content is negated by the deeper structure set up by its circulation of values. The reactionary narrative is often one characterized by circularity, whereas more "revolutionary" stories, such as those of Perrault (compare "Little Tom Thumb," for example, with any of the Grimm tales), terminate with the objects of value in different positions in the structures of meaning implicit in the narrative.

The oppositions established between heroes and traitors in *Metropolis,* however, do not exist in an ideological vacuum. Lang's film is a profoundly mythic text, inscribing itself in several streams of cultural discourse. We will examine here two cultural contexts of the film and also its possible insertion into the psychoanalytic system of discourse. We might divide the cultural contexts of the film into two groups dealing with political and scientific distinctions on the axis human/mechanical and with cultural and religious distinctions on the axis Christian/mystical-alchemical, both groups being parallel to the division of actants in the text into heroes and traitors.

The montage which opens the film gives an exposition of the complex of meanings which we can label "mechanical." At the most evident level of meaning this is clear from the denotative content of the shots, most of which depict parts of stylized machines. The motion of these machines is of two sorts, circular and back-and-forth, which are like two themes structuring the montage. The heavily rhythmic element introduced by the lateral motion and the circularity of the turning wheels prepare the introduction in the montage of a clock face, its shape duplicating the circular composition of many of the preceding shots and the rhythmic jerking of its hands echoing the others. The montage concludes with a shot of a whistle blowing; a title identifies "The Day Shift" which is seen in the next shot entering the elevators to descend to the worker city. It is not merely machinery which is identified with the traitors and which oppresses the workers — it is also the concept of *time,* the necessary base of the cluster of meanings which we have designated as "mechanical." Time is the measure of the repetitive effort required of the proletariat. On the other hand the "pleasure garden" in which Freder initially plays with the dark-haired girl (as opposed to Maria's lightness) is characterized precisely by being out of time, as well as removed from all types of machinery.

The opposition between the mechanical and the human is present also in the nature of the film's protagonists. Of the three principal traitors in *Metropolis,* only Joh Fredersen, who will be transformed into a hero at the film's end, is wholly human. The robot is, obviously, a machine, but Rotwang is also in part, having lost his right hand and replaced it with a mechanical one during the robot's construction. Thus the inventor is an embodiment of this central tension: he is half human and half machine, on the metonymic level of the hands. It is, significantly, his right, mechanical hand which Fredersen shakes after first seeing the robot in action. Shortly afterward, Fredersen also shakes the robot's hand; his transformation to hero will be signalled at the end of the film by his shaking for the first time a fully human hand, that of the foreman.

This master opposition is also present in a less consistent manner in methods of transportation depicted in the film. When the workers, oppressed by the ruling class, go to and from work they use the elevators, helping agents for the traitors, whereas when they descend to the catacombs to hear Maria they do so on foot. When the workers go as traitor to destroy the machines, their position as actant is underlined by their use of the elevators — the very sort of machinery which they wish to eliminate. Freder, Maria, and Josaphat take the children to the upper levels by purely "human" effort. These oppositions inscribe themselves in an almost Marxist discourse; they therefore contribute to the paradoxical nature of the film. The deep narrative structure, which we can justly characterize as reactionary, belies the contexts into which the production of this meaning is inserted.

A second sort of discourse alluded to in *Metropolis* is of a religious dimension. This is most evident in the names of the protagonists, Joh Fredersen ("John" in the English titles does not suggest "Jehova" as well as the German), Maria, Josaphat (Joseph in the American version), and Freder, who is most often referred to simply as "the son" or "Joh Fredersen's son." (Josaphat, we might add, has a less important role than Maria, the Father, and the Son, as befits the Western religious tradition.)

But there is a consistent opposition present between the vague Christianity present in so much of the film and another tradition, mystical and alchemical, most evident in the connotations produced by the presentation of Rotwang. He is portrayed as a sort of medieval sorcerer (and his robot will be burned like a witch); compared to the archetypically Aryan appearances of Freder and Maria the inventor looks distinctly Semitic. On his door and above the robot in his laboratory is a five-pointed star. He lives alone apart from the rest of society. His "science" is occult and solitary.

The opposing, Christian tradition is most apparent in Maria and Freder. The latter, working at the curious circular machine during his second visit to the machine rooms, is quite clearly crucified on the hands of the clock face which appears behind the controls. Maria is clearly and uncomplicatedly associated with Christian teachings. In the catacombs, when she relates the tale of the Tower of Babel there emerges a curious juxtaposition of the Christian and mystic elements opposed in the text. Maria stands in front of numerous crucifixes, viewed reverently from below by the workers. As the shots appear which illustrate her story (differentiated from surrounding shots by a circular masking) it is apparent that the builders of the tower are visually and verbally equated with the tradition represented by Rotwang, that of the arrogant and occult "scholar." Even the clothing worn by the planners of the tower is similar to that of the inventor.

There is also a third manner in which the text, though less directly this time, may be viewed as inserting itself into larger contexts, into an "intertextual space." This aspect of *Metropolis* is composed of structures analyzable in psychoanalytic terms. We will mention here only Oedipal aspects of the film and the presence of elements suggesting a sort of "death wish." Through the cultural and political grids we have referred to above a three-membered "family" is created. Fredersen, as leader of society and as a "Jehova" figure, becomes the Father. Freder, as the ruler's son, as representative of the workers, and as Christ, is the Son. Finally Maria, in her religious context and as spiritual creator of Freder and the workers — for it is she who reveals to them their respective *manques,* creating them as individual consciousnesses — is the Mother. Freder, to negate and assume the power of the Father, must have access to the Mother — which is precisely what is prevented by the abduction of Maria. He will see the robot in Maria's image in the hands of his father, which of course produces his lack of power (castration). Thus the film portrays an individual and collective, Oedipal and primal revolt against the Father, for Maria is also Mother to the masses. The father is retained at the end of the film only in a partially castrated form (he *kneels* on the ground while his son fights Rotwang). That Fredersen is not killed outright, but merely stripped of some of his power which is transmitted only to the Son and not to the workers indicates the repressed, compromised nature of the Oedipal conflict in *Metropolis.*

But the film, and indeed most of Lang's work, lends itself also to an analysis in terms of life and death instincts. The preservation of culture itself is at stake in the prevention of Fredersen's projected destruction of the workers. There is a persistent identification in the film of the machines and hence the traitors with death, both of the individual and of the structure of society. This is further identified with the pagan/mystic tradition, as when Freder sees the accident in the central power room as a sacrifice to the god Moloch. In a curious way this death tendency is portrayed as belonging to nature as opposed to culture (this of course is perfectly consistent with Freud's thought). Thus when the central powerhouse is destroyed, it is the released *water* which threatens to kill the children. Culture is always dangerously near a breakdown under the forces of nature. The maintenance of culture is the responsibility of the heroes. In most of Lang's work, particularly in his German silent period, there exist powerful forces for the end of culture, individuals whose goal is total destruction: Mabuse in *Dr. Mabuse the Gambler* or Haghi in *Spione* are perhaps the clearest examples.

Whether one wishes to consider these cultural and psychoanalytic contexts of the inscription of narrativity in *Metropolis* as primary or secondary as compared to "deeper" structures of the text depends purely on the perspective chosen for the analysis. In this study we have attempted to give more or less equal weight to the various levels of elaboration posited by Greimas. At the "deepest" level are the elementary structures of meaning which, anthropomorphized, produce the notions of "actions" and "characters" which with insertion into larger contexts are elaborated into the immediately accessible narration. In this analysis we have stopped short of considering the nature of the inscription of the film itself, how the text produces meaning from moment to moment: codes of lighting or representation of actions, the function of titles, methods of editing and composition, etc. This would be another aspect of the study of the text and an extremely interesting one. Hopefully, however, through this limited work on the profoundly resonant text of *Metropolis* we have suggested some of the levels of structuration involved in the analysis of the production of meaning through narration.

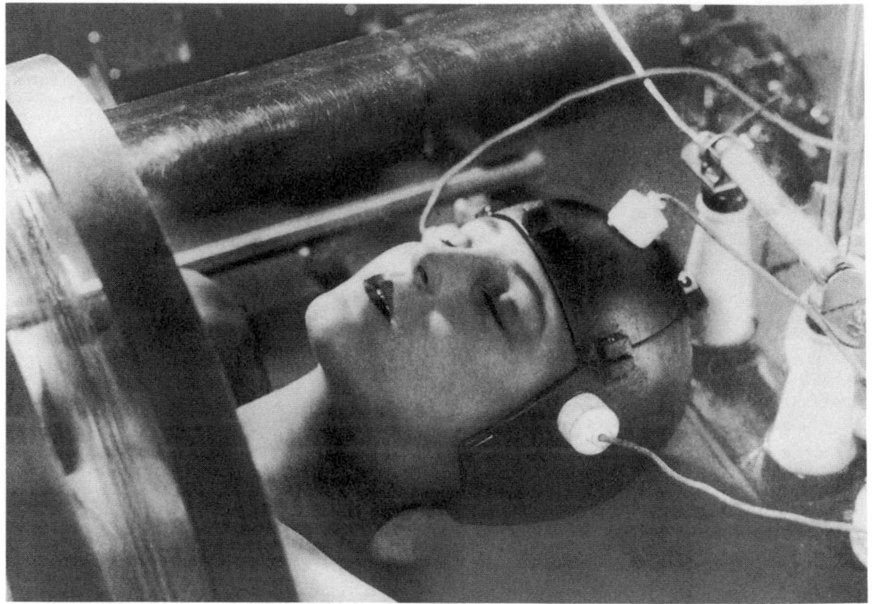

17. Helm between virgin and robot: the transformation scene. [Deutsches Institut für Filmkunde, Frankfurt]

Science, Machines, and Gender

*Ludmilla Jordanova**

THERE HAVE BEEN CERTAIN MOMENTS that stand out in retrospect because they gave rise to statements about the nature of rational or scientific power that were so compelling, forceful or frightening that they gripped the imagination of generations and provided a general reference point for subsequent debate. Easily the best-known example of such a work is Mary Shelley's *Frankenstein* (1818), subsequently immortalized in virtually every literary and artistic genre.[1] In American culture the short stories of Edgar Allan Poe and Nathaniel Hawthorne have had a similar if less dramatic impact. The famous German silent film *Metropolis* (1926) should be seen in this context. It mobilized a number of familiar themes — tradition versus modernity, labour versus capital, men versus machines — around a sentimental story line, and equally important, it produced visual images of unusually compelling intensity. The scene where the inventor makes a robot in the likeness of a woman is certainly one of the most memorable moments in the history of film. In this essay I want to show how Lang's film deployed ideas about the relationships between science and gender. In order to appreciate how *Metropolis* is related to the themes and traditions related to these issues, we shall have to examine its mode of production and its content in some detail.

When *Metropolis* received its much publicized Berlin première early in 1927, the critics and public alike were hostile to it. Many commentators found the ending of the film banal and unsatisfying, although they generally praised the modern images of machines and buildings that

---

* Reprinted from Ludmilla Jordanova, *Sexual Visions. Images of Gender in Science and Medicine between the Eighteenth and Twentieth Centuries* (New York: Harvester Wheatsheaf, 1989) by permission of the author.

[1] The literature on Frankenstein is extremely extensive. Items relevant to the themes of this essay include M. Hindle's "Introduction" to Mary Shelley, *Frankenstein* (Harmondsworth: Penguin Books, 1986); P. Brooks, "Godlike Science/Unhallowed Arts; Language and Monstrosity in Frankenstein," *New Literary History* 9 (1978), 591–605; M. Poovey, "My Hideous Progeny: Mary Shelley and the Feminization of Romanticism," *Proceedings of the Modern Language Association* 95 (1980), 332–47; P. O'Flinn, "Production and Reproduction: The Case of Frankenstein," *Literature and History* 9 (1983), 194–213; A. K. Mellor, "Frankenstein: A Feminist Critique of Science," in G. Levine, ed., *One Culture: Essays in Science and Literature* (Madison: U of Wisconsin P, 1987) 287–312; A. K. Mellor, "Possessing Nature," in A. K. Mellor, ed., *Romanticism and Feminism* (Bloomington: Indiana UP, 1988); 220–32; and D. Musselwhite, *Partings Welded Together: Politics and Desire in the Nineteenth Century Novel.* (London: Methuen, 1987), Chapter Three.

continue to be a source of admiration. *Metropolis* is a complicated and confused film. It drew, however, on some important themes relating to work, industrial organization and the nature of science that were particularly characteristic of European thought in the 1920s. Furthermore, it put these themes into play through a plot which hinges on the nature of femininity — especially its twin aspects, virginity and overt sexuality — and on the role of woman as the social and political bedrock of stable societies. This association of gender with analyses of science was far from novel; it mobilized traditions which linked women with passion and superstition, and men with reason and knowledge, women with religion and sorcery, men with science and management, women with humanity, men with destruction, women with sexuality, men with the lust for power.

The story of *Metropolis* concerns a city-cum-industry run by Joh Fredersen in which the workers are reduced to a faceless mass of exploited bodies. A young woman, Maria, comforts them with reassurances that a saviour and mediator will come to deliver them from their anguish. Freder, the boss's son, sees Maria, falls in love with her and casts himself in the role of the people's deliverer and critic of his father. His father, however, learns that discontent is spreading among the workers and decides to enlist the help of Rotwang, the inventor, who has been working on a robot "in the image of man, that never tires or makes a mistake."[2] Fredersen discovers that the workers are meeting secretly in the old catacombs to hear Maria talk to them about prayer and patience. After taking Fredersen to the catacombs to see Maria in action for himself, Rotwang captures Maria, imprisons her in his house and makes, at the boss's request, a robot in her exact likeness. The robot is then programmed to incite the workers to revolt because Fredersen is looking for an excuse to use violence against them. Their uprising wreaks havoc and has the inadvertent effect of flooding the underground city where the workers live, thus putting in jeopardy the lives of their children. When they finally realize this, the workers, thinking she has destroyed their children, pursue Maria. In fact, they capture the robot, and burn it as a witch, thereby revealing its true nature — a machine not a person. Rotwang chases the real Maria onto the roof of the cathedral, from where he falls to his death after Freder goes to her rescue and fights him off. Maria, father and son are reconciled, and a workers' leader comes forward in the same spirit. It was, after all,

[2] This intertitle is to be found in Fritz Lang, *Metropolis* (1973, Reprint, London: Faber and Faber, 1989), 47.

Fredersen's son, aided by Maria, who had saved their children. The boss is symbolically united to the workers by a handshake at the end of the film.

To understand the film we need to know something of its conditions of production. Fritz Lang (1890–1976) was born in Austria and had trained as an architect and artist before turning to the film industry, in which he worked as an actor and scriptwriter, coming to prominence as a director in the 1920s. Lang thought of setting a film in a futuristic city during a visit to New York in 1924. His wife and close collaborator, Thea von Harbou (1888–1954) then wrote a novel upon which the film in turn was based.[3] The original film shown in Germany was much longer than the version currently available and apparently contained characters and events from the novel which are now missing. The version we know as made for the United States and was considerably altered. No copies of the original are known to exist. To speak of the film as "Lang's" therefore constitutes a simplification; it was the work of many hands, but it is impossible to know exactly what the terms of the collaboration were or what the effect of the cuts was. In his later years as an exile in the United States, Lang was quick to criticize *Metropolis* and its romantic, simplistic ending.[4] Although all these points lead to interpretative problems, they do not undermine the possibility of an historical analysis of *Metropolis,* which need not depend on Lang's special status as the main creator of the film. When I mention Lang in this chapter I do so partly as a matter of linguistic convenience to avoid the necessity of saying "the team that made *Metropolis*" and partly as a reflection of the critical literature most of which focuses on Lang.

It may be useful at this point to note the main respects in which the novel and the film (as it is known) diverge. In the novel, Fredersen and Rotwang are locked in mutual hatred over their love for Hel, Freder's mother, who had died when her son was born. Fredersen "stole" Hel from Rotwang. Von Harbou situated Rotwang in an ancient magical tradition by explaining the uniqueness of his house — a medieval island in a sea of skyscrapers — in terms of an earlier occupant who had possessed awesome occult powers. Similarly, she accounts for the anomalous survival of a Gothic cathedral in a hyper-modern city

[3] Von Harbou, *Metropolis,* first published in 1927. She had already been a stage actress and was an established author by the time *Metropolis* was written. [Editors' Note: Holger Bachmann's account of the genesis of the film in the introduction takes account of evidence not available at the time that Jordanova's essay was written.]

[4] Lang's opinion on film endings was expressed in "Happily Ever After," *Penguin Film Review* 5 (1948), 22–29, an interview where Lang criticized *Metropolis.* See G. D. Phillips, "Fritz Lang on *Metropolis,*" in T. R. Atkins, ed., *Science Fiction Films* (New York, 1976), 19–27.

through the power of the group of monks who still run it. Furthermore, Fredersen has a mother from whom he is estranged because she disapproves of his general conduct. His reconciliation with her concludes the book and carries with it a pledge that he will reform, rebuild and redeem Metropolis. In the novel, Rotwang's death results from his belief that Maria, whom he sees in the cathedral, is his beloved Hel; he cannot understand why she flees from him — a mistake which is comprehensible only in the context of a fight he has had earlier with Fredersen. When he regains consciousness following this, he believes himself dead, and so goes in search of his lost love. At the level of the plot, therefore, the novel is fuller and more consistent than the film and contains significantly different emphases. The use of florid religious imagery is much more elaborate, the references to father-son conflict more overt, and the symbolism generally more highly developed. It is possible that the differences stem from a complex combination of the cuts referred to above, the generic differences between novel and film, and the challenge of transforming verbal into visual images.

The difficulties in interpreting the film are of two main kinds. The first stem from the peculiar historical circumstances of pre-Nazi Germany, the use of films as instruments of Nazi propaganda and the attempt to come to terms with fascism following the Second World War. This issue is often reduced to a concern with the question, "Was Lang in general, and his work in *Metropolis* in particular, marked by the same ideological tendencies that led to the rise of fascism?" In other words, is it necessary to find ways of dismissing them as morally and politically tainted? This drive for moral clarity has led, for example, to a debate about whether Rotwang is a precursor of the reviled Jewish figures of later Nazi films — a point to which we shall return. The "problem" of Lang has been solved in a number of ways, one of which is to attribute blame for any apparently unsound ideological tendencies in his films to the contributions of Thea von Harbou, who remained in Germany after Lang left, and was an active film-maker under Hitler.[5] Yet, to pose the question of Lang's political views in this way is to make assumptions about the second interpretative issue — the relationship between cultural products such as film and the historical setting in

[5] See, for instance, Kracauer, *From Caligari to Hitler* (Princeton, Princeton UP, 1947), 162.

which they are made. Theoretically this is a particularly hard issue to deal with, and few attempts have been made to do so.[6]

To simplify, the issue is whether Lang was merely reflecting general, even unconscious tendencies in his own culture, the very ones that made Hitler's rise to power possible, or whether he was putting forward the views of a specific group with a coherent ideological perspective. Another possibility, although not one I support, that Lang's is a highly idiosyncratic vision, is little entertained because critics generally wish either to exonerate him from or implicate him in broader movements of the 1920s. I am not, of course, advocating a view of him or of the film as unique, since one of my purposes in analyzing *Metropolis* is to place it in a broad cultural context. But it is, I think, unsatisfactory to see him either as a passive reflector of his environment or as the mouthpiece of a particular group. For the moment a more general difficulty, reflecting the current state of scholarship, should be borne in mind. If we take it for granted that cultural artefacts are in some sense socially produced, then we need to search out and lay bare the various levels of mediation between economy, society and culture. For the case of Weimar Germany I have not been able to discover a literature that carries out such a job.

Of course, the standard cultural histories of the period make many assertions about these relationships, based on various theoretical suppositions and prejudices, but they fail to work out the links in any systematic way. For example, in his highly acclaimed work, *Weimar Culture,* Peter Gay locates *Metropolis* among works which portray "the revenge of the father." He finds it a film "calculated mainly to sow confusion," a "tasteless extravaganza" and "a repulsive film." He concludes his account of *Metropolis,* "The revenge of the father and the omnipotence of the mother were twin aspects of the Weimar scene, both equally destructive to youth."[7] Such an approach clearly cannot shed light on the highly specific fashion in which the film portrays the workplace and the labour process. We can juxtapose this portrayal with what is known about labour conditions, wage settlements and the intro-

---

[6] The only serious attempt I know of to undertake such an analysis of *Metropolis* is J. Tulloch, "Genetic Structuralism And The Cinema: A Look at Fritz Lang's *Metropolis,*" *Australian Journal of Screen Theory* 1 (1976), 3–50.

[7] *Weimar Culture: The Outsider as Insider* (Harmondsworth: Penguin, 1974) 148–9. See also W. Laqueur, *Weimar: A Cultural History 1918–1933* (London: Weidenfeld & Nicolson, 1974); E. Rhode, *Tower of Babel: Speculations on the Cinema* (London: Weidenfeld & Nicolson, 1966), 85–105; P. Monaco, *Cinema and Society: France and Germany during the Twenties* (New York, Oxford and Amsterdam: Elsevier, 1976), 118, 124, 128–9; J. D. Barlow *German Expressionist Film* (Boston: Twayne, 1982), 118–33; and Kracauer, *From Caligari to Hitler,* 162–4, for other attempts to link the film with the prevailing mood of Weimar Germany.

duction of industrial rationalization in the period. The links between these two levels, the material conditions and the representation, need to be systematically examined. I have, however, been unable to locate any rigorous attempts to look at how labour was represented in a variety of cultural settings (art, film, theatre, fiction, social theory) and to offer an overall interpretation of the way labour-capital relations were treated. What is said about this later on must therefore remain somewhat speculative.

The difficulties of interpreting a film produced in such a fraught context mean that we must be especially careful about attributing a moral position to its director. This is in part because such positions are rarely articulated unambiguously, and also because it is hard to know how the ordinary public understood the film at the time it was produced. The opinions of critics, while illuminating, are not necessarily representative. If we want to make assertions about *Metropolis* as an expression of the conscious and unconscious tendencies of its time, it helps to have some independent means of assessing what these tendencies were. My point is that these are frequently inferred by hindsight, starting from the subsequent ascendancy of fascism. This teleological approach is understandable, since our need to distance and purify ourselves from the Nazis is still very strong, as the persistent popularity of films about the Second World War containing stereotyped Germans testifies; yet it is also unhelpful.

Cultural histories of Weimar that mention *Metropolis* generally present it in terms of crises of belief and identity, highlighting the religious and Oedipal themes. The film certainly explored a number of easily recognizable Christian themes: Maria, the Virgin-Mother; a son striving to save the world; a stern, almighty father; the virtues of patience and prayer; the necessity for suffering in order to overcome evil. These were even more heavily underscored in the novel, in which Fredersen is locked in conflict with the monks of the Gothic cathedral, who believe that doomsday has come when the city is in turmoil. Furthermore, Fredersen himself experiences the cataclysm as an occasion for repentance and he seeks to become the new redeemer of Metropolis. In the film, the use of crosses in the catacombs where Maria gives solace to the workers, of a halo of light around her head, of the Tower of Babel parable and even the frequent use of triangular motifs (the Trinity) further reveal an indebtedness to traditional religious language. Equally evident is the Oedipal theme. Freder rebels against and wishes to destroy his father. Indeed, in her novel Thea von Harbou wrote explicitly of Freder's parricidal drive. Historians have found the conflict between father and son revealing of the general cultural crisis of Weimar. Hence the ending of the film — in which father and son are reconciled, yet without any radical change in the power structure being on the cards — appears especially prescient of the rise of totalitarian power.

My concern here is with the deployment of science and technology within the film, and particularly with the ways these are related to magic and tradition on the one hand, and the dual nature of female sexuality on the other. Those who have emphasized science and technology often classify *Metropolis* as "science fiction," a genre defined in the *Oxford Companion to English Literature* as "a class of prose narrative which assumes an imaginary technological or scientific advance, or depends upon an imaginary and spectacular change in the human environment."[8] At first sight the use of the robot supports the status of *Metropolis* as science fiction. Yet *Metropolis* was conceived as an expression, if a somewhat exaggerated one, of a city life already firmly rooted in American culture. The robot, in the sense of an artificially made human being, relates as much to ancient myth as it does to a projected future, and Lang's film, like von Harbou's novel, is striking for the persistence of historical reference. The clothes are not futuristic but contemporary or traditional, the language and value systems are those of the 1920s and its parent culture, the modes of transport those in common use. Even the machines, which might possibly evoke an idea of "technological or scientific advance," exist as much as primitive deities as modern marvels. In short, to categorize *Metropolis* as science fiction draws our attention away from its use of modern science and technology in dynamic interplay with magic and tradition. The film lays bare the exceedingly fragile boundaries between good and bad science, good and bad beliefs, good and bad machines, and good and bad women.

Four topics of particular importance are raised in the film: industry, science and technology, city life and modernism, and they all contain implications about gender. *Metropolis* is set in a city which is also a single industrial plant with one man in charge of everything. The workers service the machines, which require constant attention; thus, while both human labour and mechanical power are required to keep the Metropolis going, the former are subservient to the latter. The (male) worker must keep up with the machine, and this is unambiguously shown as the source of excessive fatigue over long shifts.

Two themes prominent in early twentieth-century debates about industrial organization are evoked in *Metropolis*: scientific management in its broadest sense and the role of corporations. As a movement, scien-

---

[8] See also Atkins, *Science Fiction Films*, and S. Jenkins, ed., *Fritz Lang: The Image and the Look* (London: British Film Institute, 1981), esp. 82.

tific management is commonly linked with the American engineer Frederick Winslow Taylor (1856–1915), whose work became widely known in America in 1910 as a result of a government inquiry, and whose *Principles of Scientific Management* (1911) had been translated into German in 1913. Taylorism built on earlier moves towards "systematic management," which had stressed the importance of a system of management for directing and controlling production. Such streamlining of administration, through centralizing and standardizing managerial tasks to avoid wasted effort, is forcefully expressed in the depiction of Fredersen's austere, highly automated and efficient office. As developed by Taylor, the theory of scientific management was strongly committed to rationality and efficiency. It also entailed finding the best person for each task, breaking down jobs into their constituent tasks in order to analyze how each one could be undertaken in the most efficient manner and then training the workmen to use this (and only this) approach. Taylor and his followers maintained that their methods dramatically increased efficiency and so productivity. Something of the flavour of Taylor's system can be gleaned from his remark that "[the] work [of handling pig iron] is so crude and elementary in its nature that the writer firmly believes that it would be possible to train an intelligent gorilla so as to become a more efficient pig-iron handler than any man can be."[9]

The implication — occasionally made explicitly by Taylor, that less "human" men make better workers — is clearly taken up and exaggerated in *Metropolis*, where the labourers move in a senseless mass, devoid of individuality. They are shown to be dominated and even enslaved by time, their bodies drawn beyond physiological efficiency — the goal of Taylorism — into stupor. The shifts in *Metropolis* last ten hours, and the clocks appropriately have a ten-hour face. Not only was working to fixed time schedules central to early industrialization, but scientific management extended this through the emphasis on

---

[9] F. W. Taylor, *The Principles of Scientific Management* (New York: Harper, 1911), 40. See also J. A. Litterer, "Systematic Management: The Search For Order And Integration," *Business History Review* 35 (1961), 461–76; D. Nelson, "Scientific Management, Systematic Management, and Labor, 1880–1915," *Business History Review*, 48: (1974), 479–500; C. S. Maier, "Between Taylorism and Technocracy: European Ideologies and the Vision Of Industrial Productivity in the 1920s," *Journal of Contemporary History* 5 (1970), 27–61; and H. S. Person, 'Scientific Management', *Encyclopedia of the Social Sciences* 13–14 (1930), 603–8.

the timed task, the importance of avoiding wasted effort, the need for production schedules and the setting of wage rates and bonus systems.[10]

Metropolis thus captured some aspects of scientific management — the subservience of people to the work process and the tyranny of time — and exaggerated them, as in a caricature, to heighten the viewer's sense of industrial inhumanity. Other central features of scientific management, however, find no expression in *Metropolis.* Two silences in particular stand out. First, the role of management and of technical expertise was central to Taylorism, which was unthinkable without both the enthusiastic co-operation of the managerial strata and the expertise of engineers. These groups of middle-class professionals are never seen in the film, yet in the social vision of scientific management they played a crucial part, for reasons which will become clear when the second silence has been identified. This concerns rewards for work. Taylor and his followers believed that fair wages were of the utmost importance and that higher productivity was directly in the workers' interest, because it would lead to higher wages. The reasoning behind this was perfectly plain — higher incomes undermined class solidarity, enhanced social mobility, and through the power to consume that better incomes offered, drew working people into a middle-class life style. In theory at least the lure of moving into the professional and managerial classes would undermine any possible discontents.

Of course, the discourse of scientific management itself was not free from tensions and inconsistencies. The goal of a classless, stable society fitted ill with the emphasis on the intense specialization of work that Taylorism required and with Taylor's own sense of the animality of manual workers. Significantly, *Metropolis* portrayed work as physically demanding rather than as requiring specialized skills, while the workers are never shown making products or having and spending money. In stark contrast to the rich, the workers are exhausted, walk like zombies, get killed in industrial accidents, work in hot, steamy conditions, and thus lead miserable lives. In these respects they are closer to slaves than to the modern workers scientific management sought to create.

During the 1920s there was intense concern with the growth of large industrial complexes and monopolies as these assumed ever greater political and economic power. Metropolis was just such a body — a single giant unit, city-state and factory rolled into one. Corporatism constituted an ideology rooted in the transfer of power away "from elected representatives or a career bureaucracy to the major organized forces of

---

[10] The classic statement remains: E. P. Thompson "Time, Work Discipline and Industrial Capitalism," *Past and Present* 38 (1967), 56–97.

European society and economy."[11] This shift has been associated with a weakening of parliamentary democracy, the growth of private power and an erosion of the distinction between the public and private sectors, and the development of centralized bargaining procedures in which labour leaders played a significant role. One historian has argued that Germany was moving clearly towards corporatism during the 1920s, a trend he identified with conservatism.[12]

Aspects of these themes are certainly explored by Lang. In *Metropolis* there is no political structure in which people can participate, hence any distinction between public and private — one of the traditional foundation stones of participatory democracy — is totally inapplicable. If we understand private power as suggesting both the ascendancy of particular interests and the dominance of individuals, then Fredersen represents such power. There is no hint of bargaining between major groups in the film, not least because labour has no voice, being reduced, literally, to a collection of faceless bodies. They require the managerial "head" of Metropolis to direct them. The city-factory is thus a corporate entity in a particularly direct way, in that the film presents it as a single organism, requiring head, hand and heart to work together for it to survive. The ending may be thought to hold out the promise of a negotiated settlement, but this can be no more than conjecture, since the emphasis is sentimental, not practical. Furthermore, the workers are portrayed in distinctly unflattering terms; they are unable to distinguish the false from the true Maria; they can easily be roused to violence that is potentially injurious to their own families; they lust after revenge against (the robot) Maria; and they become instantly docile once their children are known to be safe. Certainly many of these points contribute towards an important point that the film makes. The work structures of Metropolis are shown to be sterile and destructive at all levels of the hierarchy because they lack human sentiment — presented as a distinctively feminine trait in contrast to the masculinized production system.

It could be argued that the portrait of labour and its control in *Metropolis* merely served to highlight the degradation of the whole system, and so sharpen a critique of modern industrialism. It is also likely that Lang took up certain themes that appealed to him dramatically, and developed them in an extreme form, partly for visual effect. There is no

---

[11] C. S. Maier, *Recasting Bourgeois Europe: Stabilization in France, Germany and Italy in the Decade after World War I* (Princeton: Princeton UP, 1975), 9.

[12] Maier, *Recasting Bourgeois Europe*, 13.

reason why he and his co-workers should have felt bound to produce a logically or politically consistent whole. We cannot, indeed should not, look to *Metropolis* for insights about corporatism and scientific management in Weimar Germany. But the film does reveal something of the nexus of tensions and problems that industrial development was seen to be spawning, particularly concerning the relationships between (male) workers and machines and the reduced human potential of industrial workers, seen as a loss of positive feminine attributes. In addition it suggests a number of specific social and cultural themes through which the anxiety over "the modern" was focused.

Clearly, it would have been impossible for themes around modernity to be taken up in *Metropolis* without science and technology occupying a visible position. The film treated three modern themes in a way that owes less to contemporary events than to well-established literary and artistic motifs; fear of machines; the creation of artificial "man," and the "mad" scientist. In order to pursue these more fully we will have to undertake a number of short detours. It will be easier to draw out the distinctiveness of *Metropolis* if we can establish some points of comparison. A variety of candidates invite comparison with *Metropolis*, including Villiers de L'Isle-Adam's novel *L'Eve future* (1886). This concerns the fabrication, by the inventor Thomas Edison, of an android that is an ideal woman. There are some evident similarities with Lang's film here.[13] No less relevant are Mary Shelley's *Frankenstein* (1818) and Nathaniel Hawthorne's *The Birth-mark* (1843), both of which will be discussed shortly.

These juxtapositions may seem curious and open to two specific objections; that both involve literary productions unsuitable for comparison with a film, and that they were produced in very different socio-cultural settings from *Metropolis*. In answer to the first objection it is appropriate to again point out that the film was itself first conceived as a novel,[14] which we can locate with respect to literary traditions, and also that, as a silent film, its narrative structure, which relies heavily on the text shown on the screen, retains a marked literary character. To the second it may be said that the general influence of *Frankenstein* is so

---

[13] On Villiers, see A. Michelson, "On The Eve Of The Future: The Reasonable Facsimile and the Philosophical Toy," *October* 29 (1984), 3–22, and C. Bernheimer, "Huysmans: Writing Against (Female) Nature," in S. R. Suleiman, ed., *The Female Body in Western Culture* (Cambridge, MA: Harvard UP, 1986), 373–86. The latter deals with Villiers *en passant*, but the themes of the article as a whole are nevertheless highly relevant.

[14] [Editors' Note: There is now doubt about this, see Bachmann's introduction in this volume. Jordanova's point about the literariness of the film's sources stands, however.]

extensive that its treatment of similar themes — making people, and power-seeking science — forces the comparison upon us. The same cannot be claimed, however, of Hawthorne's short story, written in the early 1840s. Certainly he was well aware of the Gothic tradition, but my reasons for choosing this work are somewhat different. It contains, in an exceptionally concentrated form, many of the themes I am considering here. It is not necessary to postulate Hawthorne's direct influence upon Lang for his writings to illuminate the general linkages between science, medicine and gender. Indeed, the example of Hawthorne reveals how very widely dispersed the language of power, control, domination, penetration, and masculinity was.

The fear of machines is present in two distinct forms in *Metropolis*. We have already mentioned how the machines the workers service also dominate and control them; this is the first form that a fear of machines takes. Apparently machines keep the city going, although exactly how they do so remains unspecified. Their importance is none the less dramatically demonstrated when the workers wreck them in anger and flooding of their homes results. The film drew on a naive faith in technology and simultaneously expressed a primitive fear of machines when these are transformed into monsters, named after non-Christian deities, who swallow up workers, just as primitive gods demanded the constant sacrifice of human victims.[15] Either way, the machines are rendered omnipotent — either because of modern technology or because of irrational belief — and therefore they are to be feared. It may be helpful to put this in the context of the "cataclysmic" novel tradition, since, according to one commentator:

> novelists attributed the upheaval to class struggle, and that in turn was traced to the failure of industrial society to work out institutions that would protect the working man from enslavement to the very technology that, in more utopian visions, was supposed to free man from hunger and drudgery.[16]

This suggests the double character of machines in their capacity to both liberate and enslave. There is another kind of duality in relation to machines in the film. On the one hand, they are part of its modern aesthetic, presenting visual challenges and delights to Lang as they did to

---

[15] Names used in the film include Ganesha, Baal, Moloch, Mahomet, Golgoth, and Juggernaut.

[16] T. Stoehr, *Hawthorne's Mad Scientists: Pseudoscience and Social Science in Nineteenth-century Life and Letters* (Hamden, CN: Archon Books, 1978), 269.

many artists of the period.[17] On the other hand, they presented an ugly side, being demanding and vengeful, the agents of death. Such ambivalence about machines was in no way confined to the 1920s, although it may have been fuelled by contemporary industrial developments and a general concern about "modernity."[18]

The second form in which the fear of machines emerges in the film is through the robot, a highly specific mechanical type that is best considered in connection with how the film treats the making of an artificial person. *Metropolis* draws on old traditions concerning the artificial production of human beings. It is true that this is achieved not directly from organic remains, as in *Frankenstein*, nor by means of sculpture, as in the Pygmalion myth, but via a robot and elaborate machinery. From the imagery of the dissecting room and charnel house in Shelley's novel, we have moved to that of the physics and chemistry laboratory. When Rotwang the inventor creates the false Maria, it is flashing lights, flasks and electrical phenomena which we see. Frankenstein also used electricity to animate his creature, but here the similarities end. Whereas his monster bears the visible marks of his unnatural creation, Rotwang achieves a complete human likeness. There are two quite different notions of alien presence here; the first is alien because hideous, the second because evil, insidious and undetectable. Where Frankenstein initially saw himself as a benign father, Rotwang deliberately created an agent of destruction. The larger projects that gave birth to the two creatures were also quite different. Frankenstein was possessed by a desire to fathom the secrets of (female) nature. Rotwang, too, may have had these goals, but the viewer is not informed of them. Rather his boast is that he has made "a machine in the image of man, that never tires or makes a mistake," the prototype for "the workers of the future — the machine men!"[19] His work is thus explicitly linked to the labour process, to automated production. Rotwang set himself up as a godlike figure, as of course Frankenstein also did; both usurped the female procreative role. However, the former parodied God's creation of the human race by making machines in the image of man, whereas the latter did so by making a hideous distortion of man.

The question of the similarities between human beings and machines was not a new concern of the early twentieth century but went

---

[17] R. Banham, "Machine Aesthetic," *Architectural Review* 117 (1995), 25–8 and the article "Machine Aesthetic," in A. Bullock and O. Stallybrass, eds., *Fontana Dictionary of Modern Thought* (London: Fontana, 1977), 361; this quotes van Doesburg's claim to have coined the phrase "machine aesthetic" in 1921.

[18] See M. Berman, *All That is Solid Melts into Air: The Experience of Modernity* (London: Verso, 1983).

[19] See note 2 above.

back to debates about "man-machine" that became intense in the seventeenth century with Descartes' assertions that animals are automata. During the eighteenth century La Mettrie's *The Man Machine* (1748) caused a veritable sensation. Subsequently, many scientific and medical investigations explored the mechanistic aspects of human anatomy and physiology.[20] Yet these debates did not strike at the same deep-seated anxieties as *Metropolis,* in which the fear of automation and hence of total control over and manipulation of daily existence seems to be the animating concern:

> The technical superiority of the machine, by transforming mere efficiency into a human ideal, has set in motion a convergence between itself and man which tends, on the one hand to lift the robot to a sort of sub-human role, and on the other to assimilate man to the machine not only in the biological or psycho-physiological sense, but also in relation to his values and conduct. . . . The obsessive *leitmotiv,* . . . of human civilization being threatened by a robot takeover, would seem thus to betray symbolically a widespread fear of the automatization of life.[21]

Metropolis added another dimension to this fear by making the robot a seductive woman. It thereby becomes insidious in a particularly threatening way, by luring men through desire. The machine appears feminine even before the scientist makes it into "Maria," since it has a distinctively womanly overall body shape. The result is two different forms of danger — technological and sexual — riveted together. The whole motif of the robot is portrayed in modern terms, visually speaking, in dramatic contrast to Rotwang himself.

Rotwang looks not like a modern scientist but like a hermit who knows about magic and alchemy; he wears a long gown, has a somewhat demented manner, owns old books, and lives in a medieval house nestled incongruously in the modern city and harbouring mysterious secrets. It is easy to see here how Rotwang recalls literary precedents such as Frankenstein and Faust and also Aylmer in Hawthorne's *The Birth-mark.* It has been suggested that the "mad scientist" is a literary type in Gothic and Utopian novels, and there do indeed appear to be a number of recurrent themes that bear not only on *Metropolis* but also on the relationships between science, medicine, and gender. Five issues

---

[20] A useful survey of these developments is A. Vartanian, "Man-Machine From The Greeks To The Computer," in P. Weiner, ed., *Dictionary of the History of Ideas,* vol. 3 (New York: Scribner, 1973), 131–46.

[21] Vartanian, "Man-Machine," 146.

in relation to the "mad scientist" are of especial importance here: masculinity; power, control, and over-reaching; secrecy; experimentalism; and science and magic. These issues can be presented exceptionally vividly through a brief discussion of *The Birth-mark*.

The story concerns a passionately enthusiastic natural philosopher, Aylmer, and his beautiful young wife, Georgiana, who has a small mark on one of her cheeks. In her husband's opinion it is an increasingly troubling blemish on her otherwise perfect form. She eventually agrees to let him remove it, which, after much arduous experimental work, he is able to do — at the cost of her life. Here, then, is the classic tale of the over-reacher, and the affinities with *Frankenstein* are obvious. The differences are equally instructive. Although we can understand Shelley's tale in terms of the masculine desire to dominate nature, Frankenstein did not directly work on woman as Aylmer and Rotwang did.[22] Hawthorne brings the gender question to the fore by making the experimenter and subject husband and wife, and by explicitly addressing the relationship between love of knowledge and love of a person:

> [Aylmer] had devoted himself, however, too unreservedly to scientific studies, ever to be weaned from them by any second passion. His love for his young wife might prove the stronger of the two; but it could only be by intertwining itself with his love of science, and uniting the strength of the latter to its own.[23]

The passionate engagement with "deep science" is characteristic of the over-reacher, and as the novel version of *Metropolis* shows, the relationship between Rotwang and Maria had an erotic dimension, even if based on mistaken identity. In the film, the way he stalks her in the catacombs and then abducts her suggests sexually predatory behaviour. The fact that these scientists are men is essential not only to the plot but to the sexual dynamic that is integral to power over nature.

Rotwang, Aylmer, and Frankenstein are all perfectly clear about the power and control they seek. The equation between knowledge, power, and danger is made openly. This theme is brought into particular prominence in *Metropolis* because the link with political authority is so direct — Rotwang is working for Fredersen, and Fredersen has total power in Metropolis. However, acquiring power over nature is not represented as a public matter; rather, it is repeatedly associated with secrecy. In *Frankenstein* much is made of his "midnight labours," and the

---

[22] I am, of course, well aware that Frankenstein began work on a female companion for his monster, work that he later destroyed. Nonetheless, the plot hinges on his relationship with the unnamed male being he created initially.

[23] Hawthorne, *Selected Tales and Sketches*, ed. M. J. Colacurcio (Harmondsworth: Penguin Books, 1987), 259.

need for concealment dominated his whole mentality. Aylmer too worked only with a trusted helper and was horrified when his wife ventured into the laboratory. His entire enterprise is shown as a quest for nature's secrets, secrets that he finds it impossible to penetrate: "our great creative Mother, while she amuses us with apparently working in the broadest sunshine, is yet severely careful to keep her own secrets . . . like a jealous patentee."[24] It follows that those who wish for her secrets must be both cunning and secretive themselves. Rotwang is no exception to this pattern. He works in seclusion in a house easily turned into a prison for the real Maria, while an air of mystery hangs around him and his abode. The sense of secrecy is fed by the involvement of such over-reachers with difficult, dangerous, even transgressive experiments. The strong emphasis on an experimental approach comes from a number of sources — the perception of alchemy as a paradigm of over-ambitious knowledge, the association with magic, and the vividness with which experiment evokes the idea of prising secrets from nature. It also allows the "mad scientist" to be portrayed as active, interventionist, as visibly moved by his passion for knowledge.

This passion for knowledge is never uncritically depicted. Possibly the association with magic serves to establish that something not quite legitimate is going on, indeed that it has profane qualities. The form of the profanity is, of course, important. The affront to nature and to God is generally clear. Such a search for knowledge is also profane because it is inappropriate to the human condition — a point Hawthorne repeatedly and eloquently made since it is Aylmer's abhorrence of his wife's "fatal flaw of humanity" that drives him beyond the bounds of normal behaviour to a denial of the reality of disease and death.[25] "He was confident in his science, and felt that he could draw a magic circle round her," in other words, Aylmer wanted more of natural philosophy than it could reasonably give, he wanted magical control.[26] In Rotwang's case, too, we are encouraged to think of a mixture of science and magic — his appearance, his bizarre medieval house which included a modern laboratory, the symbols on the doors.

---

[24] Hawthorne, *Selected Tales*, 265.

[25] Hawthorne, *Selected Tales*, 261.

[26] Hawthorne, *Selected Tales*, 266.

And yet, Rotwang displays a unique characteristic, certainly not shared by either Frankenstein or Aylmer — he is successful.[27] He actually achieved what he claimed he could, the robot did look like Maria, she did do as she was told. His knowledge was made palpably real. The problem, so far as the plot of *Metropolis* is concerned is that he served an evil master, for it was in Fredersen's interests that he made the robot, and it was Fredersen's plan gone awry that caused disaster. Perhaps this is to exaggerate the differences, for it is true that like other "mad scientists" Rotwang is presented as obsessive, as possessed by a passionate love of, or lust for, power and knowledge that led to his downfall. Furthermore, the idea for the robot had clearly come to him long before Fredersen asked for his help. Rotwang is a complex figure who displayed prodigious intellectual powers, which even Fredersen respected and which were of infinite value in the modern Metropolis. Yet he also manifested the archaic powers of a sorcerer. In this respect he resembled the machines, at once suggestive of modern power and of primitive evil.

The exploration of modernity in *Metropolis* was undertaken as much through the idea of the city as through science and technology. If early twentieth-century thinkers wanted to voice reservations about the times in which they lived, the city offered an attractive vehicle for their doubts. The city could stand for a multitude of discontents, including, crime, decadence and immorality, as it had done for centuries. Yet, for equally long, the city had also represented positive values such as learning, civilization and enlightenment. In *Metropolis,* Lang highlighted modern, high-rise architecture, advanced transport systems and vertical structure of the city as a representation of its social hierarchy. He was particularly keen in *Metropolis* to find novel cinematic ways of conveying the immense height of the buildings.[28]

What contemporary commentators found troublesome about city life, particularly in the United States, was the close proximity between different social, religious and ethnic groups. It was perceived as a location which threatened communities, for these could hardly hold together amidst the insistent mobility of urban life. Some who have written about Lang have pointed to distrust of the city as a characteristic of German conservative thought in the 1920s. Yet contemporaries found other meanings in modern city life apart from the threat of social disintegration, including a kind of exhilaration which went with being

---

[27] Faust too was successful, but only with the help of Mephistopheles. Rotwang is *seen* to do it all himself, although it would be possible to interpret the film as implying that he had magical assistance.

[28] J. Elderfield, "Metropolis," *Studio International,* no. 103 (1972), 196–9.

free from the oppressive intimacy of rural or small town life.[29] By contrast, Lang showed the Metropolis not as a place where groups mingle promiscuously but as one where they are rigidly segregated. The public areas are only for an elite whose composition is never specified and whose behaviour vividly evokes the decadent pleasure-seeking with which the Weimar period is so often associated.

However, there can be no doubt that the city stood for modern life, or that modernity was an important feature of the film. The modernity is conveyed in a number of ways, which do not always sit easily together. The self-indulgent merrymaking of the privileged elite was one way of suggesting it; others were the modern architecture, the industrial machinery, the transport systems and Fredersen's bare, functional office. These must be seen, however, in relation to the ancient catacombs, Rotwang's medieval house, the Gothic cathedral and the eighteenth-century costumes in which the gilded youth of Metropolis besport themselves. Thus the film does not present a simple futuristic or modernistic scenario, but sets up a dynamic between old and new. It is worth remembering how very controversial, socially and politically, simple functionalist architecture was at this time, and that the underlying issue was not only stylistic preference but an entire world-view.[30]

In so far as *Metropolis* rests on a world-view, it is organicism and not the culture of the modern that provides a unifying theme. "Organicism" is not a straightforward concept, and many different claims have been advanced under its name. In relation to *Metropolis*, two strands of organicist thought are relevant, and they are summarized in the following propositions: "the parts cannot be understood if considered in isolation from the whole" and "the parts are dynamically interrelated or interde-

---

[29] See G. Simmel, "The Metropolis And Mental Life," (first published in 1903) in D. Levine, ed., *Georg Simmel on Sociability and Social Forms* (Chicago, 1971), 324–39, esp. 332–3.

[30] A convenient way of appreciating the implications of new styles of the period is through the Bauhaus; see the exhibition catalogue *Fifty Years Bauhaus* (London, 1968), especially the section on architecture, 145–210. B. Fletcher's *A History of Architecture* (London: Butterworths, 1975), contains some examples of factory design, 1246, 1264–71 and 1290. Lang's aesthetic can also usefully be placed in the context of precisionist art; see *The Precisionist View in American Art* (Minneapolis Exhibition Catalogue, 1960), esp. 19 (Spencer, "City Walls"), 28–37 (section on "Urban Themes") and 38–41 (pictures under the themes "Reflections of an Industrial Society" and "The Solid Geometry of Industry").

pendent."[31] Frequent allusions are made in the film to the need for an integrated harmony between different parts of the body: "Between the brain that plans and the hands that build, there must be a mediator," "It is the heart that must bring about an understanding between them." The film ends in fact with the following title: "There can be no understanding between the hands and the brain unless the heart acts as mediator."[32] These statements imply that a society must function as a whole system, just as an organism does, and that social unity is a prized value. Yet this is put forward in a context of intense exploitation and extreme division of labour, a fragmentation the organicist formulation does not seek to challenge. The concern with bringing together head and hands (both masculine) indicates a deep fear of splitting in the social order which will be mended not by ending the original divisions but by binding groups together in some unspecified way through the language of emotions and sentiment (both feminine). The organicist discourse in *Metropolis* works, then, at two levels: the first stresses harmonious relations among the elements of a social system, while the second registers divisions and hierarchy. The point about the hierarchy, however, is that each stratum depends on the others and therefore has no autonomous existence.

Visually, the distinction between the different levels is powerfully conveyed. The workers wear sombre clothes and live below ground where it is dark, while the elite live high up, travel in aeroplanes, wear pale clothes and experience the open air. The brain, the organ of calculation and hard thinking, is visually expressed in silent-film style by the exaggerated reactions and facial contortions of Fredersen and Freder. The workers, on the other hand, are purely physical; they are "hands," and hands in another sense when they are shown moving dials on clocklike machines, their arms like the hands of a clock. Not only does the life of the mind not exist for them, but they are barely differentiated from one another. The ballet-like presentation of work, which shows highly abstract movements, heightens this sense that mechanical coordination between identical elements represents the sum total of life for the majority of the inhabitants of Metropolis who trudge to and from work in serried ranks. The congruence between organicism and silent-film technique extends to Maria, who as the "heart" of the system, constantly presses her hands to her breast.

[31] D. C. Phillips, "Organicism in The Late Nineteenth and Early Twentieth Centuries," *Journal of the History of Ideas* 31 (1970), 413; see also G. Saccaro-Battisti, "Changing Metaphors of Political Structures," *Journal of the History of Ideas* 44 (1983), 31–54.

[32] Lang, *Metropolis*, 60 and 130.

All the workers appear to be male, so that for the most part Maria is the only woman we see. The women workers/workers' wives become visible only when the masses rebel and then become alarmed about the fate of their children. The whole plot in fact rests on the potentially disruptive presence of Maria. Indeed, right at the beginning it is clear that, as a fount of feeling, she will not accept a regime based on heartless exploitation. Her good, pure femininity — she is both virgin and mother — is an essential part of the organicist vision, for it enables her to be the "heart" of the city. It is equally important that the robot be her double — outwardly identical but inwardly her opposite. Femininity is thereby split into two; pure, good chastity and sensual, corrupt depravity. Gender comes to play a complex role in the film. The real business of life, whether it is labour or running Metropolis is done by men, yet they lack some essential element to make them whole, and it is this ingredient which good femininity can contribute. So that although reason and sentiment could be seen as opposed to one another, they are also complementary.

But what of the destructive side of femininity? Full sensuality was presented as a form of unreason closely akin to mass fury and mass decadence, which are incompatible with male reason. Its fate was to be identified as witchcraft and suitably annihilated. The robot built by Rotwang, a master of knowledge, is portrayed as the antithesis of that knowledge. It should be pointed out that the paradox is sharpened by the robot looking unmistakably feminine, as we noted earlier, before it became "Maria," suggesting that the destructive machine and the destructive side of female sexuality are identified with one another. Some commentators have dealt with this problem by suggesting that Rotwang is the black magician — as already mentioned, the precursor of the evil Jew of Nazi films. Equally, if not more plausibly, he could be seen in the traditions of hermits, alchemists, philosophers and anatomists, shown in paintings, such as those by Joseph Wright of Derby, as old men wearing robes, whose knowledge isolates them from others. The pentagram, shown on Rotwang's front door and in his laboratory, is, when inverted, a sign of witchcraft and inverted human nature. The term "seal of Solomon" is also used, but this is in fact six-pointed, unlike the shapes shown in the film.[33]

---

[33] On Rotwang as "sub-Aryan," see Rhode, *Tower of Babel*, 97. Tulloch, "Genetic Structuralism," 27 links Rotwang, anti-semitism and Solomon's seal. On Joseph Wright's figures, see B. Nicolson, *Joseph Wright of Derby. Painter of Light* (London: Routledge and Kegan Paul, 1968). The inverted pentagram is explained in J. C. Coo-

To identify Rotwang with bad magic is to say that the power he had was wholly illegitimate and came from his attempts to do things that are beyond the proper province of the human being. There is certainly some truth in this, yet his power was genuine in the sense that it really worked. He has a level of understanding which, it is implied, was unique and was highly valued by Fredersen. Rotwang cannot simply be a magician, then; he is also a scientist and inventor who grapples with the real world not the realms of fantasy. Indeed, if he were simply a wizard, the film would be far less interesting, not least because Fredersen's invitation to Rotwang to help him solve his political problems would seem less plausible. The alliance between political power and power over nature was forceful indeed, but legitimate power and knowledge could all too easily enter an unacceptable, illegitimate domain. The boundary between good and bad was perilously fragile.

Metropolis is an exploration of pure power. Fredersen has complete authority and control, just as Rotwang can command nature's forces. Yet both men find their power challenged because, the film implies, it was incomplete psychologically, lacking feminine sympathy. The plot resolved this by eliminating Rotwang and by giving Fredersen the capacity to empathize. His power — social, political, economic and technological — remained intact, but something was added to it to make it whole. This something was unambiguously identified as a feminine virtue, though some men, such as Freder, possessed it. The need for good femininity to fill the lacunae in male power was reinforced by the fact that Freder has no mother to mediate between him and his father, so Maria had to assume this role. She did so not directly but indirectly by creating tenderness in the son who then tried to pass it on to his father in order to bring his father to sympathize with the workers. The film thus works with a number of different kinds of power and the relationships between them; the power of the emotions (Maria and Freder), of the capacity to control nature (Rotwang), of absolute political authority (Fredersen), of wanton destruction (the robot, the masses and the monstrous machines).

Metropolis reveals much about the relationship between science and technology and other forms of power; or rather, science and technology offer Lang a verbal and visual language with which to speak about social relationships and political structures. The relationship between mental and manual labour is identical with that between rulers and

---

per, *An Illustrated Encyclopaedia of Traditional Symbols* (London: Thames and Hudson, 1978), 128.

ruled; the unifying force is the highly mechanized factory, which is also the state — an organic social system. The visual language is that of vertical hierarchy; the verbal image that of physiological systems. Femininity, triggering sexual attraction, is the dynamic element introducing change into the system through Freder being drawn to Maria, a woman of the people. In the end, only Maria can offer the quality, heart, which will reconcile head and hand and make the state truly organic. If the feminine disrupts, it also heals. Women do not represent a unitary power, but a force easily fragmented into opposites; nurturing chastity and disrupting sensuality.

In a similar fashion, scientific knowledge can split into genuine reason and illegitimate knowledge/magic, and technology potentially contains both the all-powerful, efficient machines and the monsters who claim the lives of men. When concepts split in this way they generate tensions — because the relationship between the two elements may be obscure and troublesome, and because each element can easily be transformed into the other, creating instability. Such unstable splits threaten to destroy the organic state; they require bridging. Likewise, there should be links between labour and capital. The bridges do not undermine the divisions they span but rather provide an illusion of cohesion.

Lang's film is best described as a caricature of modern life which exaggerates certain aspects to bring them to our attention. This method is most successful in relation to the workers. The denial of individuality, the fusion of man and machine, workers going to and from work in mindless synchrony, and the obsession with time and efficiency have been noted in critiques of capitalism since the time of the romantic writer and historian, Thomas Carlyle.[34] But it remains an open question what Lang and his co-workers really believed about these features of modern life. The film seems to have a conservative, palliative ending, in that master and workers are reconciled without anything being said about real material improvement. The conclusion constitutes a romantic promise, while the reality is that the organic system is preserved intact and, of course, remains hierarchical and exploitative. The use of organicist imagery, and the extended religious analogies surrounding Maria in particular, leave all the important political questions not even raised, let alone answered.

It would be wrong, however, to allow the banality of the ending to colour our reactions to the entire film. Commentators are virtually unanimous in finding the striking visual effects Lang deployed a bril-

---

[34] See, for instance, *Past and Present*, first published 1843.

liant success. This is not, I think, to "reduce" discussion of the film to purely aesthetic terms but to acknowledge the source of its impact. Visual images play a crucial role in exploring and working with the themes discussed in this chapter. They express, often in historically specific ways, something of the power, authority and control that knowledge of nature offers. These complex visual languages speak to our imagination and are all the more important because they do so, since they readily combine with taken-for-granted assumptions about such issues as gender, just as *Metropolis* does. It is the very fact that the intertwining of science and gender was so generally accessible to cinema audiences that makes the film worthy of historical attention.

18. Advertising still of Maria with the children of Metropolis: Freder's first sight of her. [Deutsches Institut für Filmkunde, Frankfurt]

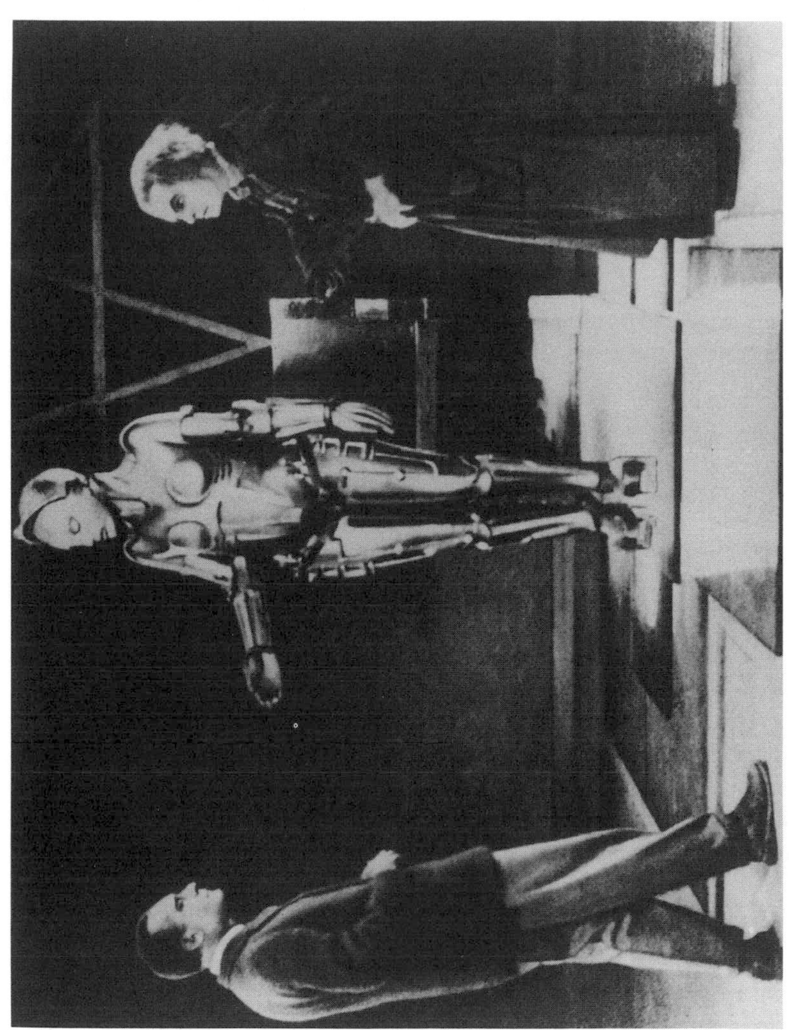

19. Fredersen's first encounter with the Maria robot.
[Deutsches Institut für Filmkunde, Frankfurt]

The Vamp and the Machine

Fritz Lang's *Metropolis*

*Andreas Huyssen**

FRITZ LANG'S FAMOUS AND INFAMOUS EXTRAVAGANZA *Metropolis* has never had a good press. While its visual qualities have been praised,[1] its content, more often than not, has been condemned as simplistic, ill-conceived, or plain reactionary. When the film was first released in the United States in 1927, Randolph Bartlett, the *New York Times* critic, reproached the director for his "lack of interest in dramatic verity" and for his "ineptitude" in providing plot motivation, thus justifying the heavy re-editing of the film for American audiences.[2] In Germany, critic Axel Eggebrecht condemned *Metropolis* as a mystifying distortion of the "unshakeable dialectic of the class struggle" and as a monumental panegyric to Stresemann's Germany.[3] Eggebrecht's critique, focusing as it does on the emphatic reconciliation of capital and labour at the end of the film, has been reiterated untold times by critics on the left. And indeed, if we take class and power relations in a modern technological society to be the only theme of the film, then we have to concur with these critics. We would also have to agree with Siegfried Kracauer's observation concerning the affinity that exists between the film's ideological punch line, "The heart mediates between hand and brain," and the fascist "art" of propaganda that, in Goebbels' words, was geared "to win the heart of a people and to keep it."[4] Kracauer pointedly concluded his comments on *Metropolis* with Lang's own words describing a meeting of the filmmaker with Goebbels that took place shortly after Hitler's rise to power: "'He [Goebbels] told me that, many years before, he and the Führer had seen my picture *Metropolis* in

---

* Reprinted from Andreas Huyssen, *After the Great Divide. Modernism, Mass Culture, Postmodernism* (London: Macmillan, 1988) by permission of the author, Indiana UP and The Macmillan Press.

[1] Cf. Paul M. Jensen, "Metropolis: The Film and the Book," in Fritz Lang, *Metropolis* (New York: Simon & Schuster), 13; Lotte Eisner, *The Haunted Screen* (Berkeley: U of California P, 1969), 223–236.

[2] [Editors' Note: See Part One of this volume for the full text of Bartlett's piece.]

[3] Stresemann was one of the leading "reformist" politicians of the stabilization phase of the Weimar Republic after 1923. Axel Eggebrecht, "Metropolis," *Die Welt am Abend*, 12 January, 1927.

[4] Goebbels at the Nuremberg Party Convention of 1934.

a small town, and Hitler had said at that time that he wanted me to make the Nazi pictures.'"[5]

One problem with such ideology critiques based on notions of class and political economy is that they tend to blur the political differences between the Weimar Republic and the Third Reich by suggesting that social-democratic reformism inexorably contributed to Hitler's rise to power. The more important problem with this approach is that it remains blind to other aspects which are at least as important to the film's social imaginary, especially since they are clearly foregrounded in the narrative. While the traditional ideology critique is not false, its blind spots lock us into a one-dimensional reading of the film which fails to come to terms with the fascination *Metropolis* has always exerted on audiences. This fascination, I would argue, has to do precisely with those elements of the narrative which critics have consistently shrugged aside. Thus the love story between Freder, son of the Master of Metropolis, and Maria, the woman of the depths who preaches peace and social harmony to the workers, has been dismissed as sentimental and childish (Eisner, Jensen); the elaborate recreation of Maria as a machine-vamp in Rotwang's laboratory has been called counterproductive to the flow of events (Kracauer); certain actions of the mechanical vamp such as the belly dance have been called extraneous and inexplicable (Jensen); and the medieval religious-alchemical symbolism of the film has been criticized as inadequate for the portrayal of a future — or, for that matter, present — urban life (Eggebrecht). I am suggesting, however, that it is precisely the doubling of Maria, the use of religious symbolism, the embodiment of technology in a woman-robot and Freder's complex relationship to women and machines, sexuality and technology, which give us a key to the film's social and ideological imaginary. Even though Kracauer's concrete analysis of *Metropolis* remained blind to this constitutive mesh of technology and sexuality in the film, he was essentially correct when he wrote in *From Caligari to Hitler*: "*Metropolis* was rich in subterranean content that, like contraband, had crossed the borders of consciousness without being questioned."[6] The problem is how to define this subterranean content, a task that Kracauer does not even begin to tackle in his analysis of the film.

Of course the critics' attention has always been drawn to the film's powerful sequences involving images of technology, which, to a large degree, control the flow of the narrative.

- The film begins with a series of shots of the great machines of Metropolis moving and turning in inexorable rhythms.

---

[5] Siegfried Kracauer, *From Caligari to Hitler* (Princeton, Princeton UP, 1947), 164.

[6] Kracauer, *From Caligari to Hitler*, 164.

• The machine room where Freder witnesses the violent explosion and has his vision of technology as Moloch devouring its victims, and the sun-like spinning disk of the central power-house present technology as an autonomous deified force demanding worship, surrender, and ritual sacrifice.

• The imagery of the tower of Babel (the machine centre of Metropolis is actually called the New Tower of Babel) relates technology to myth and legend. The biblical myth is used to construct the ideological message about the division of labour into the hands that build and the brains that plan and conceive, a division of which, as the film suggests, must be overcome.

• The capital/labour conflict is present in the sequences showing the Master of Metropolis in his control and communications center and the workers in the machine room, with the machines being subservient to the master but enslaving the workers.

• Finally, and perhaps most importantly, technology is embodied in a female robot, a machine-vamp who leads the workers on a rampage and is subsequently burned at the stake.

Eggebrecht and Kracauer were certainly correct in relating Lang's representation of technology to the machine-cult of the 1920s which is also manifest in the literature and the art of *Neue Sachlichkeit*.[7] In my view, however, it is not enough to locate the film within the parameters of *Neue Sachlichkeit* only. The simple fact that stylistically *Metropolis* has usually and mainly been regarded as an expressionist film may give us a clue. And indeed, if one calls expressionism's attitude toward technology to mind, one begins to see that the film actually vacillates between two opposing views of modern technology which were both part of Weimar culture. The expressionist view emphasizes technology's oppressive and destructive potential and is clearly rooted in the experiences and irrepressible memories of the mechanized battlefields of World War I. During the 1920s and especially during the stabilization phase of the Weimar Republic this expressionist view was slowly replaced by the technology cult of the *Neue Sachlichkeit* and its unbridled confidence in technical progress and social engineering. Both these views inform the film. Thus on the one hand, *Metropolis* is strongly indebted to Georg Kaiser's expressionist play about technology, *Gas* (1918–1920). In both works the primary technology is energy, gas and electricity respectively, and the industrial accident sequence in *Me-*

---

[7] On the *Neue Sachlichkeit* see John Willett, *Art and Politics in the Weimar Period: The New Sobriety, 1917–1933* (New York: Pantheon Books, 1978). On the machine-cult of the 1920s see Helmut Lethen, *Neue Sachlichkeit 1924–1932* (Stuttgart: Metzler, 1970) and Teresa de Lauretis et al., eds., *The Technological Imagination* (Madison, WN: The Coda Press, 1980), especially the section "Machines, Myths, and Marxism."

tropolis is remarkably similar to the explosion of the gas works in act I of Kaiser's play. But, on the other hand, the shots of the city Metropolis, with its canyon-like walls rising far above street level and with its bridges and elevated roads thrown between towering factories and office buildings are reminiscent of Hannah Höch's dadaist photomontages and of scores of industrial and urban landscape paintings of the *Neue Sachlichkeit* (Karl Grossberg, Georg Scholz, Oskar Nerlinger).

Historically and stylistically then Lang's *Metropolis,* which was conceived in 1924 during a visit to the United States (including New York) and released in January 1927, is a syncretist mixture of expressionism and *Neue Sachlichkeit,* and, more significantly, a syncretist mixture of the two diametrically opposed views of technology we can ascribe to these two movements. More precisely, the film works through this conflict and tries to resolve it. Ultimately the film, even though it pretends to hold on to the humanitarian anti-technological ethos of expressionism, comes down on the side of *Neue Sachlichkeit,* and the machine vamp plays the crucial role in resolving a seemingly irreconcilable contradiction. For his indictment of modern technology as oppressive and destructive, which prevails in most of the narrative, Lang ironically relies on one of the most novel cinematic techniques. Schüfftan's *Spiegeltechnik,* a technique which by using a camera with two lenses, focuses two separate images, those of models and actors, onto a single strip of film.[8] As I shall argue later, doubling, mirroring and projecting not only constitute the technological make-up of this film, but they lie at the very core of the psychic and visual processes that underlie its narrative.

The Machine-Woman: A Historical Digression

To my knowledge, the motif of the machine-woman in *Metropolis* has never been analyzed in any depth. In his recent reinterpretation of *Metropolis,* Stephen Jenkins has taken an important step by pushing the question of the significance of the female presence in Lang's films to the forefront.[9] Although many of Jenkins's observations about Maria and Freder are correct, his analysis is deficient in three areas: his reading remains too narrowly Oedipal moving as it does from Maria's initial threat to the Law of the Father to her and Freder's reintegration into Metropolis's system of domination; secondly, Jenkins never problematizes Lang's representations of technology and thus remains oblivious to

---

[8] [Editors' Note: see Bachmann' introduction, and Rittau in Part One of this volume for further detail on this technique.]

[9] Stephen Jenkins, "Lang: Fear and Desire," in S. Jenkins, ed., *Fritz Lang: The Image and the Look* (London: British Film Institute, 1981), 38–124, esp. 82–7.

that central political and ideological debate of the 1920s; and thirdly, he never explores the question how or why male fantasies about women and sexuality are interlaced with visions of technology in the film. It is my contention that only by focusing on the mechanical vamp can we fully comprehend the cohesion of meanings that the film transports.

Why indeed does the robot, the *Maschinenmensch* created by the inventor-magician Rotwang and intended to replace the human workers appear with the body features of a woman? After all, the world of technology has always been the world of men, while woman has been considered to be outside of technology, a part of nature, as it were. It is too simple to suggest, as does, that the vamp's main function is to represent the threat of castration to Freder; that purpose could have been achieved by other narrative means, and it also leaves unanswered the question of what technology may have to do with female sexuality and castration anxiety. Precisely the fact that Fritz Lang does not feel the need to explain the female features of Rotwang's robot shows that a pattern, a long standing tradition is being recycled here, a tradition that is not at all hard to detect, and in which the *Maschinenmensch*, more often than not, is presented as woman.

A historical digression is in order.[10] In 1748 the French doctor Julien Offray de la Mettrie, in a book entitled *L'Homme machine*, described the human being as a machine composed of a series of distinct, mechanically moving parts, and he concluded that the body is nothing but a clock, subject as all other matter to the laws of mechanics. This extreme materialist view with its denial of emotion and subjectivity served politically in the eighteenth century to attack the legitimacy claims of feudal clericalism and the absolutist state. It was hoped that once the metaphysical instances, which church and state resorted to as devices of legitimizing their power, were revealed as fraud they would become obsolete. At the same time, however, and despite their revolutionary implications such materialist theories ultimately led to the notion of a blindly functioning world machine, a gigantic automaton, the origins and meaning of which were beyond human understanding. Consciousness and subjectivity were degraded to mere functions of a global mechanism. The determination of social life by metaphysical legitimations of power was replaced by the determination through the laws of nature. The age of modern technology and its legitimatory apparatuses had begun.

It is no coincidence that in the same age literally hundreds of mechanics attempted to construct human automata who could walk and

[10] In the following I am indebted to Peter Gendolla, *Die lebenden Maschinen: Zur Geschichte der Maschinenmenschen bei Jean Paul, E. T. A. Hofmmann und Villiers de l'Isle-Adam* (Marburg: Guttandin und Hoppe, 1980).

dance, draw and sing, play the flute or the piano, and whose performances became a major attraction in the courts and cities of eighteenth-century Europe. Androids and robots such as Vaucanson's flutist or Jacquet-Droz's organ player captured the imagination of the times and seemed to embody the realization of an age-old human dream. With the subsequent systematic introduction of labouring machines, which propelled the industrial revolution, the culture of androids declined. But it is precisely at that time, at the turn of the eighteenth to the nineteenth century, that literature appropriates the subject matter transforming it significantly. The android is no longer seen as testimony to the genius of mechanical invention; it rather becomes a nightmare, a threat to human life. In the machine-man writers begin to discover horrifying traits which resemble those of real people. Their theme is not so much the mechanically constructed automaton itself, but rather the threat it poses to live human beings. It is not hard to see that this literary phenomenon reflects the increasing technologization of human nature and the human body which reached a new stage in the early nineteenth century.

While the android builders of the eighteenth century did not seem to have an overriding preference for either sex (the number of male and female androids seems to be more or less balanced), it is striking to see how the later literature prefers machine-women to machine-men.[11] Historically, then, we can conclude that as soon as the machine came to be perceived as a demonic inexplicable threat and as harbinger of chaos and destruction — a view which typically characterizes many nineteenth century reactions to the railroad to give but one major example[12] — writers began to imagine the *Maschinenmensch* as woman. There are grounds to suspect that we are facing here a complex process of projection and displacement. The fears and perceptual anxieties emanating from ever more powerful machines are recast and reconstructed in terms of the male fear of female sexuality, reflecting, in the Freudian account, the male's castration anxiety. This projection was relatively

---

[11] Examples would be Jean Paul's *Ehefrau aus bloßem Holz* (1789), Achim von Arnim's Bella in *Isabella von Ägypten* (1800), E. T. A. Hoffmann's Olympia in *Der Sandmann* (1815), and Villiers de l'Isle-Adam's Hadaly in *L'Eve future* (1886), a novel that strongly influenced Thea von Harbou in the writing of *Metropolis*. More recent examples would be Stanislav Lem's *The Mask* (1974), the puppet mistress in Fellini's *Casanova* (1976/77), and a number of works in the Franco-German art exhibit *Les machines célibataires* (1975).

[12] The disruptions which the early railroads inflicted upon the human perceptions of time and space have been magnificently analyzed by Wolfgang Schivelbusch in his book *Geschichte der Eisenbahnreise: Zur Industrialisierung von Raum und Zeit* (Munich: Hanser, 1977); an English translation has been published by Urizen. See also Leo Marx, *The Machine in the Garden: Technology and the Pastoral Ideal in America* (New York: Oxford UP, 1964).

easy to make; although woman had traditionally been seen as standing in a closer relationship to nature than man, nature itself, since the eighteenth century, had come to be interpreted as a gigantic machine. Woman, nature, machine had become a mesh of significations all of which had one thing in common: otherness; by their very existence they raised fears and threatened male authority and control.

The Ultimate Technological Fantasy: Creation without Mother

With that hypothesis in mind let us return to *Metropolis*. As I indicated before, the film does not provide an answer to the question of why the robot is a woman; it takes the machine-woman for granted and presents her as quasi-natural. Thea von Harbou's novel, however, on which the film is based, is quite explicit. In the novel, Rotwang explains why he created a female robot rather than the machine *men* Fredersen had ordered as replacements of living labour. Rotwang says: "Every man-creator makes himself a woman. I do not believe that humbug about the first human being a man. If a male god created the world . . . then he certainly created woman first."[13] This passage does not seem to fit my hypothesis that the machine-woman typically reflects the double male fear of technology and of woman. On the contrary, the passage rather suggests that the machine-woman results from the more or less sublimated sexual desires of her male creator. We are reminded of the Pygmalion myth in which the woman, far from threatening the man, remains passive and subordinated. But this contradiction is easily resolved if we see male control as the common denominator in both instances. After all, Rotwang creates the android as an artifact, as an initially lifeless object which he can then control and dominate.

Clearly the issue here is not just the male's sexual desire for woman. It is the much deeper libidinal desire to create that other, woman, thus depriving it of its otherness. It is the desire to perform this ultimate task which has always eluded technological man. In the drive toward ever greater technological domination of nature, Metropolis' master-engineer must attempt to create woman, a being which, according to the male's view, resists technologization by its very "nature." Simply by virtue of natural biological reproduction, woman had maintained a qualitative distance to the realm of technical production which only produces lifeless goods. By creating a female android, Rotwang fulfils the male phantasm of a creation without mother; but more than that, he produces not just any natural life, but woman herself, the epitome of nature. The nature/culture split seems healed. The most complete technologization of

[13] Thea von Harbou, *Metropolis* (New York: Ace Books, 1963), 54.

nature appears as re-naturalization, as a progress back to nature. Man is at long last alone and at one with himself.

Of course it is an imaginary solution. And it is a solution that does violence to a real woman. The real Maria has to be subdued and exploited so that the robot, by way of male magic, can be instilled with life, a motif, which is fairly symptomatic of the whole tradition. The context of the film makes it clear that in every respect, it is male domination and control which are at stake: control of the real Maria who, in ways still to be discussed, represents a threat to the world of high technology and its system of psychic and sexual repression; domination of the woman-robot by Rotwang who orders his creature to perform certain tasks; control of the labour process by the Master of Metropolis who plans to replace inherently uncontrollable living labor by robots; and, finally, control of the workers' actions through Fredersen's cunning use of the machine-woman, the false Maria.

On this plane, then, the film suggests a simple and deeply problematic homology between woman and technology, a homology which results from male projections: Just as man invents and constructs technological artifacts which are to serve him and fulfil his desires, so woman, as she has been socially invented and constructed by man, is expected to reflect man's needs and to serve her master. Furthermore, just as the technological artifact is considered to be the quasi-natural extension of man's natural abilities (the lever replacing muscle power, the computer expanding brain power), so woman, in male perspective, is considered to be the natural vessel of man's reproductive capacity, a mere bodily extension of the male's procreative powers. But neither technology nor woman can ever be seen as solely a natural extension of man's abilities. They are always also qualitatively different and thus threatening in their otherness. It is this threat of otherness that causes male anxiety and reinforces the urge to control and dominate that which is other.

Virgin and Vamp: Displacing the Double Threat

The otherness of woman is represented in the film in two traditional images of femininity — the virgin and the vamp, images which are both focused on sexuality. Although both the virgin and the vamp are imaginary constructions, male-imagined "ideal types" belonging to the realm Silvia Bovenschen has described as *"Imaginierte Weiblichkeit,"*[14] they are built up from a real core of social, physiological, and psycho-

[14] Silvia Bovenschen, *Die imaginierte Weiblichkeit: Exemplarische Untersuchungen zu kulturgeschichtlichen und literarischen Präsentationsformen des Weiblichen* (Frankfurt am Main: Suhrkamp, 1979).

logical traits specific to women and should not be dismissed simply as yet another form of false consciousness. What is most interesting about *Metropolis* is the fact that in both forms, femininity, imagined as it is from the male perspective, poses a threat to the male world of high technology, efficiency, and instrumental rationality. Although the film does everything in terms of plot development and ideological substance to neutralize this threat and to re-establish male control in Metropolis, the threat can clearly be perceived as such throughout the film. First, there is the challenge that the real Maria poses to Fredersen, the Master of Metropolis. She prophesies the reign of the heart, i.e., of affection, emotion, and nurturing. Significantly, she is first introduced leading a group of ragged workers' children into the pleasure gardens of Metropolis' *jeunesse dorée*, suggesting both childbearing ability and motherly nurturing. But she also alienates Freder from his father by introducing him to the misery of working-class life. While at the end of the film Maria has become a pawn of the system, at the beginning she clearly represents a threat to the Master of Metropolis. This shows in the sequence where Fredersen, led by Rotwang, secretly observes Maria preaching to the workers in the catacombs. The very fact that Fredersen did not know of the existence of the catacombs deep underneath the city proves that there is something here which escapes his control. Looking through an aperture in a wall high above the assembly at the bottom of the cavern, Fredersen listens to Maria preaching peace and acquiescence to the workers, not revolt. Prophesying the eventual reconciliation between the masters and the slaves she states: "Between the brain that plans and the hands that build, there must be a mediator." And: "It is the heart that must bring about an understanding between them." Rather than perceiving this notion as a welcome ideological veil to cover up the conflict between labour and capital, masters and slaves (that is certainly the way Hitler and Goebbels read the film), Fredersen backs away from the aperture and, with a stern face and his fists plunged into his pockets, he orders Rotwang to make his robot in the likeness of Maria. Then he clenches one fist in the air and continues: "Hide the girl in your house, I will send the robot down to the workers, to sow discord among them and destroy their confidence in Maria." In social and ideological terms this reaction is inexplicable, since Maria, similar to Brecht's Saint Joan of the Stockyards, preaches social peace. But in psychological terms Fredersen's wish to disrupt Maria's influence on the workers makes perfect sense. The threat that he perceives has nothing to do with the potential of organized workers' resistance. It has, however, a lot to do with his fear of emotion, of affection, of nurturing, that is, of all that which is said to be embodied in woman, and which is indeed embodied in Maria.

The result of Fredersen's fear of femininity, of emotion and nurturing, is the male fantasy of the machine-woman who, in the film, embodies two age old patriarchal images of women which, again, are hooked up with two homologous views of technology. In the machine-woman, technology and woman appear as creations and/or cult objects of the male imagination. The myth of the dualistic nature of woman as either asexual virgin-mother or prostitute-vamp is projected onto technology which appears as either neutral and obedient or as inherently threatening and out-of-control. On the one hand, there is the image of the docile, sexually passive woman, the woman who is subservient to man's needs and who reflects the image which the master projects of her. The perfect embodiment of this stereotype in the film is the machine-woman of the earlier sequences when she obeys her master's wishes and follows his commands. Technology seems completely under male control and functions as intended as an extension of man's desires. But even here control is tenuous. We understand that Rotwang has lost a hand constructing his machine. And when the robot advances toward Fredersen, who stands with his back to the camera, and extends her hand to greet him Fredersen is taken aback, and recoils in alarm, a direct parallel to his first spontaneous physical reaction to Maria. Later Rotwang transforms the obedient asexual robot into Maria's living double, and Fredersen sends her down to the workers as an *agent provocateur*. She now appears as the prostitute-vamp, the harbinger of chaos, embodying that threatening female sexuality which was absent (or under control) in the robot. Of course, the potent sexuality of the vamp is as much a male fantasy as the asexuality of the virgin-mother. And, indeed, the mechanical vamp is at first as dependent on and obedient to Fredersen as the faceless robot was to Rotwang. But there is a significant ambiguity here. Although the vamp acts as an agent of Fredersen's manipulation of the workers, she also calls forth libidinal forces which end up threatening Fredersen's rule and the whole social fabric of Metropolis and which therefore have to be purged before order and control can be re-established. This view of the vamp's sexuality posing a threat to male rule and control, which is inscribed in the film, corresponds precisely to the notion of technology running out-of-control and unleashing its destructive potential on humanity. After all, the vamp of the film *is* a technological artifact upon which a specifically male view of destructive female sexuality has been projected.

The Male Gaze and the Dialectic of Discipline and Desire

It is in this context of technology and female sexuality that certain sequences of the film, which have often been called extraneous, assume their full meaning. The mechanical vamp, made to look exactly like

Maria, the virgin-mother-lover figure is presented to an all male gathering in a spectacular mise-en-scène which Rotwang has arranged in order to prove that nobody will be able to tell the machine from a human being. In steam and light the false Maria emerges from a huge ornamental urn and then performs a seductive strip-tease attracting the lustful gaze of the assembled male guests. This gaze is effectively filmed as an agitated montage of their eyes staring into the camera. Cinematically, this is one of the film's most interesting sequences, and it casts a significant light on earlier sequences involving appearances of Maria and the robot. The montage of male eyes staring at the false Maria when she emerges from her cauldron and begins to cast off her clothes illustrates how the male gaze actually constitutes the female body on the screen. It is as if we were witnessing the second, public creation of the robot, her flesh, skin, and body not only being revealed, but constituted by the desire of male vision. Looking back now on earlier sequences it becomes clear how the eye of the camera always places the spectator in a position occupied by the men in the film: the workers looking spell-bound at Maria preaching from her candle-lit altar; Fredersen, his back to the camera, staring at Rotwang's robot; Rotwang's flashlight pinning Maria down in the caverns, and symbolically raping her; and, finally, the transference of Maria's bodily features onto the metallic robot under the controlling surveillance of Rotwang's gaze. Woman appears as a projection of the male gaze, and this male gaze is ultimately that of the camera, of another machine. In the mentioned sequences, vision is identified as male vision. In Lang's narrative, the male eye, which is always simultaneously the mechanical eye of the camera, constructs its female object as a technological artifact (i.e., as a robot) and then makes it come to life through multiple instances of male vision inscribed into the narrative. This gaze is an ambiguous mesh of desires: desire to control, desire to rape, and ultimately desire to kill, that finds *its* gratification in the burning of the robot.

It is also significant that the artificial woman is constructed from the inside out. First Rotwang constructs the mechanical "inner" woman; external features such as flesh, skin, and hair are added on in a second stage when the body features of the real Maria are transferred to or projected onto the robot in an elaborate chemical and electric spectacle. This technical process in which woman is divided and fragmented into inner and outer nature is later mirrored in the subsequent stages of the vamp's destruction: the outer features of the vamp burn away on the stake until only the mechanical insides are left and we again see the metallic robot of the earlier scenes. My point here is not only that construction and destruction of the female body are intimately linked in *Metropolis*. Beyond that, it is male vision which puts together and disassembles woman's body, thus denying woman her identity and making her into an object of projection and manipulation. What is interesting about Lang's *Metropolis* is not so much that Lang uses the male gaze in the described way. Practically all traditional narrative cinema treats woman's body as a projection of male vision. What is interesting, however, is that by thematizing male gaze and vision in the described way the film lays open a fundamental filmic convention usually covered up by narrative cinema.

But there is more to it than that. Lang's film may lead us to speculate whether the dominance of vision *per se* in our culture may not be a fundamental problem rather than a positive contribution to the advance of civilization as Norbert Elias would have it in his study of the civilizing process.[15] Actually Elias' sources themselves are open to alternative interpretations. He quotes for example from an eighteenth century etiquette manual, La Salle's *Civilité* (1774): "Children like to touch clothes and other things that please them with their hands. This urge must be corrected, and they must be taught to touch all they see only with their eyes." And then Elias concludes as follows: "It has been shown elsewhere how the use of the sense of smell, the tendency to sniff at food or other things, comes to be restricted as something animal-like. Here we see one of the interconnections through which a different sense organ, the eye, takes on a very specific significance in civilized society. In a similar way to the ear, and perhaps even more so, it becomes a mediator of pleasure, precisely because the direct satisfaction of the desire for pleasure has been hemmed in by a multitude of barriers and prohibitions."[16] The language both in the source and in Elias' text is revealing. Corrections, barriers, prohibition — the terms indicate that there is more at stake here than the satisfaction of desire or the progress of civilization. It is of course Michel Foucault who, in his analysis of modernization processes, has shown in *Discipline and Punish* how vision and the gaze have increasingly become means of control and discipline.[17] While Elias and Foucault differ in their evaluation of the observed phenomena, their micrological research on vision corroborates Adorno and Horkheimer's macrological thesis that the domination of outer nature via science and technology in capitalist society is dialectically and in-

---

[15] *The Civilizing Process: The Development of Manners* (Urizen Books: New York, 1978).

[16] Elias, *The Civilizing Process,* 203.

[17] Michel Foucault, *Discipline and Punish,* trans. Alan Sheridan (Harmondsworth: Penguin Books, 1977).

exorably linked with the domination of inner nature, one's own as well as that of others.[18]

I would argue that it is precisely this dialectic that is the subterranean context of Lang's *Metropolis*. Vision as pleasure and desire has to be subdued and manipulated so that vision as technical and social control can emerge triumphant. On this level, the film pits the loving, nurturing gaze of Maria against the steely, controlled and controlling gaze of the Master of Metropolis. In the beginning Maria eludes his control since the catacombs are the only place in Metropolis remaining outside of the panoptic control system of the Tower; if only for that she must be punished and subdued. Beyond that, her "inner nature" is replaced by the machine. Ironically, however, the attempt to replace the real woman by the machine-woman fails, and Rotwang and Fredersen have to face the return of the repressed. Once Maria has become a machine or, which is the other side of the process, the machine has appropriated Maria's external appearance, she again begins to elude her master's control. It seems that in whatever form woman cannot be controlled. True, the robot Maria does perform the task she has been programmed to do. In an inflammatory speech supported by sensual body language she seduces the male workers and leads them to the rampage in the machine rooms. In these sequences, the expressionist fear of a threatening technology which oppresses workers is displaced and reconstructed as the threat female sexuality poses to men and, ironically, to technology. Thus the machine-woman, who is no longer recognized as a machine, makes all men lose control: both the upperclass men who lust after her at the belly-dance party, and who, later, run deliriously with her through the streets of Metropolis shouting "Let's watch the world going to the devil," and the workers in the catacombs whom she turns into a raging machine-destroying mob. Significantly, the riot is joined by the workers' wives who are shown for the first time in the film — in a state of hysteria and frenzy. The mob scenes thus take on connotations of a raging femininity which represents *the* major threat not only to the great machines, but to male domination in general. The threat of technology has successfully been replaced by the threat of woman. But while the machines only threatened the men who worked them the unleashed force of female sexuality, represented by the vamp and the working-class women,[19] endangers the whole system of Metropolis, up-

---

[18] See Max Horkheimer, *Eclipse of Reason* (New York: Oxford UP, 1947) and Theodor W. Adorno and Max Horkheimer, *Dialectic of Enlightenment*, trans. John Cumming (London: Verso, 1997).

[19] In his thorough analysis of the Freikorps literature of the early Weimar Republic Klaus Theweleit has shown how in the presentation of proletarian women the themes of revolution and threatening sexuality are consistently interwoven. The way in

town and downtown, masters and slaves, and especially the workers' children who were abandoned underground to the floods unleashed by the destruction of the central powerhouse.

The Female Minotaur as Technology-Out-of-Control

Cliché has had it that sexually women are passive by nature and that the sexually active woman is abnormal, if not dangerous and destructive. The machine vamp in *Metropolis* of course embodies the unity of an active and destructive female sexuality and the destructive potential of technology. This pairing of the woman with the machine is in no way unique to Lang's film. Apart from the literary examples I cited earlier, it can be found in numerous nineteenth century allegorical representations of technology and industry as woman.[20] More interesting for my purposes here, however, is Jean Veber's early twentieth century painting entitled "Allégorie sur la machine dévoreuse des hommes."[21] In the right half of the painting we see a gigantic flywheel which throws up and devours dozens of dwarf-like men. A large rod connected with the flywheel moves to and fro into a metal box on which a giant woman is sitting naked, with parted legs and smiling demonically. Clearly the painting is an allegory of sexual intercourse, of a destructive female sexuality unleashed upon men. It suggests that the woman has appropriated the phallic power and activity of the machine and that she now turns this power violently against men. It is easy to see that the allegory is indicative of male sexual anxieties, of the fear of an uncontrolled female potency, of the vagina dentata, of castration by woman. Whereas in this painting woman and machine are not identical, but stand in a relationship allegorizing a specific kind of female sexuality as imagined and feared by men, woman and machine are collapsed into one in the machine-vamp of *Metropolis*. Since the painting is sexually more explicit, it can help us unearth another major aspect of the film's subterranean content. What Eduard Fuchs, the famous art collector and art

---

which Lang places the working-class women in his film corroborates Theweleit's findings. Klaus Theweleit, *Männerphantasien: Frauen, Fluten, Körper, Geschichte,* vol. 1 (Frankfurt am Main: Verlag Roter Stern, 1977), esp. 217–28.

[20] See Cäcilia Rentmeister, "Berufsverbot für die Musen," *Ästhetik und Kommunikation* 25 (September 1976), 92–112.

[21] "Allegory of the Men-Devouring Machine." Veber's painting is discussed in Rentmeister's essay (see previous note) in relation to Georg Scholz' painting "Fleisch und Eisen" of 1923, a painting that can be attributed to the *Neue Sachlichkeit*; it is also discussed in Theweleit, *Männerphantasien,* vol. 1, 454.

critic, said about Veber's allegorical painting in 1906, he could have said as well, with even more justification, of the machine-vamp in *Metropolis*: "Woman is the symbol of that terrifying, secret power of the machine that rolls over anything that comes under its wheels, smashes that which gets caught in its cranks, shafts, and belts, and destroys those who attempt to halt the turning of its wheels. And, vice versa, the machine, which coldly, cruelly and relentlessly sacrifices hecatombs of men as if they were nothing, is the symbol of the man-strangling Minotaur-like nature of woman."[22] A perfect summary of male mystifications of female sexuality as technology-out-of-control!

Exorcism of the Witch Machine

In light of Veber's painting and Fuchs' interpretation, even earlier sequences of the film assume a different meaning. In her first appearance Maria, accompanied by the workers' children, seems to represent only the stereotypical innocent virgin-mother figure, devoid of sexuality. Such an interpretation is certainly in character, but it is nevertheless only one side of the story. It is significant, I think, that Freder's first gaze at Maria is heavily loaded with sexual connotations. Just before their encounter, Freder is playfully chasing a young woman back and forth around a fountain splashing water at her. Finally they collide in front of the fountain. Freder takes her in his arms, bends over her, and is about to kiss her when the doors open and Maria enters with the children. Freder releases the woman in his arms and in point of view shot stares raptured at Maria. This context of Maria's appearance as well as the hazed iris effect surrounding Maria as Freder gazes at her clearly indicate that Maria has instantaneously become an object of desire. To be sure, the passions she arouses in Freder are different from the playful sexuality suggested by the preceding sequence, but they are anything but asexual. The use of water imagery can give us another cue here. Just as the floods of the later sequences allegorize female frenzy (the proletarian women) and threatening female sexuality (the vamp), the fountain assumes sexual meaning as well. Except that here the water imagery suggests a controlled, channelled and non-threatening sexuality, the playful kind that is permitted in Metropolis. Similarly, the choreography of body movements in the fountain scene emphasizes geometry, symmetry and control, aspects which also inform the preceding track race sequence in the Masterman Stadium which was later cut from the film. Both athletics and the sexual games of the Eternal Gardens are presented as carefree, but controlled diversions of Me-

---

[22] Eduard Fuchs, *Die Frau in der Karikatur* (Munich: Langen, 1906), 262. Translation by A.H.

tropolis' gilded youth. These scenes show us the upper-class equivalent of Lang's ornamental treatment of the workers in geometric, mechanically moving columns.[23] Already here Maria clearly disrupts the status quo. In response to her appearance Freder's body movements and gestures assume a new quality. From this point he becomes all impulse and desire, charges blindly from place to place, and seems unable to keep his body under control. Even more importantly, it is in pursuit of Maria that Freder descends underground and ends up in the vast machine halls of Metropolis. Whether she has "led" him there or not, the narrative links Freder's first exposure to the great machines with his sexual desire, a link which becomes even more manifest in the explosion sequence. For all of the subsequent events in the machine room actually mirror Freder's internal situation. The temperature rises relentlessly above the danger point and the machines run out of human control. Several blasts throw workers off the scaffoldings. Steam whirls and bodies fly through the air. Then comes a sequence in which Freder, in a total state of shock, begins to hallucinate. In his vision, the aperture high up in the belly of the great machine, in which we can see revolving cranks, changes into a grotesque mask-like face with a gaping mouth equipped with two rows of teeth. A column of half-naked workers moves up the pyramid-like steps, and two priests standing on either side of the fiery and blinding abyss supervise several muscular slaves who hurl worker after worker against the gleaming cranks which keep rising and falling amid clouds of smoke and steam. Of course, the meaning of Freder's nightmarish hallucination is quite clear: technology as moloch demanding the sacrifice of human lives. But that is not all. If we assume that Freder in pursuit of Maria is still sexually aroused, and if we remember that his second hallucination in the film deals explicitly with sexuality (that of the machine-vamp Maria), we may want to see the imagery in this sequence as a first indication of the vagina dentata theme, of castration anxiety, of the male fear of uncontrolled female potency displaced to technology.

Such an interpretation has implications for the way in which we perceive the real Maria. Rather than keeping the "good," asexual virgin Maria categorically apart from the "evil" sexual vamp,[24] we become aware of the dialectical relationship of these two stereotypes. On the level of sexual politics, the point of the film is precisely to subdue and to control this threatening and explosive female sexuality which is in-

---

[23] On the cultural and political implications of Lang's ornamental style in *Metropolis*, see Siegfried Kracauer, "The Mass Ornament," *New German Critique* 5 (spring 1975), 67–76.

[24] See Robert A. Armour, *Fritz Lang* (Boston: Twayne, 1977), 29.

herently and potentially there in any women, even the virgin. It is in this context that the elaborate sequence portraying the laboratory creation of the machine-vamp is — contrary to Kracauer's claims — absolutely essential for a full understanding of the technology/sexuality link in the film. After Rotwang has brought Maria under his control, he proceeds to take her apart, to disassemble and to deconstruct her. In a complicated chemical and electrical process he filters her sexuality out of her and projects it onto the lifeless robot who then comes alive as the vamp Maria. The sexuality of the vamp is thus the sexuality of the real woman Maria transformed by a process of male projections onto the machine. After this draining experience, the real Maria is no longer the active enterprising woman of before, but assumes the role of a helpless mother figure who is totally dependent on male support. Thus in the flood sequences she seems paralyzed and has to wait for Freder to save the children, and in the end again she has to be saved from Rotwang's hands.

Just as Maria, under the male gaze, has been disassembled and doubly reconstructed as a docile sexless mother figure and as a potent destructive vamp who is then burnt at the stake, so Freder's desires have to be disentangled and controlled, and the sexual element purged. This happens mainly in the sequences following Freder's encounter with the false Maria in his father's arms. Freder suffers a physical and mental breakdown. During recovery in bed he hallucinates with terrified wide open eyes precisely that *mise-en-scène* of the vamp which Rotwang had set up on that same evening. Although this sequence can be read according to the Freudian account of the primal scene, the castration threat of the father, and the Oedipal conflict, such a reading remains too limited. The goal of the narrative here is not just to bring Freder back under the Law of the Father by resolving the Oedipal conflict;[25] it is rather to associate all male sexual desire for women with the threat of castration. This becomes amply clear as Freder's hallucination ends with a vision of the cathedral sculptures of the Seven Deadly Sins. As the central figure of Death moves toward Freder/the camera/the spectator swinging his scythe, Freder screams in horror and sinks back into his pillows.

The fact that Freder has learned his lesson and has been healed from sexual desire shows when he reappears in the catacombs and attempts to expose the false Maria and to keep her from seducing the workers. Separating the false, sexual Maria from the real Maria in his mind suggests that he is now working actively against his own sexual desires. This point is allegorically emphasized by his successful struggle against

---

[25] That is the way Jenkins reads the sequence, "Lang, Fear and Desire," 86.

the floods inundating the workers' quarters where he saves Maria and the children. By the end of the film, Maria is no longer an object of sexual desire for Freder. Sexuality is back under control just as technology has been purged of its destructive, evil, that is, "sexual," element through the burning of the witch machine.

It is, then, as if the expressionist fear of technology and male perceptions of a threatening female sexuality had been both exorcised and reaffirmed by this metaphoric witch-burning, which, as all witch burnings, guarantees the return of the repressed. It is as if the destructive potential of modern technology, which the expressionists rightfully feared, had to be displaced and projected onto the machine-woman so that it could be metaphorically purged. After the dangers of a mystified technology have been translated into the dangers an equally mystified female sexuality poses to men, the witch could be burnt at the stake and, by implication, technology could be purged of its threatening aspects. What remains is the serene view of technology as a harbinger of social progress. The transition from expressionism to the *Neue Sachlichkeit* is complete. The conflict of labour and capital — such was the belief of the *Neue Sachlichkeit* and such is the implicit message of the film — would be solved through technological progress. The notion that the heart has to mediate between the hands and the brain is nothing but a lingering residue of expressionism, an ideological veil that covers up the persisting domination of labour by capital and high technology, the persisting domination of woman by the male gaze and the re-established repression of female and male sexuality. The final shots of the film with their visual separation of the workers from their masters and with the resumed ornamental treatment of human bodies in motion show that the hands and the brain are as separate as ever. Henry Ford's infamous categorization of humankind into the many hands and the few brains, as it was laid out in his immensely popular autobiography, reigns supreme. It is well-known how German fascism reconciled the hands and the brain, labour and capital. By then, Fritz Lang was already in exile.

20. Fredersen's office in the New Tower of Babel.
[Deutsches Institut für Filmkunde, Frankfurt]

The Mediation of Technology and Gender

Metropolis, Nazism, Modernism*

R. L. Rutsky

IF, AS MANY HAVE CLAIMED, AESTHETIC MODERNISM can be defined by its relation to technology, perhaps no other single work condenses so many aspects of this relationship as Fritz Lang's *Metropolis* (1926). There, modernism's fears of and fascination with technology are given over-determined representation. Andreas Huyssen, in one of the more perceptive analyses of *Metropolis*, has argued that the film is an attempt to resolve "two diametrically opposed views of technology:" an "expressionist view" that emphasises "technology's oppressive and destructive potential" and the "unbridled confidence in technical progress and social engineering" of "the technology cult of the *Neue Sachlichkeit*."[1] Huyssen has elsewhere suggested that the whole of the twentieth-century avant-garde may be defined by its experience — positive or negative — of technology.[2] Yet, viewing *Metropolis*, much less modernism in general, in terms of a dialectic between utopian and dystopian views of technology may obscure as much as it clarifies. It makes little sense, for example, to categorise Italian futurists, Soviet constructivists, and architects of the German *Werkbund* simply in terms of their technological utopianism. Although these movements do tend to see technology positively, their views of technology — of what technology is — are obviously different. Similarly, not all views of modern technology as dystopian define technology in the same way. Given these differences, it may be more helpful to distinguish between a rationalist, functionalist notion of technology and a notion that emphasizes the irrational, chaotic, and even the destructive aspects of technology, that sees it as a dynamic, shocking, almost libidinal force. Both of these conceptions of technology may be seen as either utopian or dystopian. If the technological utopianism of the *Neue Sachlichkeit* depends on a functionalist conception, the Italian futurists embrace a

---

* Reprinted from *New German Critique* 60 (fall 1993), 3–32, by permission of the author and publishers.

[1] Andreas Huyssen, "The Vamp and the Machine: Fritz Lang's *Metropolis*," see page 204 above.

[2] Huyssen, "The Hidden Dialectic: Avantgarde — Technology — Mass Culture," *After the Great Divide: Modernism, Mass Culture, Postmodernism* (Bloomington: Indiana UP, 1986), 10.

technology that they see as dynamic and irrational. In *Metropolis,* on the other hand, both of these "technological aesthetics" are presented, contrary to Huyssen's view, as dystopian. Indeed, it is only to the extent that these two dystopian notions of technology can be "mediated" and synthesized that a utopian technology becomes possible. The desire for this mediation serves to structure not only *Metropolis,* but much of modernism. It is also the basis for the often-noted connections between *Metropolis* and Nazism.

In *Metropolis,* this mediation can be seen in the triadic "head, heart, and hands" metaphor that structures the film, as it did Thea von Harbou's novel, from which the film's scenario was adapted.[3] As the "head" or "brain of Metropolis," Joh Fredersen is presented as a figure of almost superhuman (or inhuman) rationality and efficiency. The architect of Metropolis, he designs and constructs his "utopian" technological city along strictly rational and functionalist lines. Also built into the city's utilitarian design, however, is a Benthamite, and indeed panoptical, system of control. More precisely, this system, with its hierarchical structure, is closely related to the systems of "scientific management" devised by Frederick W. Taylor and put into practice by Henry Ford.[4] As in Taylorist and Fordist organizational charts, this structure can itself be represented as a triangle, with Fredersen at its "head."

In this system, workers must adapt themselves to a functional, technological rationality; they must function like machines, in lockstep and geometric formation, their individual identities lost. Thus, the "hands" of Metropolis become, like Rotwang's prosthetic hand, mechanical and replaceable. What is figured by this mechanization is an alienation of the social or political body; the hands are "cut off" from the utopian

---

[3] [Editors' Note: Rutsky here sketches in the circumstances of the background, genesis, and afterlife of the film, which the reader will find covered in full detail elsewhere in this volume. Having paid tribute to the restoration work of Patalas, he continues:]

> It is worth noting, however, that the sub-plots and motivations restored to the film by these reconstructions can also be found in von Harbou's novel, which I have found extremely helpful to my interpretation of the film. Throughout this essay I have drawn material not only from the edited and the reconstructed versions of the film, but also from the novel: Thea von Harbou, *Metropolis* (Boston: Gregg Press, 1975; reprint of 1929 edition published by The Reader's Library).

[4] Taylor's *Principles Of Scientific Management* was published in 1911. Ford's first assembly line started not long after. For an account of the importance of Taylor's and Ford's ideas for cinema, and for a host of other interesting ideas, see Peter Wollen, "Cinema/Americanism/The Robot," *New Formations* 8 (summer 1989), 7–34.

plans of the brain.[5] This dismembered or fragmented social body is seen as inorganic, technological, dead. The workers appear robotic and zombie-like, lacking the spirit and emotions that define human life. Fredersen himself is shown as rigid and mechanical, as lacking a human spirit and human emotions (e.g. the firing of his secretary). The "reanimation" of this body will therefore require a "mediator" who will bring these alienated, mechanical parts together, restoring the spirit of life and creating an organic whole. This mediating third term, necessary to bring the brain and the hands together, will itself be a symbol of wholeness and spirit — the heart.[6] Only Freder, as the mediating heart between his father and the workers, can succeed in rejoining the brain and the hands.

Overlaid on the triad of "head, heart, and hands" is the all-too-obvious Christian symbolism of the son as the intercessor between God the father and humanity. Freder is quite explicitly presented as a Christ figure; he descends to the workers' level and takes the place of an exhausted worker, where he suffers and is "crucified" on the control dial of the "Pater Noster" machine, crying out to his father for relief. Yet Freder's role as the son/saviour also involves him in another Christian symbolic triad, one which includes not only his father, Joh (Jehovah), Fredersen, but the virginal mother-figure of Maria (Mary). Here, it would seem, Maria stands as the representative of the positive aspects of the workers/humanity, just as the false Maria seems to embody their negative side. Between the symbolic triangle of father/son/humanity and that of Jehovah/Christ/Mary, however, there is a certain slippage, a set of displacements that will continue to disrupt the symbolic structure of *Metropolis*.

The first displacement is that, however much Maria represents the workers, it is difficult to align her with the "hands." In contrast to the sensuality of her evil double, there is little about Maria that can be associated with the physical. Her role, in fact, seems more like that which Goethe, at the close of *Faust II*, famously ascribes to the "Holy Virgin, Mother Queen:" "The Eternal-Feminine [that] draws us upwards."[7] Thus apotheosized, Maria comes to take a place similar to that in the Christian Trinity of the Holy Spirit.

---

[5] The workers, as Maria notes in the parable of the Tower of Babel, know "nothing of the dream of those who planned the tower."

[6] This triadic structure has deep roots in German philosophy; it should recall not only Hegel, but Kant's three Critiques as well.

[7] This connection is supported by the Faustian overtones that appear throughout *Metropolis* — particularly in relation to the Fredersen character — and that are considerably clearer in Thea von Harbou's novel, as they apparently were in the original version of the film.

In terms of the "head, heart, hands" typology, Maria's spirituality makes her much more a representative of the "heart" than of the "hands." She personifies, even more than Freder, the emotive and spiritual dimensions that are excluded from Fredersen's world of rationality and efficiency. Similarly, the false Maria represents a demonic spirit or nature, a "dark heart" harbouring the irrational, destructive side of the emotions. Thus, contrary to both von Harbou's premise and the repeated assertions of commentators, the heart (or the emotive/spiritual) does not mediate between the brain and the hands. The hands, in fact, are excluded, "cut off," from the process of mediation; the workers are presented simply as "manipulable" tools, as a technology equally susceptible to the emotional machinations of the false Maria as to the rationalized mechanization of Fredersen. The concluding handshake between Fredersen and the representative of the workers occurs after the fact; the actual mediation having taken place, instead, between brain and heart, rationality and emotion, the scientific and the magico-spiritual. The reconciliation of *these* opposing terms is the true ideological project of *Metropolis,* and it is to this end that Freder, rather than Maria, must play the role of the mediator.

This attempt at reconciliation is also presented as a mediation of paternal and maternal, masculine and feminine. It is hardly surprising, therefore, that the character relations, plot, and structure of *Metropolis* are dominated by the figure of the Oedipal triangle. In *Metropolis,* however, the basic Oedipal triangle has been subjected to a certain amount of condensation and displacement; it has, first of all, been split into two separate but interconnected triangles; the triad of Fredersen/Maria/Freder, and the Fredersen/Hel/Rotwang triangle which was excised from the film for its American release.[8] In the first, the maternal figure of Maria stands in for Freder's mother, Hel. The resemblance between the two is such that Rotwang, in his derangement near the end of the film, will mistake Maria for Hel. Yet Maria is herself doubled by the robot Maria, and it is the sight of her embrace with his father that sends

[8] The so-called "Hel sub-plot" was removed by the film's American editors. [Editors' Note: see Bartlett in Part One of this volume.] The relationship between Fredersen, Rotwang, and Hel has been made clear, however, by Patalas's reconstruction in "*Metropolis,* Scene 103," trans. Miriam Hansen, *Camera Obscura* 15 (autumn 1986), 165–72, and can also be seen in the Moroder version of the film, as well as in von Harbou's novel. Hel, although loved by Rotwang, succumbed to Fredersen's will and went away with him. She died giving birth to Freder, but the novel suggests that it was actually Fredersen's excessive love and her own guilt over leaving Rotwang that killed her. This information obviously gives the motivation for many of Rotwang's seemingly pointless actions in the film, including his actions at the end of the film where, thinking he has died, he goes in search of Hel and, mistaking Maria for her, attempts to carry Maria off.

Freder into traumatized illness and hallucinations. Freder's mistaken interpretation of this embrace replicates the situation of Fredersen's "theft" of Hel from Rotwang. Indeed, as Roger Dadoun has suggested, Rotwang is the counterpart of Freder; he plays the role of the "bad son," the "rebellious rival son" castrated by the father; "his severed hand is punishment for his filial curiosity and establishes a female component of his personality."[9] Freder also has a "female component," which is made clear in von Harbou's novel, where Freder's difference from his father — his "soft heart" — is explained by the fact that he "is Hel's son."[10] In the film, this "femininity" — which allows him to mediate between masculine and feminine, brain and heart — is manifested in his ability to sympathize (for instance, with the secretary, Josaphat) and in his highly emotional reactions, emphasized by Gustav Fröhlich's hyperkinetic acting style. Thus, Freder's femininity is presented as something that is part of him, part of an integrated (or mediated) whole; he is *both* Hel's *and* Fredersen's son: "Freder is Hel's son. Yes . . . that means he has a soft heart. But he is yours too, Joh. That means he has a skull of steel."[11] Freder's ability to resolve or mediate the Oedipal triangles of *Metropolis* is premised upon his status as a whole; since he combines both brain and heart, masculine and feminine, he lacks nothing. On the other hand (the one that has been cut off), Rotwang's femininity is not presented as the result of a mediated wholeness but of a lack — a lack produced by the injunction of the law of the father, who necessarily possessed what Rotwang lacks; the woman/mother but also the phallus. Even Rotwang's name suggests a femininity based on lack, on an artifice designed to cover this lack: *Rot-wang* means, literally, red cheek [*Wangenrot*, rouge], but the association of *Röte* with blood also suggests Rotwang's symbolic castration (the loss of his hand/phallus), which is covered over by an artificial, mechanical substitution. Moreover, Rotwang's madness, his "evil," is attributed to the loss of Hel to the father-figure Fredersen, just as Freder's perception of the loss of Maria to his father provokes illness and hallucinations. Yet in neither case are these disruptions of the rational, phallic order based simply upon a "feminine" lack; rather, the source of these disruptions is a "feminine" artifice, and irrational mechanical substitute, a technological simulacrum: the false Maria.

The black, mechanical form of Rotwang's female robot — its form is feminine even before its birth, or rebirth, in the figure of Maria —

---

[9] Roger Dadoun, "*Metropolis*: Mother City — 'Mittler' — Hitler," trans. Arthur Goldhammer, *Camera Obscura* 15 (autumn 1986), 149.

[10] von Harbou, *Metropolis*, 157.

[11] von Harbou, *Metropolis*, 157.

serves to replace his lost love Hel, just as his black prosthetic hand replaces his lost one. Unlike Fredersen, whose possession of the woman/mother takes place under the imprimatur of a paternal, phallic law, Rotwang must piece together a simulated, mechanical copy, onto which he will conjure the shape, and the inverted spirit of the woman/mother Rotwang, in other words, invests this technological replacement not only with an electrical, but with an emotional/spiritual charge, thereby duplicating the structure of the fetish. The technological object — itself defined by its reproducibility, by its status as a substitute — therefore stands in for both the mother and the phallus. Dadoun notes that the robot Maria can be seen to represent, on the one hand, "the severed phallus of Rotwang"[12] and, on the other, "the female genitals," the reaction to which "indicates horror of the female organ and . . . horror of sexuality" in general.[13] The robot is represented as a sexuality or physicality that has been "cut off" from the organic body, and "hand" severed from the brain and heart. Presented as fetishistic, masturbatory, and destructive, it is like the hand of Death which, intercut with the scenes of Freder's hallucinations and the false Maria's exotic dance, both plays a phallic, thigh-bone flute and swings a castrating scythe. The false Maria represents the condensation of a sexuality and a technology whose demonic or uncanny life is the product of a fetishization in which a necessarily alienated object (both sexual and technological) takes on the status of, is substituted for, an organic whole.

A similar fetishization occurs in Freder's vision of the machine as Moloch, where the spectre of an alienated technology again appears in the form of a demonic mechanical life. Yet while the robot Maria figures a technology and a sexuality that are presented as irrationally destructive and out of control, the uncanny technological life of the Moloch-machine seems to be the result of too much rationality, too much control. What is fetishized here is Fredersen's overly rational, scientific management, his urge to dominate, to control, to use and consume. As the representation of this dominating technological rationality, the Moloch-machine does indeed treat the workers as objects to be used, controlled, possessed, and, quite literally, consumed. Similarly, Fredersen treats the woman/mother as an object to be stolen and possessed; it is his obsessive, "too strong" love for Hel that is said, in von Harbou's novel, to have caused her death. Within the ideological strictures of *Metropolis*, the controlling, technological rationality of the Moloch-machine can only be presented in terms of a phallic paternal

---

[12] Dadoun, "*Metropolis*: Mother City," 146.

[13] Dadoun, "*Metropolis*: Mother City," 153.

law (it is, after all, identified — in von Harbou's novel — as the Pater Noster machine). The irrational technology of Rotwang's robot is necessarily figured, on the other (prosthetic) hand, as castrated, castrating, deadly, and feminine.

It is worth noting here the extent to which these gendered technologies correspond to the poles suggested by Kracauer in *From Caligari to Hitler*: "alternative images of tyrannic rule and instinct-governed chaos."[14] Moreover, as Kracauer has so clearly observed, this "torturing alternative" will haunt not only *Metropolis* and the German silent cinema but German society in general. It can be seen here that Huyssen's analysis of *Metropolis* in terms of a tension between a tyrannical, *Neue Sachlichkeit* technologism and expressionist fears of a chaotic, irrational technology is, to a large degree, an extension of Kracauer's basic thesis. Huyssen seems to draw even more on Klaus Theweleit's *Male Fantasies*, a work that, in exploring the relations between *Freikorps* psychology and German society, shows the extent to which Kracauer's tyranny/chaos division was cast in the terms of male and female, of a patriarchal order threatened by a chaotic, engulfing feminine other.[15] Theweleit sees this otherness as a representation of the unconscious and, following Deleuze and Guattari, notes that although it is frequently figured in terms of "floods," "streams," and "bodily fluids," it is also connected to the machine; "the unconscious is a flow and a desiring-machine."[16] Yet, curiously, Theweleit sees the "negativization of the 'mechanical'" in *Metropolis* only in connection to Fredersen's machines, which are, along with the working "masses," relegated to subterranean (that is, unconscious) levels;[17] he therefore overlooks the obvious connection between the "negativized" feminine machinery of the false Maria and the floods which she provokes. Huyssen, on the other hand, clearly recognizes the condensation in the false Maria of the (expressionist) fear of an irrational, out-of-control technology and the fears of a chaotic, engulfing female sexuality. In his reading, however, the condensation of these fears in "the machine-woman" only takes place so that, by destroying the false Maria, "technology could be purged of its threatening aspects," thus completing the transition from an expressionist view of technology as irrational and destructive to the

---

[14] Siegfried Kracauer, *From Caligari to Hitler: A Psychological History of the German Film* (Princeton: Princeton UP, 1947) 107.

[15] Klaus Theweleit, *Male Fantasies*, 2 vols., trans. Stephen Conway, Erica Carter and Chris Turner (Minneapolis: U of Minnesota P, 1987, 1989).

[16] Theweleit, *Male Fantasies*, vol. 1, 255.

[17] Theweleit, *Male Fantasies*, vol. 1, 257.

Neue Sachlichkeit's "serene view of technology as a harbinger of social progress."[18]

Underlying these similar readings, however, is an even more crucial point of agreement; in each, the affirmation of a tyrannical, patriarchal technological order, exemplified in *Metropolis*, is seen as analogous to, or foreshadowing, the Nazi rise to power. Theweleit's work, of course is explicitly concerned with this analogy. Similarly, this analogy is presented in the very title of Kracauer's work, and is made abundantly clear when he closes his discussion of *Metropolis* with the now famous story of how Hitler, much impressed by *Metropolis*, had wanted Lang to make Nazi films.[19] Huyssen, in closing his analysis of the film, echoes this sentiment: "It is well-known how German fascism reconciled the hands and the brain, labour and capital."[20]

The point of contention in this essay is not, however, the connection of *Metropolis*, or German cinema, or German culture more generally, to German fascism. It contends, rather, that the fascistic implications of these cultural forms lie not in the affirmation of a tyrannical, masculine order over a chaotic feminine other, or in the privileging of a *Neue Sachlichkeit* view of technology over an expressionist view, but in their desire for a mediation which would restore coherence to an alienated, technologized modern world split by these dystopian alternatives. In *Metropolis* it is not simply the feminine false Maria but also Fredersen's functionalist, male technology — the Moloch-machine — that is presented as dystopian, as a terrifying machine-come-to-life. It is precisely their engenderment that makes these technologies dystopian: the feminine and the masculine machine are each presented as a threat to the "mediated" organic wholeness of the brain, heart, and hands. Each is defined as a fetish, as the substitution of a "severed," "dead," partial object — both sexual and technological — for a whole, "living" subject. Indeed gender itself comes to be seen as a fetish.

Yet, if the film figures these gendered technologies — and gender itself — as alienated, split, or severed, it also suggests that they are two sides of the same problem: the alienation or repression of the organic wholeness of nature (both an internal, "human" nature and an external nature) that takes place in a technological modernity. This technological modernity is itself seen as split between an overly rational technology that represses (or mechanizes) the natural and a return of this repressed nature in the form of a chaotic, and often supernatural, technology. This view of modernity is not, however limited to *Metropolis*. It is par-

---

18 Huyssen, "The Vamp and the Machine," see page 215 above.

19 Kracauer, *From Caligari to Hitler*, 81.

20 Huyssen, "The Vamp and the Machine," see page 215 above.

ticularly apparent in those films which Kracauer discusses that, like *Metropolis,* concern the artificial or technological creation of life.

In his summary of Wegener's now lost first version of *The Golem* (1914), Kracauer observes that "the legend behind the film was the medieval Jewish one in which Rabbi Loew of Prague infuses life into a Golem, a statue he had made of clay, by putting a magic sign on its heart."[21] In the film, the clay statue is rediscovered in modern times and comes into the hands of an antique dealer, who succeeds in reanimating it and makes it his servant. Unfortunately, the Golem "falls in love with the daughter of his masters" and, infuriated by her horrified rejection of him, becomes a "raging monster."[22] The Golem's life, which, like Rotwang's creation of the robot Maria, is associated with ancient, magical, or occult powers, is artificial, technological. Like Rotwang's robot, as well as the workers of *Metropolis,* the Golem is initially a purely mechanical instrument or tool, a "dead" technological object, without a spirit or soul. Yet, also like the workers of *Metropolis,* the Golem yearns for wholeness, for spiritual and emotional fulfilment, for love; he is therefore drawn to the daughter of the antique dealer, much as the workers are drawn to Maria. It is the frustration of this fulfilment that leads him to become, much like the false Maria and the workers in their revolt, a "raging monster," libidinal, chaotic, destructive. In both films, this monstrosity results from an artificial or technological life in which love, the spirit or soul, the spiritual/emotional aspects of life, have been repressed — a repression which leads to a return of the repressed in the form of a monstrous, uncanny life or spirit.

While the Golem has obvious similarities to both the workers and the robot of *Metropolis,* the 1916 film *Homunculus* presents a character who makes clearer the connection between the instrumentalizing repression of Fredersen and the return of the repressed in the robot Maria and the workers' revolt. The initial stages of this story are similar to those of *The Golem.* Homunculus is, in Kracauer's words, "an artificial product" who has been "generated in a retort" by a "famous scientist." Although he becomes "a man of sparkling intellect and indomitable will," he is haunted by his artificial origins. Feeling like an outcast, he yearns for love, but people are horrified by him and say, "It is Homunculus, the man without a soul, the devil's servant — a monster!"[23] Resentful, he becomes a repressive dictator, even disguising himself as a worker in order to incite riots that will give him the opportunity to crush the workers. Fredersen, it should be remembered, attempts to

21 Kracauer, *From Caligari to Hitler,* 31.

22 Kracauer, *From Caligari to Hitler,* 31.

23 Kracauer, *From Caligari to Hitler,* 32.

employ a similar strategy with the false Maria. Yet if the false Maria's destructive, libidinal life is the uncanny other half of Fredersen's repressive rationality and will, the two are combined in the figure of Homunculus. He is both a tyrant and a chaotic, destructive force. Both of these aspects seem to be linked to his lack of human emotion and spirit, of a soul, which is reflected, as Kracauer notes, in "his inability to offer and receive love." Unlike Fredersen, however, Homunculus's lack of humanity is the result of the artificial status of his life. Like both the tyrannical Moloch-machine and the anarchic false Maria, he is a technological simulacrum, a fetish that threatens to replace a fully organic life. Although Homunculus's origins are scientific-technological, like those of Fredersen's Moloch-Machine, it is worth noting that his end, like that of the false Maria, is one that is generally associated with the supernatural or occult: while she is burned as a witch, he will be struck by a thunderbolt.

Clearly, these films, like *Metropolis,* represent a certain anxiety about modernity, about the "domination of nature" by a modern scientific-technological rationality. This technological rationality is presented as a tyrannical will whose attempts to "master and possess" nature lead to a repression of nature, to the alienation or severing of humanity from (its) nature. It is, then, the repression of this nature, whether it is figured in terms of organicism, love, emotion, spirituality, or as a human spirit or soul, that defines modernity as lacking, as "split."[24] This split, moreover, is represented as gendered, as the repression of a feminine nature by a tyrannical, masculine technological will. Thus, these films' anxiety about modernity is cast precisely in Oedipal terms as the imposition of a technological law of the father, that is, as a castration anxiety.

Yet castration cuts, as it were, two ways. On the one hand is the castrated body; on the other, the castrated genitalia. In the first case, one is left with a body without desire, a purely automatic or mechanical body — "dead," without a spirit or soul. This is the state of those somnambulists, hypnotic victims, and other zombie-like figures that recur so frequently in the Germany silent cinema. The Golem (prior to falling in love), Rotwang's robot (prior to its transformation into the false Maria), and the workers of *Metropolis* (prior to their revolt) can all be included in this category. The second case, then, often seems to follow from the first: desire divorced from the body seems to yield a kind of

---

[24] Although the scope of this essay does not allow a detailed treatment of this point, it would be remiss not to mention the extent to which this sense of a "split" or divided modernity is related to, and indeed dependent upon, the German experience of World War I. Theweleit's work, of course, makes this experience a central point in his analysis of German culture between the wars.

pure libido, a monstrous, out-of-control sexuality, a madness of "instinct-governed chaos" that seems to take pleasure in destruction.[25] Thus, the mechanical body becomes monstrous; the somnambulist becomes the vamp.[26]

Despite the relation suggested by his own description, Kracauer continues to pose the somnambulist and the vamp on either side of his tyranny/chaos division — as unrelated, alternative modes, rather than as two sides of the same "cut." For him, a mechanical or somnambulistic life is the result of tyranny, he sees the relationship of Caligari and Cesare, Mabuse and his minions, Nosferatu and his victims, as the relationship of the tyrant and the masses. Thus, the masses become the tools of the tyrant, obedient to his will. The vamp, on the other hand, is a representative of an "instinct-driven chaos" that is associated with a complete lack of authority, leading to wild passions, social degeneration, and violence. Kracauer's reading of Fredersen as the tyrant of *Metropolis* would then seem, according to his schema, to demand that Rotwang, like the false Maria and the rebellious workers, be read as representing the instinctual and chaotic. Such a reading would, however require one to neglect the fact that Rotwang shares many more similarities with Kracauer's supernatural tyrant figures than does Fredersen: his association with magic, the loss of his love, his symbolic castration and his madness, even the fact that Rudolf Klein-Rogge played both Rotwang and Mabuse. Upon examination, in fact, it becomes clear that Kracauer's tyrant figures are often shot through with the instinctual and the chaotic. The "slippage" from Fredersen's tyrannical overrationality to the deranged and chaotic tyrant figure of Rotwang may be seen as analogous to the "descent" into madness and/or the supernatural of such scientists, doctors, and men of "sparkling intellect and indomitable will" as Caligari, Mabuse, and Homunculus. In each of these cases, there is a representation of an attempt to master and possess nature — one that often involves a Frankensteinian creation of an artificial or technological life — that is presented as excessive and

---

[25] See Thomas Elaesser's "Social Mobility and the Fantastic: German Silent Cinema," *Wide Angle* 5 no. 2 (1982), 14–25, where Elsaesser reads the figure of "the Double" in German silent cinema both as a displacement of the "fear of proletarianization" or (industrialization) and as the return of a repressed social history "in the form of the uncanny and fantastic."

[26] This relationship between the robot/somnambulist and the monster/vamp is made even clearer in Kracauer's description of *Alraune* (1928), whose title character (also played by Brigitte Helm, the actress who portrays *Metropolis's* Maria) has been created by an artificial impregnation; for Kracauer, she is precisely a "*somnambulant vamp* with seductive and empty features, [who] ruins all those who are in love with her, and at the end destroys herself" (Kracauer, *From Caligari to Hitler*, 153–4, italics added).

tyrannical. It exceeds the bounds of the natural, of the human, and slips into chaos and madness, evoking the supernatural or the uncanny. Here again, Kracauer's examples make clear that in these films, contrary to his thesis, tyranny and chaos are related, and their relationship is presented as that of a tyrannical repression and a chaotic return of the repressed.

These films do not, as Kracauer, Huyssen, and Theweleit suggest, simply privilege tyranny over chaos, masculine over feminine, a utopian view of technology over a dystopian view. Rather, it is precisely the "split" between these poles — a division "engendered" by a repressive technological modernity — that they see as dystopian. These films represent a desire for a mediation, an attempt to "heal" the (castration) "wound" of modernity, to overcome — and undo — the Oedipal-technological repression that is seen to engender and divide the modern subject. In *Metropolis*, the mediation of this gendered and technological dystopian division is given its most precise representation: a mediation that resolves the split between a repressive, overly rational technological law of the father and an irrational, uncanny, and occult feminine technology by reintegrating a repressed feminine nature of spirit (the heart) and a masculine rationality and will (the brain). Only through such a mediation, *Metropolis* suggests, can a "severed" modern life be restored to wholeness. This restoration occurs even at an etymological level: the lost etymological significance of metropolis as "mother-city" is reintegrated into the functional, modern metropolis of the Father.[27]

Metropolis suggests that this utopian "restoration project" will involve a mediation of not only dystopian technological poles (the Moloch-machine and the false Maria), but also of the conflicting architectural styles of the *Neue Sachlichkeit* (the New Tower of Babel) and expressionism (Rotwang's house, the Cathedral). This conflict was a topic of considerable debate in German architectural circles in the years immediately preceding the making of *Metropolis*, a fact that could hardly have been lost on Lang, who once trained as an architect. This debate, as Kenneth Frampton has observed, manifested itself in the "ideological split" within the *Deutsche Werkbund* between "the collective acceptance of normative form [*Typisierung*], on the one hand, and the individually asserted, expressive 'will to form' [*Kunstwollen*] on the other."[28] Central to the notion of normative types was the idea of the

---

[27] On *Metropolis* as mother-city, see Dadoun. Although he suggests a link between the notion of the mother-city and Hitler, he omits the connection between mother-city and Hitler's references to Germany as "the Motherland."

[28] Kenneth Frampton, *Modern Architecture: A Critical History* (London: Thames and Hudson, 1985), 116. This division between the typical and the "will to form" echoes the two antagonistic aspects of William Worringer's cultural model, as presented in

"tectonic object," which, as Frampton notes, "was an irreducible building element functioning as a basic unit of architectural language."[29] On the other hand, the projection of an architectural "will to form" was to take place according to an atectonic rather than a tectonic principle: instead of depending on standardized, basic geometrical units of architectural language, the architect was to create "pure organic forms" that could be regarded "as a literature without an alphabet."[30]

It is not difficult, then, to see the connection between the idea of normative form and the tectonic, *Neue Sachlichkeit* aesthetics of Fredersen's Metropolis. One can easily imagine the words of Hermann Muthesius, one of the great champions of normative types, in the mouth of Fredersen: "Essentially, architecture tends toward the typical. The type discards the extraordinary and establishes order."[31] Yet in *Metropolis,* this tendency toward standardization and rationalized order, manifested in the abstract, tectonic forms of the city's architecture, is clearly presented as repressive. The repressed architectural elements are precisely those that display a marked tendency toward expressionist, atectonic, and "organic," rather than "abstract," forms: Rotwang's house, the catacombs, the Gothic cathedral, and, in the novel, the house of Fredersen's mother. In distinction to the normative forms and glass-and-steel construction of the *Neue Sachlichkeit,* these forms are irregular; their curved and non-parallel lines, their non-Euclidean geometry, suggest an architecture derived from natural processes and materials (wood and stone). This "organicism" is particularly apparent in their interiors, in the shadowy, irregular concaves of Maria's cavern and Rotwang's house, which, it should be remembered, are interconnected. These dark vaginal spaces are secret, occult; they are hidden from the technological surveillance of Fredersen's scientific management. They seem to hide a power that has been repressed by Fredersen's functional, technologically rationalized world, a power that is figured in the connection of these structures to the spiritual, to the religious or the magical.

---

his widely read *Abstraktion und Einfühlung* [Abstraction and Empathy, 1908]. Against the tendency towards abstract types, Worringer posed, and popularized, a notion of empathy as the projection of an individual creative will into the art object, thus conflating psychologist Theodor Lippo's idea of *Einfühlung* with art-historian Alois Riegel's notion of *Kunstwollen.*

[29] Frampton, *Modern Architecture,* 114.

[30] Frampton, *Modern Architecture,* 98.

[31] Frampton, *Modern Architecture,* 114.

Only the house of Fredersen's mother, which appears in von Harbou's novel but not in the film, seems not to share these occult connotations. Indeed, its organic connection to nature seems entirely simple and familiar: "a farmhouse, one-storied, thatch-roofed, overshadowed by a walnut tree . . . [with] a garden full of lilies and hollyhocks, full of sweet peas and poppies and nasturtiums."[32] Yet, as an almost perfect example of that style of architecture known as *Heimatstil*, a style whose organic connotations would later allow an easy match with Nazi rhetoric of "blood and soil," this house can be connected to the other structures by the curious semantic ambiguity that surrounds those words based on the German root *Heim* (home). On the one hand, words like *Heimat* (home, native land or country) and *heimisch* (of the home, domestic, local) convey a sense of familiarity, connection, and intimacy. On the other hand, *heimlich* (secret, furtive) and *Heimtücke* (treachery) carry a sense of being hidden or concealed. In his article on "The 'Uncanny,'" Freud observed this kind of ambiguity within the word *heimlich* itself, which, he noted, could mean — or, at one time at least, did mean — both "familiar" or "intimate" and "concealed" or "secret."[33] The sense of *heimlich* as concealment seems in fact to have led to its association with notions that might seem the very opposite of home: magic, the occult, ghosts (*Heimsuchen*: to haunt). As Freud notes, *heimlich* comes to be "identical with its opposite, *unheimlich* (the uncanny)." Thus, the entire cluster of words based on *Heim* seems charged with an ambiguity similar to that which has so often been ascribed to the woman or mother.[34]

In *Metropolis*, the familiarity and warmth of the home of the "good" mother can be contrasted to the darkness, occult symbols, and secret passages of Rotwang's house, which also shares a number of the characteristics of *Heimatstil*. The haunted, uncanny life of Rotwang's house, with its doors that open and close of their own accord, is merely the inversion of the intimate, organic connectedness of Fredersen's mother's house, just as the false Maria is the uncanny, inverted spirit of the good Maria. *Metropolis* demonstrates that the uncanny is the inverted form of the familiar, or, as Freud puts it, the return of "something familiar and

---

[32] von Harbou, *Metropolis*, 154. Interestingly, in the novel, Fredersen has had the house transplanted, garden and all, to the top of one of the city's skyscrapers.

[33] Sigmund Freud, "'The Uncanny,'" *The Standard Edition of the Complete Psychological Works*, trans. and ed. James Strachey et al., vol. 17 (London: Hogarth Press, 1955), 217–52.

[34] Freud notes, "It often happens that male patients declare that they feel there is something uncanny about the female genital organs. This *unheimlich* place, however, is the entrance to the former *Heim* [home] of all human beings," (Freud, "'The Uncanny,'" 245). Translation adapted by R.R.

old-established in the mind that has been estranged only by the process of repression."[35] It is worth noting here, in fact, that *Metropolis's* distinction of expressionist and *Neue Sachlichkeit* architectural elements is cast precisely in terms of the "old" versus the "modern," the mother's home, Rotwang's house, Maria's catacomb church, and the Gothic cathedral are all characterized as "old," as more ancient than the modern city that surrounds them. This opposition of an architectural modernity and an older tradition — linked to the magico-spiritual, the organic, and the feminine — is in accordance with Lang's claim to have imagined the film as a "conflict" between modern science and technology on the one hand and the occult or magical on the other. The film suggests, moreover, that it is the repression of this older magical element by a rationalized technological modernity that brings about — or, much like Frankenstein, brings to life — its inverted, uncanny form.

The idea of modernity repressing an older, more magical way of thinking was, however, hardly original to *Metropolis*: both Freud and Max Weber had advanced such ideas not long before *Metropolis* was made. For Weber, the "disenchantment of the world" was linked to a formal (or technological) rationality in which needs were "expressed in numerical calculable terms."[36] This rationalization of the world was, for Weber, fundamental to both modern science and technology and to modern capitalism. Freud also conceived the modern scientific, materialistic outlook in terms of its ability to "surmount "the old, animistic conception of the universe, which was characterized by the idea that the world was peopled with the spirits of human beings, and by the narcissistic overestimation of subjective mental processes."[37] If, however, *Metropolis* accepts this notion of modernity's repression of an older, magico-spiritual conception of the world, it certainly does not affirm it: it figures this repression in terms of loss, division, and alienation, as a sense of *homelessness* [*Heimatloskeit*]. What *Metropolis* strives for is precisely a restoration of a "familiar" sense of "enchantment" and connection to nature that strongly parallels *Heimatstil's* emphasis on "home" and the "familiar," on the older, "*rooted* values of an agrarian craft economy." [38]

Yet this restoration of the home and the familiar is not simply an abandonment of modernity in favour of the ancient, the natural, the spiritual. Rather, *Metropolis* aspires to a mediation of the masculine

[35] Freud, '"The Uncanny,"' 241. Translation adapted by R.R.

[36] Max Weber, *The Theory of Social and Economic Organization,* trans. A. M. Henderson and Talcott Parsons (New York: Oxford UP, 1947), 185.

[37] Freud, '"The Uncanny,"' 240. Translation adapted by R.R.

[38] Frampton, *Modern Architecture,* 216.

technological will of modernity with an ancient feminine spirit or nature. Here, once again, the ending of von Harbou's novel makes explicit what is only implied in the film. In the novel, a chastened Joh Fredersen goes to the home of his mother, where he speaks of recognizing in Freder's face the faces of Hel, Maria, and the masses. Fredersen's repression of the workers is linked to his oppressive love of Hel and to the paternal domination of a feminine nature. His reconciliation with this feminine nature is therefore figured as a *return to home*: as his mother tells him, "I received this letter from Hel before she died. She asked me to give it to you, when, as she said, you had found your way home to me and yourself."[39]

The character of this "home" to which Fredersen returns is, perhaps, made clear by the letter itself, which speaks of Hel's "everlasting love" and ends with a quotation from the Bible: "Lo, I am with you always, even unto the end of the world." It is in an eternal, spiritualized feminine love — much like Goethe's eternal-feminine — that the masculine, rational will finds its resolution, its completion, its destiny or home. In rediscovering this feminine spirit, Fredersen (at least in von Harbou's novel) accomplishes a mediation in which his repressive, paternal rationality is spiritualized and overcome — a sublation that was already implicit in the mediated persona of his son Freder. The relegitimation of Fredersen's (and presumably, after him, Freder's) leadership at the end of the film is not simply an affirmation of a tyrannical masculine technological order; it is based on the mediation of this patriarchal order with an eternal-feminine spirit.

If, moreover, one takes seriously the idea of a linkage between *Metropolis* and National Socialism, this reading of the film suggests that Hitler's appeal was also founded on a mediatory logic, on the idea of the leader as mediator. Dadoun makes this connection when he notes the striking similarity of *Mittler* (mediator) and Hitler. The appeal of Hitler and the Nazis was founded on the desire for wholeness; their followers, as Theweleit notes, were

> The not-yet-fully born, men who had always been left wanting; and where was the party that would offer them more? It was certainly not the rationalist-paternalist Communist Party . . . .
>
> [These men] submit to orders and connect into sites that promise to eliminate what they experience as lack. The word thy repeatedly scream at the party congress is "whole" — heil, heil, heil — and this is precisely what the party makes them. They are no longer broken;

[39] von Harbou, *Metropolis,* 249.

> and they will remain whole into infinity. Eternal life takes place in the here-and-now . . . really and truly.[40]

As Theweleit makes clear, the wholeness that Hitler and the Nazis promise is cast in opposition to a "rationalist-paternalist" communism, which could only be associated with the alienating, mechanizing effects of a technological modernity. The Nazi wholeness involves a mediation of this repressive modernity (the "here-and-now") with a repressed "eternal" spirit: the spirit of Germany. What the leader-mediator offers is a restoration of this ancient spirit: a re-spiritualization, a "re-enchantment," that will "reanimate" a "dead," technologized modern world. National Socialism is cast precisely as the "rebirth" of the German spirit (*die Deutsche Renaissance*), a "rebirth" with obvious appeal to those whom Theweleit calls "the not-yet-fully born."

In this scenario of rebirth, Hitler seems at times to be represented as both father and mother, embodying both a "steely" paternal will and a spiritual-maternal emotionality and love (for Germany and the German people). Certainly, his vision of National Socialism combines both of these attributes: "It will be unchangeable in its doctrine, hard as steel in its organization, supple and adaptable in its tactics, in its entirety, however, it will be like a religious order."[41] In this context, it is worth noting how Adorno's analysis of fascist appeal points precisely to Freud's suggestion that the unconscious "love relationships" that underlie group psychology are often expressed "through the mediation of some religious image in the love of whom the members unite and whose all-embracing love they are supposed to imitate in their attitude towards one another."[42] In Adorno's view, however, this concept of love is replaced (repressed?) in modern fascism by the "threatening authority" of the primal father; the notion of love is therefore "relegated to the abstract notion of *Germany* and seldom mentioned without the epithet of 'fanatical' through which even this love obtain(s) a ring of hostility and aggressiveness against those not encompassed by it." Yet the "relegating" of this concept of love to "the abstract notion of *Germany*" would hardly seem to reduce its efficacy, particularly in view of the logic of Hess's pronouncement that "Hitler is Germany, and Germany is Hitler." Here, yet again, a representation of Nazism in terms of a tyrannical and castrating patriarchal will neglects the extent to which the appeal of

---

[40] Theweleit, *Male Fantasies*, vol. 2, 410–12.

[41] From Hitler's speech at the closing rally of the 1934 Nuremberg Convention, recorded in Riefenstahl's *Triumph of the Will* (1935).

[42] Theodor W. Adorno, "Freudian Theory and the Pattern of Fascist Propaganda," *The Essential Frankfurt School Reader*, eds. Andrew Arato and Eike Gebhardt (New York: Continuum, 1982), 123.

National Socialism and Hitler drew on religious-spiritual notions of love, the German spirit, *Heimat*, etc., which were seen as linked to an "eternal-feminine." As Walter Langer has observed, "although Germans, as a whole, invariably refer to Germany as the 'Fatherland,' Hitler almost always refers to it as the 'Motherland' . . . ."[43] Along similar lines, Anton Kaes, writing of Helma Sanders-Brahms's *Germany, Pale Mother*, notes that the film, and the Brecht poem from which it takes its title, are part of "a tradition that goes back to the late Romantic poet Heinrich Heine [in which] Germany appears as the mother,"[44] In the film, Kaes argues, Sanders-Brahms attempts to distinguish between "the National Socialists of her film, the fathers who go to war: Germany as the father's land" and "the German people, Germania, the 'pale mother.'"[45] It was precisely this kind of gendered division that the Nazis sought to overcome through mediation.

This mediation is to take place through the person of the *Führer*, who, like Freder in *Metropolis*, combines the will of the father (the "skull of steel") with the eternal-feminine spirit and emotions of the mother (the "soft-heart"). This conjunction may help to explain the seemingly paradoxical character of the Hitler persona, which ranges from an aloof, implacable sternness to the almost quivering emotionality displayed in many of his speeches. Hitler's impassioned responses and gestures often seem to parallel Freder's hyper-emotional reactions, which served in *Metropolis*, as previously noted, to indicate the "feminine" aspect of his character. The parallels also suggest that Hitler's mediation of paternal and maternal qualities is based less on a parental position than on that, as with Freder, of the son. Theweleit has argued a similar position, noting that the *Führer* "embodies not paternal power but the common desire of sons."[46] Yet, as is well-known, what sons desire is not simply, as Theweleit claims, access to the father's power, but also access to that which is forbidden by the father's power: the realm of the mother. What the *Führer* and Freder promise, then, is access to both the resolution of a gendered modernity into an *androgynous* whole — the National Socialist state. It is a resolution that takes place neither simply in the name of the father nor solely in the name of the Holy Spirit, but in the name of the son: the name, that is, of the mediator.

---

[43] Walter C. Langer, *The Mind of Adolf Hitler* (New York: Basic Books, 1972), 153.

[44] Anton Kaes, *From* Hitler *to* Heimat*: The Return of History as Film* (Cambridge, MA: Harvard UP, 1989), 147.

[45] Kaes, *From* Hitler *to* Heimat, 148.

[46] Theweleit, *Male Fantasies*, vol. 2, 373.

If it is quite explicitly the name of the mediator (*Mittler*) that enables the resolution of *Metropolis*, it is the name *Hitler* that guarantees the National Socialist (re)solution: "The Party is Hitler," says Hess at the end of *Triumph of the Will*, "Hitler is Germany, and Germany is Hitler." It is through Hitler that an alienated, modern Germany is to be reinfused with the eternal German spirit, mediated, made whole transformed into a restored — i.e. National Socialist — Germany. This mediation of a technological modernity and an eternal spirit — like Freder's mediation of head and heart, masculine and feminine — is supposed to resolve the split between a repressive technological rationality or will and a repressed, technologized nature or spirit.

The conception of modernity as split or alienated by a repressive technological rationality has a considerable history; it can be seen in Schiller's analysis of the modern condition, where "the wheel" of technological rationality splits "man's being," repressing a part of human nature:

> With the monotonous noise of the wheel he drives everlastingly in his ears, [Man] never develops the harmony of his being, and instead of imprinting humanity upon his nature he becomes merely the imprint of his occupation, his science.[47]

For Schiller, this repression of (human) nature produces a mechanical, robot-like copy or "imprint": an artificial, technologized nature. At the same time, however, Schiller sees in a technologized modern nature what can only be described as a return of the repressed: a return of those chaotic, out-of-control and clearly libidinal "impulses" which are, for Schiller, connected to the "nature" of the working "masses":

> Among the lower and more numerous classes we find crude, lawless impulses which . . . are hastening with ungovernable fury to their brutal satisfaction . . . Society uncontrolled, instead of hastening upward into organic life, is relapsing into its original elements.[48]

It is not difficult to recognise in Schiller's view of a divided, technologized modern world the figures of tyranny and "instinct-governed chaos," as well as those of the robot/somnambulist and the monster/vamp. An even more striking similarity, perhaps, is Schiller's desire for a mediation of these divisions. For Schiller, however, the mediator — whose task, as Peter Bürger notes, will be "to put back to-

---

[47] Frederich Schiller, *On the Aesthetic Education of Man*, trans. Reginald Snell (New York: Unger, 1965), 40.

[48] Schiller, *On the Aesthetic Education of Man*, 35.

gether the 'halves' of man that have been torn asunder"[49] — will not be the heart, but art: "we must be at liberty to restore by means of a higher Art this wholeness in our nature which Art [i.e. artifice, technology] has destroyed."[50] For Kant and Hegel, too, the aesthetic realm is defined in terms of mediation, as that which, as Hegel puts it, "stands in the *middle*."[51]

The aesthetic realm is defined explicitly in opposition to the technological. In contrast to the dead, partial, technological object, which has no intrinsic meaning or purpose, the aesthetic object is seen as an organic whole, as having, like a living thing, its own, internal meaning and purpose.[52] The aesthetic object is not presented as an object at all, but as a living subject, with its own spirit or soul, its own "aura." As Benjamin would later note, "To perceive the aura of an object we look at means to invest it with the ability to look at us in return."[53] Art itself comes to represent that old sense of magico-spiritual enchantment or animism, of an eternal spirit, repressed by the modern, technological world.

It may seem that such a conception of art (or of the aesthetic), cast as it is in opposition to the technological and to modernity itself, could have no place in aesthetic modernism or, to the extent that it did appear, could only be represented as nostalgic or regressive. Yet, aesthetic modernism is from its very beginning caught up in a desire to mediate between the eternal and the modern, the magico-spiritual and the technological — a desire, one might say to spiritualize, or rather, to *aestheticize*, the modern and the technological. Baudelaire, despite his openness to the artifice and "shocks" of a technologised, modern nature (i.e., the city), saw the need for a mediation of this "transitory" modernity with an abstract, eternal spirit. He defined his art in terms of its power to "distil the eternal from the transitory," to combine two "halves" —

---

[49] Peter Bürger, *Theory of the Avant-Garde,* trans. Michael Shaw (Minneapolis, U of Minnesota P, 1984), 45.

[50] Schiller, *On the Aesthetic Education of Man,* 45.

[51] G. W. F. Hegel, *Aesthetics: Lectures on Fine Arts,* trans. T. M. Knox (Oxford: Clarendon, 1975), 38.

[52] Hegel expresses this view of "art as organic" quite clearly while summarizing Kant's aesthetics, with which on this point he obviously agrees: "the beautiful . . . exists as purposeful in itself, without means and end showing themselves separated as different aspects of it. The purpose of the limbs, for example, of an organism is the life which exists as actual in the limbs themselves; separated they cease to be limbs. For in a living thing purpose and the material for its realization are so directly united that it exists only in so far as its purpose dwells in it" (Hegel, *Aesthetics,* 59).

[53] Walter Benjamin, "On Some Motifs in Baudelaire," in *Illuminations,* trans. Harry Zohn (New York: Schocken, 1969), 188.

"the ephemeral, the fugitive, the contingent" and "the eternal and the immutable" — into "a completely viable whole."[54]

This conception of art as a mediation of the modern technological world and an abstract, eternal spirituality will appear in various guises throughout modernism. Contrary to the prevailing "functionalist" view of modernist art and architecture, modernism has frequently presented itself in religious or spiritual terms, as is explicitly the case in, for example, Neo-Plasticism, early *de Stijl*, Suprematism, expressionist architecture, and the early Bauhaus.[55] In contrast to Baudelaire, one can also observe in movement such as these the demand — noted by Peter Bürger — that "art becomes practical."[56] These attempts to, as Bürger puts it, "organize a new life praxis from a basis in art" will therefore frequently be translated into efforts to "re-spiritualise" or "reunify" the modern technologized world. If, however it is art (or the artist) that is to reunify society, to make it (spiritually) whole, this unification will itself be cast as a mediation of art and technology.

Not surprisingly, these demands for a "practical" aesthetic mediation of/with the modern technological world are particularly influential in architecture. With German architectural circles, this desire for mediation will transcend the previously noted poles of expressionism and the *Neue Sachlichkeit*, although it will be differently inflected by each. This difference can be stated in terms of these movements' differing views of technology: while the *Neue Sachlichkeit* tends to affirm an abstract aesthetic based on a rationalist, functionalist notion of technology (a technologized aesthetic), expressionism attempts to subordinate what it sees as an irrational and divisive technology to a spiritualized, holistic aesthetic (an aestheticized technology). In the present context however it is the expressionist tendency to spiritualize or aestheticize technology (and modernity in general) that is most instructive. This tendency is exemplified in Bruno Taut's Glass Pavilion, designed for the Cologne *Werkbund* exhibition of 1914. Inscribed with mystical aphorisms from Paul Scheerbart's *Glasarchitektur*, the Glass Pavilion was intended to serve as the *Kultursymbol* of a spiritual renewal in which a more practical, democratic art would be the basis for a new societal unity. Yet Taut's utopian aspirations were, as Frampton has observed, tied to certain medieval models, particularly the Gothic cathedral:

[54] Charles Baudelaire, "The Painter of Modern Life," *The Painter of Modern Life and Other Essays*, trans. Jonathan Mayne (London: Phaidon, 1964), 12–13.

[55] The concern with abstraction in these movements was based less on notions of technological rationality or functionalism than on the idea of abstract, geometrical forms that they conceived in neo-Platonic terms, as universal and eternal. Neo-Plasticism and early *de Stijl* were also heavily influenced by Theosophy.

[56] Bürger, *Theory of the Avant-Garde*, 49.

> According to Taut this crystalline structure . . . had been designed in the spirit of a Gothic cathedral. It was in effect a *Stadtkrone* or "city crown," that pyramidal form postulated by Taut as the universal paradigm of all religious building, which together with the faith it would inspire was an essential urban element for the restructuring of society.[57]

This notion of the *Stadtkrone,* of "a new religious building capable of unifying the creative energy of the society as in the Middle Ages," was to prove extremely influential.[58] It would dominate the "Utopian Correspondence" exchanged in 1919–20 by the architects of the Glass Chain, whose members included Walter Gropius. It would manifest itself not only in Mendelsohn's Einstein Tower but in Hans Poelzig's *Grosses Schauspielhaus* for Max Reinhardt. It would even appear prominently in the proclamation of the Weimar Bauhaus, both in Feininger's woodcut of "The Cathedral of Socialism" and in Gropius's call for a "new building of the future, which will embrace architecture and sculpture and painting in one unity and which will rise one day toward heaven from the hands of a million workers like the crystal symbol of a new faith."[59]

The unifying effect of the *Stadtkrone* was based precisely on its mediatory capacity, its ability to reintegrate an "older" spirituality, associated with the Gothic cathedral and medieval society, into the here-and-now of a technological modernity. The glass or crystalline tower was figured as kind of spiritual radio receiver — both antenna and crystal tuner — for "tuning in with the cosmos," to use Ernst Bloch's trenchant phrase.[60] If, however, Bloch was well aware of the "incredible problems of a *'Gothic style' within the crystal*"[61] of mediating "spiritualized," organic forms and abstract, rationalist geometry; such a mediation was at the heart of the utopian dream of an aestheticized modern city, presided over by a symbolic new cathedral, the "Cathedral of the Future."

---

[57] Frampton, *Modern Architecture,* 116.

[58] Frampton, *Modern Architecture,* 118. For an interesting reading of the Gothic cathedral, which echoes and amplifies many of the ideas expressed here, see William Worringer's *Form in Gothic* (New York: Schocken, 1964), a work which, as Worringer notes, is a kind of sequel to his *Abstraction and Empathy* (see note 28).

[59] Walter Gropius, "Program of the Staatliche Bauhaus in Weimar," *The Bauhaus: Weimar, Dessau, Berlin, Chicago,* ed. Hans M. Wingler, trans. Wolfgang Jabs and Basil Gilbert (Cambridge, MA: MIT Press. 1969), 31.

[60] Ernst Bloch, "Building in Empty Space," *The Utopian Function of Art and Literature,* trans. Jack Zipes and Frank Mecklenburg (Cambridge, MA: MIT Press, 1988), 195.

[61] Bloch, "Building in Empty Space," 197.

If this dream of a mediated, aestheticized modern city reached perhaps its fullest representation in *Metropolis*, it was only in National Socialism that the idea of an aestheticized modernity would achieve its culmination: what Walter Benjamin would refer to as the "aestheticization of politics" — or more precisely, the aestheticization of the modern state. This is the dream of a spiritualized, organic state machinery; it is the dream of a modern state become a home — familiar, whole, enchanted — the dream of a state with *an aura*. For the Nazis, the state itself was to become the cathedral of the future, in which the ancient spirit of the German people would be restored to an alienated modernity through the artist-leader's mediation, as an expression of his "will to form."[62]

This vision of the state as a work of art and of the leader as its artist had, in fact, been expressed by Joseph Goebbels as early as 1929 in a now well-known passage of his novel, *Michael*:

> Art is an expression of feeling. The artist is distinguished from the non-artist by the fact that he can give expression to what he feels. In some form or another: the one in images, the other in tone, the third in words, the fourth in manner — or even in historical form. The statesman is also an artist. For him, the people represent nothing different than what the stone represented for the sculptor. The leader and the led [*Führer und Masse*] presents no more of a problem than, for instance, the painter and colour.
>
> Politics is the plastic art of the state, just as painting is the plastic art of colour. This is why politics without the people, or even against the people, is sheer nonsense. To form a People out of the masses, and a State out of the People, this has always been the deepest sense of a true politics.[63]

There can be no denying the extent to which the Nazis realized these monumental "artistic" ambitions, or the role played in this realization

---

[62] See Joseph Goebbels's description of the "expression" of this cathedral of the future in his novel, *Michael*:

> As the man above us spoke, stone rolled upon stone, building the *cathedral of the future*. For years, something had been living inside me: it now took shape and became palpable.
>
> Revelation! Revelation!
>
> In the midst of ruin, a single man had dared to stand and raise the banner high [italics added].

Michael: ein deutsches Schicksal in Tagebuchblättern (Munich: Eher, 1942, reprint of 1929 edition), 102.

[63] Goebbels, *Michael*, 21. For a parallel discussion of the Nazi state as a *Gesamtkunstwerk* see Philippe Lacoue-Labarthe, *Heidegger Art and Politics*, trans. Chris Turner (Oxford: Blackwell, 1990).

by what Goebbels would term "the creative art of modern political propaganda." The ability of this "art" to "win the heart of a people and keep it" was, as Goebbels implicitly acknowledges, based on its mediatory capacity, on its combination of "modern," technological forms with the spirit of the German people:

> The shining flame of our enthusiasm . . . alone gives light and warmth to the creative art of modern political propaganda. Rising from the depths of the people, this art must always descend back to it and find its power there. Power based on guns may be a good thing; it is, however, better and more gratifying to win the heart of a people and to keep it.[64]

This passage, taken from Goebbels' speech at the 1934 Nuremberg Party Convention, plays a major role in Kracauer's explication of both *Metropolis* and Leni Riefenstahl's film of that convention, *Triumph of the Will*. He notes that the final scene of *Metropolis* "confirms the analogy between the industrialist [Fredersen] and Goebbels," and all the more, presumably, the analogy between Fredersen and Hitler:

> If in this scene the heart really triumphed over tyrannical power, its triumph would dispose of the all-devouring decorative scheme that in the rest of *Metropolis* marks the industrialist's claim to omnipotence. Artist that he was, Lang could not possibly overlook the antagonism between the breakthrough of intrinsic human emotions and his ornamental patterns. Nevertheless, he maintains these patterns up to the very end: the workers advance in the form of a wedge-shaped, strictly symmetrical procession which points towards the industrialist standing on the portal steps of the cathedral. The whole composition denotes that the industrialist acknowledges the heart for the purpose of manipulating it; that he does not give up his power, but will expand it over a realm not yet annexed — the realm of the collective soul.[65]

The crucial point in Kracauer's reading of the film, and his analogous reading of *Triumph of the Will*, is that the basis of Nazism is a subordination of "the heart," associated with "intrinsic human emotions" and "the realm of the collective soul," to a tyrannical, technological (or "industrial") will, represented by the geometrical forms of the mass ornament.[66]

---

[64] From *Triumph of the Will*.

[65] Kracauer, *From Caligari to Hitler*, 164.

[66] It is worth noting that in his 1927 essay on "The Mass Ornament," Kracauer argues that capitalism, with which he associates the mass ornament, "does not rationalize too much but *too little*." Thus, "the weight granted to reason in the ornament is . . . an illusion," an abstract, empty, formal rationality that allows "uncontrolled nature [to grow] prodigiously under the pretence of rational expression." For Kracauer, only

Despite its wide acceptance by later critics, Kracauer's reading here, as this essay has attempted to show, misunderstands the appeal of these films, and of Nazism itself. The basis of this appeal is not a "desire for tyranny" — an idea that would extend even the most pessimistic conceptions of false consciousness — but precisely a desire for a sense of wholeness, of *Heimat*. The "aesthetic" mediation of brain and heart, rationality and human emotions, masculine and feminine, modern technology and an ancient or eternal spirituality, is not simply "an ideological veil," hiding the "truth" of Nazi desire; this mediation is itself the "truth" of National Socialism's appeal.[67] Goebbels and Hitler did not admire *Metropolis* because, as Huyssen suggests, they saw its notion of mediation "as a welcome ideological veil to cover up the conflict between labour and capital;"[68] rather, they saw the mediation itself as a "true" expression of National Socialist goals and ideology.

From this perspective, *Metropolis's* final scene does indeed represent a mediation of a tyrannical, patriarchal, technological rationality with an ancient, repressed feminine spirit or nature. This mediation is evident in the very organization of the scene, which places a repentant Fredersen, his hair turned white, between the abstract, tectonic formation of workers in the foreground and the organic, atectonic form of the cathedral in the background. These aspects have, of course, already been mediated in the white-clad person of Freder, whose task it is to bring about the final joining of hands between the worker's representative and his father — a joining which, framed by the doors of the cathedral behind them, restores the feminine emotionality and spirituality represented by Maria (who stands, off-screen, to the other). Through

---

a "true reason," one that is capable of "encompassing human beings," could overcome the formal rationality of the mass ornament. This "human reason" would allow "ornaments" based not on the rationalized form of "the masses," but in the "organic life" of "the people." Siegfried Kracauer, "The Mass Ornament," *New German Critique* 5 (spring 1975), 67–76.

One cannot help but be struck here by the similarity between Kracauer's notion of a human reason — which would apparently reintegrate (synthesize?) an empty, modern rationalization with organic, human concerns — and the desire for a mediation of rationality and nature, the technological and the organic, in *Metropolis* and Nazism. This is not, of course, to conflate Kracauer's thinking with Nazi ideology, but merely to suggest that what blinds Kracauer to the ideological appeal of *Metropolis* and Nazism is precisely the similarity of that appeal (with its basis in a desire for mediation) to his own clearly Hegelian, point of view.

[67] This truth, is of course, ideological, as is the desire for wholeness that is its basis.

[68] Huyssen, "The Vamp and the Machine," see page 206 above.

this mediatory aesthetic, then, the "mass ornament" is re-connected to its spiritual and emotional nature, to its "eternal-feminine" home

A similar mediatory aesthetic inflects the archtectonics of *Triumph of the Will*. Here again, commentators following Kracauer have tended to see the massing of crowds into abstract, geometrical patters as indicative of a rationalization or mechanization, a triumph of a technological rationality or will. Such an interpretation neglects the fact that these crowds are not presented, as in *Metropolis*, as dispirited, soulless robots or somnambulists, but as just the opposite: a re-unified, re-spiritualized German people, a people to whom the ancient German spirit, soul or nature has been restored. The abstract modernist architectonic of the mass ornament is mediated with a familiar, older spirit, a sense of organic or natural connection, of *Heimat*, which is represented by the "organic," Gothic architecture of the ancient city of Nuremberg, with its connotations of past German glories. In *Triumph of the Will*, "even Nuremberg's ancient stone buildings," its "steeples, sculptures, gables and venerable facades,"[69] are mobilized in the service of the National Socialist symbology of mediation and restoration. In this "restoration," the modern architectonic of the mass ornament and the ancient atectonic forms of Nuremberg's Gothic cathedrals and buildings are mediated and reassembled into the "aestheticized" form of the Nazi Cathedral of the Future.

It is in this figurative cathedral that one finds the true architecture of National Socialism, the *Stadtkrone* through which the divisions of the modern world are to be mediated and the German spirit restored, the German people re-unified. The architecture of this cathedral combines the forms of both the *Neue Sachlichkeit* and expressionism; it represents itself as modern and technological on the one hand, and, on the other hand, as the heir to a mythical Aryan tradition, of which the Gothic cathedrals are a part. Perhaps the single most accurate representation of this imaginary structure can be found in Albert Speer's so-called "cathedral of light," a luminous "structure" formed from banners and the beams of searchlights, which can be seen in *Triumph of the Will* when Hitler addresses the assembled *Amtswalter* [party functionaries].[70] The "architecture" of Speer's "cathedral" can be seen as the logical extension of the premises of Taut's Glass Pavilion: a religious structure that, unbounded by material constraints, is open to both the cosmos and the

---

[69] Kracauer, *From Caligari to Hitler*, 301–2.

[70] Speer's story of the background of the "cathedral of light" can be found in *Inside the Third Reich*, trans. Richard & Clara Winston (New York: Macmillan Co., 1970), 58–59.

people — thus allowing it to serve as a kind of aesthetic focal point, mediating between the celestial and the modern world.[71]

Yet as Kenneth Frampton has noted, Speer's "cathedral of light" was itself subordinated to the demands of another art, an art which was, even more than architecture, central to the Nazi effort to aestheticize the modern, technological world:

> Leni Riefenstahl's documentary film of the Nuremberg rally of 1934, *Triumph des Willens,* was the first occasion on which architecture, in the form of Speer's temporary setting, was pressed into the service of cinematic propaganda. Henceforth Speer's designs for stadia at Nuremberg were determined as much by camera angles as by architectural criteria.[72]

What Frampton's point demonstrates, is that Speer's "cathedral" was as much a cinematic as an architectural construction. Its tendency to the cinematic was not, however, implicit simply in its *mise-en-scène,* but also in its ability to serve as the very figure of cinema: at once a projection of light, lens, and a screen. Is not *Triumph of the Will* itself figured as a "cathedral of light," a luminous aesthetic structure in which an ancient spirit and a modern technology are focused in the figure of Hitler the mediator, Hitler the artist of the National Socialist state?[73] This art (of the state, of politics) was, as Syberberg has suggested, precisely *cinematic*: "Hitler created war only for the newsreels. To see his own epic Hollywood movie."[74] Gilles Deleuze has similarly noted that "up to

---

[71] This notion of a "connection" to the cosmos, to an eternal, celestial realm of the spirit, recurs constantly in Nazi symbology. It can be seen, for example, in the architectural eagle that hovers over Hitler in Speer's "cathedral of light"in the often-noted aerial shots of Hitler's plane at the beginning of *Triumph of the Will,* as well as in the film's final shot, where the men of the S.A. (the name itself [*Sturmabteilung*] alluding to the heavens) appear to march — in formation, as a mass ornament — into the clouds. It is, in fact, worth comparing this shot to the final scene of *Metropolis*: in both, the mass ornament is not portrayed as a purely abstract, mechanical form, but becomes a form reinfused with a "technology" reanimated by a spiritual aspect, a soul or aura. It thus becomes a "living" aesthetic whole.

[72] Frampton, *Modern Architecture,* 218.

[73] This desire for an aesthetic, and indeed cinematic, mediation of the ancient and modern can also be seen in the cinema of the Third Reich as a whole. As Peter Reichel has noted, Nazi audiences were fascinated not only with historical films centred on famous German leaders, scientists and artists of the past, but also with the future, with science fiction films, many of which show the influence of *Metropolis.* See Peter Reichel, "Das Medium, das die Herzen erobert: Der Film," in *Der schöne Schein des Dritten Reiches: Faszination und Gewalt des Faschismus* (Munich: Hanser, 1991).

[74] "Hans Jürgen Syberberg — A Cycle Concluded," *The Filmex Society Newsletter* 7 (June 1979), 3.

the end Nazism thinks of itself in competition with Hollywood."[75] Anton Kaes confirms this point by drawing attention to Goebbels's "cinematic" vision — near the very end of the war — of the future of the Nazi state: "in a hundred years' time they will be showing a fine colour film of the terrible days we are living through. Wouldn't you like to play a part in that film? Hold out now, so that a hundred years hence the audience will not hoot and whistle when you appear on the screen."[76]

Perhaps it was only in terms of cinema, in terms of the "art" of "cinematic propaganda," that the imaginary "structure" of the Nazi Cathedral of the Future could be fully brought "to life," projected as a unifying aesthetic vision. If the glass or crystal cathedral was figured as a kind of radio receiver, the Cathedral of the Future could only be a gigantic cinema hall, or rather, the art of cinema itself, projected onto the world as a mediated, aestheticized, and luminous totality, the ultimate *Gesamtkunstwerk.*[77]

The insistence on viewing this totalitarian art as merely a delusion, an ideological "screen" which hides the obscene truth of Nazi tyranny, misrecognizes the extent to which this tyranny is in fact based on such an aesthetic of wholeness and mediation, in which the divisive repression of a technological, patriarchal law is to be overcome.[78] The violent, oppressive tyranny of Nazism is not based on an identification with the technological law of the father, but precisely on a refusal of this identification: on the denial of differences, of the technologies of difference. Difference, like technology itself, is either to be mediated into an aesthetic whole or excluded and destroyed. So too for the technology of cinema, which should, as Goebbels noted of *Triumph of the Will,* overcome the instrumentality of "mere propaganda" and "lift up the harsh

---

[75] Gilles Deleuze, *Cinema 2: The Time-Image,* trans. Hugh Tomlinson and Robert Galeta (Minneapolis: U of Minnesota P, 1989), 264.

[76] Quoted in Kaes, *From* Hitler *to* Heimat, 4.

[77] The extent to which modernism is "haunted" by this "spirit" of aesthetic wholeness can be seen in the repeatedly voiced desire for a "total work of art," from Mallard's Total Book to Wagner's *Gesamtkunstwerk* to Bazin's "myth of total cinema," as well as in the "alliance of the arts under the wing of a great architecture" announced in the manifesto of the *Arbeitsrat für Kunst* and repeated in Gropius's Bauhaus manifesto.

[78] In contrast to the Nazi view, see Jacques Lacan, "Aggressivity in Psychoanalysis," *Ecrits,* trans. Alan Sheriden (New York: Norton, 1977), 8–29, where he notes the connection of aggressivity to an imaginary wholeness. For Lacan, moreover, it is precisely through Oedipal identification that this aggressivity is to be transcended.

rhythm of our great epoch to eminent heights of artistic achievement."[79] Even in this statement, one can discern the figures of a paternal technological (or instrumental) rationality drawn upwards by an eternal-feminine spirit in which it finds its mediation, its destiny, its home. It is only on the basis of this aesthetic mediation (of technology, of difference) that the tyranny and the horror of Nazism are made possible, only in the name of an androgynous mediator, through whom difference is denied.

[79] Richard Barsam, *Film Guide to* Triumph of the Will (Bloomington: Indiana UP, 1975), 67.

Part Four

METROPOLIS NOW

21. Lang rehearsing the dance sequence.
[Deutsches Institut für Filmkunde, Frankfurt]

22. A rare still of Helm's seductive dance as the robot. [Deutsches Institut für Filmkunde, Frankfurt]

Canning the Uncanny

The Construction of Visual Desire in *Metropolis*

Andrew Webber

As a film that is generally understood as inaugurating a key form of genre cinema, science fiction, *Metropolis* employs many of the sorts of stylisations that characterise the genre film. The melodrama and the thrills of genre films reveal in their most drastic form the sorts of structures that are embedded in all types of film viewing. Above all, a film like *Metropolis* appeals to fantasy as a fundamentally ambivalent structure, one that combines erotic lure with spectacles of aggression. That is, *Metropolis* works rhythmically between visual pleasure and unpleasure, and by that rhythm interchanges and redefines them. The film projects the sort of fantasy that Freudian psychoanalysis exposes in dreams and other psychic scenarios, one that is bound up in a dialectic between eros and the death drive.

While film, and genre films in particular, can be seen to rely on the manipulation of this dialectic, it is a notoriously unreliable mechanism. This can be shown by the rules of play in the *fort-da* game that has often been understood as a model for the fantasy projections of the cinema. This is the game which Freud, in *Jenseits des Lustprinzips* (Beyond the Pleasure Principle, 1920), describes his grandson playing: casting a cotton-reel into and out of view in compensation for the absence of his mother.[1] The game represents desire as imbricated in the movement between presence and absence. The reel can at best re-present the mother by association, in a metonymic fashion; it is a fetish, standing in for, and aiming to cover over, a fundamental lack. The logic of the game is thus marked by the rhythmic impulse of lack. The pleasure of *da* is always constructed through the unpleasure of *fort*, and the control which the viewer has over the play of projection between the two is at best conditional. This visual game played with a cotton-reel can be understood as a prototype for the more elaborate games played with and by the film reel in the cinematic machine, projecting and presenting, hiding and seeking to show.

While *Metropolis* can be said to play to the rhythm of *fort-da* in a give-and-take excitement which is designed to be contained in the satisfaction of total presence at the end, I am interested here in showing

[1] *Standard Edition of the Complete Psychological Works of Sigmund Freud*, ed. and trans. James Strachey et al, vol.18 (London: Hogarth Press, 1955), 14–17.

how problematic any such containment or canning is. The different forms of the *fort-da* played in succession by Freud's grandson testify to its interminable character, and the versions played out in *Metropolis* will be seen to exceed the term which is engineered for them. My analysis of the failure of the apparatus of control will focus on a particular form of the Freudian fantasy: voyeuristic spectacle. My contention is that for spectators both on- and off-screen, the voyeuristic desire on show here is always the at once alluring and threatening desire of the other. While voyeurism depends for its pleasure upon control, control in the desire of the other is always liable to be arrogated to the indeterminate agency of the other's desire. In exposing the subjection of visual desire to the other, *Metropolis* will be seen to exhibit various aspects of what might be called the cinematic uncanny, as it projects the spectacle of desire into the territory beyond the pleasure principle.

Metropolis is only the most industrialized form of a fantasy structure that informs much expressionist film.[2] Classic expressionist films such as *Caligari* (1919) or *Nosferatu* (1922) certainly operate with voyeuristic fantasies of electrifying otherness. And both emphasize agencies of control over that otherness. But the authorities, scientific and political, that exercise control are found wanting, and the experimental control over the fantastic devices is in fact exceeded by what is released in the final picture. The conventions of the uncanny are established, only to become in their turn subject to uncanny otherness, to excesses of meaning over which they have no proper control.

Caligari, Nosferatu, and *Metropolis* not only exhibit the excesses of the uncanny, but they seek to work it in analogous ways. Notwithstanding evident differences of style, they feature comparable modes of the *construction* of visual desire. This is most evident in the ways in which the fantasies that they mobilise are built into fantasy architectures: the painted sets of *Caligari,* the Gothic arches of *Nosferatu,* and the futuristic urban technology of *Metropolis.* In each case, the architectural construction of the visual field sets the scene for a construction of desire, a desire whose uncanny, constructed object is, respectively, a somnambulistic automaton, a grotesquely prosthetic and made-up vampire, and a robot.

What all three films have in common, therefore, is the figuration of their own make-up as fantastic constructions. There is a compelling case for viewing the uncanny body that is brought to life in each of the films as having a *mise-en-abyme* function. That is, what is engineered or oth-

---

[2] While there is considerable debate about the usefulness of the term *expressionist film,* I use it for convenience here to categorize those films made in Germany in and around the twenties that feature, in various ways, the projection of subjective fantasies.

erwise experimentally projected into life is always also figuring the celluloid body of the film medium, specifically film in its fantasy forms.

In his pioneering study *Theory of Film*, subtitled *The Redemption of Physical Reality*, Siegfried Kracauer suggests that the film medium has a special role to play by effecting some sort of metaphysical conversion of the material into the imaginary.[3] Fantasy is seen as the privileged form of this transfiguration. But Kracauer also recognises that the transfigured body may not entirely work, that it will also tend to display a certain staginess. The figures of the fantastic are, in other words, inevitably produced *ex machina*: out of the cinema's theatrical machine. All the fantasy and dream scenes of expressionist cinema, the heavens, haunted houses, circuses, fairs, variety halls and so forth, are marked by this ambivalent appeal to fantastic illusion and to the awareness of its construction.

Eisenstein is only partly on the mark when he applies his constructivist critique to *Caligari*, and by extension the fantasy features of expressionist film in general, as "this barbaric carnival of the destruction of the healthy human infancy of our art."[4] For Eisenstein, Caligarist film as showground for decadent fantasies and pathological pleasures represents the carnivalesque not as a radical subversion of systems of power but as sustaining the feudal structures of the political status quo. In fact, the frequently retrogressive scenarios of *Caligari* and its ilk may be analysed as the fantasy constructions of a political or social unconscious. The demons, vampires, and golems let loose upon society would thus be seen as conjured up or engineered by repressed desires. And the fact that they frequently do reveal the apparatus behind their fantasies, representing, perhaps in spite of themselves, the construction of what is on show, opens up the possibility of the sort of critical distance that Eisenstein would promote. In other words, as much as expressionist film may appear to produce totalized fantasies, it frequently operates variations on the sort of montage which is used by Eisenstein and other exponents of the political avant-garde to defamiliarize the cinematic medium and make the cine-eye see critically. By scrutinizing the material montage, the *ex machina* construction of a body, which is the focus of *Metropolis*, and the function of that body in the broader construction of the film fantasy, we will see that the carnivalesque apparatus does not work quite as totally as Eisenstein's analysis might suggest.

At the same time, as we shall see, the elaborately constructed interplay of visual objects and desiring looks on screen in *Caligari*, *Nos-*

---

[3] Princeton NJ: Princeton UP, 1997.

[4] Sergei Eisenstein, *Film Form: Essays in Film Theory* (New York: Harcourt/Brace, 1949), 203.

feratu, or *Metropolis* exposes as much as it solicits the voyeuristic fantasising of the onlooker. Construction at once facilitates what might be called the cinematic unconscious, the unsurpassed potency of the medium in playing to the desire for fantasy, and sets it apart as other, as a fabricated mise-en-scène. The cinematic apparatus serves multiple desires. To borrow the model elaborated by Deleuze and Guattari in their *Anti-Oedipus*, film can be understood as a key form of desiring machine.[5] It is a complex apparatus for the working of desire, producing the visual terrorism of the slasher, the voyeuristic thrills of the peepshow, the lure of the fetish. It does the work of constructing or reconstructing the conventions of desire and gender in their most visually seductive forms, but also, as we shall see, of deconstructing the symbolic and performative structures that support them. The desiring machine does not straightforwardly serve straightforward desires.

The model of the desiring machine suggests a linking up of the discourses and analytic systems of psychoanalysis and economics. To use the term Freud liked to apply to the site of the unconscious, this is to posit the cinema as the *andere Schauplatz*, the other scene or show-place of the post-industrial polis: the outlet of its dream-factory. But to what extent does the machinery of this factory produce or reproduce according to the economic models for desire of psychoanalysis? Or, to return to the fabricated pun of my title, can the psychoanalytic uncanny be understood as one of the prime products canned in the film factory? And is its production not always dysfunctional, constitutionally bound to spill out of the can?

Psychoanalytic theory is intensely reliant upon the construction of visual desire. The key scenarios of Freudian and post-Freudian theory, those which are seen as formative for the psychoanalytic subject, establish a certain mechanics of visual desire. The primal scene, the *fort-da* game, and the Lacanian mirror-stage, as different as they are in the dramatic detail of their enactment all play out a fundamental structure. They set the scene for compulsive scenarios of identification, projection, and separation. And, accordingly, they serve to construct ambivalent models of desiring practice for the infantile viewing subject.

In order to go about testing these models on *Metropolis*, it might initially be useful to set out some of the first principles of Freudian theories of visuality. In his *Drei Abhandlungen zur Sexualtheorie* (Three Essays on the Theory of Sexuality, 1905), Freud theorizes the eye as erogenous zone, divided between two drives which have the character of dialectical counterparts: *Schaulust* (pleasure in looking) and *Zeigelust*

[5] Gilles Deleuze and Félix Guattari, *Anti-Oedipus: Capitalism and Schizophrenia*, trans. Robert Hurly, Mark Seem, and Helen R. Lane (London: Athlone, 1984), especially Chapter 1.

(pleasure in showing). The fantasies of *Schaulust*, or scopophilia, are always bound up, for Freud, with the desire to show. This dialectic is seen to work through the perverse forms of the desires to show and to see: for Freud, "the exhibitionist in his unconscious is at the same time a *voyeur*."[6] These drives are partial and positional. If Freud uses the term *Einstellung*, that is, a position taken up, to describe, for instance, the point of view in a voyeuristic fantasy, then he looks forward to the function of *Einstellung* as the setting or disposition of the shot in film. This emphasises the positionality of this form of desire, the fact that it is set relative to other positions in a structure, other settings of an apparatus.

The eye is the remotest of erogenous zones: its *Einstellung* or desiring position is always at a distance, fantasizing the remote control of the visual object through the objective, held in close-up but at a distance. A notorious example of this fantasy in the film medium would be Powell's *Peeping Tom* (1960), which, by putting the perverse viewer behind the camera, suggests that the medium itself is driven by this type of fantasy. It figures the film apparatus as the particular sort of desiring machine which according to Carrouges, and as developed by Deleuze and Guattari in *Anti-Oedipus*, serves the fantasies of the single man, as bachelor machine. But the fantasy is always also subject to dysfunction. In the case of *Peeping Tom*, the bachelor machine is catastrophically terminated in a way that replicates the termination of other bachelor machinery in Hoffmann's *Der Sandmann* (The Sandman, 1817), Kafka's *In der Strafkolonie* (In the Penal Colony, 1919), or indeed *Metropolis*. In each case, the machinery fails above all in its servicing of the spectatorial gaze. In the case of film, it may seem that the viewing apparatus, apparently limitless in its powers of visual illusion and intrusion, remains prone to uncanny fears of breakdown or reversal. An example might be the experience of the voyeuristic eye, whose point of view we share, at the key-hole of Cocteau's *Sang d'un Poète* (Blood of a Poet, 1930): an eye that is caught in the act, beheld through the aperture by the eye of the other.

For Freud, visuality is also the most distinctive mode of the uncanny. If I replayed in my title Freud's word-game with *heimlich* and *unheimlich*, playing on an elision of antithesis, then it is because these apparently opposite points of view are subject, to use a suitable filmic metaphor, to cross-cutting. The familiar environment and that which lies underground in an open coffin, that which is concealed in cabinets or closets for occasional display, or confined in prison or asylum cells, laboratories or catacombs, and wont to escape, are always cross-cut in

---

[6] Freud, *Standard Edition*, vol. 7 (1953), 167.

this manner. The homely, which is constructed upon the idea of self-identity or sameness, and the unhomely otherness which exceeds and haunts it are at once radically separate and dialectically interdependent.

To *can* is to contain or to frame, locating the uncanny within some sort of construction for viewing and knowing. The uncanny is that which, according to the Freudian definition, should have remained hidden within the structures of the domestic framework but which is nonetheless exposed within and against them. The imaginary and symbolic structures of the canny or homely are always cross-cut by that which is repressed in order to sustain them. *Heimlich* is always foreshadowed by *un* as the mark of an in-built repression, where the repressed always returns. Homeground is overshadowed by the projections of *ein anderer Schauplatz,* another scene. Specifically, the overground constructions of domestic and working life in *Metropolis* are undermined by the world of the living dead, the catacombs that subtend the city. Rotwang's house and the cathedral, as Gothic overground projections of the subterranean caverns, serve as privileged sites for the incursion of the uncanny.

I shall be using cross-cutting as an apt metaphor for the uncanny operation of desire in *Metropolis* as double-edged or, in the Lacanian sense, dialectical. Desire, for Lacan, is always of the other, both aimed at what the desiring subject is and has not and always constructed according to the often dangerous desires *of* that other. This dialectical structure, in thrall to alterity, will be seen here to operate not least in the *fort-da* rhythms of the filmic structure of cross-cutting.

The original and ultimate psychoanalytic cross-cut, that of castration, derives from the otherness displayed in another of Freud's *andere Schauplätze,* the primal scene. This scene marks visual desire out as always already traversed by what, for psychoanalysis, is the unkindest cut of all. The primal scene, where the infant is witness to parental intercourse, represents the inseparability of desire and separation. It is a sort of home movie on release from the censorship of parental guidance. It is viewed surreptitiously and experienced as domestic violence. Intercourse is seen as cross-cutting, running the partners together and cutting between them in a rhythm of two-way violation. The viewer is rhythmically projected between two *Einstellungen* in a motion picture of sex and violence, directed by the compulsive structure of serial repetition. As the child views rather than directly partaking, so the gaze represents its separation, the fact that its alternating identification with the partners in the sexual display is always cross-cut. Indeed, after the model of Oedipus, it is the eye that is subject to the symbolic castration which is the price exacted by this spectacle. The voyeur is always liable to blinding, the cutting out of visual desire.

This is what marks the incursion of the uncanny into the visual field according to Freud's reading of Hoffmann's *Sandman,* whose eponymous bogey-man is an optical projectionist of desire and terror, threatening to cut out the vision of voyeuristic children. The version of the primal scene viewed through a peep-hole behind curtains in *The Sandman* may be taken as a model for the ambiguous, or cross-cut, desire which is in play in the cinematic act, above all in the horror fantasy genre.[7] For here the lure is always a construction of pleasure and unpleasure, of split identification with the victimizer and the victim, representing the uncannily split, repetitive and eroticized spectacle of the death wish. The voyeuristic *Einstellung* of *The Sandman* also sets it up as the primal scene for many of the fantasy scenarios of expressionist cinema, not least in the case of a film which, like *Metropolis,* animates the construction, in its most material sense, of desire.

Before proceeding to consider how *Metropolis* might replay the structures of the primal scene, it may be worthwhile to consider briefly the implications of Lacan's return to Freud for visuality and, in particular, the visual regime of the cinema. The first gesture in the key text, his seminar on the eye and the gaze, is towards the *Wiederholungszwang* or repetition compulsion.[8] The Lacanian reworking of this Freudian compulsion is focused on the Aristotelian figure of the *automaton.* Lacan reads *Zwang* as automatism, indicating that the alternating compulsion of the viewing subject to project vision and to draw visual objects in drives a sort of automatic machine of desire. The automatic drive of the visual, what Lacan dubs the scopic, can be said to find its privileged machinery in the film apparatus which engages the gaze of the beholder in its productions. But the Lacanian analysis would always see this machinery as compulsively failing the subject. The privileged site of the cinema, which may appear to simply project scenes as fantasy objects for the viewing subject, in fact functions as another sort of *anderer Schauplatz.* It is a show-place that is always *of the other,* where the subject is never simply her- or himself, always left wanting.

As we shall see from a closer look at the visual regime of *Metropolis,* the film always in part represents this lack as much for the characters as viewers within it as for spectators who are lured into looking in and identifying with them. For Lacan, the scopic field is always dialectically

---

[7] For a more detailed account of how these uncanny projections work in *The Sandman,* see my chapter on Hoffmann in *The Doppelgänger: Double Visions in German Literature* (Oxford: Clarendon, 1996).

[8] Jacques Lacan, "Of the Gaze as *Objet Petit a*" in *The Four Fundamental Concepts of Psycho-analysis,* ed. Jacques-Alain Miller, trans. Alan Sheridan (London: Vintage, 1998), 67.

riven between the eye of the beholding subject and what he calls the gaze, which is of the Other. You never simply see but always see as you are seen by the overseeing Other. This gaze of the Other functions as a sort of panopticon, a total surveillance that corrects the model of the all-seeing pleasure of the viewing subject. The visual fantasies of *Metropolis* are all subject to this panoptical view, represented by the technological gaze of the Father which controls the visual field.[9]

The logic of the theory of visual bipartition (the constitutional division of the viewer) means that the spectatorial subject is always also beheld by the panopticon, lured and caught up by the power of identification into its cross-cut networks and relays of looks, a system of "Einstellungen," all of which are only ever partial. The way in which the camera-eye must divide itself between view-points in the filmic space, means all sorts of double and multiple visions for the viewer who is subject to its optical machinery. The subject is thus projected into alterity, in accordance with Lacan's view that scopic desire and what the subject is given to see will always mismatch. This constitutional otherness of the scopic is represented for Lacan in serial obstacles to the total lure of the visual: frames, blind-spots, screens, masks and veils.

Lacanian theory is inevitably most interested in a particular cinematic blind-spot, the phallus. As that which, in its fleshly mould, is most intently censored, it seems destined to return in more veiled, symbolic or fetishistic forms. The phallic symbols and figures that proliferate in expressionist film represent the absence of the original as much as a substitute presence. Here, the phallic figures are recurrently figured as visualized in a double sense, seeing as well as seen. This is the function of monsters, show-figures like Cesare and Nosferatu, who are recognised as phallic forms even by critics, such as Eisner and Prawer, with no particular investment in psychoanalysis. Cesare and Nosferatu are visually fascinating, designed to transfix with their cosmetically highlighted eyes, visionary, apparently all-seeing. But this is a fantasy embodiment of the all-powerful gaze which is inevitably also lacking, prone to falling asleep, to blinding or dissolving. The monstrous fantasy of the all-seeing eye is subject, in other words, to disappearance. Desire is constructed through compulsive lack, through the visual absence of "fort," and the prime figure of visual desire is always liable to be gone. This is what the gaze as object of desire means for Lacan; like the phallus it is that from which the subject has been separated

[9] The panoptical tower of *Metropolis* can be likened to the monocular tower that beholds Harker as he arrives at Nosferatu's castle. Both constructions seem to support the authority of the phallocentric gaze, but, just as the eye of Nosferatu's tower is a socket in a phantom architecture of power, so Fredersen's panoptical look is blind to the underground world.

in order to constitute itself as subject. The monsters of expressionist fantasy films embody a gaze without aversion or taboo which must ultimately be cut if the Symbolic order and its subjects are to be sustained.

Recurrently, in expressionist film, the eye assumes the privileged object status of the phallus; what is unrepresentable in itself is replaced by the rigid stare of the naked eye. Lacan, after Freud, points up this symbolic potential by associating the phenomenon of *invidia,* the evil eye (the eye, you might say, of the horror movie) which is vampiric, voraciously feeding upon the gaze which beholds it, with the phallus as *fascinum,* the cult object in the mystery of the scopic drive. This fascinating visual object is, however, always one of di-vision, always already cross-cut. We need only refer to the anamorphic skull projected across the foreground of Holbein's *Ambassadors,* a key focus in the Lacanian seminar on the eye and the gaze. For Lacan this projection is the stain of castration which cuts across the gaze. It represents the phallus as phantom, cutting across, but also cut off from, the iconographic apparatus of the picture. The phallus acts as a memento mori, an anti-fetish cross-cutting the elaborately fetishistic image of power. According to this analysis, it is no surprise to find that the phallic figures of expressionist film, the likes of Cesare and Nosferatu, are also constructed as skeletal bodies of death. This same mortification of the phallus will be seen at work in *Metropolis.*

Films like *Caligari* or *Metropolis* appear to show master figures in apparent possession of the master signifier, the phallic object, in the shape of automata. To adopt the terminology of the fairground spectacle in *Caligari,* the showman controls the exhibition of his "Schauobjekt." According to Lacan, however, the phallus is a phantom more liable to possess the masterful subject than to be possessed. This analysis of the construction of visual desire in *Metropolis* will seek to show both the potency and the impotence of this possession.

Teresa de Lauretis, in one of the key feminist critiques of the classic psychoanalytic readings of film, suggests that they inevitably do violence to women: "the psychoanalytic vision of cinema . . . still poses woman as telos and origin of a phallic desire, as dream woman forever pursued and forever held at a distance, seen and invisible on another scene."[10] While this reads as a plausible description of the sort of fantasy that drives *Metropolis,* the question is whether a psychoanalytic vision of the film will inevitably just replay that fantasy. There is always a danger that psychoanalysis may just serve as another form of

---

[10] Teresa de Lauretis, *Alice Doesn't: Feminism, Semiotics, Cinema* (London: Macmillan, 1984), 25.

desiring machine, reproducing the phallocentric construction of gender in what it analyzes. If the present reading of *Metropolis* may inevitably appear to be phallocentric in its organisation, then it is because it wants to show how obsessively the film is enslaved to the phallus. The advanced technology of this film serves a primal, not to say primitive, form of patriarchal desire. Rather than serving the same fantasy, the advanced technology of psychoanalytic theory can be appropriated to work more ideologically to show how the fantasy is constructed and to expose its disorders. The phallic gaze that, it is argued, is so focal to the *Metropolis* fantasy is in fact also radically out of control. Psychoanalysis may, therefore, help to expose the phallocentrism of the film's spectatorial order as profoundly decentred.

If the phallic object is indeed a recurrent show-object in expressionist cinema, how then does it work as such? Its function as an object of compulsive viewing is, in different senses, constructed. In both *Caligari* and *Nosferatu,* in addition to the construction of the desired body into the architectural apparatus, the visual regime is marked by the machine-produced rhythms of optical fascination. In both cases the spectatorial eye is compulsively trained on show-objects by the hypnotic mechanics of the artificial eye. The effects of the camera iris, as it contracts and dilates, reconstruct the lure of the visual apertures of key-hole and peep-hole.

These frames for illicit viewing are combined in *Caligari* with the curtains, screens, and titles of a sort of film cabinet. The rhythmic pulling in and out of the gaze serves not least to represent self-reflexively the spectacular, hypnotic exhibit of film. Cesare, as the medium of phallic desire, also stands for the desire of the film medium. The phallic monster, as prime show-object within the show-object film, embodies at once the thrilling, potentially menacing powers of the medium and its in-built illusoriness. The self-reflexiveness of the film spectacle is marked in both films by a network of doublings and mirrorings. The doubles, decoys, effigies, and shadows which serve to proliferate the phallic figure are at once evidence of its compulsion and of its susceptibility to simulation, projection, and illusion. In *Caligari,* the frame suggests that the case of the "Schauobjekt" is but a deluded simulation, the fantasy animation of a madman, and in *Nosferatu,* the monstrously compelling body of the vampire dissolves in the light of day like the film image it is.

How, then, does the construction and animation of fantasy in *Metropolis* relate to these models? It is a film of compelling architectonic, iconographic, and choreographic visual structures and one which fantasises against this structural apparatus the mechanical reproducibility of the human form. When the glowing image of Brigitte Helm is projected onto the automaton, the act of animation simulates the processing of the human body into an alluring image that is reproduced as a body on the film screen only by means of mechanical projection. Specifically, it simulates a key form of cinematic desire, the projection of the female body as sex machine. This technological fantasy body, which is designed to serve the desires of a triangle of single men (Fredersen senior, Rotwang, and Freder) meets the specifications of the bachelor machine, suggesting that the cinematic dream factory has a particular affinity with that model of production.

What, though, is the relation of this female figure to the phallic automata of the other two films, both gendered male? Psychoanalysis provides a theoretical model for construing female figures as phallic, in particular in the shape of the archaic body of the phallic mother, associated by Freud with the castrating gaze of the Medusa.[11] The robot Maria is, of course, constructed as Mother, reconstructing the lost mother, Hel. Not only does this laboratory processing of life aim to recreate the mother, but it seeks to give birth to life without a mother. As reproduction between men, contracted by Fredersen and Rotwang, it is unsurprising that the robot should be phallicly shaped. The laboratory process simulates sex in its mounting excitement of moving parts and frothing fluids. Its key focus, however, is on the immobile object of the automaton and the rings of light which seek to electrify it into life by their massaging movement. This is a simulated sex act between phallus and hand, the hand which Rotwang has lost in his experiments and now seeks to recuperate by his manipulation of the apparatus which serves as a technological extension of the hand. And what comes in the climax of this simulation is the successful simulation of the female figure, but always in the shape of the phallus; a female figure which is above all constructed according to the psychoanalytic specifications of the fetish, that is as an object which is designed to make up for lack, a perfectly engineered prosthesis.

It is by now commonplace that the fantasy constructions of *Metropolis* are sustained by highly questionable ideological constructs. The construction of the female in the double figures of virgin mother and vamp is the centrepiece of a more general apparatus of political stylisations. What psychoanalysis might help to show is how such stylised images are fetishistically formed to satisfy dominant desires by making up for the lack in the order of the dominant ideology. If patriarchy produces for itself the ultimate phallic desiring machine, then this can

---

[11] Freud argues in his *Neue Folge der Vorlesungen zur Einführung in die Psychoanalyse* (New Introductory Lectures on Psychoanalysis, 1933) that phallic mother and Medusa are cognate figures, linked by their relation to the fear of castration (*Standard Edition*, vol. 22 (1964), 24.

be used to point up the constitutional deficiency which it is designed to overcome. This is where the machine becomes uncanny, as the prosthesis takes on a life of its own and begins to threaten the constructions of the patriarchal order.

In order to show how the desiring machine functions and dysfunctions, let us consider two sequences from the film that are, in more senses than one, structurally repetitive. They are at once twin scenes, the one a repetition of the other with a surrogate object, and internally repetitive, marked by the sorts of serial substitutions and repetitions which psychoanalysis sees as the structure of desire itself. Both represent a spectacle of desire that is uncanny; in both cases the uncanny is an intentional production effect, but it is also an effect which exceeds the intention of its creator or director. In either case the mise-en-scène focuses on the female body as constructed as an, albeit ambiguous, phallic icon by and for the male gaze, and in either case this construction produces uncanny dysfunction.

The first of the scenes takes place before the creation of the robot, but it can be viewed as part of the processing of Maria into a desiring machine, as a sort of cinematic testing. It is the scene where Rotwang chases Maria in the catacombs, the uncanny Gothic underground of Metropolis. The scene is prepared by an act of illicit spectatorship as Rotwang and Fredersen extinguish their torches and view Maria's sermon through a rough-hewn eye-shaped aperture. Maria's first appearance had been established, through Freder's point of view, as a sort of iconic projection in a halo of light, a highly cinematic form of cult imaging. From the start, Maria is established bifocally. On the one hand she acts as a visual aid, directing the gaze of others; hence her first word: "Look!" At the same time she is produced as an image of what Laura Mulvey has famously called the "to-be-looked-at-ness" of woman on screen.[12] She corresponds, in other words, to the desire that Rotwang, Caligari-like, invokes in Fredersen, as he draws back the curtain, revealing the robot in his cabinet, with the words: "Do you want to look at her?" Thus Maria, as an object of double vision, is produced to serve the dual drives of the visual field, showing and looking. She is a prime cinematic object, appealing in a dialectical fashion to *Zeigelust* and *Schaulust*.

In the underground mass, the cinematic cult is projected further, as Maria is cast as a fascinating spectacle in light, and her sermon on the tower of Babel is then relayed, as if she were screening it, in a film vision. According to this film cult logic, the viewers at the peep-hole are

---

[12] Laura Mulvey, "Visual Pleasure and Narrative Cinema," *in Film Theory and Criticism: Introductory Readings*, ed. Gerald Mast et al., 4th ed. (New York: Oxford University Press, 1992), 746–57 (750).

in the position of the projectionist, concealed in a loft. When the chase begins, this logic is sustained. The occult scientist, who will subsequently be seen creating the "film image" of Maria as robot and directing her intervention in the Metropolis story, here mounts a fantasy film of his own. He first puts out the light with his mechanical hand and then starts his light-show in the darkened auditorium of the catacombs. As he plays his torchlight over Maria's hysterically frozen or twisting body, so the projection of the female body as fantasy image on the cinema screen is mounted self-reflexively. The show within the show, akin to Caligari's cabinet, is represented not least by the throwing of her shadow as terrorized image on the wall beyond her, forcing her to see and to pursue the projection of her image as victim.[13]

The reversal of shots in this sequence ensures that the viewer experiences the thrill of the chase in cross-cut between the view-points of voyeuristic victimizer and exhibited victim. Maria is subjected as scopic object both to the direct violence of visual desire and to a more indirect coercion of her own vision as she is made to track the projection of the violating gaze. The mad projectionist incorporates stock horror film sequences into his screening of his victim as his torchlight plays over objects of terror in a form of repetitive, sadistic foreplay. The scene displays not least the desire to postpone capture through the ambiguous rhythms of repetition compulsion. This is on show, in particular, in the replay of the shot where the projectionist illuminates the skeleton and lures from his victim a gesture towards the fascinating, mortifying object. In an elaborate relay of gazes, Rotwang directs Maria's gaze onto the icon of Gothic horror, while Maria's gesture, demonstrating the presence of the object as *da*, also directs the viewer's gaze. The film within the film thus plays to the rules of the *fort-da* game in its compulsively repeated gestures of concealment and revelation. It plays between the image of life and its negative, presence and absence, and so plays a game of now you see it now you don't with the enthralled viewer on- and off-screen.

The question is whether Rotwang's private screening works straightforwardly for the pleasure of his own viewing and for the vicarious pleasure of the cinematic spectator. The psychoanalytic logic of the *fort-da* game works to challenge notions of the mastery of loss through the motions of projection. If Rotwang is put in the position of the infant here, seeking to master the loss of the "mother" Hel, through projections first of a living surrogate and then of a sophisticated toy, a

[13] Here, as elsewhere in the film, Lang exploits the cinematic potency of shadow-play. Its cinematographic role in *Metropolis* represents a key moment in the passage of this feature from the uncanny warning and haunting shadows of expressionism into the aesthetics of film noir.

sex-doll, we might wish to question the integrity of his mastership. In fact, his master's gaze is itself mortified. In accordance with Freud's model, the voyeur is also positioned here as exhibitionist, displaying his phallicized gaze to his object. But the exhibitionist is not entirely in control of what is exhibited. When we see his eyes over the torchlight from Maria's point of view, they are shadowed on either side by the blind stare of skulls. The skulls which he uses as filmic effects in his show for Maria are thus also in view and blindly viewing behind his back. If the beam of light which pins the victim down represents the gaze of the master as a phallic agency, then the absent gaze of the eye-sockets cross-cuts that gaze with the sort of phantom of castration which Lacan analyzes in the projected skull of Holbein's *Ambassadors*.

The ambiguous merging of appeals to scopophilia and necrophilia might appear then to have caught the master necromancer at his own game. As the chase culminates in the full capture of Maria's body image in the beam of light, with Rotwang crouched in the foreground, what is presented is an image which is blinded by the light for the exhibit, the exhibitionist/exhibitor, and the cinematic viewer alike. The total subjection of the female body to the projection apparatus of the phallic gaze in fact screens that gaze in a different sense. The phallicized show of the exhibitionistic exhibitor is cut at its climax, and the scopic object is revealed only fleetingly as a sort of cinematic phantom as the blinding light fades out.

If this scene represents a sort of preliminary processing of the female body into the desiring machine, then it also shows symptoms of more radical dysfunction to come. The substitute organ which is the torch, an artificial eye held as another sort of prosthesis in the substitute hand, casts light above all on the uncanny lack of control which afflicts fantasies of substitution, however masterfully they may be engineered and directed. Like the cane wielded by Caligari in the mise-en-scène of his exhibition or the whip which directs the gaze of Harker onto Nosferatu's tower, the phallic device serves to orchestrate cultish fantasies of subjection, but the ultimate spectacle, the end-term of the serial substitutions, is prone to black-out or disintegration before your very eyes. It is not for nothing that directly before the chase, Rotwang's eyes open as Fredersen's torch-light passes over his face. He is made, in other words, to be imaged himself by the projection of light and to preview the act of animation. Similarly, in the replay of the chase scene in the cathedral, Rotwang, the master hypnotist and projectionist, is himself figured as a somnambulistic automaton. Thus the process of substitution takes control of its putative master. The cult of the phallus is always cross-cut in this way.

The principal act of substitution is, of course, that of the robot for the virgin, and as the effigy's underground sedition is clearly a black-mass repetition of the cult of Maria, the chase in the catacombs is also rehearsed by the substitute in the dance scene. If the chase was a private show, the dance is a public spectacle, a light-show which appeals more directly to the model of the cinema.[14] Once more the show is directed by the artificial hand of Rotwang, as he points the gaze of Fredersen towards the stage and so demonstrates its character as a fetishistic celebration of the phallic cult. Once more this cult is mediated by a mise-en-scène operating with the erogenous effects of the artificial eye, with the gaze working as a substitute for the phallus. The male gaze in its mounting excitement is fascinated by the image of the phallic woman as exotic dancer, an image which, like the show-objects Cesare or Nosferatu, can be seen to embody the enthralment of the film medium. Film is thus projected, as it were, onto the phallic stage, suggesting that the medium is in a state of arrested development.

The show is intensely self-reflexive in its appeal to the erogenous zone of the eye. Eye-balls are projected onto the screen behind the spectacle, and the dancer arises as an excitement of the eye, emerging *ex machina*, as it were, out of a mechanized podium in the shape of an artificial eye. The construction of the show body as scopic object into the eye prepares for its production as focus for the phallic cult. The image produced here is of a classically fetishistic variety, in accordance with the specifications of Freud's essay on *Fetischismus* ("Fetishism," 1927). The archetypal instance of the fetish there is an effect of light, a *Glanz* which, through its convergence with the English "glance," becomes a compulsive visual object.[15] That is, the fetish is dialectically constituted, binding the visual subject to the visual object, the look to the show.

It is a characteristic of the fetish, however, that the consonance of *Glanz* and glance is rarely straightforward. The show-object of the dance spectacle is produced by light, but produced not least as silhouette, at once to be seen and not to be seen. According to the logic of the fetish, the body is silhouetted in the shape of the phallus, while the detail of its naked parts is teasingly uncertain. The robot can *be* the phallus for the gaze of the spectators, but it is uncertain whether or not it *has* the phallus. It corresponds in this way to what Freud classifies as the more sophisticated instances of fetishistic attachment, where the object incorporates in what he calls its "construction" at once the dis-

[14] In the novel, the projection of lights advertising the Yoshiwara club is aligned with that of the cinema.

[15] Freud, *Standard Edition*, vol. 21 (1961), 152.

avowal and the assertion of castration.[16] To develop the model from Laforgue, which Freud adopts only to question, the fetishizing of the body in the stage-show involves a partial scotomization; it is a wide-eyed show which also, however, produces blind-spots. The display of the desiring machine is produced with the sorts of strategic veiling which characterized the cult of the phallus in the ancient Mysteries. At the same time, the sequence exploits all the tricks of the strip-tease, using front- and back-lighting to conceal even as it reveals. The threat of blinding, the castration of the desiring gaze, is thus constructed into the show.

If the bachelor machine is produced *ex machina*, out of a mechanical eye, it also serves to produce an extraordinary machining of the male gaze. The screen image here maintains the machine-body transaction which runs through the film by reproducing the establishing sequence where it is machine parts which are featured in montage. The most advanced devices of the cinematic apparatus are employed to create the extraordinary split-screen montage of the enthralled eyes. On the one hand, this would appear to present an image of consuming potency for the male gaze, an erotic counterpart to the panoptical vision of the control tower. It presents a spectacle of male desire as fixated, in every sense, at the phallic stage. But this is a multiple gaze which is spinning out of control and where the mechanical splicing of the montage represents a cutting of the gaze. This is a scene which derives intertextually from the archetypal fantasy scenario of Hoffmann's *Sandman*, where the bachelor machine Olympia is also put on show as a dancer by her "father." The montage of eyes can thus be understood as reproducing the uncanny effects of the proliferation of eyes, organic and artificial, in Hoffmann's tale. This is the sort of multiplication which Freud reads as one of the key paradoxes of psychic representation, where excess is taken to represent lack. The profusion of eyes in these cut-up visual effects would thus appear to match the classic form of the Freudian uncanny: the compulsively repetitive representation of the primal lack which is castration.

This logic of excess, produced as overcompensation for the trauma of lack, is marked in other ways in the sequence. The split-screen montage is reflected by the sequential structure of the show-scene, where the images of the gyrating show-girl are cross-cut with the images of the male gaze. Cross-cutting here appears to serve the totalization of the visual fantasy in a frenzied copulation of subject and object. But the total gaze is in fact rhythmically cut up; the blinking or flashing effects, produced by brief black-outs between the parallel sequences, lend the

---

[16] Freud, *Standard Edition*, vol. 21 (1961), 156.

show the character of a *fort-da* game. The pleasure of presence is mediated by strategic cuts to the radical unpleasure of absence. What the sequence thus constructs is a version of what post-Lacanian film theory calls suture, the primary filmic structure which follows the rhythms of the *fort-da*. The viewer is rhythmically stitched into a fantasy that appeals to the totalizing power of the Imaginary. But the stitching is also a sign of the traumatic gaps which drive and structure that fantasy. The Imaginary is cross-cut by the mark of the Symbolic through its key feature, the threat of castration as a complete black-out.

What is marked on these structural levels is then realised at the climax of the mise-en-scène. The cult object rises up sitting astride a podium which is no longer the ornamental gazing eye that it was, but transformed by the raised heads of serpents into a theatrical representation of the archetypal evil eye. The bachelor machine is exposed as a technological version of the archaic menace of the phallic woman Medusa who blinds even as she enthrals the male gaze. The virile figures who carried the podium at the start of the show have duly been metamorphosed into figures of stone, the seven deadly sins from the cathedral.

The cutting of the eye-show even at its ecstatic height is replayed in the cross-cut sequence featuring Freder as a hallucinatory, illicit spectator at the show. Like Jane in *Caligari*, who finds Caligari's exhibition of the show-object Cesare when she is searching for her father, he has been invited to the skin-flick exhibition in the name of the father, whose invitation he discovers at the side of his bed. By a sort of parapraxis, the lapsed member of the club of the sons is admitted to the club of the fathers. This is the characteristic Oedipal ambivalence which Lacan finds in patriarchy and the patronymic; by a sort of trick (the card out of the father's hat) the prohibitive "nom/non du père" is switched into a licence to enjoy the father's pleasures.

The necessary price for admission to the patriarchal club is subjection to a slice of Oedipal terror. Freder's viewing position as a member by proxy is prepared by a version of the primal scene, when he is consigned to bed with a hysterical fever brought on by finding his father in a clinch with the substitute mother figure. The primal scene triggers a traumatic light-show, as Freder's gaze is assaulted by flashing lights before being subjected to a wheeling montage of staring faces. The castrating gaze of the laughing Maria is cross-cut with the blind gaze of Death, and the heavy eye-shadow on the circulating images of Maria's face simulates the eye-sockets of the death's head. This absent gaze represents the blacking out of the viewer's vision which duly ensues. The circles of light and the spinning dark sockets which feature in this hallucinatory vision on Freder's mind-screen correspond to a leitmotif which structures the film's visual regime. The circle of light as emblem of the gaze is prone to conversion into its negative, the blank and blind socket. The two converge, for example, in the earlier mind-screen fantasy when Freder sees the master-machine as Moloch. Andreas Huyssen sees this vision as a technologized version of the archaic figure of male fear, the *vagina dentata*.[17] If this is a plausible reading of this man-eating machine, then its power to devour/castrate is represented not least by the intense gaze of its eyes which are figured as part of the circuitry of spot-lights in the film. Freder is dazzled and over-exposed by the brightness of this lighting effect. The blinding circles of light are thus counterparts to the devouring socket of the mouth. Their convergence is projected by the highlighting of the Os of MOLOCH, letters that are at once circles of light and dark sockets, nullifying and castrating for the fascinated male gaze.

It is the same logic of the blinding gaze that makes the robot's light-show a preview for another form of animation, the dance of Death. As this latest fantasy film on Freder's mind-screen cuts to the cathedral, so the continuity from the eye-show is marked by the mirroring of the eye-shaped frame of the dance podium in the rose-window above Death's head.[18] The grim reaper advances, slashing at the eye of the camera, the hero, and the vicarious spectator, thus threatening a more definitive cross-cutting, or castration, of visual desire. The gyrating desiring machine is thus transformed into the automatic slashing of the sort of phallic skeleton or phantom which figured in *Caligari* and *Nosferatu*.[19] The show becomes definitively uncanny, and the spectator's vision is once more blacked out.

The trauma of the ultimate cutting out of vision is, of course, stitched up by the end of the film. The Medusa is put to the stake. The phallic construction put upon femininity has created an uncanny monster, one fit for the sort of ritual sacrifice which the phallocratic order imposes on such bewitching menaces. The robot Maria serves as a kind of final girl for the fantasy film of patriarchy, providing a further spectacle in the light-show of her burning. The Medusa has thus served the function for the male order described by Teresa de Lauretis, as one of the obstacles "man encounters on the path of life, on his way to manhood, wisdom, and power; they must be slain or defeated so that he can

---

[17] Andreas Huyssen, *"The Vamp and the Machine,"* in Part Three of this volume.

[18] A further continuity is given by the transposition of the effigies of the deadly sins from the cathedral niches to the stage. The figures of these fantasy scenes are thus subject to displacement from one "other showplace" to another.

[19] Specifically, this is the same figure as features in miniature in *Nosferatu* on the repeating clock in the castle.

go forward to fulfil his destiny — and his story."[20] While Nathaneal, the hero of Hoffmann's *Sandman,* becomes irremediably uncanny in himself, so constructed into his fantasy that the immolation of the automaton is but a prelude to his own, *Metropolis* manages to construct a more benevolent finish in its recycling of the mad-scene on the tower. In Hoffmann's tale, the uncanny alchemist and anti-father Coppola/Coppelius is left on the loose, concealed amongst the spectators of Nathaneal's suicidal fall. Here his avatar, Rotwang, is sacrificed as well as his doll, and with him the uncanny fantasy life of the patriarchal order. A new contract can thus be established between men, with the voice of femininity whispering in the ear of the heroic mediator.

Thus the uncanny is canned. Whether the final spectacle really works to contain what has been so spectacularly released along the way is another matter. When the cardinal points of the body politic — the hand, the brain, and the heart — are drawn together at the end, their union is surely overshadowed by the unspeakable master organ of the patriarchal order: the organ, which in a series of fetishistic forms, at once hidden and highlighted, has driven the plot. If the will to power represented by the phallus is effaced in the final concord, then so are the anxieties, the shades of lack, which always attend its representation. While the Medusa may not be given the last laugh in *Metropolis,* we may recall the suggestion by Hélène Cixous that this much-sacrificed monster laughs on at patriarchy and the anxieties of castration which haunt it.[21] Certainly the image of the machine Maria as Medusa, laughing as she burns, is one which exceeds the bounds of the film's diegetic order. The silent laugh of this image of excess, presenting a mockery of the constitutional lack in the order of things, echoes uncannily on, even as the film's closure is cannily engineered.

---

[20] de Lauretis, *Alice Doesn't,* 110.

[21] Hélène Cixous, "The Laugh of the Medusa," in *New French Feminisms,* ed. Elaine Marks and Isabelle de Courtivron (Amherst: Massachusetts UP, 1980), 245–64.

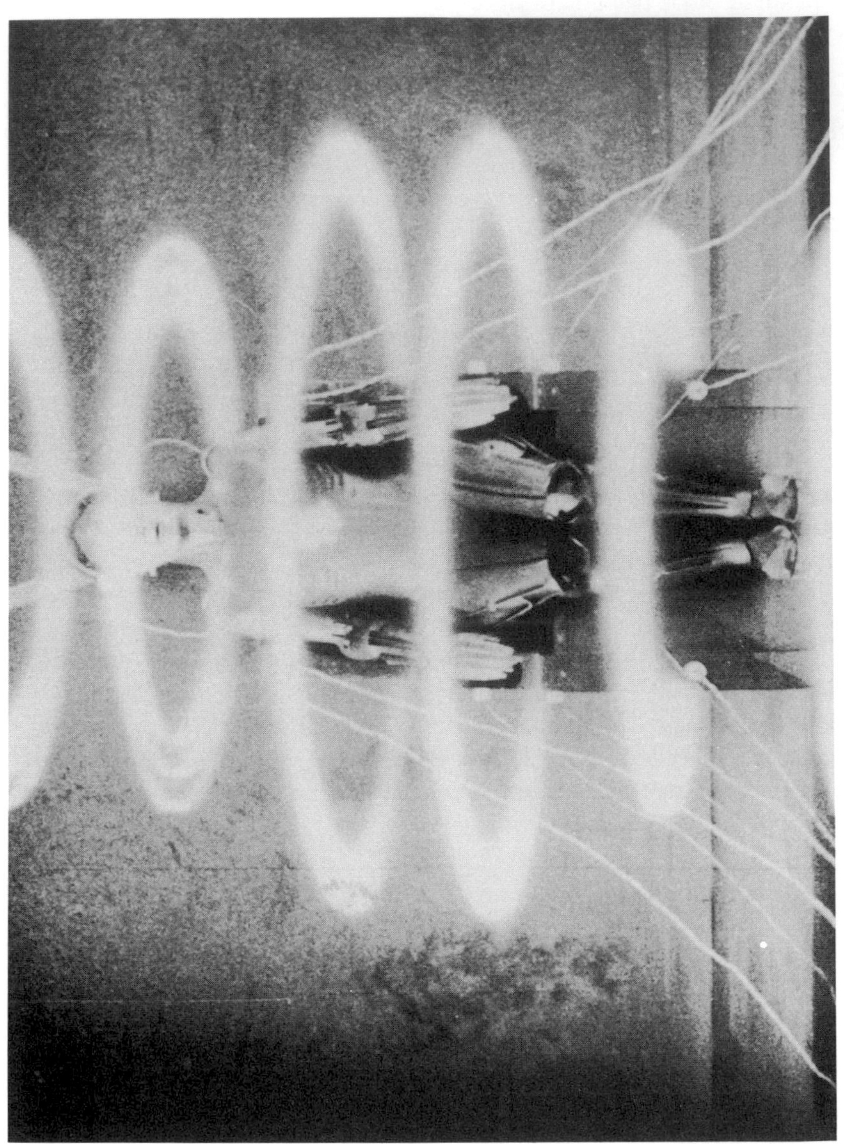

23. The robot with the light rings.
[Stiftung Deutsche Kinemathek, Berlin]

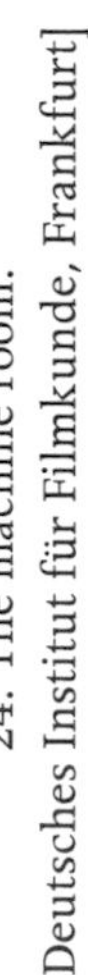

24. The machine room.
[Deutsches Institut für Filmkunde, Frankfurt]

The Imitation Game

Paralysis and Response in Fritz Lang's *Metropolis* and Contemporary Critiques of Technology

Julia Dover

IN HIS 1950 ARTICLE entitled "Computing Machinery and Intelligence," British scientist Alan Turing described an experiment in which he proposed that machines could display intelligent behavior by imitating human response. In spite of the complexities of the human brain, his famous Turing Test, or imitation game, was extremely simple: a person posed questions to two respondents via a teletype machine. One of the respondents was human, the other, a computer that was programmed to mimic the inconsistency of human response to such a degree that its behavior was indistinguishable from its human counterpart. The task of the interrogator was to determine which of the respondents was human. Invariably, the masquerading computer was selected.[1] The language Turing chooses to describe his experiments obscures the distinction between the human and the mechanical. He defines both the human brain and the digital computer as discrete state machines that employ mathematical analogies of function to operate in, as he describes, "series of jumps and clicks from one quite definite state to another."[2] Turing's imitation game blurs the comfortable hierarchy between the subjective "I" and the objective "it". Not only is the interrogator unable to differentiate human from mechanical sentience, but also the material house of agency has changed from flesh to metal and mathematics. This copycat machine was the first external and artificial seat of consciousness; a twentieth-century manifestation of an ancient struggle of mythic proportions, a struggle for the control over the geography of consciousness and identity that has transfixed the imagination since Olympus and Eden.

While Turing's creative impetus to design an operative and identical other (an internalized version of the doppelganger) can be traced back centuries, various technological innovations since the nineteenth century such as photography and cinema, robotics, digital, and virtual and genetic research, and Turing's own field of artificial intelligence have in

---

[1] Alan Turing, "Computing Intelligence and Machinery" in *Mechanical Intelligence: Collected Works of Alan Turing*, ed. D. C. Ince (Amsterdam: Elsevier, 1992), 133–60.

[2] Turing, "Computing Intelligence and Machinery," 139.

varying degrees rendered the human form into a basic unit of precise imitation. The intimate use of these technologies challenges the dialectical relationship between body and soul constituting selfhood like never before, thereby raising the stakes of the imitation game.

A large body of contemporary cultural criticism reflects a profound suspicion of the function of visual technologies which represent, mimic or reproduce the real. Just as Turing's discrete state machine unhinges consciousness from physiology, visual technologies such as television and cinema which represent the world of objects act to split the symbol from its referent, according to critics. For Jean Baudrillard, the inability to distinguish human (real) from machine which hallmarked the Turing Test holds true for our experience with images as well. He holds visual technologies responsible for the end of cultural representations which were based on an external, independent reality. According to Baudrillard, humans are locked into a Möbius strip of pure representation, what he calls hyperreality, from which there is no exit, where the differentiation between subject and object, interior and exterior, material and immaterial, experience and appearance collapse upon themselves in a cycle of perpetual "incestuous convolution."[3] Baudrillard heralds the disappearance of objects into chains of infinitely replicating hollow signs, or simulacra. In this matrix, the human being has no agency, she is held captive by the seductive verisimilitude of the illusion. Response within this framework is dangerous, indeed ultimately impossible; all that remains is "an immense uncertainty."[4] Baudrillard speaks for a large number of cultural critics when he explains that there is an immoral perversity, even a pornography within mimesis: "it is precisely when it appears most truthful, most faithful and most in conformity to reality that the image is most diabolical."[5] Authors Neil Postman and Paul Virilio support Baudrillard's position by suggesting that consciousness is becoming a mere reflection of the machines of everyday use. These authors offer a grim prognosis for the future possibilities of autonomy and civil society in a machine and image-mediated environment.[6] Writings as diverse as Anne Friedberg's *Window Shopping: Cinema and the Postmodern,* John Tagg's *Burden of Representation* and *Screening the Body: Tracing Medicine's Visual Culture* by Lisa Cartwright

---

[3] Jean Baudrillard, *Xerox and Infinity* (London: Agitac, 1988), 9.

[4] Baudrillard, *Xerox and Infinity,* 14.

[5] Jean Baudrillard, *The Evil Demon of Images,* trans. P. Patton (Annandale: The Power Institute of Fine Arts, 1984), 13–14.

[6] See Neil Postman, *Amusing Ourselves to Death: Public Discourse in the Age of Television* (New York: Viking Penguin, 1986), and Paul Virilio *The Aesthetics of Disappearance,* trans. Philip Beitchman (New York: Semiotext(e), 1991), 194.

discuss the histories of visual technologies, particularly cinema, using a rhetoric of conspiracy. Vision, apparently, operates as a complex system of surveillance and discipline, in which the representation determines an authoritarian control over the spectator. Tagg examines representation in terms of their underlying rigid power structures.[7] Friedburg grounds the euphoria of the visual replica of the nineteenth century in Foucault's *régime panoptique.* She views early vision machines such as the diorama through the lens of Foucault's panopticon prison of imagined scrutiny, and describes the spectators as trapped within an imaginary illusion of immobility.[8] For Cartwright, the motion picture camera embodies the compulsion of the medical gaze to trap and embalm human life. In her words, the spectacle of cinema "reflexively documents the complex place that technologies of representation have come to occupy in the regulation and control of life and death."[9]

Conspiracy, authority, disappearance, and death: the rhetoric of contemporary critiques of replication technologies is charged with doom. Alienation of the self is regarded as a fundamental characteristic of modern identity. This alienation, or fragmentation, is created and perpetuated by the network of machine-image complexes which constructs the social realm. Betrayed by the platonic suspicion of the world of appearances, the modern individual cannot distinguish the real from the artificial, and is imprisoned in a Purgatory of inbetween. Turing's discrete state machine manifests an imitative intelligence external to the human authority which designed it. It is an "it" able to mask as an "I." Whether the "thing" is a robot, a computer or an image, it is charged with what Paul Coates refers to as an uncanny power to usurp the authority of the master by claiming the seat of identity formation using its mimetic function:

> The (filmic) image is an alienated reflection, an imitation of life that is perilously similar to the original. The man who has lost his reflection may experience terror when he observes it living its own life. The doubling of an image is a propagation that diminishes it, and the man who sees his own *Doppelgänger* has a weaker sense of his own identity than the man who does not. The same may be said of the society that

---

[7] John Tagg, *The Burden of Representation: Essays on Photographies and Histories* (London: MacMillan, 1988), 21.

[8] Anne Friedburg, *Window Shopping: Cinema and the Postmodern* (Berkeley: U of California P, 1993), 28.

[9] Lisa Cartwright, *Screening the Body: Tracing Medicine's Visual Culture* (Minneapolis: U of Minnesota P, 1995), 46.

scrutinizes itself on the cinema screen: it views the lost image of itself with near-anthropological dispassion.[10]

Critiques of visual technologies offer no avenue for creative response by the sentient subject to the ambiguity of the imitation game. This suspicion is symptomatic of a larger cultural unease with human agency in relation to the modern technological complex. In order to gain understanding of this discomfort, it becomes important to examine the rules of the imitation game on its own terms. Such investigation is crucial at a point in history when traditional concepts of self are challenged even further by new technological innovations such as genetic cloning and virtual intelligence.

The prototypic science fiction film of 1926, Fritz Lang's *Metropolis*, is a powerful laboratory of relationship between the biological subject and technological object on two levels: in the subject and style of its presentation, and in the cinematic medium itself, or the viewer's interaction with the moving images on screen. First, the film plays disturbingly with the site of consciousness and authority in the relationship of human and machine (like the Turing test). Workers, pistons and clockfaces move in Tayloristic tandem. They jump and click to the rhythm of efficiency accorded to Turing's discrete state machines. On aesthetic and narrative levels, boundaries between living (real) and artificial are interchangeable. Power gradients, hierarchies and metamorphic pathways between the biological and the mechanical become confused, as most powerfully symbolized by the spectacles of Moloch and the robot double. *Metropolis* also incorporates cultural reaction to the mimetic machine as menacing and seductive. Second, the patterns of projection and metamorphosis in the human engagement with machine as depicted in the caverns and cityscapes of *Metropolis* unfold within a larger system, the viewing complex, or what Aumont, Baudry and others have referred to mechanistically as the cinematic apparatus, or the cybernetic system of camera, image, eye, and response.[11] The spectator observes the machinations of the modern industrial complex swallow workers whole, herself implicated in a Baudrillardian battle with the Moloch of the image. From this perspective, the spectator within the cinematic apparatus is an actor whose identity is absorbed by a machine, just like Maria and her malevolent robot double: the stuff of science fiction.

---

[10] Paul Coates, *The Gorgon's Gaze: German Cinema, Expressionism and the Image of Horror* (Cambridge: Cambridge UP, 1991), 1.

[11] See Jean-Louis Baudry, "The Apparatus: Metaphysical Approaches to Reality in Cinema," *Camera Obscura* 1 (spring 1976), 104–126. Peter Wollen has also compared the cinematic medium with the content of the film: "Cinema/Americanism/The Robot." *New Formations* 8 (summer 1989), 7–34.

According to Susan Sontag, the genre of science fiction films is not about science, but about the aesthetics of destruction. These films are rites of acting out unmanageable cultural fears:

> In science fiction films it is by images and sounds, not words that have to be translated by the imagination, that one can participate in the fantasy of living through one's own death and more, the death of cities, the destruction of humanity itself.[12]

Science fiction films, then, project our worst nightmares onto the screen as alien and external images. Sontag also sees science fiction as the emblem of an inability to respond. The genre allows for the cultural expression of a profound loss of control, without the risk of physical implications. In examining duplication and imitation both within and without the diegetic context of *Metropolis,* my intentions are twofold. First, I offer a close reading of the mythical absorption of human consciousness by machine in Lang's film. I examine how the machine complex drains human capacity for agency by assuming an identical appearance to the people it manipulates. Within the closed filmic world of *Metropolis,* I trace the pattern of response of the people to the machine monsters which control and envelop them. Second, I bring out the symmetrical relationships between victimization and reaction in *Metropolis* as science fiction and the dynamics of the cinematic apparatus, including the malevolent relationship of the image to the viewer I have described which dominates contemporary cultural theories. I assert that the Moloch and Maria robot of *Metropolis* and Baudrillard's image apparitions are both mythic emblems of cultural incapacity as outlined in Sontag's discussions of science fiction. I present alternative avenues for engagement with the imitation which can enable Baudrillard's viewer to break out of the closed mythical world of the image as robot master.

Metropolis courts disaster by riding the fragile frontier between flesh and metal on both aesthetic and narrative levels using the conceit of the robot double. Set designs, linear camera composition and characterization in the film all function as a threatening robot complex. The cogs and engines of the machine room absorb the movement of the massed workers as material. The camera is static, the enormous frame squarely magnifies the iron bulk of factory machine, its flat, symmetrical composition infers an entrenched solidity of power. The workers have neither voice nor face; their gray uniforms and rigid, repetitive movements render them as dark spots, nuts and bolts against the well-lit and thunderous mechanical display. It is the fallibility of human ac-

---

[12] Susan Sontag, "The Imagination of Disaster," *Against Interpretation* (London: Vintage, 1961), 212.

tion which precipitates explosion. A metamorphosis occurs, the apparition of another double appears and disappears. Solid phases into gas, then back again: the machine becomes mouth, the Moloch that ingests. The master and the servant exchange morphologies. The workers with no faces are alive, but they behave as robots and they exist as functional bits. The machine is object, thing, a material other, but it shape shifts into human form. The axis of creating and becoming is confused. At this point, the dehumanization of the workers is ornamental, a matter of set design, an expressionistic background of spectacle against which the narrative will unfold. Lang's aestheticization of the worker automata acts to further dehumanize them. In *Metropolis,* then, the integrity of the self is consistently under siege. Both the narrative and the visual composition of the frame make it difficult to distinguish subject from object of imitation, to locate cause versus effect. Essentially human qualities of spontaneity and inconsistency, qualities that, incidentally, Turing designed his discrete state machine to mimic for his imitation game, are certainly not traits applicable to the actions of the workers in the texture of the frame. At the point in the film when the workers do break from their automated movements, they become destructive: physical action can have lethal consequences.

The metamorphosis of the Maria double intensifies the imitation game. The lens zooms in toward the singular form of the human being. Rotwang's theft, his experiment in replication occurs far away from the grandstand anonymity of the Moloch underworld. The camera has moved closer, the laboratory is a private and intimate stage for the violation of the self by the external world. The objects, human and other, which existed as flat units of contextual ornamentation in the Moloch sequence, have acquired depth and agency in the laboratory. The room is filled with objects which move in unpredictable ways: liquids in vessels, electrical surges, and people. In the climactic sequence of morphological displacement, the camera captures intimate and sensual detail of faces and gazes: the eyes of Rotwang, the closed eyes of Maria, the frightening impenetrable and empty eyes of the robot. The fault line of separation between human agent and automaton is immanent in its frailty and proximity to the viewer.

Metropolis reinforces patterns of authority using the geometry of frame composition. The images can be characterized by their division into balanced parts. Even though both the narrative and the editing are chaotic, the symmetrical composition of the frame acts to stabilize and reinforce. Moloch devours, Maria's life force is stolen and replaced by a demonic imitation, and the city is flooded, but the aesthetics ground the audience's response in equanimity. Maria lies inert, encased in glass as sacrificial meal along the bottom of the frame. Rotwang's invention claims dead centre as idol apex of a pyramid: in terms of composition, there is no question of where the seat of authority is. Even the scientist serves as aesthetic handmaiden to the metal god. Close up shots of beakers filled with boiling liquids, vials and electrodes dissolve into each other, into cutaways of the ravaged Maria and the robot. Dissolve again to protozoan bubbles, the shift in form is chemical, substance, material — *real*. There is an instant during this sequence when the viewer loses orientation; the direction of the energy shift becomes obscured in the montage of dissolving extreme close ups. The robot "stares" squarely through the lens with imitation eyes. The image slowly dissolves from metal into flesh. The thing assumes the appearance of a self, a familiar Maria. The real one is drained, used up, diminished. The simulation opens its eyes to devour the lens.

The Maria double of *Metropolis* evokes a contradictory sensorium of responses in the audience. The viewer is simultaneously intoxicated and horrified by the gyrations of the robot. Its human appearance seduces, its behavior as demon unsettles because it can elicit pleasure, yet it is itself beyond the experience of pleasure: it is dead. From the moment it opens its eyes, the Maria robot never ceases to be a thing, from its orgiastic display in the nightclub to its immolation. Mimetic technologies, including photography, cinema and even artificial intelligence (including Turing's discrete state machine) transfix the modern imagination in a manner similar to the viewer's fixation on the Maria robot. Cinematic images mesmerize not because they simulate the living, but because we know they are dead, as if we have seen a ghost, as if the corpse stands up and walks away, a corpse. Life is quantifiable, we know it because we embody it. Death, on the other hand, is incomprehensible. The fascination for anthropomorphic automata is macabre. It is based not on a preoccupation with immortality, but with death. Technologies of human imitation, then, are laden both with the celebration of human potential and its darker side:

> anthropomorphic design . . . also foresees our potential for enslavement, self-destruction, or even . . . our eventual obsolescence . . . . It illustrates how the trick ultimately rebounds upon the trickster, how our desires and appetites have a way of eventually eating away at us, rendering us nearly empty or lifeless beings.[13]

The Maria robot offers omnipotence and impotence at the same time. Its lure prompts a closed system of desire for the extension of power and a simultaneous fear of loss of control to perpetuate itself. This matrix of opposing forces represented in the Maria robot is the source of inertia

[13] J. P. Telotte, *Replications: A Robotic History of the Science Fiction Film* (Chicago: U of Illinois P, 1995), 5.

and weakening of human agency in the technological age. Machines in *Metropolis* drain, absorb, threaten and swallow, or conversely, they are sought out by the mob and destroyed, burnt at the stake, purged. Loss of control is always imminent. Destruction — of both template and copy — hangs in the balance. The world of *Metropolis* exists as a closed and self-perpetuating ellipsis of victimization, absorption, reaction and return to stasis. The stability of mutual slavery is dependent upon the scourge as release of tension. Just as the Tower of Babel is destroyed by those who built it, Moloch is also blown apart so that it can be rebuilt. The workers are as inextricably linked to the machines as the robot is to Maria. In the cycle of destruction, there is no space for response, no possibility for any relationship beyond slavery. In fact, *Metropolis* naturalizes slavery on all levels, down to the deep structure of the piece. The geometry of the film is circular: in the beginning, mechanized order prevails like clockwork. The industrial complex cannot tolerate the struggle of workers as human objects to reassume their integrity as subject agents. The Maria robot acts to lance the wound as a witch-burning spectacle to restore the balanced order of inertia. The workers, in their brief, frenzied escape from the cruelty of mechanized time and work, are under the impression they are free. On the steps of the cathedral, the pyramidal power structure is re-established. Maria's words, "Between the head and the hand is the heart" fall flat, and the cycle of slavery and control can recommence. The end of the film prompts a Sisyphian return to the beginning: one imagines that a whistle bows, and the workers assume their positions as prostrate sacrifices, as if the film never happened:

> The technological surface of the world these people have shaped — and that clearly shapes them — has not really changed, nor has its allure. Instead of removing the veil of these seductive forces, the people have simply lifted it and let it fall back.[14]

Decades after its initial release, *Metropolis* still manages to simultaneously impress and appall audiences. The experience of the contemporary viewer is double-edged. The highly controlled frame, the geometric, flat and expressionist forms within both reassure and please the eye. The futurist cityscapes evoke a strange nostalgia for the time in history, now passed, when it was possible to imagine the future of human progress as glorious, without implications of catastrophe. Appearances, though, are deceiving: the etheric skyscraper paradise of Fredersen's empire is fueled by a cyborg furnace, a machine complex merging metal and sinew that belches steam and bodies in subterranean caverns. The paradise and nightmare aspects of the city are embodied in

---

[14] Telotte, *Replications*, 67.

the single form of the Maria robot double. The Maria robot at once enchants and horrifies because, like the discrete state machine, it moves spontaneously to a degree where both viewer and characters within the film cannot tell the difference between the biological and the mechanical. When the mob of workers burns the robot, the viewer is not certain which aspect they seek to annihilate — the human surface or the subcutaneous machine. Traditional codes of morality are warped by shifting appearances. Neither the workers nor the viewer know who the enemy is; relief is felt by characters and audience when the order of the narrative and the hierarchies of *Metropolis* are once again restored through murder, of a kind, to match Lang's comfortable frame.

The duplicitous appearances of the machine complex in *Metropolis* are a golem image which still resonates for the contemporary viewer. The forces of technological progress which were projected as monster myth onto the cinema screen in the 1920s continue to challenge the human subject's sense of living in the world. The substance of the science fiction story of the present — the technological alien which threatens human agency — has itself transformed from the iron and coal of earlier industrial factories into bits of digital information and virtual images. The metaphoric patterns of seduction, simulation and destruction which bind people and machine within a never-ending treadmill of slavery in *Metropolis* are identical to the relationship between viewer and image in the cinematic apparatus of contemporary theoretical discussions on cinema and other visual technologies. Such a comparative analysis offers invaluable insights into the cultural context of anxiety which frames the contemporary viewing experience of *Metropolis*.

In his writing on the relation of the spectator to the image, Jacques Aumont defines the cinema apparatus as the system of regulation and control which determines the spectator's relationship to the image.[15] For theorists such as Cartwright, this regulation, as I have discussed, is motivated by an authoritarian impulse to control life and death. The term *apparatus* prompts associations with the discrete state machine — a name which Turing attributed to both brain and computer. Just as "discrete state machine" implies a cybernetic link between subject sentience and object itness, Aumont's cinematographic apparatus links a human subject with external objects (the image) in a pattern of domination within which the subject has little control. Just as movement, appearance and humanity of the workers in the *Metropolis* underworld are absorbed by a machine, and the Maria robot assumes the stolen form of

[15] J. Aumont, *The Image*, trans. C. Pajackowska (London: British Film Institute, 1997), 143.

its human victim, the image aspect of the apparatus robs the viewer of her capacity and desire, even, to distinguish the real from its simulation. Just as Maria's power of resistance is diminished when her form is stolen in the laboratory (she ceases hereafter to act as a mobilizer of human agency), in the experience of watching images, according to Coates, the imitation of reality diminishes the spectator's sense of self. The science fiction monsters of *Metropolis* metaphorically embody Jean Baudrillard's simulacrum: factory machine, robot and cinematographic image all acquire a malevolent and destructive quality by imitating the appearance of the human form, or the *real*. The creation destroys the creator. The viewer of *Metropolis,* within the paralyzing framework of contemporary theory's cinematographic apparatus, is trapped by the seductive surfaces of the images on screen, whose content of human-devouring machines and robot simulacrum reflects and *imitates,* in fact causes the viewer's own consummation by the screen. In a sense, then, the phasing of human consciousness with machine in *Metropolis* mythically projects the audience's death of self. The *object* monsters in the diegetic world of the film are the *image* monsters of the cinematographic apparatus.

Alien creatures and machine monsters of the science fiction genre must be annihilated for humans to survive; there is no room for peaceful coexistence. The disturbing power of Lang's *Metropolis* lies in its graphic aestheticization of the politics and implications of this annihilation. As I have discussed, the film's happy ending is misleading, for the destruction of the Maria robot is achieved at terrible cost. In their crazed urge to kill the Maria robot, the workers risk without thought the drowning of their children and the collapse of the city. This urge to destroy the Maria double as a witch-burning in fact entrenches the slavery of the workers. There is no room for hope or transformation (children) in this closed fear-based system. The sensuous images of *Metropolis* suffocate the viewer, for there is no possibility for escape from the cycle of absorption and disappearance of the self into the thundering machine complex, and its subsequent, inevitable destruction and return. The struggle for survival in the film is epic and Darwinian, a clash of survival of the fittest, with machine objects assuming the power and vitality of species. Ultimately, the machine complex wins; human agency remains absorbed and subverted by its own fear of the machines. Lang draws the viewer into this process by the seductive yet highly ordered composition of the frame. This closed system of destruction closely echoes the relationship of viewer to image in the cinematographic apparatus of contemporary theorists. The rhetoric of cultural theories of Baudrillard and company preclude the possibility for creative response. The viewer is trapped and absorbed by the imitation of the real that technology offers; she is paralyzed by the pleasure of the likeness, this pleasure is the poison which numbs the victim. The cycle of slavery in *Metropolis* is the same as the closed prison of hyperreality that lulls the viewer into inertia in the cinematographic apparatus. Cultural critics invest technologies which imitate human appearance or, like the Turing machine, the inconsistency of behaviour and consciousness, with a mythical power of destructive intent, over which humans have no control. In the Möbius Strip of mediated reality, automation, not autonomy, reigns. Baudrillard's conception of the relationship of human subject to mechanical object is nihilistic and fantastical. He accuses visual technologies of eroding even the desire for alternatives. This rhetoric of attack on technological objects mirrors the workers' purge of the Maria robot in *Metropolis*. Blame is placed on the technological object as agent of alienation. The image is vilified and charged with a fetishistic power to devour the viewer's consciousness. Contemporary theories create a technological monster so dangerous to human survival that it must be destroyed. Like the workers of *Metropolis*, critics of representation in a sense purge the malevolent simulacrum for their freedom. Just as the workers perpetuate their slavery to the machine complex which absorbs their identity, the urge to place blame on technological objects for the alienation which plagues modern society further paralyzes our capacities for engaged response. The closed worlds of *Metropolis* and the cinematographic apparatus of contemporary theory, then, are science fiction emblems of Sontag's notion of inadequate response. Both worlds are frightening, for they offer no resolution for the human agent beyond destruction and acquiescence. The imitation game is a matter of life and death.

The juxtaposition of a German expressionist film of the 1920s with contemporary critiques of visual technologies may appear somewhat arbitrary. It is also not my intention to reduce the rich complexity of Fritz Lang's mise en scène to a limited psychological or theoretical denominator. My analysis of the parallel systems of relationship in *Metropolis* and contemporary theories focuses on the perceptual experience of the viewer or human agent of technological objects of representation. It is perception which connects, ultimately, the film, the theoretical perspectives, with the experience of the modern sentient subject. Perception grounds the analysis in the physical process of human interaction with the objective world. Human perception is also the complex point of intersection between consciousness, or soul, and the body which constitutes the self. Through this approach, I have revealed distinct identical patterns of reaction in both filmic and theoretical worlds discussed. The symbolic, thematic and structural dimensions of the Moloch underworld and Baudrillard's conspiratorial image complex reflect and perpetuate the threat of absorption by technology, and an inability for human identity to maintain the integrity of self in a machine and image-arbitered environment. In this comparison, the objects, and ultimately the means of perception cannot be trusted: the cinema screen and the Maria robot are malevolent illusions of the real, as is the discrete state machine of Turing's imitation game. That we cannot distinguish the image from its referent as Baudrillard laments, that the workers confuse the human and robot versions of Maria, implies that the self is betrayed by its perception, and the means by which it negotiates with the world. The human subject, it seems, has merged with the objects it has created as a nightmare android which is partly biological and partly metal. The discomfort with this mingling material state of being, so powerfully represented by the mythic world of *Metropolis,* so loudly expressed by the contemporary theories I have discussed, contradicts the traditional Enlightenment celebration of science as a vehicle of control over the natural world, and the dominion of human consciousness over physical and material states. The science fiction of doom and the closed circles of return in the cyborg apparatus of *Metropolis* marks a loss of faith in the power of human agency to manipulate, even understand the external realm of objects.

Within the larger landscape of the twentieth century, though, there is good reason to fear the consequences of human perception and the urge for scientific control over the objective realm. The impetus to project the imagination upon the environment and the supremacy of Cartesian rationality which severs thought from object (products of the Enlightenment) have inflicted havoc in the twentieth century. Since 1914, that quality of human consciousness which can use technology to transcend the physical limitations of the body, time and space to colonize other dimensions has been directly implicated in disaster. Environmental hazards, over-population, and the imminence of total war have tainted the utopia of perpetual progress. Instrumental reason fueled the euphoria of the replica, the engines of the modern industrial complex and the machinery that is the subject and backdrop of *Metropolis.* The eye of instrumental reason designed technologies of mass destruction and the camera lens. The seduction of the simulacrum is a seduction of the power which accompanies supreme authority of science and reason over nature. From this perspective, the iconoclasm of contemporary theories of visual technologies appears appropriate. It is my assertion, however, that the critiques of visual technologies I have outlined are locked in a pattern of reaction which perpetuates the most destructive aspects of Enlightenment rationality which they purport to attack.

The fear of the mechanical or the image other, and especially the corresponding paralysis of the human agent to act in response to this fear are the result of a fierce objectification, both of the means and contexts of bodily perception. Philosopher Merleau-Ponty has demonstrated that this Cartesian dualism is the pearl of the Enlightenment; it fuels a hierarchical relationship of pure thought and human consciousness over the world of things, including the body. The consequence of the disassociation of mind from body, according to Merleau-Ponty, is that the body and its senses, and the realm of the external all become mechanized tools for manipulation.[16] The self, in a sense, becomes split apart, like the image from its referent, and molded into a cyborg creature of human consciousness and mechanical body bits like the Maria robot, the Moloch underworld and the cinematographic apparatus of human subject and image other. Empiricism reduced human perception to machines hundreds of years before Fritz Lang composed images of human-devouring engines and monstrous doppelgangers. When consciousness is disembodied, and the body itself is cast into a laboratory of object things, perception and engaged response, or the synthesis of thought and corporeality which grounds an empathetic relationship with the world, become impossible. This fracture of subject from object provokes action without responsibility. The external world becomes a chaos of disengaged effects over which the subject cause has no control. The effects appear to assume an agency of their own: welcome to the science fiction of carnivorous machines and Baudrillard's Evil Demon of Images.

Merleau-Ponty offers a way out of the destructive closed system of mutilated perception in *Metropolis* and contemporary theories of technology. He restores identity formation within the elastic, and essentially ambiguous complex of perception, or the matrix of the psychic, the physiological components of the human subject and the world of objects. The body of the cinematographic apparatus, then, is freed from its mechanistic bondage to the image object, and is returned to a vivifying field of experience. The sense experience of the subject (or the viewer) is the point of creative identity formation and communication with the world, an experience which Merleau-Ponty refers to as incarnate subjectivity. Meaning is created within the dialectics of this subjectivity. Resubjectifying the body and focusing on sensual perception as a vehicle of communion with the external world counteracts the paralysis of modern alienation. Like the workers of *Metropolis*, theories of conspiracy entrench their alienation and slavery to the machine com-

[16] M. Merleau-Ponty, *Phenomenology of Perception*, trans. C. Smith (London: Routledge, 1989), 199.

plex of instrumental reason by objectifying perception and locating the authority of identity formation in the alien and lifeless world of objects. While the pattern of slavery and fear in both *Metropolis* and contemporary theory is perpetual, it does offer safety from the risks and responsibility which incarnate subjectivity demand. Response, and empathetic relationship of the human subject to the external world curtails the frenzy of consumption and destruction of the environment. Human agents become guilty, automatically and implicitly, by association, and can no longer blame mythic objects for a world that falls apart. Filmic and theoretical realms can spin and perpetuate destructive patterns without immediate consequence. These realms, however, are barometers of a social and physical paralysis whose stasis is catastrophic.

25. André von Mattoni as pictured by Ufa.
[Deutsches Institut für Filmkunde, Frankfurt]

26. Gustav Fröhlich as pictured by Ufa.
[Deutsches Institut für Filmkunde, Frankfurt]

27. Freder as comic-book action hero in the American publicity.
[BFI Films: Stills, Posters and Designs]

Metropolis — The Archetypal Version

Sentimentality and Self-Control in the Reception of the Film

Ben Morgan

A Sentimental Introduction

Metropolis has a bad ending.[1] Even Lotte Eisner, one of Lang's staunchest supporters, felt forced to admit that, in the handshake between Fredersen and Grot, the film is finally "overwhelmed by the excess of emotionalism," and many critics have shared her opinion.[2] On the other hand, the applause for the film's technical achievements started literally from the moment the first images were shown at the premiere in Berlin and has hardly flagged since.[3] To cope with these two sides of the film, contemporary reviewers adopted a strategy of attributing the aspects of the film they disliked to the pen of Thea von Harbou, the scriptwriter, in this way distinguishing Lang's (or the cameraman, Karl Freund's, or the set designer, Otto Hunte's) formal masterpiece from the sentimentality they found so unpalatable. Buñuel even declared the film to be two films stitched together, one the responsibility of Lang and his technicians, which achieved a new form of visual poetry, the other the cloying amalgam that was Harbou's narrative.[4] This division of labor fell all the more easily because it was gendered, as Rudolf Arnheim's review makes explicit (to later generations, it falls easily for the different reason that Harbou stayed in Germany in 1933, joining the NSDAP

---

[1] This article was written in collaboration with Katja Lehmann. Thanks are also due to Michael Minden and Holger Bachmann for their comments and advice, and to Brigitte Capitain at the Deutsche Institut für Filmkunde in Frankfurt am Main for her enormous assistance during my visit to the Institute.

[2] Lotte Eisner, *Fritz Lang*, trans. Gertrud Mander (London: Secker & Warburg, 1976), 90.

[3] "Der Beifall setzte bei den ersten Bildern, die die riesige technische Leistung zeigten, ein und steigerte sich immer mehr." "Pressestimmen über Metropolis," *Kinematograph*, 1039 (16 January 1927), 16.

[4] Luis Buñuel, "Métropolis," *Cahiers du cinéma* 223 (August/September 1970), 20–21. The text in English translation is included in its entirety in Part One of this volume.

in 1940).[5] "Let us keep manicured fingers off socialism," Arnheim declares, for, to his misogynist eye, the deficiencies of the plot were the direct product of a woman applying her sentimental standards in the unsentimental, male realm of politics.[6] A review written by a certain H. P. in the journal *Der Bildwart* seems to have shared Arnheim's assumptions. Lang's mistake, it suggests, was to allow a woman to write the script for his technological fantasy without letting a (male) expert vet the details. At that same time, the review reveals what it was about the womanly sentimentality that the critic found so abhorrent: "Metropolis as a technological film fantasy is infantile."[7] The emotionalism was despicable because it was childlike.

With the best will in the world it is indeed hard to read Harbou's novel — with its constant, bombastic incantations and clichéed terms of description. But the film isn't the same thing as the novel (if nothing else it's been streamlined and clarified by the collective process of the "Regiesitzungen," the exhaustive production meetings with Freund, Rittau, Wilkomm, Schüfftan, Kettelhut, Hunte and Vollbrecht at Lang and Harbou's apartment).[8] Moreover, it isn't the condemnation itself that is important but the assumptions which it reveals: whatever it is that lies behind the image of the childlike woman. Around the time that these reviews were written, in the late 1920s, Freud was writing his sociological works, *The Future of an Illusion* and *Civilization and its Discontents*, the recurring theme of which was the renunciation required to be an adult (and particularly an adult man). To grow up, for these texts, is to forego the satisfaction of your wishes.[9] In the case of Freud, these wishes are understood to be primarily sexual. The reviews of *Metropolis* suggest that it's not only sex that must be regulated but the many different types of emotions grouped together in the accusations of kitsch, sentimentality, and infantility. (In another text of the period, Weber's *Science as Vocation*, it is the desire for emotionally satisfying explana-

---

[5] For details of Harbou's biography, see the entry "Thea von Harbou" in *Cinegraph: Lexikon zum deutschsprachigen Film*, ed. Hans-Michael Bock (Munich: edition text + kritik, 1984–).

[6] Rudolf Arnheim, "Metropolis (1927)," *Film Essays and Criticism*, trans. Brenda Benthien (Madison: U of Wisconsin P, 1997), 119. (The review originally appeared in *Das Stachelschwein*, 1 February 1927.)

[7] "Metropolis ist als technische Filmphantasie kindlich." H. P., "Metropolis," *Der Bildwart* 4/5 (April/May 1927), 326.

[8] Patrick McGilligan, *Fritz Lang: The Nature of the Beast* (London: Faber and Faber, 1997), 110–13.

[9] For a general discussion of these texts, see John Deigh, "Freud's later theory of civilization: Changes and implications" in *The Cambridge Companion to Freud*, ed. Jerome Neu (Cambridge: Cambridge UP, 1991), 287–308.

tions of one's place in the world that must be renounced if one is to be properly virile.)[10] The complaint that the film is at once too womanly and too childish in its approach to political and technological issues is thus a complaint that it doesn't submit to the regulation of emotions required by the world of male experts.

What is particularly striking about this complaint is the manner in which it introduces social criteria into debates about the film. One of the questions that most vexed contemporary critics was precisely that of the film's relation to society. H. G. Wells was only the most famous of a host of reviewers whose desire to read the film as a literal forecast of social developments produced a hilarious frustration.[11] Read literally, the film will inevitably seem illogical. Be it the levers that, as Paul Ickes pointed out, need the strength of a gorilla to be activated; or the leakage of steam continually evident in the machine rooms; be it the purposelessness of the technological activity (it apparently wasn't yet critically possible to say the film was *about* this purposelessness); be it the absurdity of the underground city, when all recent sociological evidence pointed to a lateral expansion of urban centers, the film conjures up an urban nightmare already out-of-date when the film was made. Did Ufa not at least have the money to take Lang to look at a modern power station, is the despairing cry of the reviewer in *Kino-Technik*.[12]

That the reviewers should approach the film sociologically was hardly to be avoided. The film was marketed as a vision of the future ("The destiny of the humanity of the year 2000"), with specifically political implications ("The tragic struggle of opposing classes has come to an end"),[13] nor is this marketing strategy exceptional, since class was one of the key frameworks for explaining social experience in the Weimar Republic (think of Piscator, for whom at least two of Lang's cast, Heinrich George and Gustav Fröhlich, had worked at the *Volksbühne*).[14] What is more striking is the reviewers' blindness to manifestations of society other than class or technology, both in the film, and in their

---

[10] Max Weber, "Science as Vocation," in *From Max Weber: Essays in Sociology*, trans. H. H. Gerth and C. Wright Mills (London: Routledge & Kegan Paul, 1948), 155.

[11] H. G. Wells, "Mr. Wells reviews a current film," see Part One of this volume. Others include the review in *Kino-Technik*, 20 February 1927, 102–3; Paul Ickes, "Metropolis," *Filmwoche*, 19 January 1927, 60–61; "Metropolis," *Der Bildwart* 4/5 (April/May 1927), 326–29; A. Kraszna-Krause, "Metropolis," *Filmtechnik*, 5 March 1927, 91–93.

[12] *Kino-Technik*, 20 February 1927, 103.

[13] "'Metropolis' Das Schicksal einer Menschheit im Jahre 2000," Parufamet Presse- und Propagandaheft [1926], unpaginated.

[14] Gustav Fröhlich, *Waren das Zeiten: Mein Film-Heldenleben* (Munich/Berlin: Herbig, 1983), 110.

own responses. Seventy years later, society is visible not only in the images of machines and class conflict, or in the architecture of Fredersen's city, but in what the characters' behaviour, the film's formal devices, and indeed the reviewers' responses reveal about the regulation of emotional life.

This aspect of the film is something later critics have been more willing to address, particularly those with an interest in psychoanalysis. There is a tendency in such readings, however, to reproduce, in a different vocabulary, the assumptions behind the original reviews. Where critics of the 1920s distanced themselves from the emotionality of the film by calling it sentimental, psychoanalytic readings distance themselves from the emotion by calling it misogynist or proto-fascist, or both. Either the film is thought to represent a purging (through the burning of the robot vamp) of those aspects of femininity which, in the critics' view, patriarchy finds threatening (as in the readings of Jenkins and Huyssen),[15] or Freder's mission to bring feeling back into the relationship between brain and hand is thought to prefigure National Socialism (as in the readings of Dadoun and Rutsky).[16] Indeed, Rutsky suggests that the film is tyrannical and proto-fascist precisely to the degree that it appeals to emotions and a desire for wholeness. In all these cases, the emotional aspect of *Metropolis* is engaged with, but only the better to demonstrate its perniciousness and ban it from discussion.

The problem with these readings is not the suggestion that the film is either misogynist or proto-fascist — the film is both to a degree — but rather the undifferentiated way in which these aspects are presented, first through the implication of an *inevitable* link between the film's images and sexism or fascism (as opposed to the argument that the film can be *appropriated* by sexist or fascist discourse); secondly, through the exclusion of any other more positive emotions. In psychoanalytic terms, this reductive attitude arises because the critics view the film too exclusively from the perspective of the father and his anxieties (anxieties which the critics understand to be his fear of woman, his fear of technology, both of them together representing a fear of castration). As long as a reading focuses on these anxieties, any interpretation of the characters of Freder and Maria will be severely limited. Freder will be constrained to conforming to his father's desires (learning to over-

---

[15] cf. Stephen Jenkins's brief analysis in "Lang: Fear and Desire," *Fritz Lang: The Image and the Look*, ed. Stephen Jenkins (London: British Film Institute., 1981), 82–87, Andreas Huyssen, "The Vamp and the Machine," see Part Three of this volume.

[16] Roger Dadoun, "Metropolis: Mother-City — 'Mittler' — Hitler," trans. Arthur Goldhammer, *Camera Obscura* 15 (autumn 1986), 137–63. R. L. Rutsky, "The Mediation of Technology and Gender: Metropolis, Nazism, Modernism," see Part Three of this volume.

come his alarming interest in Maria as her "true" nature is revealed by the robot double, as Stephen Jenkins puts it), and won't be allowed a project or perspective of his own.[17] Maria, similarly, will be permitted no autonomy but will be reduced to a collection of patriarchal images of woman: virgin preacher and robot whore. Such readings are problematic for the simple reason that the film is barely told from the father's perspective. The two characters whose imaginative world we see from the inside are Freder and, to a lesser degree, Maria. It is their subjective visions — of the technological Moloch, of the Tower of Babel — that teach us how to interpret Fredersen's social order and encourage us to stand outside it. It is their subjective visions that are (albeit problematically) vindicated in the closing moments of the film.

There appear to be no psychoanalytic readings of the film that are willing to engage with Freder and Maria on more positive terms, no-one willing to break with Fredersen's perspective and grant the other two characters autonomy. One obstacle to such a step is the sexualized vocabulary, inherited from Freud, that is used to describe Freder's emotional life: Jenkins' fear of castration, Dadoun's frantic voyeurism.[18] Alice Miller has powerfully argued that such Freudian attempts to sexualize experience misrepresent it from the perspective of an abusing parent or adult, denying the victim a voice of their own.[19] Jung offers more useful tools for an analysis of Freder because of the respect for emotional processes that underpins his work. Behind the unfashionable conviction that the unconscious develops purposefully or teleologically lies a view of emotional life that doesn't rely on control (Jung's professed aim is that the ego recognize its decentring), but rather acknowledgement and integration.[20] Similarly his technique of amplifying as opposed to decoding dream images allows the images to exist more on their own terms, rather than transforming them into so many signifiers for the Oedipal drama.[21] An analysis of the film that draws on Miller

---

[17] Jenkins, "Lang: Fear and Desire," 85–86.

[18] Jenkins, "Lang: Fear and Desire," 84; Dadoun,"Metropolis: Mother-City — 'Mittler' — Hitler," 145.

[19] Alice Miller, *Thou Shalt Not Be Aware: Society's Betrayal of the Child*, trans. Hildegarde and Hunter Hannum, 2nd ed. (London: Pluto, 1990).

[20] C. G. Jung, *Two Essays on Analytical Psychology* (London: Routledge & Kegan Paul, 1966), 131.

[21] For Jung's treatment of dreams, see his "The Practical Use of Dream-Analysis" (1934), *The Practice of Psychotherapy* (London: Routledge & Kegan Paul, 1966), 139–61. My reasons for invoking Jung are not so much the easy match of Jungian archetypes onto characters in the film as the methodological point that Jung shows more respect for emotional life than Freud, who seems predominantly to want to sexualize and control.

and Jung should be able to make more clearly visible those parts of the emotional spectrum which critics have previously occluded with their accusations of sentimentality, misogyny and nascent fascism. This in turn will clarify the film's relationship with society — that is to say, with the mechanisms for the regulation of emotional life that existed in Germany of the 1920s.

Emotion, as Carl Plantinga has argued, is something of which much film theory inspired by Brecht, Freud and Lacan is deeply suspicious, regarding it as a cause of delusion, a support for oppressive social structures or a pleasure the responsible film-goer should learn to forego.[22] Plantinga himself sketches an alternative to these theories which draws on cognitive psychology, hoping thereby to grant more space to the emotions which films address. However, the result is a truncated view of emotional life, for his cognitive analyses too quickly exclude the idea of the unconscious, and leave no space for discussion of the social mechanisms by which emotional life is regimented.[23] The emotions addressed by *Metropolis* lie too deep to be accurately represented by a vocabulary that has broken all ties with psychoanalysis, and are too bound up with society for sociological concerns not also to be included. Such a reading would both misrepresent the wishes articulated in the film, and conceal the structures that control them. In the reading of the film that follows (or of the palimpsest as Giorgio Bertellini has called it on account of the numerous versions which overlay the absent original),[24] I shall be referring to the edition (3241m in length), based on the East German restoration, which can be viewed at the Deutsches Institut für Filmkunde in Frankfurt am Main, the censor's record of intertitles, and also to the original novel.

A Psychological Reading of the Initial Encounter

As Stephen Jenkins has suggested, the plot of *Metropolis* begins the moment Maria intrudes into Freder's protected existence.[25] (The novel similarly opens with the psychological turmoil provoked in Freder by Maria's appearance.) The timing of her appearance in the film is not arbitrary. Maria appears the moment Freder is about to kiss the young

---

[22] Carl Plantinga, "Notes on Spectator Emotion and Ideological Film Criticism," in *Film Theory and Philosophy*, ed. Richard Allen and Murray Smith (Oxford: Clarendon, 1997), 372–93.

[23] For dismissal of the unconscious as a tool for discussing melodrama, see Plantinga, "Notes on Spectator Emotion," 384–85.

[24] Giorgio Bertellini, "Restoration, Genealogy and Palimpsests. On Some Historiographical Questions," see Part Two of this volume.

[25] Jenkins, "Lang: Fear and Desire," 82.

woman whom, by chasing, he has chosen as his play-mate for the day. Inasmuch as one shot can be said to prompt the next, Freder's embrace prompts Maria's appearance — she is the archetypal figure whom the kiss-to-be calls into consciousness, an impulse associated with sexuality, but at the same time immediately breaking the bounds of Freder's previous sexual experience (he pushes the other girl away and she doesn't feature again).

Maria functions as what Jung would call an anima figure.[26] (The novel underscores this by invoking the images of virgin and mother to describe Maria's face.)[27] She awakens emotional and spiritual impulses that his life of athletics competitions and sexual games has lacked up to this point. The anima may be the product of male imaginings, but as she is portrayed in the film, the anima Maria has the power to appear of her own accord, to look at Freder every bit as much as he looks at her, and then leave of her own accord. Whereas the robot is constructed by men — literally, by Rotwang, and socially, by the voyeuristic eyes of the men to whom Rotwang displays her — Maria is an autonomous figure whose origins elude explanation. Though it is fair to say that she is partly constructed by the expectations of the male eyes turned towards her (to the degree that any relationship operates through projection),[28] these glances always assume that she is already in position (just as, when it comes to saving the children, she appears to emerge from Rotwang's house of her own accord, although this might merely be a lacuna in existing versions of the film.) Rigorously speaking, we can say neither that she is a male construct, nor that she is not. We can only observe her effects.

The entrance of Maria starts Freder's quest, making him investigate a world he has not previously taken notice of. The topography of this quest (his journey downwards) is psychological. Just as Jung, in the famous dream which he took to mark his discovery of the collective unconscious, explored the different levels of a house penetrating to ever older records of human civilization,[29] so Freder's freshly awakened longing takes him down into the machine room, where he observes the regimentation and inhumanity of his father's system, and then subsequently down into the catacombs.

What Freder observes in the machine room are psychological structures (this is the way to read the otherwise senseless and technically in-

---

[26] For an introduction to the concept of the anima, see *Two Essays on Analytical Psychology*, 188–205.

[27] Thea von Harbou, *Metropolis*, (New York: Ace Books, 1963), 9.

[28] Huyssen, "The Vamp and the Machine," in Part Three of this volume.

[29] C. G. Jung, *Memories, Dreams, Reflections* (London: Fontana, 1995), 182–83.

accurate images of the labour process at the M-machine). The structures might at some point have had their origins in actual practices of work (the sort of basic habits of rational organization that Weber describes as the building blocks of the Protestant entrepreneurial mentality: submitting to regular working hours, separating the work place from the home, and business accounts from domestic accounts).[30] But by the time they have been engrained for three hundred years they have lost the goal that originally gave them meaning. The work routines are metaphors for psychological structures, the figurative representation of a rationalization that has become an end in itself.

The explosion that Freder witnesses reveals the archaic terror that underpins this rationalized ballet. The vision of the Moloch is a filmic equivalent of the compression of the archaic and the industrial on which Horkheimer and Adorno base their argument in the *Dialectic of Enlightenment*. Freder's first reaction to this horrifying spectacle is to try to intervene directly. (He runs forward as if to help, but is driven back by the explosion.) But since he appears to be almost invisible to the workers bearing stretchers, it makes sense that he should instead attempt to effect change through the channel of his father, by asking him to transform the city and raising the spectre of a possible revolt. This return to paternal authority shouldn't be read as a sign that Freder cannot exist without his father's blessing, but should rather be seen as part of a learning process — an avenue which Freder explores only to move beyond it when he is confronted with Fredersen's rigid inability to adapt. In this process, Freder gradually takes on more and more responsibility for his own development.

The next step is to submit first hand to the irrational discipline of the existing structures and so feel the pain that has previously been concealed from him by closed doors. It is striking with what ease Freder can cross over between the two levels. There are no locks or barriers, other than habit and thc blindncss this brings with it, to prevent him from exploring the layers beneath the self-assured surface. Once he has registered this pain, he can be guided further beneath the rationalized surface to the catacombs in which Maria preaches her message of reconciliation. Of course, the moment when Freder discovers the catacombs is also the moment when Fredersen discovers them too. The more conscious, controlling aspects of the psyche (Freder and Fredersen) become aware together of a layer of longing that they didn't previously perceive. (The editing of this sequence makes very clear that the two discoveries occur in parallel, as the film cuts between Freder's discovering

---

[30] Max Weber, *The Protestant Ethic and the Spirit of Capitalism*, trans. Talcott Parsons (London: Unwin, 1930), 47–78 ("The Spirit of Capitalism").

a map of the catacombs in his newly acquired overalls, and Fredersen asking Rotwang to interpret a similar map for him, followed by Freder's, and Fredersen's and Rotwang's separate progressions down towards Maria.) Fredersen is quick to perceive the power that accrues to Maria because she offers a space in which the workers can acknowledge their longing. If he is to control the workers fully he must divide them from this desire.[31] The sexualization of Maria, through her robot double, is specifically shown to be a part of this attempted repression. (Although it should also be noted that Maria is only explicitly sexual when she is on the surface, being ogled by men in evening dress at Yoshiwara. In the catacombs, and in the machine room she is not sexual, simply chaotic and as powerful as the real Maria whose place she usurps.)

More important than Fredersen's reaction, however, is Freder's. When he hears the message of reconciliation that Maria preaches, he recognizes that he is himself the mediator, looking up towards the camera and beating his chest. Maria's sermon and Freder's overwhelmed response typify exactly what critics of the film's sentimentality find so difficult. Faced with this apparent kitsch, it is easy to get distracted by the more palatable combination of sex and technology to be found in Fredersen and Rotwang's subplot, and so avoid the potentially humiliating admission that one also shares this longing. But the plot belongs to Freder and Maria. (Theirs is the narrative referred to by the motto featured in the original credits: "The mediator between the brain and the hand must be the heart.")[32] Fredersen's and Rotwang's machinations remain reactions to the disturbances provoked by Freder and Maria's developing encounter. R. L. Rutsky acknowledges the centrality of Freder and Maria's relationship, but only to denounce the integration they strive for as fascist.[33] To shift the focus away from the flashing lights of the robot's transformation, on the one hand, and the threat of fascism looming on the historical horizon, on the other, we need to bring the scene in the catacombs closer to its historical context — conceding its potential for kitsch whilst simultaneously making visible what else the scene contains.

---

[31] "I want to sew dissent between them and her. I want to destroy their faith in this woman ——." ["Ich will Zwietracht säen zwischen ihnen und ihr! Ich will ihren Glauben an diese Frau zerstören ——."] "Zulassungskarte der Film-Prüfstelle" (Berlin, 13 November 1926): Roll 4, Title 20. (Photocopy in the Deutsches Institut für Filmkunde.)

[32] "Sinnspruch: Mittler zwischen Hirn und Hände muß das Herz sein." "Zulassungskarte," immediately preceding the first roll.

[33] Rutsky, "The Mediation of Technology and Gender," see pages 238–39 above.

Communicating Intensity on Film

One way to escape the film's sentimentality would be to say that Lang didn't really mean it. This is the line taken by Thomas Elsaesser, who writes of "the impossibility of Freder fulfilling the role of mediator in anything other than a derisory or deliberately ironic fashion."[34] It is easy to see how, to a viewer in the 1980s, Gustav Fröhlich beating his breast might seem to signal irony. Fröhlich's autobiography, on the other hand, stresses that Lang despised all artificiality when working on the film, insisting on realism to the point of making his actors inflict physical damage on themselves.[35] The way Fröhlich beats his breast only emphasizes that standards of realism that Lang worked with at the end of the silent era differed from those of today. Discussions of acting in expressionist silent cinema stress the abstract and exaggerated nature of the gestures that film-makers borrowed from the expressionist stage in order to externalize inner states.[36] It seems that these exaggerated gestures could easily appear artificial and ineffective even to contemporaries. David Kuhns has recently suggested that this problem arose inevitably when abstract gestures were transferred from stage to screen, losing the "complete physical and vocal commitment" of the live actor, whose intensity alone could fill the gesticulations effectively.[37] But contemporary critics argued in slightly different terms. Rudolf Kurtz, writing in 1926, maintained that abstract acting got into difficulties as soon as naturalistic (or non-abstract) elements were allowed to slip in, muddying the abstraction.[38] Curt Wesse, writing in 1928, then suggested that such infelicitous combinations arose inevitably in film, for the camera constantly reminded the viewers that what they were look-

---

[34] *Monthly Film Bulletin,* 51 (December 1984), 364, see also the version included in Part Two of this volume..

[35] *Waren das Zeiten: Mein Film-Heldenleben* (Munich/Berlin: Herbig, 1983), 113.

[36] The most useful discussion of acting in German cinema of the 1920s is Knut Hickethier, ed., *Grenzgänger zwischen Theater und Kino: Schauspielerporträts aus dem Berlin der zwanziger Jahre* (Berlin: Ästhetik und Kommunikation, 1986), which includes a general introduction followed by essays on individual stars, including Brigitte Helm (195–212). Other discussions include: Lotte Eisner, *The Haunted Screen: Expressionism in the German Cinema and the Influence of Max Reinhardt* (London: Thames and Hudson, 1969), 137–49; Jürgen Kasten, *Der expressionistische Film: Abgefilmtes Theater oder avantgardistisches Erzählkino? Eine stil-, produktions- und rezeptionsgeschichtliche Untersuchung* (Münster: Maks Publikationen, 1990), 155–62.

[37] David F. Kuhns, *German Expressionist Theatre: The Actor and the Stage* (Cambridge: Cambridge UP, 1997), 136–37.

[38] Rudolf Kurtz, *Expressionismus und Film* (Berlin: Verlag der Lichtbildbühne, 1926), 122.

ing at was a human form not an abstract design.[39] For Wesse, the only solution was to abandon abstract gesticulation, and underplay — a theory of cinematic acting already formulated by Urban Gad, the director of Asta Nielsen films, in 1921, but not consistently put into practice until the later 1920s when film-makers came to rely more on montage and editing to convey meaning, and less on the activity of the actors themselves.[40]

Metropolis employs the same exaggerated, non-naturalistic gestural vocabulary discussed by theorists of expressionism (indeed, Lotte Eisner picks on Rudolf Klein-Rogge's depiction of Rotwang, and Brigitte Helm's frightened Maria as a clear example of expressionistic acting in film).[41] At the same time, Lang developed a number of techniques to ensure that the gestures did not degenerate into arbitrary conventions. First, he seems to have attempted to generate the intensity that Kuhns suggested was the characteristic of the expressionist stage, by a sort of methodical torturing of his actors. In a brief discussion of the art of directing which he published in *Die Filmbühne* in April 1927, he wrote of the unconditional commitment to the collective project that making a film required, and argued that the star-system militates against this commitment to the ensemble.[42] Certainly, for his work on *Metropolis*, Lang cast two unknown quantities whom he could wear down until they acted with the intensity that he required. (Helm had neither film nor theatre experience, Fröhlich had theatre and limited film experience.) The scene in the catacombs in which Fröhlich/Freder falls on his knees before Helm/Maria was rehearsed for two days in order to achieve the almost trance-like state that Lang required.[43] Patrick McGilligan's biography of Lang collects numerous further reports of the filming of *Metropolis*, all of which return to the question of Lang's emotionally demanding and manipulative working practices, as he drove his ensemble to their limits in order to generate the intensity and realism he required.[44]

Intensity in itself does not ensure emotional contact with the viewer. The face that carries the intensity must fit the emotions it expresses. Freder's role in the plot is androgynous. It falls to him to rein-

---

[39] Curt Wesse, *Großmacht Film: Das Geschöpf von Kunst und Technik* (Berlin: Deutsche Buch-Gemeinschaft, 1928), 187.

[40] Hickethier, *Grenzgänger zwischen Theater und Kino*, 39.

[41] Eisner, *The Haunted Screen*, 144.

[42] reprinted in Fred Gehler and Ullrich Kasten, eds., *Fritz Lang: Die Stimme von Metropolis* (Berlin: Henschel, 1990), 92–94.

[43] McGilligan, *Fritz Lang: The Nature of the Beast*, 116.

[44] *Fritz Lang: The Nature of the Beast*, 115–26.

tegrate the world of feeling that was previously projected entirely onto the preaching Maria. This androgynous role requires an androgynous face since the faces on the screen, especially when subjected to the almost mask-like makeup that was then still necessary for work under the studio lights, are themselves part of the meaning of the film: a sign or symbol as much as a natural face.[45] Gustav Fröhlich was cast late, replacing André von Mattoni after shooting had already begun (he was originally playing a minor role as a worker but was "spotted" on set by Harbou, who persuaded Lang to make the expensive substitution.)[46] A comparison of the faces of Mattoni and Fröhlich, or at least of the character types constructed for them by the Ufa publicity department, suggests why this substitution was necessary — although it's unlikely that Lang and Harbou would have explained their choice in these terms, but would rather have made the change intuitively because Fröhlich's face "fitted" the part better (Figs. 25 and 26). Mattoni is more conventionally masculine than Fröhlich: heavier, older, more reserved, marketed as reliable, where Fröhlich is marketed for his energy and boyishness, and his emotion. (His contribution to the promotional material released by Ufa is an article on the shooting of the love scene in the catacombs in which he recounts the grueling methods which produced the final intensity.)[47] Certainly, contemporary reviewers perceived the combination of emotion and strength that Fröhlich/Freder represented, commenting on the mixture of boyish openness and manly purpose.[48] An actor who did not embody these qualities would not be able to carry the emotional development that Freder undergoes.

As well as acting and casting, technical and formal aspects of the film support and reinforce its emotional message. An important aspect of the promotional material for *Metropolis* was the technical innovations introduced by Lang and his cameraman Karl Freund. The special issue

---

[45] Fröhlich, in his autobiography, documents the strict make-up regime to which the actors were subjected (Fröhlich, 128). For a brief discussion of the star's face as a conveyor of meaning see Theodor Adorno, "The Schema of Mass Culture," trans. Nicholas Walker, in *The Culture Industry*, ed. J. M. Bernstein (London: Routledge, 1991), 53–84 (82). Adorno, however, darkly suggests that the star's face can only convey the injunction to conform. My analysis of Gustav Fröhlich's face in *Metropolis* suggests otherwise.

[46] Fröhlich, *Waren das Zeiten*, 110.

[47] "Eine Liebeszene wird gedreht," in *Metropolis, Sondernummer des Ufa-Magazins*, ed. Stefan Lorant (Berlin: Bukwa, Presse Abteilung der Ufa, 1927), unpaginated.

[48] "Er ist aktiv lebendig, jünglinghaft-hell und männlich gesammelt zugleich. Eine sehr schöne Leistung." (*8-Uhr-Abendblatt*.) "Jung, hell, lodernd, trifft er den Übergang vom weichlichen Millionärssohn zum Charakter, zum Manne, mit einer überraschenden Deutlichkeit." (*Neue Berliner Zeitung*.) Both quoted in "Pressestimmen über Metropolis," *Kinematograph*, 1039 (16 January 1927), 16–18.

of the *Ufa-Magazin* devoted to the film included an article attributed to Karl Freund entitled: "How it was done," and an editorial contribution called "The Flying Camera." The Karl Freund article was reproduced in the press book, and Freund contributed other similar articles to the press at the time of the film's release.[49] Particularly the article "The Flying Camera" stresses the degree to which Freund wanted the camera directly to reproduce the subjective experiences of the characters, hence the famous swinging of the camera to coincide with the moment of the explosion in the workers' city during the flood. The character whose subjective experience we share most is Freder's, through the trick photography of the Moloch, or of the ten-hour clock with which he struggles when working his shift, or of the sensation of falling occasioned by the sight of his father with the (false) Maria, but also through more straightforward point-of-view editing, as when we pass with Freder for the second time into the steam of the machine rooms. Equally important for the catacomb scene, however, is that the camera also show the scene from Maria's point of view. The charge of the scene is intensified by the fact that Freder and Maria look at each other. The effect of eye contact is generated by the darting eye movements made by Maria (in response to the question "Where is the mediator," and answered in the next shot by Freder. This is reinforced by positioning the camera higher than Freder (on a smaller trolley as a production still taken by Horst von Harbou reveals),[50] so that we appear to be looking down at him from the vantage point of Maria's stage.

Even more important than the plot, acting, casting and camerawork, however, is the *mise-en-scène*, the creation and deployment of a fictional topography through the use of sets and lighting. This can be perceived most clearly if *Metropolis* is compared with another film, in order to see what particularly characterizes its creation of a fictional world. The film *Michael*, directed for Ufa by the Danish director Carl Theodor Dreyer and released in September 1924, is in many ways comparable.[51] Originally scripted by von Harbou (who adapted a novel by Hermann

---

[49] Karl Freund, "Wie es gemacht wurde," and "Die fliegende Kamera," in *Metropolis, Sondernummer des Ufa-Magazins* (unpaginated). Karl Freund, "Zauberin Kamera," *Illustrierte Film-Zeitung*, 20 January 1927, 1. Karl Freund, "Meine Arbeit am Metropolis," *B. Z. am Mittag*, 7 January 1927.

[50] Claude-Jean Philippe, *Metropolis un film de Fritz Lang: Images d'un tournage* (Paris: Centre National de la Photographie, 1985), 62.

[51] My source of information is the press-cuttings file on the film at the Deutsche Institut für Filmkunde. Filmographic details are also available in Reinhold Keiner, *Thea von Harbou und der deutsche Film bis 1933* (Hildesheim: Georg Olms, 1984).

Bang),[52] and shot by Karl Freund, it similarly tells the story of a young man whose love for a woman leads him to break with the world of a father-figure. However, the film creates its fictional world in a very different way. The film is set almost entirely in the apartment and studio of a late nineteenth-century artist, and is shot in many scenes merely through the alternation of facial expressions, exploiting what David Bordwell has called "the spatial and narrative authority of the soulfully expressive human face" in a way typical of Dreyer's early films.[53] There are large amounts of dialogue (169 intertitles for a film 1966m long — a title every 11.7 meters, compared with *Metropolis*: 193 for 4189m — a title every 21.7m) which are conveyed through a combination of intertitles and close-ups of the characters in the conversation. As the contemporary reviewers noted, Dreyer's aim was a particular kind of realism: a psychological drama presented with understated acting in sets which recreate a familiar milieu with an impressive attention to detail.[54] The film nevertheless occasionally requires a heightening of its realist surface to recreate the emotional intensity of the situations and push beyond the close-ups and tableaux that are otherwise its main devices.[55] Here Karl Freund's camera came to Dreyer's aid. The review in *Lichtbildbühne* records that one particular transition (the switch from light to shadows to demonstrate the inner anguish of the mentor when he is abandoned by Michael on the occasion of his greatest public success) provoked spontaneous applause in the premiere.[56] Similarly, to convey the intensity of the scene in which it is Michael, not the Master who is able to complete the Countess's portrait by painting her eyes, the film employs what at the time was close to trick photography, alternating shots of Michael and the Countess, using an early zoom technique to home in on Michael's intently staring face, and reducing what we see of the Countess shot by shot until we see only her eyes.

Lang's technique for conveying the intensity of the exchanges between Freder and Maria is different. Dreyer creates intensity by breaking with his understated, naturalist style to employ a special effect: the Master cast in shadow in a way that is only loosely motivated by the ac-

---

[52] Dreyer claimed not to have used von Harbou's script for the shooting, but the film still shares key elements with her script. Keiner, *Thea von Harbou,* 139.

[53] David Bordwell, *The Films of Carl Theodor Dreyer* (Berkeley: U of California P, 1981), 59.

[54] For a collation of contemporary reviews see "Kritiken zu dem Decla-Ufa-Film 'Michael,'" *Kinematograph,* 921 (12 October 1924).

[55] For a discussion of Dreyer's deployment of close-up and tableaux, see Bordwell, *The Films of Carl Theodor Dreyer,* 37–59: "Early Films: The Construction of Space."

[56] *Lichtbildbühne,* 27 September 1924, quoted in *Kinematograph,* 921.

tion (one could explain the darkness by lights being switched off as the party finishes but we're not shown this); or the zoom effect introduced for Michael's painting. Intensity is created by transgressing the terms otherwise established by the mise-en-scène, and deploying camera and lighting symbolically. Lang has no such division between the realist and the symbolic — everything in the film is both. The action is set in an entirely symbolic landscape — a geography of the soul — but within this setting rules of spatial continuity are almost always observed; special effects either serve to reinforce this sense of spatial continuity, such as the movement of the camera during explosions, or they are presented explicitly as a subjective impression, such as the vision of the Moloch, or the male eyes ogling the dancing robot. This changes the way Lang's characters are situated. The world in which Dreyer's characters move is merely an explanatory backdrop — the artist's milieu explains why we are being shown a story of this intensity and, with the homosexual relationship, potential transgressiveness — but it doesn't itself express the intensity, except in those moments where unexpectedly a special effect is used. The world of *Metropolis*, on the other hand, is inseparable from the characters' experience, with each setting embodying a life-style, attitude or psychological state. There are brief moments when characters confront each other in abstract space (Maria's face looking into the camera/Freder from a grey background at two points in the Eternal Gardens, Freder's face looking up the camera/Maria from a dark background in the catacombs), but the close-ups are exactly situated by the shots before and after, and, more importantly, the emotional intensity conveyed by the face is not achieved by a sudden change of style. The abstract close-up only adds to a meaning already articulated by the symbolic setting. The meaning of the first encounter between Freder and Maria in the Eternal Gardens is reinforced by what remains visible in the frame in all the other shots — the artificial garden behind Freder, Freder's clothes and companion, the children around Maria. Similarly, in the catacombs the archaic walls, the crosses, Freder's worker's uniform, and the other workers visible in the frame all amplify the encounter. Nor is it not merely the fact that the objects are visible, but the way they are visible that creates the emotional quality of the scene. In his article on the magic camera, Karl Freund comments on the degree to which he used lighting to create the contrasting atmospheres and textures of the film's different locales (Eternal Gardens, machine rooms, catacombs).[57] In the artificial world that the film creates, no part of the frame is background, no part of the frame is there merely to suggest the naturalness of the fictional world

---

[57] "Zauberin Kamera," *Illustrierte Film-Zeitung*, 20 January 1927, 1.

(nothing is there for the Barthesian "effect of the real"). Everything is there to convey the story of Freder's emotional development, the fantastical story of his unexpected summoning by Maria, and ensuing transformation. As Patrice Petro suggests in a different context, the mise-en-scène itself becomes part of the studied intensification and emotional language of the film.[58]

One contemporary critic grasped just this. Writing anonymously a year or so after the film's premiere, he (or she) commented that *Metropolis* wasn't idle entertainment but was dealing with a specific filmic problem: that of inventing a fantastical form appropriate to the fantastical themes.[59] This argument has left behind the accusation of sentimentality and attempts instead to grasp how the technical and formal innovations of the film are in fact anchored in the archetypal content. Buñuel's two films, for this critic, have merged back into stereoscopic unity. (Significantly, this comment appears in an article that particularly addresses the issue of Lang and von Harbou's collaboration, finding in their working relationship a model of collective creativity.)[60] Yet this level of understanding for the project of the film remains an isolated example. To understand why there was so little critical understanding for the efforts of Lang, von Harbou, Freund and the other technicians to let the audience share the subjective experiences of the protagonists, we need to look more closely at attitudes to cinema in the Weimar Republic.

Problems of Reception, Structures of Self-Control

Ironically, *Michael* was held by contemporary critics to have succeeded on precisely the ground on which *Metropolis* was thought so dismally to have failed. *Michael* was consistently praised for the combination of restraint and intensity to be found in the direction, acting and camerawork, while the movie was cited as proof that the cinematic medium can lift itself to the heights of art.[61] The reason for this success seems in

---

[58] Patrice Petro, *Joyless Streets: Women and Melodramatic Representation in Weimar Germany* (Princeton: Princeton UP, 1989), 32.

[59] "Viele sahen in 'Metropolis' eine Spielerei und erkannten nicht, daß es hier um die Lösung eines Problems ging, das in seinen letzten Konsequenzen bis heute noch gar nicht klar erkannt ist, daß Lang nämlich den ersten praktischen Versuch machte, phantastische Themen in noch phantastischere Bilder zu zwingen." "Fritz Lang inszeniert, Thea von Harbou schreibt," *Film-Magazin*, 10 (4 March 1928), 6.

[60] *Film-Magazin*, 10 (4 March 1928), 7.

[61] See for instance the reviews of *8Uhr-Abendblatt*, *Berliner Lokal-Anzeiger*, ("Jeder Rest von Kientopp wurde hier überwunden,") *Berliner Börsen-Zeitung*, *Neue Preußische Zeitung*, *Die Welt am Montag* and *Lichtbildbühne* ("Was hier geschaffen ist,

no little measure to have been the milieu in which the film was set. The reviews return again and again to notions of the genius, isolation and passion of the artist figure, to explain the story whilst at the same time situating it at a distance that requires no direct engagement. Emotions were permissible, indeed laudable, where they could be recognized and labeled as belonging to the aesthetic sphere (or at least to an artist) rather than the sphere of everyday life. *Metropolis*, on the other hand, failed because it did not confine emotional life to the realm of art, denying the viewer the easy escape of labeling feelings as aesthetic, and so forcing them to reach instead for the pejorative categories of the womanly or infantile.

At the same time, both the institution of cinema, and the fluid gender roles during the particular phase of the Weimar Republic in which *Metropolis* was produced, provided a space for emotions that didn't strictly conform to these segregations. An introduction to the cinema published in 1928 by Curt Wesse reveals what it meant for a man to step into the darkened space of the cinema in Weimar Germany. The author contrasts cinema with the experience of going to the theatre. Theatre is a public occasion for which one dresses formally, takes one's wife and submits to social scrutiny. The cinema is in contrast a place where one can escape the scrutiny of one's person and one's relationships: "A visit to the cinema is in contrast not a society or personal affair, but has more of a social character: the cinema-goer sinks into the masses and, freed from the responsibilities of his public persona, wants to catch as much as possible of the intimate affairs of the people whom the indiscreet camera makes appear before us on the screen."[62] This description of cinema prefigures Benjamin's essay on mechanical reproduction. Here too cinema represents an escape from one's identity as bourgeois subject into the liberating collectivity of the masses.[63] But where in the Benjamin essay, the cinematic spectator is released directly

bedeutet eine Kulturtat ersten Ranges"), reprinted in "Kritiken zu dem Decla-Ufa-Film 'Michael,'" *Kinematograph*, 921 (12 October 1924).

[62] "Der Besuch des Kinos ist nicht mehr eine gesellschaftliche und persönliche Angelegenheit, er hat mehr einen sozialen Charakter: der Besucher taucht in der Masse unter und will nun, befreit von den Verantwortlichkeiten seiner Person, recht viel von den persönlichen Angelegenheiten der Leute erhaschen, die uns die indiskrete Kamera auf der Leinwand erscheinen läßt," Wesse, 272.

[63] Walter Benjamin, "The Work of Art in the Age of Mechanical Reproduction," *Illuminations*, trans. Harry Zohn (London: Fontana, 1973), 211–44 (227–28 and 231–34).

into the clean air of revolutionary politics, Wesse's description is more ambiguous and as a consequence more revealing. Whilst it starts with the same clear contrast between the personal and the collective that Benjamin will later draw on, it then introduces another layer, one which seems more specifically psychological: the release from regimentation by one's public persona, and the voyeuristic pleasure at other people's experiences which this release permits. Wesse's text has little of the verve of Benjamin's grand theory, but rather collates a cross section of ideas about the cinema available in the later 1920s. But it's precisely this looser organization that gives the text its value as a historical document.[64] The text reveals the layer of personal, psychological structures that Benjamin brushes over in his desire to portray film as a political force, and suggests that cinema is as important for the psychological economy as it is for the political. It shows how the cinema was explicitly experienced as a space in which emotional life could exist unpoliced by the social expectations embodied in one's public or social persona.

It would be easy to suggest that all that emerged in the darkened space of the cinema was the lurid voyeurism that Wesse's text seems itself partly to evoke. But to assume that social identity polices only aggressivity and sex is to take either a very rosy view of structures of subjectivity and or an unnecessarily Freudian view of repressed emotions. The release from public identity could equally offer space to more positive attributes: vulnerability and emotionality in the stereotypical man, a sense of agency and self-sufficiency in the stereotypical woman. This could especially be the case in a context, such as that of Germany in the 1920s, in which gender roles were themselves open to re-negotiation. Patrice Petro's survey of the illustrated press of the Weimar Republic reinforces the degree to which, in the later 1920s, male and female roles (at least for growing middle class) were both more fluid and more equal, an androgynous woman accompanied by an equally androgynous man.[65] For Petro, this confirms the inadequacy of any discussion of Weimar cinema that doesn't acknowledge the potential for differing responses from different viewers with different expectations or life-styles.

Petro's main aim is to make visible the responses of female viewers which she thinks discussions of Weimar cinema have often occluded by focusing too exclusively on the battered and disempowered male

---

[64] For a brief discussion of Wesse's book, which situates it in the context of writing about film in the Weimar Republic, see Sabine Hake, *Cinema's Third Machine: Writing on Film in Germany 1907–1933* (Lincoln: U of Nebraska P, 1993), 281–82.

[65] Petro, *Joyless Streets*, Chapter Three.

subject taken to be emblematic of the Weimar Republic. As part of her attempt to differentiate, she lists three images of male subjects represented in films of the period and apparently addressed to different viewers.[66] The impotent and symbolically defeated male, such as Emil Jannings in *Der letzte Mann* (The Last Laugh, 1924) or *Der blaue Engel* (The Blue Angel, 1930) which addresses the male subject-in-crisis of the Weimar Republic: a passive, homoerotic male, to be found in those films which explicitly deal with gay relationships, as in *Anders als die Andern* (Different from the Others, 1919) and *Geschlecht in Fesseln* (Sex in Chains, 1928), but also in Murnau's *Faust* (1926), which addresses a viewer willing to bring to bear on a film the same aestheticized view of the male body that he would bring to bear on a painting. Finally, she lists the type to be found in melodramas of the period: a passive eroticized male viewed in the film itself specifically by women. This last type is the type which, in her view, speaks most clearly to the stronger, androgynous woman of the mid-1920s, opening a space for "an alternative conception of female spectatorship and visual pleasure,"[67] as the viewer's gaze is given the space to be contemplative and to absorb the emotional implications of a situation before the narrative hurries her along.

This list of male types leaves no room for Gustav Fröhlich's Freder: for a male who is both emotional and active, who discovers agency precisely to the degree that he acknowledges the emotional and spiritual impulses embodied by Maria. This seems to be a type that it is hard to perceive, indeed it was completely invisible to the artists preparing publicity for the film's American release, whose drawings transformed Freder into a more conventionally masculine, domineering comic-book hero (Figure 27).[68] It seems to have been visible, however, to those German reviewers who commented favourably on Fröhlich's combination of boyish openness and masculine strength. If it is added to Petro's list, it becomes all the more apparent that the emotions released in the darkened space of Weimar cinema are unlikely to have been merely voyeuristic. At the same time, the chorus of dismissal directed by other critics against the film suggests that these emotions were not uncontroversial. To many reviewers it was still unthinkable to admit to the

---

[66] Petro, *Joyless Streets*, 155–58.

[67] Petro, *Joyless Streets*, 158.

[68] Karin Bruns, *Kinomythen 1920–1945. Die Filmentwürfe der Thea von Harbou* (Stuttgart: Metzler, 1995), similarly reduces Freder to what she calls an engineer type: "Wichtigste handelnde Figur bleibt . . . der symbolische Entwurf Ingenieur, der technische Held" (Bruns, *Kinomythen*, 89). In this reading, Freder's emotional quest is rendered invisible, replaced by a hysterical obsession with creation (Bruns, *Kinomythen*, 96). Freder is assimilated to Rotwang.

longings embodied by the film's love-story. Even the darkened space was not enough to let them fully cast off their public persona, as Benjamin's theory confirms ten years later by the way it obscures the personal dimension of such a release to emphasize instead the — safer, more masculine — realm of the political collective.

This self-policing did not only occur in the audience. It could occur also in the very film that brought emotions to the surface — which brings us back to the bad ending of *Metropolis*. Although the film acknowledges the emotional intensity of Freder and Maria's relationship, there is no reason to believe that the men and women who produced the film were any more perfectly enlightened than the audiences that watched it. They too shared the structures of self-policing that make the acknowledgement of such emotions seem so scandalous, as one sees in the anecdotes that Fröhlich tells about the making of *Metropolis* (he was so offended by a reviewer commenting that he had a womanly beauty that he resolved wherever possible to avoid make-up on camera in order to prevent the feminization of his features), or in Brigitte Helm's statement that she lived and identified with the robot vamp far more than she did with the saint, or in the fact that Lang's methodical torturings did as much to prop up his own sense of authority as they did to induce openness and realism in his actors and crew.[69]

The consequence of this self-policing is that the film doesn't keep its promise. Its makers were unable to follow through the development whose origins they had so clearly represented, and became distracted instead by the generation of suspense. To show this we need finally to recapitulate what remains of Freder's story. When Freder returns from the catacombs, he initially doesn't find Maria (who doesn't show up for their rendez-vous in the Cathedral), but rather the image of Maria created by his father and Rotwang: the sexualized, chaotic Maria with whom Fredersen wishes to distract and control the work force. This image of Maria causes Freder's collapse (captured in the free-fall image), as Freder's new point of orientation is removed, and he is plagued by the hallucinatory images of the robot Maria and Death. However, Josaphat returns to help him reorient himself, and lead him back down to the catacombs to confront the false Maria. If he was briefly confused by Maria's double, he is no longer. In the catacombs, he unhesitatingly denounces the robot.

These sequences show an important obstacle to Freder's quest — the way in which emotional life is recast in sexual or destructive terms so as to demonize and exclude it (a trick which only works in a society with

[69] Fröhlich, *Waren das Zeiten*, 128. Helm: interview in the *Prager Presse*, 22 July 1927, quoted in Andrea Böhm, "Brigitte Helm: Heilige und Vamp," in Hickethier, *Grenzgänger*, 196; McGilligan, *Fritz Lang. The Nature of the Beast*, 117–18.

a long tradition of denigrating sex). With Josaphat's help, Freder remains clear and finds Maria in time for the three of them to rescue the children. During this process, Freder's father learns that the disruption he has instigated has cost him his son. The anguish at losing Freder, which is only reinforced when Fredersen watches him struggling with Rotwang on the cathedral roof, dissolves the inhuman rigidity that his son had previously been unable to break through and paves the way for the final reconciliation.

This reconciliation feels false because it has not been fully prepared (a fact which can't merely be explained by the missing footage, since the censor's record contains no intertitles that would prepare it more fully). Apart from the brief outburst when Slim ("Der Schmale") tells him he is not the only man mourning the loss of a son, Fredersen is never confronted with his destructiveness, neither does he fully engage with the work force. In the novel, Grot, the foreman figure, is trampled to death when the workers break into the so-called Heart-Machine.[70] In the film he survives to make the impassioned claim that the workers have destroyed the machines on which their lives depend. The purposelessness of the machines is something many reviewers remarked on. When Grot, in contrast, speaks out in their name, he speaks for Fredersen. Indeed, before the moment when Fredersen orders him to allow the destruction of the machine rooms, Grot has appeared as Fredersen's man, bringing the mysterious plans of the catacombs to his office to report. When Fredersen is reconciled with the foreman, he is reconciled with someone from whom he has barely been alienated.

This false reconciliation has consistently provoked critics. But its flaw is not that it is sentimental, but that it is not sentimental enough. It doesn't follow through the story of Freder's emotional transformation. This story is finally interrupted the moment Maria unexpectedly disappears after she, Freder and Josaphat have escorted the children into the "House of Sons." At this point, all plot development (the confrontation of the two Marias, the confrontation between Fredersen and Freder, and Fredersen and the workers, the acknowledgement of the real Maria's power) is replaced by action for its own sake: Freder's fear that Maria is being burnt, and the chase of Maria by Rotwang. Such suspense is a strategy for emotional control: a strategy of distraction.

The term distraction is used by all of Kracauer, Benjamin, and Horkheimer and Adorno in their discussions of film. For Kracauer and Benjamin, it is a positive term, describing the political or proto-political

[70] von Harbou, *Metropolis*, 165.

consciousness that they both believe the cinema to generate.[71] For Horkheimer and Adorno, in contrast, it explains the mystificatory potential of film, the power of film to prevent the viewers from having thoughts of their own.[72] There are two problems with Horkheimer and Adorno's argument. The first is their tendency to derive arguments about film from what they believe to be its technical properties. (In this case, the mere fact that film is edited out of sequences of shots leads to its depriving the spectator of thinking time.) The second is their emphasis on rationality at the expense of emotion as an antidote to film's mystificatory powers. Suitably modified, however, their critique well fits the privileging of slick editing over emotional analysis to be found towards the end of *Metropolis.* The tension generated by the catastrophe and ensuing chase takes up the viewer's emotional involvement to expend it in agitation. As Adorno noted in a later text, however, a mystificatory film contains its own antidote in so far as it must awaken and address the very emotions it wants to harness through distraction.[73] The viewer doesn't have to accept the film's ending. The closing suspense can instead itself be criticized as a mechanism of emotional regulation similar to those evident in the critical reception of films during the 1920s. Such a critique will ensure that the positive impulses of the film are not occluded: Freder's summoning by Maria and recognition of emotional responsibility, Maria's strength, purpose and emotional clarity, and finally the affection that exists between Freder and Josaphat alongside Freder's relationship with Maria. *Metropolis* as a film both criticizes and reinforces structures of emotional regulation. There is no reason for the viewer to reinforce this reinforcement.

---

[71] Siegfried Kracauer, "The Cult of Distraction,"in *The Mass Ornament: Weimar Essays,* trans. Thomas Y. Levin (Cambridge, MA: Harvard UP, 1995), 323–328; Walter Benjamin, in W. B., "The Work of Art in the Age of Mechanical Reproduction," *Illuminations,* trans. Harry Zohn (London: Fontana, 1973), 211–44.

[72] Max Horkheimer and Theodor W. Adorno, *Dialectic of Enlightenment,* trans. John Cumming (London: Allen Lane, 1973), 126–27.

[73] Theodor Adorno, "Transparencies on film," trans. Thomas Y. Levin, in T. A., *The Culture Industry,* ed. J. M. Bernstein (London: Routledge, 1991), 154–61 (156–57).

Selected References on *Metropolis*, Lang, and Related Topics

This list of references is not intended to be exhaustive but to provide a useful research resource for those interested in *Metropolis* and its various contexts. Complete bibliographical information relating to the documentation and the individual essays in this volume is provided either in the texts themselves or in the form of footnotes. The essays reprinted in this volume are not listed below.

There are several websites dedicated to *Metropolis*. Of these the most authoritative is Michael Organ's "*Metropolis*. Bibliography and Checklist of Resources," at http://www.uow.edu.au/~morgan/Metroa.html.

Adorno, Theodor W. "The Schema of Mass Culture." Trans. Nicholas Walker. In Theodor W. Adorno. *The Culture Industry. Selected Essays on Mass Culture*, ed. J. M. Bernstein, 53–84. London: Routledge, 1991.

Adorno, Theodor W. "Transparencies on Film." Trans. Thomas Y. Levin. In *The Culture Industry. Selected Essays on Mass Culture*, ed. J. M. Bernstein, 154–61. London: Routledge, 1991.

Altman, Rick. "The Silence of the Silents." *The Musical Quarterly* 80, no. 4 (1997): 648–718.

Armour, Robert A. *Fritz Lang*. Boston: Twayne, 1977.

Arnheim, Rudolf. "Metropolis (1927)." In *Rudolf Arnheim. Kritiken und Aufsätze zum Film*, ed. Helmut H. Diedrichs, 184–86. Munich: Fischer, 1977. English in *R. A. Film Essays and Criticism*, trans. Brenda Benthien, 118–19. Madison: U of Wisconsin P, 1997.

Bachmann, Holger. *"Über die Heide ins Herz der Nation." Theodor Storms Novelle "Zur Chronik von Grieshuus" und ihre Verfilmung durch die Ufa*. Essen: Die blaue Eule, 1996.

Barlow, J. D. *German Expressionist Film*. Boston: Twayne, 1982.

Bartetzko, Dieter. "Ordnung und Chaos. Fritz Langs Filme und das dritte Reich." In *Illusionen in Stein*, ed. Bartetzko, 243–274. Reinbek: Rowohlt, 1985.

Bellour, Raymond. "On Fritz Lang." In *Fritz Lang, The Image and the Look*, ed. S. Jenkins, 26–37. London: British Film Institute, 1981.

Berletto, Paulo. *Fritz Lang: "Metropolis."* Torino: Lindau, 1990.

Bock, Hans-Michael and Michael Töteberg, eds. *Das Ufa-Buch: Kunst und Krisen, Stars und Regisseure, Wirtschaft und Politik*. Frankfurt: Zweitausendeins, 1992.

Bogdanovich, Peter. *Fritz Lang in America*. London: Studio Vista, 1967.

Borde, Raymond. "La Restauration des Films: Problèmes Ethiques." *Archives* 1 (September/October 1986): 1–10.

Bowser, Eileen "Some Principles of Film Restoration." *Griffithiana* 38–39 (October 1990): 172–73.

Bruns, Karin. *Kinomythen 1920–1945: Die Filmentwürfe der Thea von Harbou.* Stuttgart: Metzler, 1995.

Cieutat, Brigitte. "Fritz Lang 'Morodernisé', ou, L'art du détournement." *Positif,* no. 285 (November 1984): 12–14.

Cieutat, Brigitte. "Le symbolisme des figures géométriques dans *Métropolis.*" *Positif,* no. 365/366 (July/August1991): 133–36.

Coates, Paul. *The Gorgon's Gaze: German Cinema, Expressionism and the Image of Horror.* Cambridge: Cambridge UP, 1991.

Codelli, Lorenzo, "Entretien avec Enno Patalas, conservateur de la Cinémathèque de Munich, sur *Métropolis* et quelques autres films de Fritz Lang." *Positif,* no.285 (Novembre 1984): 15–20.

Dadoun, Roger. *"Metropolis*: Mother City — 'Mittler' — Hitler." Trans. Arthur Goldhammer. *Camera Obscura* 15 (autumn 1986): 136–64.

de Lauretis, Teresa et al., eds. *The Technological Imagination.* Madison, WI: The Coda Press, 1980.

Eisner, Lotte. *The Haunted Screen: Expressionism in the German Cinema and the Influence of Max Reinhardt.* Trans. Roger Greaves. London: Thames and Hudson, 1969.

Eisner, Lotte, *Fritz Lang.* Trans. Gertrud Mander. London: Secker & Warburg, 1976.

Elsaesser, Thomas. "Social Mobility and the Fantastic: German Silent Cinema." *Wide Angle* 5, no.2 (1982): 14–25.

Elsaesser, Thomas. "Film History and Visual Pleasure: Weimar Cinema." In *Cinema Histories/Cinema Practices,* ed. Patricia Mellencamp and Philip Rosen, 47–84. Frederick: University Publications of America, 1984.

Fröhlich, Gustav. *Waren das Zeiten: Mein Film-Heldenleben.* Munich: Herbig, 1983.

Gandert, Gero, ed. *Der Film der Weimarer Republik: ein Handbuch der zeitgenössischen Kritik.* Berlin: de Gruyter, 1993.

Gehler, Friedrich and Ullrich Kasten, eds. *Fritz Lang: Die Stimme von Metropolis.* Berlin: Henschel, 1990.

Giesen, Rolf. *Special Effects.* Berlin: edition 8½, 1985.

Gösta, Werner. "Fritz Lang and Goebbels — Myths and Facts." *Film Quarterly* 43 (summer 1990), 1989/90: 24–27.

Grossman, Atina. "*Girlkultur* or Thoroughly Rationalized Female: A New Woman in Weimar Germany?" In *Women in Culture and Politics: A Century of Change,* ed. Judith Friedlander et al, 62–82. Bloomington: Indiana UP, 1986.

Grossman, Atina. "The New Woman and the Rationalization of Sexuality in Weimar Germany." In *Powers of Desire: The Politics of Sexuality.* ed. Ann Snitow, Christine Stansell, and Sharon Thompson, 153–71. New York: Monthly Review Press, 1983.

Hake, Sabine. *Cinema's Third Machine: Writing on Film in Germany 1907–1933.* Lincoln: U of Nebraska P, 1993.

Harbou, Thea von. *Metropolis.* Berlin: August Scherl, 1927. Reprinted ed. with an afterword by Herbert W. Franke. Frankfurt am Main: Ullstein, 1984.

Harbou, Thea von. *Metropolis.* Anonymous English translation. London: Hutchinson, 1927.

"Thea von Harbou" in *Cinegraph: Lexikon zum deutschsprachigen Film,* ed. Hans-Michael Bock. Munich: edition text + kritik, 1984-. Unpaginated looseleaf publication.

Herf, Jeffrey. *Reactionary Modernism: Technology, Culture, and Politics in Weimar and the Third Reich.* Cambridge: Cambridge UP, 1984.

Hickethier, Knut, ed. *Grenzgänger zwischen Theater und Kino: Schauspielerporträts aus dem Berlin der zwanziger Jahre.* Berlin: Ästhetik und Kommunikation, 1986.

Huyssen, Andreas. *After the Great Divide: Modernism, Mass Culture, Postmodernism.* Bloomington: Indiana UP, 1986.

Huyssen, Andreas. "Mass Culture as Woman: Modernism's Other." In *Studies in Entertainment: Critical Approaches to Mass Culture,* ed. Tania Modleski, 188–207. Bloomington: Indiana UP, 1986.

Jaeger, Klaus, Horst-Diether Kalbfleisch, Helmut Regel, eds. *Der Weg ins Dritte Reich: Deutscher Film und Weimars Ende.* Oberhausen: Verlag Karl Maria Laufen, 1974.

Jenkins, Stephen. "Lang: Fear and Desire." In *Fritz Lang: The Image and the Look,* ed. Stephen Jenkins, 38–124. London: British Film Institute, 1981.

Jensen, Paul M. *The Cinema of Fritz Lang.* New York/London: A. S. Barnes, 1969.

Jensen, Paul. M. "Metropolis," *Film Heritage* 2, no.3 (winter 1967/68): 22–28.

Kaes, Anton. *From* Hitler *to* Heimat*: The Return of History as Film.* Cambridge, MA: Harvard UP, 1989.

Kaes, Anton. "Film in der Weimarer Republik." In *Geschichte des deutschen Films.* ed. Wolfgang Jacobsen, Anton Kaes, Hans Helmut Prinzler. Stuttgart: Metzler, 1993.

Kaplan E. Ann. *Fritz Lang. A Guide to References and Resources.* Boston, MA: G. K. Hall & Co, 1981.

Kasten, Jürgen. *Der expressionistische Film: Abgefilmtes Theater oder avantgardistisches Erzählkino? Eine stil-, produktions- und rezeptionsgeschichtliche Untersuchung.* Münster: Maks Publikationen, 1990.

Kasten, Jürgen. *Film schreiben. Eine Geschichte des Drehbuchs.* Vienna: Hora, 1990.

Keiner, Reinhold. *Thea von Harbou und der deutsche Film bis 1933.* Hildesheim: Georg Olms, 1984.

Kirchhartz, Andrea. "Produit-détruit-reconstruit: l'histoire de *Métropolis* et de sa restauration." *1895. Revue de l'Association française de recherche sur l'histoire du cinéma.* 19 (décembre 1995): 19–33.

Korte, Helmut, ed. *Film und Realität in der Weimarer Republik.* Munich: Hanser, 1978.

Kracauer, Siegfried. *The Mass Ornament: Weimar Essays.* Trans. Thomas Y. Levin. Cambridge, MA: Harvard UP, 1995.

Kracauer, Siegfried. *From Caligari to Hitler.* Princeton: Princeton UP, 1947.

Kreimeier, Klaus, *Die Ufa-Story. Geschichte eines Filmkonzerns.* 2nd ed. Munich: Heyne, 1995.

Kuhns, David F. *German Expressionist Theatre: The Actor and the Stage.* Cambridge: Cambridge UP, 1997.

Kurtz, Rudolf. *Expressionismus und Film.* Berlin: Verlag der Lichtbildbühne, 1926.

Laberge, Yves. "Une mémoire filmique défaillante: oublis et plans manquants dans la version sonorisée (1984) du film *Métropolis* (1927) de Fritz Lang." *Champs visuels. Revue interdisciplinaire de recherches sur l'image* 4 (février 1997): 135–46.

Laberge, Yves. "Le retour de *Métropolis*: une idéologie subversive au service d'une autre." In *Théâtre et cinéma: un miroir de l'Allemagne. Études littéraires,* 133–56. Sainte-Foy: Presse de l'Université Laval, 1985.

Lang, Fritz. *Metropolis.* 1973. Reprint, London: Faber and Faber, 1989.

Lang, Fritz."Was ich in Amerika sah — Neuyork und Los Angeles." *Film-Kurier,* 11 December 1924: unpaginated.

Lang, Fritz. "Was lieben und hassen wir am amerikanischen Film?" *Deutsche Filmwoche,* 2 October 1925: 35.

Lang, Fritz. "Wege des großen Spielfilms." *Die literarische Welt* 40 (1 October 1926): 5–6.

Lethen, Helmut. *Neue Sachlichkeit 1924–1932.* Stuttgart:Metzler, 1970.

Lungstrum, Janet. "Metropolis and the Technosexual Woman of German Modernity." In *Women in the Metropolis. Gender and Modernity in Weimar Culture,* ed. Katharina von Ankum, 128–44. Berkeley, Los Angeles, London: U of California P, 1997.

Maibohm, Ludwig. *Fritz Lang und seine Filme.* 2nd ed. Munich: Heyne, 1985.

McCormick, Richard W. "From Caligari to Dietrich: Sexual, Social and Cinematic Discourses in Weimar Film." *Signs* 18, no.3 (1993): 644–48.

McGilligan, Patrick. *Fritz Lang: The Nature of the Beast.* London: Faber and Faber, 1997.

Mellencamp, Patricia. "Oedipus and the Robot in *Metropolis.*" *Enclitic* 5, no.1 (spring 1981): 20–42.

Metz , Christian. *The Imaginary Signifier: Psychoanalysis and the Cinema.* Trans. Celia Britton et al. Bloomington: Indiana UP, 1981.

Monaco, Paul, *Cinema and Society: France and Germany During the Twenties.* New York: Elsevier, 1976.

Murray, Bruce A. *Film and the German Left in the Weimar Republic: From Caligari to Kuhle Wampe*. Austin: U of Texas P, 1990.

Murray, Bruce A. and Christopher J. Wickham, eds. *Framing the Past: The Historiography of German Cinema and Television*. Carbondale: Southern Illinois UP, 1992.

Ott, Frederic, W. *The Films of Fritz Lang*. Secaucus: Citadel, 1979.

Owens, Nancy. "Image and Object: Hegel, Madonna, Metropolis." *Spectator* 12, no.2 (spring 1992): 58–63.

Patalas, Enno. "*Metropolis*, Scene 103." Trans. Miriam Hansen. *Camera Obscura* 15 (autumn 1986), 165–73.

Patalas, Enno, "Metropolis in/aus Trümmern," In *Fritz Lang. Eine Publikation des Münchener Filmmuseums und des Münchener Filmzentrums E. V.*, ed Fritz Göttler, 15–17. Munich: Münchener Filmmuseum, 1988.

Petro, Patrice. *Joyless Streets: Women and Melodramatic Representation in Weimar Germany*. Princeton: Princeton UP, 1989.

Plummer, Thomas, ed. *Film and Politics in the Weimar Republic*. New York: Holmes and Meier, 1982.

Pommer, Erich. "Geschäftsfilm und künstlerischer Film." *Der Film* 50 (10 December 1922).

Prouty, Howard H. "*Metropolis*." In *Magill Survey of Cinema Silent Films*, vol. 2, ed. Frank N. Magill, 733–44. Englewood Cliffs NJ, Salem Press, 1982.

Reichel, Peter. *Der schöne Schein des Dritten Reiches: Faszination und Gewalt des Faschismus*. Munich: Hanser, 1991.

Roth, Lane. "Metropolis, the Lights Fantastic: Semiotic Analysis Of Lighting Codes in Relation to Character and Theme." *Literature/Film Quarterly* 6, no.4 (fall 1978): 342–46.

Saunders, Thomas J. "History in the Making: Weimar Cinema and National Identity." In *Framing the Past. The Historiography of German Cinema and Television*, ed. Bruce A. Murray and Christopher J. Wickham, 42–67. Carbondale: Southern Illinois UP, 1992.

Scherpe, Klaus R., ed. *Die Unwirklichkeit der Städte: Großstadtdarstellungen zwischen Moderne und Postmoderne*. Reinbek: Rowohlt, 1988.

Seltzer, Mark. *Bodies & Machines*. London: Routledge, 1992.

Sturm, Georges. "Für Hel, ein Denkmal, kein Platz." *Bulletin CICIM* 9 (1984): 54–78.

Sturm, Georges. "Auf der Suche nach der verlorenen Szene." *Bulletin CICIM* 5–6 (1983): 88–95.

Telotte, J. P. *Replications: A Robotic History of the Science Fiction Film*. Chicago: U of Illinois P, 1995.

Töteberg, Michael. *Fritz Lang* 3rd ed. Reinbek: Rowohlt, 1994.

Traub, Hans. *Die Ufa: Ein Beitrag zur Entwicklungsgeschichte des deutschen Filmschaffens*. Berlin: Ufa-Buchverlag, 1943.

Tudor, Andrew. *Image and Influence*. London: George Allen & Unwin, 1974.

Tulloch, John. "Genetic Structuralism and the Cinema: A Look at Fritz Lang's *Metropolis*." *Australian Journal of Screen Theory* 1 (1976): 3–50.

Turner, Graeme. *Film as Social Practice* 2nd ed. London: Routledge, 1992.

Usai, Paolo Cherchi, ed. *Burning Passions. An Introduction to the Study of Silent Cinema*. London: British Film Institute, 1994.

Wang, Wilfried. "Geometrie und Raster: Der mechanisierte Mensch." In *Expressionismus und Neue Sachlichkeit: Moderne Architektur in Deutschland 1900 bis 1945*, ed. Vittorio Lampugnani and Romana Scheider, 32–49. Stuttgart: Hatje,1994.

Willett, John. *Art and Politics in the Weimar Period: The New Sobriety, 1917–1933*. New York: Pantheon Books, 1978.

Wollen, Peter. "Cinema/Americanism/The Robot." *New Formations* 8 (summer 1989): 7–34.

The Editors

HOLGER BACHMANN's Cambridge doctoral dissertation dealt with Arthur Schnitzler's contribution to the early film industry. He has published articles on English and German literature and linguistics and on contemporary film. His study of Ufa's 1925 silent film adaptation of Theodor Storm's novella *The Chronicles of the Grey House,* entitled *Über die Heide ins Herz der Nation,* was published in 1996. He works for an asset management company in Frankfurt.

MICHAEL MINDEN is University Lecturer at the University of Cambridge and a Fellow of Jesus College, where he teaches German literature and film. He has published articles on a wide range of topics in German literature and cinema. His most recent book is *The German Bildungsroman: Incest and Inheritance* (1997).

The Contributors

GIORGIO BERTELLINI is the author of the monograph *Emir Kusturica* (1996). He is currently completing his dissertation on ethnic film spectatorship in New York City at the turn of the century. Bertellini has contributed to numerous film journals and collections of essays on film. He has taught Film Studies at NYU, UC Davis, CUNY-Queens College, and the School of Visual Arts (New York).

JULIA DOVER read Communications Studies at Concordia University, Montreal and European Literature at the University of Cambridge. She is currently studying Film Production at the London International Film School.

THOMAS ELSAESSER, who is Professor of Film and TV Studies at the University of Amsterdam, has published extensively on German cinema. His books include *New German Cinema: A History* (1989) and *Weimar Cinema and After: Germany's Historical Imaginary* (2000). He is preparing a monograph on *Metropolis* for the British Film Institute.

ANDREAS HUYSSEN is Villard Professor of German and Comparative Literature at Columbia University. He has published extensively on German literature and on intellectual and cultural history. Among his books are *After the Great Divide: Modernism, Mass Culture, Postmodernism* (1986) and *Twilight Memories: Marking Time in a Culture of Amnesia* (1995).

LUDMILLA JORDANOVA is Professor of Visual Arts in the Department of World Art Studies and Museology at the University of East Anglia. She has published widely in literary, medical, scientific and intellectual history. Her most recent books are *Nature Displayed: Gender, Science and Medicine 1760–1820* (1999) and *History in Practice* (2000).

BEN MORGAN is Newton Trust Lecturer in German at the University of Cambridge and a Fellow of Emmanuel College. He has published many articles on German intellectual history and contemporary German literature, and he is currently working on a history of the regulation of emotions from Meister Eckhart to the present.

ENNO PATALAS is the co-author of *Geschichte des Films* (1973), a standard work on the history of cinema. He was formerly the director of the Munich *Filmmuseum* and very much involved in the restoration of early German films, including *Metropolis*. He was technical advisor to the 1984 Giorgio Moroder version of Lang's film.

R. L. RUTSKY is Assistant Professor in the Department of Film, Television, and Theatre at University of Notre Dame. He has published widely in the field of the relation between technology and aesthetics. His book *High Techne: Art and Technology from the Machine Aesthetic to the Posthuman*, was published in 1999.

ANDREW WEBBER is University Lecturer in German at the University of Cambridge and a Fellow of Churchill College. He has published widely in the field of German literature and film. His most recent book is *The Doppelgänger: Double Visions In German Literature* (1996), and he is currently working on a book on Thomas Bernhard.

ALAN WILLIAMS is Professor of French and Cinema Studies at Rutgers University (New Brunswick, New Jersey). He has written extensively on film, especially French and American film history. He is the author of *Republic of Images: A History of French Filmmaking* (1992) and the editor of the forthcoming *Film and Nationalism* for Rutgers UP.

Index